D1454398

PROBLEMS IN EQUINE MEDICINE

PROBLEMS IN EQUINE MEDICINE

Edited by

CHRISTOPHER M. BROWN, B.V.Sc., Ph.D.
Professor
Department of Large Animal Clinical Sciences
Michigan State University
East Lansing, MI

Lea & Febiger   1989   Philadelphia • London

Lea & Febiger
600 Washington Square
Philadelphia, PA 19106-4198
U.S.A.
(215) 922-1330

Lea & Febiger (UK) Ltd.
145a Croydon Road
Beckenham, Kent BR3 3RB
U.K.

Library of Congress Cataloging in Publication Data

Problems in equine medicine.

Includes index.
1. Horses—Diseases—Diagnosis. I. Brown,
Christopher M. [DNLM: 1. Horse Diseases—
diagnosis. SF 951 P962]
SF951.P95 1989 636.1'089'6075 88-27255
ISBN 0-8121-1171-0

PRINTED IN THE UNITED STATES OF AMERICA

Print number: 5 4 3 2 1

DEDICATION

To my parents, who fostered and encouraged my academic development, and to Tony King, Jim Pinsent, and Jim Holmes, who gave me a philosophy about veterinary medicine and taught me to apply it.

PREFACE

Clinicians in referral centers daily receive calls from colleagues in general practice seeking advice on the management of their patients. Frequently they do not ask what the best treatment is for a particular disease, but rather describe a horse's problem in terms of clinical signs and laboratory data, and then ask, "What do you think?" Their questions, and similar ones from students, were the motivation for producing this book. *Problems in Equine Medicine* is not meant to help solve *all* medical problems encountered in equine practice, instead concentrating on common ones. Even so, it is not totally comprehensive. For example, apart from the chapter on the neonate, it concentrates on the adult horse. For logistical reasons some problems, such as those with dermatologic signs, could not be included.

The book is directed toward anyone who treats horses with medical problems, but it will probably be most useful to students and those less experienced in equine medicine. The experienced practitioner will find much common knowledge here, but knowledge that is presented with a different emphasis.

I originally planned to write the entire text myself, but the overwhelming task would have precluded a timely completion of the book. I have been very lucky to have the help of 13 authors providing expertise in various areas. I am very grateful to them for their help and patience during some of the delays. In addition, I have had the good fortune to work with an outstanding group of equine clinicians and residents at Michigan State, who have been a constant source of guidance and advice. They practice the highest standards and expect them of others. Finally, it is the horses who have taught us about their diseases, and our students who have fostered that learning.

The production of the book has been encouraged and facilitated by the staff at Lea & Febiger. I thank them for their patient assistance.

Christopher M. Brown
East Lansing, Michigan

CONTRIBUTORS

Frank M. Andrews, D.V.M., M.S.
Assistant Professor, Research Associate
Department of Rural Practice
College of Veterinary Medicine
University of Tennessee
Knoxville, TN

Warwick A. Arden, B.V.Sc.
Assistant Professor
Department of Large Animal Clinical
  Sciences
College of Veterinary Medicine
Michigan State University
East Lansing, MI

Christopher M. Brown, B.V.Sc., Ph.D.
Professor
Department of Large Animal Clinical
  Sciences
Michigan State University
East Lansing, MI

G. Kent Carter, D.V.M., M.S.
Assistant Professor
College of Veterinary Medicine
Texas Veterinary Medicine Center
Texas A & M University
College Station, TX

Benjamin J. Darien, M.S., D.V.M.
Instructor
Department of Large Animal Clinical
  Sciences
College of Veterinary Medicine
Michigan State University
East Lansing, MI

Thomas P. Mullaney, M.V.B., Ph.D.
Associate Professor
Department of Pathology
College of Veterinary Medicine
Michigan State University,
East Lansing, MI

Michael J. Murray, D.V.M., M.S.
Assistant Professor of Medicine
Virginia-Maryland Regional College of
  Veterinary Medicine
Leesburg, VA

Michael W. O'Callaghan, B.V.Sc., Ph.D.
Associate Professor
Department of Surgery
School of Veterinary Medicine
Tufts University
North Grafton, MA

Erwin G. Pearson, D.V.M.
Associate Professor
College of Veterinary Medicine
Oregon State University
Corvallis, OR

Stephen M. Reed, D.V.M.
Associate Professor of Equine Medicine
Department of Veterinary Clinical Sciences
College of Veterinary Medicine
Ohio State University
Columbus, OH

Virginia B. Reef, D.V.M.
Assistant Professor of Medicine
New Bolton Center
University of Pennsylvania
Kennett Square, PA

Allen J. Roussel, Jr., D.V.M., M.S.
Assistant Professor
College of Veterinary Medicine
Texas University Medicine Center
Texas A & M University
College Station, TX

Ioana Sonea, D.V.M.
Graduate Assistant
College of Veterinary Medicine
Michigan State University
East Lansing, MI

Pamela C. Wagner, D.V.M., M.S.
Associate Professor
School of Veterinary Medicine
Tufts University
North Grafton, MA

CONTENTS

chapter 1

UNDERSTANDING AND MANAGEMENT OF PROBLEMS AND OWNERS

Christopher M. Brown

Of all of the species of animals that veterinarians treat, none has such a diversity of sizes, breeds, uses, and owners as the horse. Horses range in weight from less than 50 kg to over 1000 kg. They range in value from less than $100 to over $50,000,000. Their uses include companionship, racing, pulling, jumping, breeding, entertaining, and in some areas meat production. The veterinarian is challenged to know both the diseases of the horse and their significance in different horses. In addition, a wide range of "owner-related" factors have a direct and indirect impact on the understanding and management of problems in equine medicine (Fig. 1–1).

UNDERSTANDING NORMALITY

Owners and other laypersons can recognize grossly abnormal situations such as the severely dyspneic animal or the emaciated foal just as easily as trained veterinarians. The major challenge to the equine practitioner is to detect more subtle problems, to determine if a particular

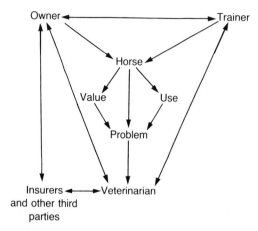

Fig. 1–1. Factors in understanding and managing problems in equine medicine.

horse is normal or abnormal, and if abnormal to determine whether the abnormalities are significant.

Some parameters such as rectal temperature and resting pulse rate have a normal range, often ±2 standard deviations of the mean. Such established ranges must be used only as rough guides, however; so many factors, such as age, breed, sex, and state of excitement, can influence physiologic variables in horses that the values must be interpreted in the context. For example, a pulse rate of 80 beats/minute is considered a serious sign in a colicky horse (Chapter 4). However, such a value obtained from a colicky horse that had just been unloaded after a 2-hour trailer ride to a clinic would be less important. If after 30 minutes of rest the pulse had come down to 50, the situation would be less serious.

Most clinical pathologic data can be expressed as a mean and a normal range. Again, many factors (age, breed, sex, stage of training, pregnancy, and lactation) can influence these values and hence their interpretation. Some of the most variable laboratory data are obtained from hematologic investigations in horses, particularly the red cell series (Chapter 13). In addition, often large differences exist between the "normal" ranges from different laboratories. A high value from one may be within the middle of the range for another. If possible, all evaluations should be done by the same laboratory for a particular patient, and preferably for a particular veterinary practice.

One of the major problems with published normal values is that owners, trainers, and often veterinarians regard the values as absolute limits. Any deviation, however small, is regarded as a serious problem, one that should be investigated. This attitude often leads to the investigation of a problem based on laboratory data alone, rather than on a specifically identified medical complaint. One common "problem" encountered in performance horses, particularly racehorses, is a persistently elevated value for serum aspartate aminotransferase, often only 50 to 60 units above the normal maximum. These "problem" animals can be identified on routine serum biochemical screening or during their evaluation for poor athletic performance (Chapter 17). Although these elevations might reflect some ongoing pathophysiologic process, they might reflect no more than recent muscular activity. Published ranges are only guides, and the significance of a deviation can be determined only when all pertinent clinical and other findings are evaluated.

Whereas, despite their limitations, values for physiologic parameters and laboratory data do provide a definite reference point from which to work, unfortunately other important variables have no such reference. These are the subjective assessments of attitude and behavior. Nevertheless, obvious deviations are detected even by the most inexperienced. Often, minor changes in disposition are more likely to be detected by those who work with the particular horse than by the veterinarian making a first examination. Regrettably, often the complaint is that the animal is "just not right"—appetite may be slightly depressed and the horse less active. Veterinarians who have worked with horses for many years will often be able to detect these subtle changes more readily than their less-experienced colleagues. Unfortunately, this ability is acquired only with time.

Another area of subjectivity is the evaluation of auscultatory findings from the heart, lungs, and abdomen. Again, familiarity based on experience allows the confidence to establish a subjective opinion of normality. The horse's body conformation, degree of excitement, and dietary history will influence what can be heard.

UNDERSTANDING THE PROBLEM AND ITS SIGNIFICANCE

Rarely is a horse presented for veterinary evaluation because the owner knows it has a specific disease, such as atrial fibrillation or protozoal myelitis. Owners and trainers can merely cite "poor performance" or "weakness behind." The veterinarian's understanding of the horse's problems is based initially on the presenting complaint and is expanded by a complete and accurate history. The quality of the history can vary; if the horse was acquired recently, previous problems might be unknown. Also, the owner might not be very knowledgeable about equine matters, or the trainer might not be honest, fearing some blame for the problem.

After acquiring the history the veterinarian should have some idea of the problems from the owner's perspective and should begin to formulate some ideas on possible causes and methods of evaluation. He or she should avoid latching on to one aspect of the history or problem and locking into a diagnosis prematurely. It is well to remember that "common things occur commonly; the unusual is to be expected; and the rare is as scarce as rocking horse manure!" The veterinarian should

concentrate on the most likely problem but keep an open mind to other possibilities.

The problem is further refined by a thorough physical examination and additional diagnostic testing. By this point the veterinarian should understand the problem.

Although many problems in equine medicine can be pursued to great depth, such measures are not always justified. The veterinarian must understand the value and use of the horse before advising the owner to pursue the problem and invest in the workup. The veterinarian has a responsibility not only to the client, but also to the horse. A course of investigation or therapy should not be recommended if the horse will not benefit. A period of discomfort for the horse is justified if a reasonable period of normal useful life will probably follow. The definition of "useful" in this context lies with the owner. For example, though a racehorse with severe pulmonary hemorrhage and pulmonary abscesses might not be salvageable for racing, therapy might be justified if the owner would like to cure it and retire it to pasture. On the other hand, the owner might be interested only in having a horse that can be returned to normal function as either an athlete or a breeding animal.

At varying points during the investigation of the problem the veterinarian might be able to advise the owner on the horse's future, even though the problem has not been fully explained. For example, the history of a 10-year-old racehorse might indicate that its performance has been progressively worsening over the last 4 years, such that the horse is unable to compete effectively, and several standard investigations have failed to uncover the cause. At the outset the client could be told that the "problem" might not be worth pursuing if a curable or manageable problem will probably not be found. Similarly, if after partial investigation, some understanding of the problem is obtained but the next steps in the assessment would be significantly more expensive, the value of the horse, as determined by the owner, will determine if the problem should be pursued further. Commonly the client will determine a maximum that can be spent on the horse, and on that basis the veterinarian has to decide what type of evaluation should be undertaken. If a horse is insured, the insurance company might insist on a full evaluation in order to meet the conditions of the policy.

Even if the problem is defined and understood, to determine its significance requires somewhat detailed knowledge of the use of the horse, either current or proposed. The same problems have different significances in different horses. For example, chronic low-grade lung disease could be the ruin of 4-year-old standardbred racehorse, but could be completely unimportant in a 15-year-old Belgian broodmare. The veterinarian must be able to understand these variations if the client is to be advised accurately.

UNDERSTANDING THE OWNER

The veterinarian might have more difficulty understanding the owner's position than the horse's medical problem. While horses are mostly utilitarian, often a bond develops. The sentimental value of the horse often exceeds the monetary value, and an owner will often spend much more than the worth of the animal on its evaluation and treatment. For others the decision is entirely economic, and the horse is merely part of a business. The veterinarian needs to appreciate the position of the owner when evaluating the situation. The equine practitioner can play a role similar to veterinarians in small-animal practice, those in agricultural practice, or a combination of both.

Successful assessment and management of equine medical problems requires a thorough understanding of owners and their expectations. Veterinarians often understand their long-time clients well. They can relate to the clients' problems and their interpretations of the horses' problems. However, developing a good understanding of a new client's expertise and objectivity as a horse owner in one 20- to 30-minute visit is not easy. If the horse has an apparently complex problem, it is worthwhile to spend equal time getting to understand the client and getting to understand the horse's problem.

Horse ownership is continually expanding, and the number of first-time horse owners is increasing. Many problems encountered in equine practice are the results of ignorance. New owners seek advice from a variety of sources. The veterinarian, whose services usually have to be paid for, is often low on the list of possible sources for advice. Friends, neighbors, feed merchants, and tack shop owners are often relied on for information first. Advice is often confusing and conflicting.

Many horse owners will "shop around" with their problem, seeking a solution. Frequently a horse with a chronic or recurrent problem has been seen by more than one veterinarian. Owners do not always inform the current veterinarian that others have tried and, in the owner's opinion, failed. Owners are often motivated by frustration, but they should be encouraged to share their ideas about other opinions. If possible, the information should be obtained from the other veterinarian.

No client will be satisfied if he or she has no trust in the opinion of the veterinarian. It is vital to establish a good client-veterinarian relationship at the outset. The client has to believe that his best interests and those of his horse are being served. Owners of horses with chronic problems often resent the veterinary profession. Having invested time and money, they may still have a problem horse.

Such an attitude, if perceived, is worthwhile exploring with the client. Veterinarians, particularly the newly qualified, often feel responsible for the failure to diagnose or resolve a problem, and the perceptive client can lose confidence in the veterinarian. The veterinarian should be honest and tell the client what can and cannot be done, and how much it will cost. Disappointment develops only when expectations exceed achievements. If the client is unhappy or reluctant, the veterinarian could recommend a second opinion, perhaps a local colleague or someone at a referral clinic. Referral should also be suggested if the veterinarian is unable, because of lack of facilities or expertise, to pursue a problem adequately. A referral should also be arranged if the client spontaneously requests it. For whatever reason, if a referral is arranged every effort should be made to ensure that all pertinent information is transmitted to the receiving veterinarian.

chapter 2

CHRONIC WEIGHT LOSS

Christopher M. Brown

The maintenance of a normal and constant body weight is a balance between input and output (Fig. 2–1). The input is the nutrients in the diet; the output is the sum of nutrients used for exercise and body functions, nutrients ingested but neither digested nor absorbed, and nutrients absorbed but subsequently lost in feces, urine, or sweat. Understanding this balance makes solving the problem of chronic weight loss fairly straightforward.

DEFINITION

Owners vary tremendously in their concern about weight loss in their horses. Some will seek veterinary advice when no one else would consider the animal to be anything other than healthy. Others will wait until the horse is almost emaciated before asking for help. Equally variable are owners' estimates of weight lost, and the rate of weight loss. Owners have been known to report a weight loss of several hundred pounds often in 1 to 2

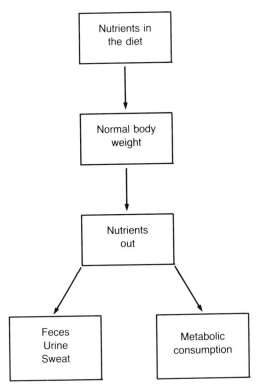

Fig. 2–1. Balance between input and output needed to maintain normal and constant body weight.

POSSIBLE CAUSES

Chronic weight loss in horses can result from specific diseases or syndromes. Generally speaking, horses become thin because of lack of food, water, or both, or poor quality of food and water; failure to eat or swallow food; failure to digest or absorb food; increased or abnormal loss of nutrients once absorbed; and increased utilization of nutrients once absorbed (see Table 2–1).

CLINICAL EVALUATION (Fig. 2–2)

As indicated above, owners vary in their concern for, and awareness of, the severity of a horse's weight loss. An accurate history is valuable in determining which of the probable causes of weight loss should be given most consideration. The standard of management should be evaluated on the farm.

Is the horse stabled individually or kept at pasture with a large group? The environment of the stabled horse is easier to examine. Observation of the individual at pasture with a large group is less accurate and less reliable. Owners might be embarrassed that they have a thin horse and be less than open in describing feeding and management practices, as they are concerned that they will appear to have been negligent. This concern sometimes accounts for the assertion that the horse became very thin very quickly; while the horse has not, the owner might have been less observant than he or she would have wished. Equally, if the owner is an absentee, the farm manager or trainer might attempt to mislead or to conceal information, again to avoid being considered negligent.

The history should establish the age of the horse, its use, and the duration of ownership; the diet and medical program, including parasite control and dental prophylaxis; the duration and severity

weeks or even days! Although knowing the correct weight for a horse would be a useful part of any equine health maintenance program, usually the weight is not available. Measuring tapes that estimate the weight from girth dimensions only approximate the actual weight and cannot be relied on for an accurate assessment. Determining whether the horse is losing weight is sometimes easy from physical findings and an accurate history; in other cases establishing the severity of the problem, or even if a problem exists at all, is difficult.

Whatever the indications and suggestions from the owner, chronic weight loss should be investigated when a horse has noticeably lost weight and not regained it, or has continued to lose weight over 4 to 5 weeks.

TABLE 2–1. CHRONIC WEIGHT LOSS IN ADULT HORSES

Major Causes	Minor Causes	Specific Disease
Lack of nutrients or poor-quality nutrients		Starvation
Failure to eat offered food	Unpalatable food	Contaminated or spoiled food
	Inability to eat	Neurologic lesions Dental disease Fractured jaw
	Inability to swallow	Neurologic lesions Pharyngeal masses
	Chronic pain	Chronic arthritis Chronic laminitis Gastric ulceration Nonhealing wounds
	Chronic infection	Equine infectious anemia Internal abscesses Endocarditis Brucellosis
	Chronic lung diseases	Heaves
	Neoplasia	Squamous cell carcinoma of the stomach Any internal neoplasm of significant size
Failure to absorb ingested nutrients	Small-bowel maldigestion/malabsorption	Lymphosarcoma Lymphocytic/plasmacytic enteritis Granulomatous enteritis Eosinophilic enteritis Reduced arterial blood flow secondary to parasite damage
	Large-bowel dysfunction	Same as for small bowel, parasitic damage to bowel wall
Increased loss of nutrients once absorbed	Protein-losing enteropathy	Granulomatous enteritis Chronic bowel ulceration, e.g., phenylbutazone toxicity Parasitic damage
	Renal disease	Immune-mediated glomerular damage
	Sequestration in body spaces	Peritonitis Pleuritis
Increased metabolic activity	Physiologic increases	Increased work load Pregnancy Lactation
	Pathophysiologic alterations	Hyperthyroidism (rare) Cushing's syndrome Liver disease

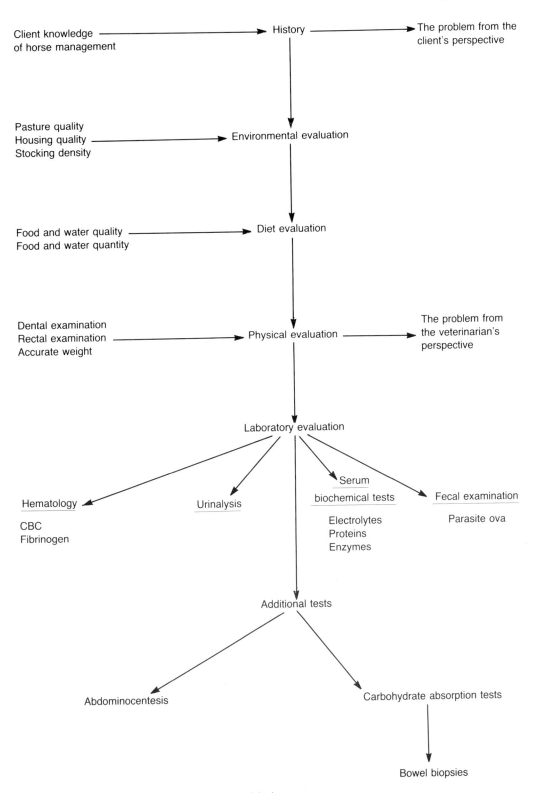

Fig. 2–2. Evaluation of a horse with chronic weight loss.

of the problem; and the presence of any other affected animals on the premises. Many new horse owners are poorly informed about the basics of horse management. *Many thin horses, particularly of the "backyard" variety, are products of malnutrition, poor dental care, overwork, and enteric parasitism.* Spending time with an owner in general discussion and strolling about the premises can be as useful as a detailed examination of the patient and elaborate laboratory tests. All that may be needed is basic advice on horse management and preventive medicine.

The horse should be observed in its environment and a detailed physical examination performed. If initial superficial examination does not reveal an obvious cause of the problem, blood and fecal samples can be taken to establish a minimum laboratory data base. The veterinarian should perform routine hematology including a fibrinogen; serum biochemistries, including blood urea, sodium, potassium, chloride, total protein, and albumin/globulin fractions; and 9 varieties of serum enzymes, most usefully sorbitol dehydrogenase, aspartate aminotransferase, and gamma glutamyltranspeptidase. The feces should be examined for parasite eggs.

Having obtained a reasonable understanding of the problem from the client's point of view, and hopefully to some degree from the patient's, one can ask specific questions to determine the cause of weight loss (Fig. 2–3). Additional tests and questions can be raised as the investigation proceeds.

IS THE HORSE BEING FED?

As mentioned above, standards of horse management vary tremendously. Because many owners believe that they are feeding an adequate diet, a verbal report is not sufficient. Ideally, the veterinarian should make a direct estimate of what is being fed. How

much hay, how much grain, and of what quality? What is the quality of pasture? What is the stocking density? An initial on-site investigation of a weight loss problem is better than an evaluation in a clinic or hospital to answer these questions.

The average 450-kg (1000-lb) horse at rest requires about 16.0 Mcals (67.2 MJ)/day to maintain normal body weight. This energy can be provided by 8 to 10 kg of hay and 2 to 4 kg of grain. When the workload increases or the metabolic status changes, such as occurs in pregnancy or lactation, demands increase accordingly. The nutritional needs of horses vary. Some are "easy-keepers" and maintain body weight on a low plane of nutrition, and others are "hard-keepers" and always require more food than their peers to maintain body weight.

Horses require clean, free-choice water. Weight loss ensues when water is restricted, partially because of concomitant reduced food intake. Water restriction can occur in hot, arid areas, when water freezes, or when water is provided in buckets that are refilled only once or twice a day. The average horse needs about 20 to 30 L of fresh water a day when doing light work in a temperate climate. Again, weight loss can occur if an increased need for water produced by increased work load, lactation, or increased environmental temperature is not met.

IS THE HORSE EATING WHAT HAS BEEN OFFERED?

This question is easier to answer when the horse is housed individually than when it is kept on pasture, particularly if it is fed with other horses. Groups of horses establish a social order, and newly introduced horses can have difficulty in establishing themselves. They might be prevented from getting enough food by more dominant horses. A history of recent introduction into a well-established group of horses can therefore be significant. If an individual horse in a group is the only

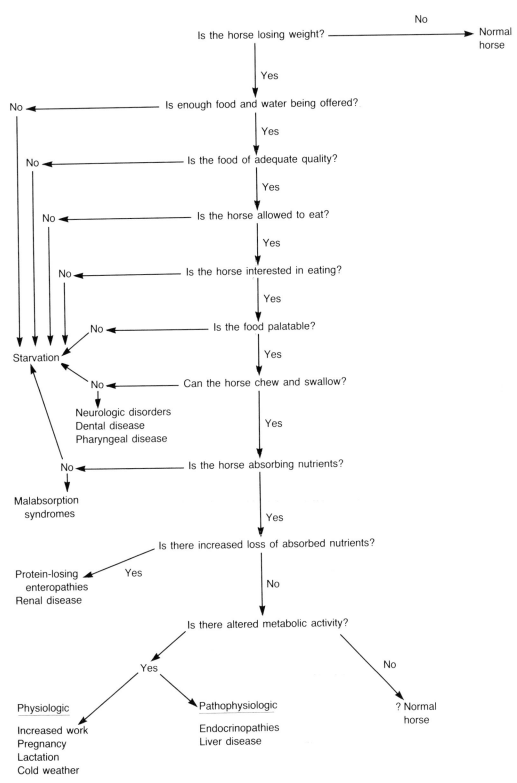

Fig. 2–3. Causes of chronic weight loss.

one losing weight, separating it from the group and feeding it individually allows for closer observation and monitoring of food intake. Some horses are "slow eaters" without any organic lesions, requiring two or three times as long as other horses to eat the same amount of food. In competitive situations these animals do not fare well.

There are, however, many reasons why horses will refuse food or are unable to eat when food is offered to them, leading to weight loss.

Palatability. Palatability becomes a problem when hay or grain has become spoiled or contaminated with various agents. For palatability to be a significant cause of weight loss, a whole batch of feed that is used over several weeks would have to be involved. Usually several horses will refuse to eat contaminated or spoiled feed. The presence on the farm of many thin horses apparently provided with an adequate amount of food might indicate a palatability problem. Horses' feed refusal patterns vary, however. For example, grain contaminated with monensin is eaten readily by some horses and refused by others. Hence, not all horses might be affected. Palatability is more difficult to determine if only one animal is kept. If the animal appears interested in food but then refuses to eat, or starts eating bedding straw in preference to hay, reduced palatability should be suspected. The owner should try a dietary change and see if food refusal stops.

Prehension, Chewing, and Swallowing. These functions are integrated, and abnormalities in one or more can lead to reduced food intake and loss of weight (see Chapter 6). Prehension relies on good motor control of the facial muscles and tongue together with sensory input from the lips, oral mucosa, and vision. Facial paralysis, either bilateral or unilateral, can interfere with the prehension of

food, as can total or partial tongue paralysis. Causes of damage to cranial nerves VII and XII include trauma and ascending infections from the guttural pouches. In addition, some horses with polyneuritis equi have cranial nerve lesions. Central nervous lesions such as neoplasms and abscesses and protozoal myelitis can cause varying cranial nerve signs, which can affect prehension. Similar central nervous damage can occur with aberrant parasitic migration through the brain stem. Affected horses are interested in eating and place their muzzles into the grain and hay and attempt to grasp food. Their success depends on the severity of the lesion. Significant weight loss can develop. Blind horses in familiar environments usually find food without problems.

Difficulty with chewing will result when the muscles of mastication are paralyzed, following damage to cranial nerve V either bilaterally or unilaterally. The causes are similar to those of cranial nerve VII damage. Most commonly, however, abnormal chewing and difficult chewing in horses is caused by severe dental disease. This develops in various circumstances. In the young growing horse, erupting molars, premolars, and retained deciduous premolars ("caps") can lead to a sore and painful mouth that makes chewing slow and inefficient. In older horses, particularly those with some degree of dental malalignment, abnormal wear can lead to development of sharp points on the cheek teeth that cause abrasions to the buccal mucosa and the tongue, making chewing painful. In old horses, severely worn teeth can develop periodontal disease, leading to alveolitis and pain. In addition, if the teeth of animals with advanced dental disease are more sensitive to cold, the horse might refuse to drink cold water. The reduced water intake may have an additional effect on body weight.

Any painful condition affecting the mouth will lead to difficulty in chewing or reluctance to eat. Severe oral ulceration, such as that occurring with phenylbutazone toxicity, can cause problems. Traumatic lesions, particularly fractures to the mandible or maxilla, are chronically painful, interfere with eating, and lead to weight loss.

Difficulty in swallowing can result from neurologic damage. The complex swallowing reflex relies on the integration of several motor and sensory pathways. The cranial nerves involved include VII, IX, X, and XII. In addition, space-occupying lesions of the pharynx or retropharyngeal region can also lead to difficulty in swallowing, as can central nervous lesions.

Watching the horse eat and examining the stall for evidence of partially chewed food is useful in any case of weight loss. Any suggestion of abnormality indicates need for a detailed examination of the oral cavity. Particular attention should be paid to the teeth. Sharp points can be removed by rasping (floating), although simple points on the teeth do not usually cause severe weight loss. Retained "caps" in young horses can be removed. If dental disease is advanced, radiography might be indicated to evaluate the problem more accurately. Radiography of the pharynx together with endoscopy might be needed if a pharyngeal dysfunction is suspected.

Chronic Painful Conditions. These conditions include chronic severe arthritis, chronic laminitis, deep nonhealing wounds, and invasive tumors. In addition to the depression caused by the pain and resulting partial anorexia, some of these lesions reduce the horse's mobility. Such horses at pasture are reluctant to move about and graze and hence further reduce their food intake. Analgesic therapy together with specific treatment for the problem might lead to increased food intake and reversal of weight loss.

Chronic Infections. Infections such as equine infectious anemia (EIA), internal abscesses, and pleuritis can lead to recurrent fevers, depression, and partial anorexia. Clinical signs will vary and clinical pathology will often be non-specific. All infected horses are anemic to some degree; chronic bacterial infections usually cause a leukocytosis with mature neutrophilia. Serum fibrinogen is usually elevated in these cases. Abdominocentesis, rectal examination, thoracic percussion, thoracocentesis, and radiography can localize the site of the problem. Successful treatment of chronic deep-seated infections depends on identifying the cause and selecting appropriate antimicrobial agents (see Chapter 15). Animals suspected of having chronic EIA, which is not treatable, should be tested by the gel diffusion test (Coggin's test).

Severe Chronic Lung Disease. "Heaves" is often associated with marked weight loss, usually because of reduced food intake. These severely dyspneic horses are reluctant to move about; already making a tremendous effort to breathe, they do not, or cannot, take sufficient time to eat enough to maintain body weight. In addition, the increased work of breathing for these animals increases energy demand, accelerating the weight loss. Although owners believe that the aerophagia exhibited by some of these animals leads to digestive dysfunction with increased flatulence ("broken wind"), the increased air in the gastrointestinal tract probably does not have a significant effect on digestion and absorption and hence body weight. Specific management and therapy of lung disease is covered elsewhere (Chapter 7).

Neoplasia. Neoplasia, particularly of the gastrointestinal tract, is also associated with weight loss. Some of this weight loss is due to reduced intake, resulting from systemic effects caused by substances produced by the tumor, from pain caused by the tumor, or from physical obstruction, e.g., in the pharynx. Some of the weight loss might be due to maldigestion or malabsorption caused by the neoplasia. In addition, large tumors have significant metabolic demands that consume nutrients.

In many of these chronic conditions, appetite for all foods is not affected in the same way. For some unknown reason, horses with chronic debilitating illness will continue to eat hay or graze grass, but will refuse to eat grain.

IS THE HORSE DIGESTING AND ABSORBING WHAT IT EATS?

For the most part, dietary protein, fat, and noncellulose carbohydrate are digested in and absorbed by the equine small intestine. Any undigested or unabsorbed materials are broken down by cecal and colonic microorganisms, and breakdown products are absorbed predominantly as volatile fatty acids in the large bowel. Undigested material, particularly fiber, is lost in the feces. Dysfunction of one or more of these parts of the gastrointestinal tract can lead to maldigestion, malabsorption, or both.

Our knowledge concerning specific mechanisms of maldigestion in adult horses is poor. Pancreatic disease and dysfunction appear to be extremely rare, based on a low incidence of pathologic changes encountered at necropsy. Specific brush-border enzyme deficiencies have not been described in adult horses, and maldigestion per se can only be inferred from the histologic appearance of the gut in some thin horses. On the other hand, small-intestine malabsorption syndromes have been documented in adult horses and are usually characterized by a deficiency or impairment in the absorption of d-xylose, glucose, or both.

Typically, horses with maldigestion eat normal or increased amounts and have progressive weight loss extending over weeks to months. The animals are bright and alert in the early stages of the condition and often remain so until severely debilitated. If small-intestine dysfunction is the only problem, they usually will not develop diarrhea; the large bowel is capable of controlling fecal water in spite of the increased osmotic load imposed by the malfunctioning small intestine. However, if small-intestine dysfunction is severe, say greater than 80%, or if the large bowel is also involved in the disease, diarrhea can be a clinical sign.

Small-Intestine Malabsorption

Specifically, several diseases of the small intestine can produce small-intestine malabsorption (and possible maldigestion). These include diffuse lymphosarcoma of the small intestine, eosinophilic infiltration, plasmacytic/lymphocytic infiltration, granulomatous enteritis, and possibly reduced blood flow secondary to parasitic damage to the arterial blood supply. The causes of conditions other than parasitic lesions are not known, although granulomatous enteritis has some of the histologic features of human immune-mediated granulomatous disorders such as Crohn's disease, and occasional cases can be associated with avian tuberculosis infections.

Diagnostic Evaluation. The cause of small-intestine malabsorption cannot be determined by clinical examination or by routine laboratory data. Rectal examination might reveal that the lymph nodes at the origin of the cranial mesenteric artery are palpably enlarged in horses with intestinal lymphosarcoma or granulomatous enteritis; however, these nodes are felt easily in all thin horses because of the loss of surrounding mesenteric fat. Normal nodes about 2 to 3 cm feel like a bunch of widely spaced grapes. When pathologically enlarged, they can be two to three times normal size, often about the size of an egg.

Laboratory Tests. The blood can be normal, or the patient can have a mild anemia with a packed cell volume of about 27% (0.27 L/L). Even in lymphosarcoma the white cell series is usually normal, although in cases of severe parasitism or eosinophilic infiltration a mild peripheral eosinophilia can be present. Routinely assayed serum enzymes are usually normal, but the specific isoenzyme of alkaline phosphatase associated with gut can be elevated in some cases. These isoenzymes are not measured in many veterinary laboratories, however, and this test is far from specific. It merely indicates some form of gastrointestinal disorder, not its location or nature. In cases without diarrhea, serum electrolyte concentrations are usually normal, although serum calcium concentration can be elevated in some cases of equine lymphosarcoma. Serum protein concentrations are usually normal, although if protein-losing enteropathy is a feature, as in some cases of granulomatous enteritis, hypoalbuminemia can be present. Serum globulin can be elevated in chronic inflammatory disorders, and beta-globulins are often elevated in parasitized animals. These animals have an elevation of IgGT. However, because these elevations are not specific for parasitic infestations, they are supportive data. Lymphosarcoma is one of the few diseases associated with low or undetectable serum IgM in adult horses.

Abdominal fluid obtained by paracentesis is often unremarkable in these malabsorbing horses. Lymphosarcoma rarely exfoliates into the peritoneal fluid; the disease is often confined to the bowel wall and drainage lymph nodes. A normal fluid sample does not rule out a diagnosis of neoplasia. In granulomatous enteritis the phagocytic activity of peritoneal mesothelial cells has been reported to be increased. However, assay of this activity is not routinely available and has not become established in the evaluation of suspected granulomatous enteritis cases. Eosinophils can be present in higher numbers when severe parasitism is involved, or eosinophilic infiltrates are present in the bowel wall. Horses that are eating well and losing weight without any striking clinical or laboratory findings are candidates for the assessment of monosaccharide absorption, using glucose, d-xylose, or both.

The oral glucose tolerance test as an indicator of small-intestine absorptive function has several practical advantages, but also several theoretical disadvantages. Glucose is inexpensive, readily available, and easily assayed in suitable samples by most laboratories. However, because it is a normal body metabolite, its serum concentration will be influenced not only by its rate of absorption from the gut, but also by the metabolic status of the horse, which in turn can be influenced by endocrine factors, themselves determined by both internal and external factors. For the general practitioner, however, the oral glucose tolerance test is a good beginning for the assessment of small-intestine absorption in an adult horse.

The test is simple to perform. The horse is fasted of food and water for 12 hours before and during the test. A 20% glucose solution is administered via stomach tube, at a dosage equivalent to 1 g of glucose/kg body weight. Blood samples are collected at zero time and hourly for 6 hours. In a normal horse, serum glucose will double from a mean of about 90 mg/dl to about 180 mg/dl at 1 to 2 hours after dosing (Fig. 2–4). Malabsorption is not implied unless the curve is "flat" or markedly reduced (Fig. 2–4). In any horse with a questionable curve the test should be repeated, or d-xylose absorption testing should be done.

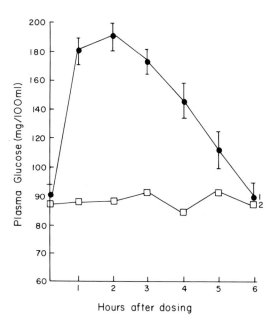

Fig. 2–4. Plasma glucose concentrations in normal horses (●) and a horse with small intestinal malabsorption (□) following an oral dose of glucose at a dosage of 1 g/kg body weight.

D-xylose is a pentose sugar not normally present in equine serum in significant amounts. In the short term its serum concentration is not influenced by metabolic status. A large amount is excreted unchanged in the urine. As it is not greatly influenced by other factors, the serum concentration of d-xylose after oral dosage is a good indicator of its absorption by the small intestine. The test has disadvantages; the compound is more expensive than glucose and not as readily available, and the assay of serum d-xylose concentrations is not widely available. Because the test is no longer routinely used in human medical practice, local medical laboratories do not usually offer the assay. Generally, the test can be performed only at or close to a veterinary clinical pathology laboratory.

The test protocol is similar to that for the oral glucose test. The fasted horse is dosed with a 10% solution of d-xylose at the dosage equivalent to 0.5 g d-xylose/kg body weight. Samples are taken at time zero and then hourly for 6 hours. Serum d-xylose should reach about 20 mg/dl by the first hour (Fig. 2–5). A "flat" curve indicates malabsorption; low curves are equivocal, and the test should be repeated, perhaps a few weeks later if the disease is progressive.

In both the oral glucose tolerance test and the d-xylose absorption test, flat or low curves can indicate small-intestine malabsorption. However, several other possibilities should be considered when interpreting these absorption tests. First, laboratory error in the assay of the sugar can occur. Second, the sugar has to be delivered to the small intestine in order to be absorbed; if the animal has not been adequately fasted and food is still present in the stomach, food will mix with the solution and absorb it, and the glucose or d-xylose will be delivered at a reduced rate and concentration to the small intestine. Lower serum concentrations will ensue.

Although a 12-hour fast is considered to be adequate to achieve gastric emptying, fiberoptic gastroendoscopy has revealed significant amounts of food in

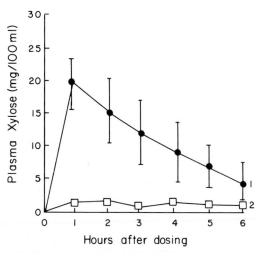

Fig. 2–5. Plasma d-xylose concentrations in normal horses (●) and a horse with small intestinal malabsorption (□) following an oral dose of d-xylose at a dosage of 0.5 g/kg body weight.

horses' stomachs after a 12-hour fast. In some horses up to 24 hours is needed before the stomach is empty. Any obstructive lesion that could influence gastric emptying could lead to reduced delivery of the agent to the stomach, and hence low or flat curves. These lesions include pyloric stenosis, gastric granulomas, and gastric neoplasms. Pyloric stenosis is a fairly rare condition in adult horses but can occur secondarily to scar tissue contraction following gastric ulceration. In addition, space-occupying lesions outside the pylorus, such as neoplasms or abscesses in local lymph nodes, can press against the pylorus and cause obstruction.

Gastric granulomas 2 to 3 cm in diameter are fairly common in horses, usually associated with infestations with Habronema larvae. They do not usually interfere with gastric emptying. Occasionally, however, large granulomas that involve the pylorus can develop. Affected horses can have low or flat curves. Gastric neoplasia is not common in horses, although squamous cell carcinomas are well documented; other tumors are very rare. The squamous cell carcinomas usually arise at the margo plicatus and can become huge, almost obliterating the lumen of the stomach. Again, a low or flat absorption curve would be anticipated. Some horses with large gastric neoplasms exhibit signs of abdominal discomfort when intubated and fluid is infused into their stomachs. Presumably, gastric capacity is reduced.

In addition to physical obstruction, these gastric granulomas and neoplasms could lead to alterations in gastric motility, causing delayed emptying. Data on gastric motility in horses is limited, and none exists on the pathophysiology of equine gastric motility. Perhaps conditions such as chronic grass disease cause reduced motility, giving these animals low or flat curves.

The oral glucose tolerance test and the d-xylose absorption test are also influenced by the horse's immediate previous dietary experience. Experimentally, horses that have been on a predominantly low-energy diet appear to absorb more, or at least to have higher peaks to their curves, than the same animals on a high-energy diet. The diet must be considered when interpreting a d-xylose absorption test, particularly if the results are equivocal. The reason for these curve differences is not understood. Reduced absorption might be caused by the gastric or small-intestine fermentation of the sugars by enteric bacteria, the population of which could be influenced by the diet. Or it might be related to the horse's endocrine status, particularly that of insulin, which again could be determined by recent dietary history.

Special Tests. Further evaluation of apparent malabsorption is indicated if a definitive diagnosis is required; the absorption tests merely suggest one of several conditions, including delayed gastric emptying, small-bowel infiltrative diseases, and reduced bowel perfusion secondary to parasitic damage. A few clinics have the facilities to perform fiberoptic gastroduodenoscopy in large standing horses. This technique allows for direct visualization of the stomach, pylorus, and proximal duodenum. Also, a few clinics can perform small mucosal biopsies, which might be adequate to determine the presence of small-bowel disease.

An alternative, more expensive, and more risky procedure is an exploratory laparotomy. This allows for a direct examination of the abdominal contents and related structures. Several full-thickness biopsies can be taken from along the wall of the small intestine and also from drainage lymph nodes. Several gut biopsies should be taken because the disease might not be diffuse, and a single sample might miss an affected area. Histopathologic evaluation of the biopsies might define the problem and suggest possible therapy. The cranial mesenteric artery and its branches can be examined for evidence of parasitic infection. These malabsorbing horses are often thin and are not good surgical candidates. Many heal poorly postoperatively, although some do well.

Treatment. Therapy for small-intestine malabsorption syndromes in horses is not well evaluated. With lymphosarcoma, the long-term prognosis is poor. Although horses might respond initially to prednisolone, 1 mg/kg body weight intramuscularly once a day, this response is not usually sustained. To my knowledge, additional chemotherapeutic protocols have not been evaluated in horses. If the biopsy indicates non-neoplastic lymphocytic-plasmacytic infiltration of the bowel, a similar steroid regimen might be helpful: initial therapy for 3 to 4 weeks at 1.0 mg/kg prednisolone intramuscularly. The dosage should be gradually reduced if the horse responds. Weekly weighings are needed to assess the response. By the fifth or sixth week the goal should be an alternate-day dosage of 0.5 or 0.25 mg/kg, to be gradually tailed off over the next 4 to 5 weeks. Total therapy should last about 12 weeks, although some animals might need low maintenance therapy.

These guidelines for therapy are based on personal experience with a small number of cases. If therapy is successful, absorption test results might return to the normal range.

If eosinophilic infiltrates predominate according to histopathology, or if cranial mesenteric parasitic lesions are suspected based on physical examination, ivermectin can be given at therapeutic dosages to kill any strongyle parasites, larvae or adults, involved. In addition, if eosinophilic bowel infiltration is detected, a steroid regimen similar to that outlined above should be considered, if

not immediately, then after the effects of ivermectin have been assessed.

Approach to Testing. An approach using exploratory laparotomy, biopsy, and therapy is theoretically the most logical and complete. However, economic and other factors might dictate a more empirical method of handling small-intestine malabsorption problems. The owner might chose to limit testing to d-xylose or oral glucose tolerance tests, without pursuing further diagnosis. However, different causes of malabsorption have different prognoses. An animal whose malabsorption is caused by a neoplasm has a poor prognosis, no matter what therapy is used. A non-neoplastic infiltration of the bowel might respond to steroids. Parasitic infestation of the bowel or its blood supply can respond to anthelmintic therapy.

The best approach is probably to treat the horse with larvicidal doses of anthelmintics and wait 2 to 3 three weeks (if the disease is not progressing at such a rate that waiting before further treatment would threaten the life of the horse). If the horse shows little response to ivermectin, a course of prednisolone could be tried, as outlined above. The facts and risks of the empirical method of treatment should be explained to the client. Immunosuppression of a horse might allow other, possibly fatal diseases to develop. However, because many of these animals will die if nothing is done, the choices are often very limited. In the final analysis, the extent to which a diagnosis is pursued depends on the severity of the problem, the need for the owner to have a definitive diagnosis, and sometimes external influences such as insurers and their agents.

Even after performance of laparotomy and biopsy, a definitive diagnosis is not guaranteed. A horse can have an abnormally low d-xylose curve and yet have a histologically normal small bowel when sampled at laparotomy. Four possible reasons exist: the d-xylose assay might contain laboratory error; reduced gastric emptying or sugar fermentation can occur (see above); the biopsy might not sample a diseased piece of bowel; and the bowel might be functionally abnormal without any histologic change. Although I have not encountered a functionally abnormal but histologically normal bowel for certain, I have suspected as much after evaluating some animals at necropsy and not finding any other reason for their apparently reduced absorption.

Large-Bowel Maldigestion and Malabsorption

Large-bowel maldigestion and malabsorption could lead to chronic weight loss, but how frequently is not known. Certainly, in cases in which granulomatous enteritis or lymphosarcoma involves the cecum and colon, one could expect significant large-bowel dysfunction and reduced absorption of volatile fatty acids. Severe large-bowel disease can lead to weight loss, usually with chronic diarrhea. However, chronic diarrhea per se is not indicative of total large-bowel malabsorption. Many horses with chronic diarrhea maintain adequate body weight with a normal food intake. Malabsorption and weight loss is probably caused by parasitism of the large bowel, particularly infection with small strongyles, both adults and larvae. In addition, protein-losing enteropathy can be associated with parasitism, and parasites can directly consume the host's protein. A good anthelmintic regimen is usually indicated in a horse with chronic weight loss. Even if fecal evaluation for eggs is negative, significant damage can be done by larval forms and immature adults.

IS THERE AN INCREASED LOSS OF NUTRIENTS ONCE ABSORBED?

A horse can be eating well, digesting and absorbing food, and yet be losing weight. Weight loss can result from increased loss of nutrients through two major routes, the gastrointestinal tract and the kidneys. In addition, significantly large amounts of protein can be "lost" to the body by accumulation in the pleural or peritoneal cavities when the horse has active pleuritis or peritonitis. Affected animals are also usually febrile and anorexic, which significantly contributes to weight loss.

Protein-losing enteropathies affect both the large and the small bowel. Maldigestion and malabsorption also usually contribute to weight loss. Protein-losing enteropathies include granulomatous enteritis, severe parasitism, and chronic ulcerative lesions such as those induced by chronic phenylbutazone toxicity. I have encountered horses with large chronic ulcerative lesions involving 30 to 40 cm of the large colon. Salmonellae have been isolated from these lesions, but because diarrhea is not always present in these horses, the role of salmonellae in the cause of the problem is not clear. Weight loss results from loss of large amounts of protein from these large, open, ulcerated areas.

All of these situations are marked by continued loss of plasma proteins, and in many cases by abnormal absorption as well. Laboratory data are not specific. Mild anemia can be present, and chronic inflammation can be reflected by a moderate leukocytosis. Serum chemistries can be unremarkable, with the exception of a low serum protein, particularly albumin, which can fall below 1 g/dl. In some cases, inflammation can lead to an elevated globulin, or at least can maintain globulin within the normal range.

If severe hypoalbuminemia produces ventral and limb edema, specific tests for liver and kidney dysfunction should be performed to determine the cause of the low albumin levels. Abdominal fluid analysis is not usually helpful. Protein-losing enteropathy should be suspected in an animal that is eating well but losing weight and is hypoalbuminemic without evidence of liver or kidney dysfunction.

Biopsy via laparotomy of the small and large bowel can be helpful in refining the diagnosis but involves risks. Biopsy of the rectal mucosa taken through the anus using an endometrial biopsy instrument, useful only if the enteropathy is generalized, is safe. If the cause of the protein-losing enteropathy can be identified specifically, treatment can be determined more appropriately. If phenylbutazone toxicity is suspected, cessation of therapy and time might be all that is necessary. If parasites are responsible, anthelmintics might help, but because severe bowel damage can have developed, a slow response to therapy should be expected. Severe, extensive ulcerative areas resist treatment. Empirical therapy with oral "gastrointestinal protectants" is usually useless. Specific antibiotic therapy against salmonellae is equally unrewarding. If the problem is considered to be due to granulomatous enteritis, steroid therapy, as outlined above, can be helpful in some cases.

Generally speaking, cases of protein-losing gastroenteropathy carry a poor prognosis in adult horses, particularly if they cannot be accounted for by phenylbutazone toxicity or parasitism.

Renal disease, which can be immune-mediated, can lead to significant protein loss, and this proteinuria accounts for some of the weight loss encountered. In addition, affected horses are usually azotemic, depressed, and anorexic. Thus, they have an accelerated loss of nutrients in the urine and a markedly reduced intake. The clinical signs associated with chronic renal disease include depression, anorexia, and polydipsia and polyuria with weight loss. Peripheral limb and ventral edema can develop secondary to the marked hypoalbuminemia in advanced cases. Additionally, the animals can be anemic, hypochloremic, hyponatremic, and hypercalcemic. Urinalysis is often helpful with massive proteinuria and little or no evidence of urinary tract inflammation (see Chapter 12).

IS THERE AN INCREASED OR ABNORMAL USE OF NUTRIENTS?

Increased metabolic activity, induced by increased work or other normal physiologic states, will lead to weight loss unless the diet is adjusted accordingly. Pathophysiologic states also can lead to increased use of absorbed nutrients, leading to weight loss.

As pointed out, new horse owners often are unaware of the dietary needs of their horses. Though they may be providing an adequate amount of food to meet the needs of maintenance and light work in the winter months, they often do not increase or alter the ration in the summer when they begin to work the horse more vigorously and regularly. Careful enquiry may be needed to determine if drastic changes have taken place in the work schedule. Other owners do not feed adequate amounts to their horses during the cold winter months. They might merely turn them out into pasture and forget about them.

Some horses always lose weight when kept in full work and remain lean throughout the work period. Though horses are grazers, designed to eat little and often, horses in heavy training schedules are fed occasionally and in large amounts. It might be that they cannot take in enough calories to meet their increased needs. This appears to be particularly true for some endurance horses trained to travel distances of 50 to 80 km/

day. Such horses are often remarkably lean, but are fit and healthy and perform well throughout the season. Their owners might not be concerned with the condition of the animal. Others may request a full evaluation, including laboratory tests to determine what is wrong. They are often reluctant to take the animal out of training to see if the lost weight is regained. Thin, hard-working horses are often not abnormal in medical terms, and all investigations can turn up negative findings. This lack of findings is reassuring to some owners but unacceptable to others, who regard their veterinarian as a failure for not identifying the problem.

Many breeding stallions lose weight during the breeding season and gain it back again in the fall and winter. How much of this loss is due to increased metabolic rate and calorie consumption, and how much to reduced intake is speculative. Certainly, many stallions fret and worry throughout the season and do not eat as well as during the off-season.

Late pregnancy and lactation also increase demand for nutrients, and weight loss results if dietary adjustments are not made. A pregnant mare needs about 20% more nutrients in late pregnancy than for normal maintenance, and at peak lactation requires up to 50% more. Again, failure to make dietary adjustments is more likely with first-time, inexperienced horse owners. Advice and monitoring of the feeding program is often all that is needed.

Apart from these physiologically induced states of increased demand, in some rare diseases abnormal metabolic function results in weight loss. Hyperthyroidism leads to a generalized increase in total metabolic activity and subsequent weight loss. Well-documented cases are rare, and thyroid hormonal assay, together with stimulation tests, is indicated if hyperthyroidism is suspected. Horses with Cushing's syndrome also lose weight. These animals have a variety of endocrine abnormalities secondary to neoplasia of the intermediate lobe of the pituitary. These abnormalities include hyperadrenocorticosteroidism, which results in marked hyperglycemia and glucosuria. Large amounts of glucose are lost in the urine, causing negative energy balance. These patients usually have other, more marked clinical problems overshadowing their weight loss. They are polydipsic and polyuric, they often have chronic laminitis, and they suffer from chronic recurrent infections. Their coats grow so long that they might mask the weight loss on casual visual examination. They appear thin only if they are clipped out or a hand is run along their backs. Laboratory data and ancillary tests will characterize these patients (see Chapter 12).

Lastly, chronic liver disease is often associated with chronic weight loss (see Chapter 14). However, not all horses with chronic liver disease are icteric. The weight loss of chronic liver disease is due not only to severe metabolic derangements, but also to reduced intake resulting from the marked depression in these patients. Clinically, the animals are variably depressed, are occasionally icteric, can have ventral edema, and can be photosensitive over their white or nonpigmented skin. Severe cases can show signs of hepatic encephalopathy with aimless wandering, head pressing, and convulsions.

Clinical pathologic data vary, depending on the phase of the disease when blood samples are taken. Hypoalbuminemia is often present. Serum enzymes, sorbitol dehydrogenase, aspartate aminotransferase, and particularly gamma glutamyltranspeptidase can be elevated to varying degrees. Sulfobromophthaline clearance is usually increased. A liver biopsy is indicated for a definitive diagnosis. Specific therapy is not available, but many horses will eventually recover if placed on a diet of grass hay (see Chapter 14).

SUPPLEMENTAL READING

Bolton, J.R., et al.: Normal and abnormal d-xylose absorption in the horse. Cornell Vet.,66:183–197, 1976.

Jacobs, K.A., and Bolton, J.R.: Effects of diet on the oral glucose tolerance test in the horse. J. Am. Vet. Med. Assoc. 180:884–886, 1982.

Jacobs, K.A., et al.: Effects of diet on the normal d-xylose absorption test in the horse. Am. J. Vet. Res. 43:1856–1858, 1982.

Lewis, L.D.: Feeding and care of the horse. Philadelphia, Lea & Febiger, 1982.

Roberts, M.C.: Malabsorption syndromes in the horse. Compend. Contin. Educ., 7:S637–S647, 1985.

Rumbaugh, G.E., Smith, B.P., and Carlson, G.P.: Internal abdominal abscesses in the horse: A study of 25 cases. J. Am. Vet. Med. Assoc., 172:304–309, 1978.

chapter 3

DIARRHEA

Michael J. Murray

Diarrhea in the horse is the passage of fecal material with an increased water content. It can range from soft, formed stools with a mild to moderate increase in water content, to a projectile fluid that contains minimal solid matter. The passage of excessive water in the feces reflects disruption of the normal balance of fluid and electrolyte secretion and absorption in the intestinal tract. In foals, diarrhea can result from disorders affecting the small intestine, the large intestine, or both, whereas in adult horses, diarrhea results almost exclusively from disorders of the large intestine. Diarrhea can cause significant losses of water, electrolytes, and buffer, and it is often accompanied by local and systemic inflammatory responses. The effects of several inflammatory mediators can further compromise the patient who is already dehydrated, depleted of electrolytes, and acidotic.

NORMAL PHYSIOLOGY OF THE EQUINE DIGESTIVE SYSTEM

Gastric physiology of foals is poorly understood. The neonatal diet consists entirely of milk, which coagulates prior to passage into the small intestine. The digestion and absorption of water, electrolytes and trace minerals, lactose, protein, fat, and vitamins occurs almost exclusively in the small intestine. During the first few weeks of a foal's life, the digestive system develops the ability to process a wide variety of feed materials. The foal becomes coprophagic in its first days, ingesting the mare's manure soon after the mare defecates. The manure inoculates the foal's undeveloped large intestine with the bacteria and protozoa required for the digestion of cellulose, and with its ingestion begins ingestion of grass and hay.

Over the next few weeks the large intestine develops rapidly, both physically and physiologically. As the foal continues to grow, the fermentation of feed into volatile fatty acids by the flora of the large intestine provides a significant source of energy. Additionally, the balance of fluid and electrolyte absorption and secretion in the large intestine becomes a major factor, along with renal function, in the overall regulation of total body fluid, electrolytes, and buffer homeostasis.

The primary function of the fully developed large intestine of the horse is the production and absorption of volatile fatty acids by microbial digestion of soluble and insoluble carbohydrates. Transport mechanisms in the large intestine have evolved to perform three major functions: absorption of volatile fatty acids, which is associated with the transport of water, sodium, chloride, hydrogen ions, and bicarbonate across the mucosa; maintenance of luminal pH between 6.8 and 7.2; and maintenance of luminal osmolality at approximately 300 mOsm. The regulation of luminal pH and osmolality maintains an environment that supports the population of microorganisms that synthesize volatile fatty acids.

Most of the microbial fermentation of carbohydrates to volatile fatty acids occurs in the cecum, ventral colon, and dorsal colon. Much of the ingested soluble carbohydrate (starch) is fermented to propionic acid in the cecum and large colon. Fermentation of the insoluble carbohydrate (cellulose) occurs primarily in the ventral and dorsal colons. The principal volatile fatty acids produced from the fermentation of cellulose are acetic acid and butyric acid, with the majority being acetic acid. The volatile fatty acids are absorbed from the lumen of the intestine and transported to the liver and peripheral tissues, where they provide up to 75% of the energy needed.

The transport of fluid and electrolytes across the intestinal mucosal epithelium is governed by passive and active forces. The sum of these forces determines whether there is net absorption from or secretion into the lumen. Passive forces regulating fluid and electrolyte transport include the intrinsic permeability of the intestinal epithelial cells, the osmotic pressure gradient exerted by intestinal lumen contents, the electric potential difference across the intestinal epithelial cells, the concentration gradient of solutes across the intestinal epithelial cell, and the pH of the luminal contents. The absorption and secretion of fluid and electrolytes is governed by many processes at the cellular and microvascular levels. These dynamic processes act with the fluctuations in the absorption and secretion of fluid and electrolytes that occur throughout the day in the equine colon.

In a 450-kg horse, the cecum receives an average of 60 L of fluid from the small intestine daily, with only 4 to 5 L being excreted in the feces. Also, 35 L are secreted into the lumen of the large intestine daily. Thus, 90 L of fluid are absorbed daily by the cecum, large colon, and small colon. This volume of fluid is more than three times the plasma volume.

Because digested material is retained within the large colon for several days, volatile fatty acids, primarily acetate, are produced and absorbed continuously. However, in ponies fed twice daily, definite cyclic changes in water and electrolyte transport occurred in conjunction with the production and absorption of volatile fatty acids derived from microbial fermentation of the most recently ingested feed. Based on the data from several reports, a model describing the digestive physiology based on equids fed twice daily has been proposed.

Luminal acetate increases during the first 8 hours after feeding, associated with the net secretion of sodium and water into the lumen of the colon. Acetate directly inhibits the absorption of sodium in the equine colon, possibly by inhibiting a sodium/hydrogen ion exchange process. Only the undissociated form of acetate (acetic acid) can be absorbed, and at the normal cecal and colonic pH of 6.8, 99% of acetic acid is in the dissociated, anionic state (acetate). However, in the lumen, CO_2 is hydrated to form carbonic acid, which dissociates into bicarbonate and hydrogen ion. The hydrogen ion can combine with acetate to form acetic acid, which is then absorbed into the colonic epithelial cell. As acetic acid is absorbed, a net accumulation of bicarbonate occurs in the lumen, secondary to absorption of hydrogen ions produced by the hydration of CO_2, and secretion of bicarbonate into the lumen from the mucosal epithelial cell occurs via a chloride/bicarbonate exchange mechanism. Thus, the period of volatile fatty acid production is marked by fluid secretion into the lumen to buffer the osmotically active volatile fatty acids, bicarbonate accumulation in the lumen, which maintains a slightly acidic pH, and absorption of volatile fatty acids.

During the period 8 to 12 hours after feeding, the processes described generally reverse. In conjunction with a decreasing acetate concentration in the large colon, sodium and water absorption is restored. Secretion of hydrogen ion into the lumen, via restoration of the sodium/hydrogen ion exchange mechanism, buffers the accumulated bicarbonate in the lumen, producing CO_2, which diffuses across the mucosal cell into the blood. Thus, the bicarbonate that accumulated within the lumen of the colon during the volatile fatty acids absorptive phase is reclaimed and absorbed as CO_2. The majority of the water not reabsorbed from the large colon is then reabsorbed in the small colon.

Thus, despite a tremendous flux of fluid and ions across the epithelium of the cecum and large colon throughout the day, the horse is able to achieve net absorption of essential volatile fatty acids and to retain water, ions, bicarbonate, and hydrogen ion sufficient to maintain fluid, electrolyte, and acid-base homeostasis.

PATHOPHYSIOLOGY

The pathophysiology of diarrhea is complex and differs with the cause. The onset of diarrhea can reflect decreased absorption of fluid and electrolytes, their active or passive increased secretion, or both. Frequently, local and systemic inflammatory responses accompany the diarrhea.

The pathophysiologic processes in diarrhea will be discussed in the context of alterations in the microvasculature of the intestine, agents that cause secretion at the cellular level, inflammatory mediators, which affect the intestine at both cellular and microvascular sites, and endocrine mediators. In adult horses with diarrhea, these changes relate to the large intestine; in foals they can relate to the small intestine, large intestine, or both. Alterations in colonic physiology will be stressed, because most cases of equine diarrhea reflect colonic disorders. Knowing the interaction of the physiologic mechanisms will aid the clinician in directing therapeutic plans toward the pathophysiologic process.

MICROVASCULAR CHANGES

Although the balance between secretion and absorption in the normal intestinal microvasculature is delicate, the interstitium allows for expansion and contraction of the interstitial space (i.e., increased and decreased hydration); this potential is termed the edema safety factor. However, the changes that can occur in the large intestine secondary to colitis can disrupt this balance and negate the safety factor. Inflammatory mediators such as endotoxin, oxygen radicals, histamine, and bradykinin increase the capillary endothelium's permeability to macromolecules and promote an increase in the movement of protein-rich capillary filtrate into the interstitium, which can alter the characteristics of the interstitial gel matrix. Alteration can lead to protein exudation into the intestinal lumen and a plasma protein deficit, which exacerbates the movement of fluid from capillaries into the interstitium. In cats, prostaglandin E_1 (PGE_1) induces intestinal fluid secretion and protein exudation into the intestinal lumen.

With severe hypoproteinemia, the capillary oncotic pressure can be decreased as much as 50%, leading to an increased capillary filtration rate and increased fluid movement into the interstitium. Interstitial compliance is lost, resulting in progressive tissue edema and protein loss.

An increase in the filtration coefficients of the capillaries, that is, the rate at which water can pass through them, can increase interstitial fluid. Agents that cause such an increase include histamine, bradykinin, PGE_1, and cholera toxin. These increase filtration either by in-creasing the size or number of pores within the capillary endothelium (histamine, bradykinin), or by increasing the number of perfused capillaries (PGE_1, cholera toxin). Thus, the combination of increased capillary permeability to macromolecules, hypoproteinemia, and increased capillary perfusion can lead to a profound movement of protein-rich fluid through the interstitium and eventually into the bowel lumen.

SECRETORY MEDIATORS

Bacterial enterotoxins are proteins produced by bacteria such as Escherichia coli, Salmonella, Shigella, and Vibrio cholerae. These toxins interact with intestinal epithelial cells and cause secretion of fluid and electrolytes into the intestinal lumen by increasing intestinal mucosal cyclic guanosine monophosphate (heat-stable enterotoxins), or by increasing cyclic adenosine monophosphate (cAMP) (heat-labile enterotoxins). Cholera toxin is clinically significant only in humans, although an in vitro study demonstrated that it caused an increase in cAMP in isolated equine colonic mucosa. Salmonella enterotoxin caused fluid secretion in isolated colon segments in vivo. Although E. coli that produce heat-stable or heat-labile enterotoxins have been isolated from foals with diarrhea, at present it is not known if these or other enterotoxins are important in the initiation of diarrhea in foals or adult horses.

The results of several studies suggest that prostaglandins are involved in intestinal fluid secretion. Oral administration of prostaglandin E_1 in humans can cause diarrhea. Increased mucosal prostaglandins E_1, E_2, and thromboxane A_2 have been measured in humans with colitis. Following treatment with sulfasalazine, a drug that inhibits prostaglandin synthesis, human patients that responded with a decrease in fecal fluid output also had a decrease in colonic mucosal prostaglandin levels.

INFLAMMATION

A variety of inflammatory cells and mediators affect the equine colon. In the normal colon, mast cells are situated along the basement membrane of crypt epithelial cells. Aggregates of lymphocytes are interspersed throughout the colon, and lymphocytes and plasma cells freely migrate through the mucosa. Frequently, eosinophils infiltrate the mucosa in response to parasitic migration and problably other antigenic stimuli. In cases of acute colitis, large numbers of neutrophils infiltrate the submucosa and mucosa. Additionally, monocytes are recruited, producing a complex cellular inflammatory and immunologic response.

Signs of endotoxemia frequently accompany, or even precede, diarrhea in horses. Lipid A is responsible for endotoxic activity of bacterial lipopolysaccharide (LPS). Endotoxins produce fever, leukopenia, thrombocytopenia, damage to vascular endothelium, and coagulopathies and cause impairment of cardiopulmonary function. In addition, endotoxin administration in the equine species causes pulmonary hypertension, hypoxemia, lactic acidosis, and transient diarrhea. Circulating endotoxin has been detected in horses with clinical salmonellosis and in horses with diarrhea in which Salmonella was not isolated. Thus, endotoxin appears to be involved in many of the abnormalities occurring in horses with acute diarrhea.

The process by which inflammatory cells damage bacteria also can damage host tissues. Complement activation and phagocytosis of bacteria by macrophages and neutrophils stimulate metabolic changes in these phagocytic cells, resulting in a 2- to 20-fold increase in cellular oxygen consumption and increased glucose metabolism through the hexose-monophosphate shunt. This increase promotes a rapid generation of oxygen radicals (O_2^-) and hydrogen peroxide (H_2O_2). Oxygen radicals and hydrogen peroxide react with iron to form hydroxyl radicals, highly unstable and biologically active oxygen radicals.

Hydroxyl radicals cause tissue injury by peroxidation of lipid in cell membranes, leading to cell death and further propagation of hydroxyl radicals. Hydroxyl radicals break down the collagen-hyaluronic acid interstitial matrix and damage capillary endothelial cells, thus disrupting an important regulation of tissue hydration.

Prostaglandins, in addition to having a secretory effect, are likely to be involved in the intestinal inflammatory response. In laboratory animals, inoculation of the intestine with viable Salmonella causes an increase in intestinal mucosal cell prostaglandin E. Pretreatment with the nonsteroidal anti-inflammatory drug (NSAID) indomethacin minimizes the inflammatory response and intestinal fluid secretion secondary to Salmonella infection.

Another group of arachidonic acid metabolites, leukotrienes, might also be involved in the pathophysiology of the inflammatory response in colitis. Leukotriene B_4, which is a potent chemotactic factor for neutrophils, has been shown to have enhanced synthesis in colon mucosal biopsies from humans with ulcerative colitis. Rabbit colonic mucosa responds to the leukotriene 5-HPETE by an increase in chloride secretion.

Another product of an inflammatory response is bradykinin, which is present as an inactive precursor in tissue and is activated by stimuli associated with inflammation and tissue damage. In laboratory animals, bradykinin causes an increased chloride secretion from colonic epithelium. This effect appears to be mediated through the release of arachidonic acid and seems to involve both prostaglandins and leukotrienes.

ENDOCRINE MEDIATORS

The gastrointestinal endocrine system of the horse has been evaluated partially, but its role in the initiation and maintenance of diarrhea is not known. Two hormones that could have a role are vasoactive intestinal peptide (VIP) and 5-hydroxytryptamine (serotonin). In other species, VIP causes an increase in colonic epithelial cAMP and causes profound fluid and electrolyte secretion. Intravenous VIP administration in human volunteers caused a profuse, watery diarrhea within 4 hours, and VIP has been implicated in the pathogenesis of pancreatic cholera in humans.

Experimentally, serotonin has been demonstrated to be released from enterochromaffin cells secondary to cholera toxin exposure and to have a role in the secretory diarrhea associated with narcotic withdrawal. Serotonin's mechanism in the development of diarrhea might involve stimulation of local prostaglandin synthesis.

TYPES

ACUTE DIARRHEA

Causes

Foals. The causes of acute diarrhea differ somewhat in foals (see Chapter 19) and adult horses, although agents that cause colitis, such as Salmonella, affect foals and adults alike. The causes of diarrhea in foals have been characterized as nutritional, parasitic, viral, bacterial, or antibiotic. Nutritional diarrhea results from overingestion of milk, or in the case of orphan foals, ingestion of a poorly digestible milk replacer. Undigested or nonabsorbed sugars and proteins are osmotically active, initiating passive secretion into the small and large intestines. The excess fluid presented to the incompletely developed large intestine cannot be reabsorbed, and diarrhea results.

Several parasites can cause diarrhea in foals, including Parascaris equorum, the L_3 stage of Strongylus vulgaris, Strongyloides westeri, and possibly Cryptosporidia. Diarrhea caused by Strongyloides westeri is frequently associated with outbreaks on farms, although the overall prevalence of Strongyloides-induced diarrhea is not great.

The prevalence of rotavirus diarrhea in foals is unknown, but it has been documented as being very high on certain farms. It primarily affects foals less than 2 months of age, causing a profuse diarrhea with moderate to severe dehydration, electrolyte deficits, and metabolic acidosis. The disease can progress rapidly and can ultimately be fatal. Rotavirus destroys the tips of small-intestinal villi, leading to malabsorption of osmotically active sugars and peptides, particularly lactose. The profuse nature of the diarrhea suggests an active secretory process as well, possibly as a result of a secondary bacterial infection.

Coronavirus, adenovirus, and parvovirus have been associated with diarrhea in foals but are not thought to be common causes of diarrhea.

Salmonella species cause severe enterocolitis in foals, and diarrhea can occur in foals with primary Salmonella septicemia. Enteropathogenic E. coli are generally assumed to cause diarrhea in foals, but the specific virulence factors such as adhesion pili associated with colibacillosis in other species have not been characterized in strains of E. coli isolated from foals. Rhodococcus equi is associated with diarrhea in foals, secondary to mesenteric and intestinal abscess formation and peritonitis.

Diarrhea can result from the oral administration of antimicrobials in foals. Antimicrobials are most typically involved in trimethoprim-sulfa combinations, erythromycin, and penicillins. The diarrhea associated with the use of erythromycin has been observed with erythromycin base and erythromycin stearate, both of which are poorly absorbed by the intestine. In my experience, erythromycin estolate, which is better absorbed and is thus more effective as an antimicrobial, has not been associated with diarrhea. Most antimicrobial-associated diarrhea in foals is mild to moderate and resolves when oral administration of the drug is discontinued.

Foals with clinical or endoscopic evidence of gastric ulcers often have diarrhea. Frequently, the diarrhea resolves within 24 to 48 hours of therapy with a histamine type 2 receptor antagonist. Many such foals are treated with several medications, and a specific pathogen, such as rotavirus, can be the primary cause of diarrhea; in other cases there appears to be a direct association between the diarrhea and the gastric lesions. In such cases, the diarrhea resolves shortly after initiating the histamine type 2 receptor antagonist. Potential mechanisms of the diarrhea include increased acid load to the small intestine, with damage to the superficial mucosa and malabsorption, and an endocrine-mediated diarrhea, with potential involvement of vasoactive intestinal peptide, somatostatin, and gastrin.

Juveniles and Adults. The documented causes of diarrhea are more limited in juvenile and adult horses than in foals. *The cause of the diarrhea is frequently not determined*, in spite of extensive testing. The most frequently diagnosed infectious cause of diarrhea in horses is Salmonella, although in some areas Ehrlichia risticii may be a more common cause. Salmonellae have several virulence factors that contribute to invasiveness, to the fluid secretory response, and to the host's local and systemic inflammatory response. A large number of Salmonella serotypes have been isolated from cases of equine colitis, but S. typhimurium, S. agona, and S. anatum are among the most frequently isolated. Salmonellae are ubiquitous in the environment, and from 1 to 5% of asymptomatic horses tested shed Salmonella in the feces.

Salmonellosis is characterized by an acute, septic colitis, resulting in profuse diarrhea. In many cases, with treatment, the severe diarrhea and associated metabolic disorders improve within 7 to 10 days of the onset of illness. Horses that have severe diarrhea and septicemia for 14 days or longer are unlikely to survive, even with intensive therapy. Other clinical syndromes of salmonellosis include fever and leukopenia, colic, and proximal enteritis with gastric reflux.

Ehrlichia risticii is the causative agent of equine monocytic ehrlichiosis (Potomac horse fever). The organism is an obligate intracellular parasite, localizing primarily in peripheral monocytes and macrophages. The organism has been observed ultrastructurally in colonic and small-intestinal epithelial cells and in colonic mast cells. The pathophysiology of the disease is poorly understood, although horses infected with Ehrlichia risticii often have clinical signs and complications similar to horses with salmonellosis. Clinical signs of endotoxemia and septicemia, including fever, leukopenia, congested mucous membranes, and hypercoagulability, occur with both diseases. Laminitis is a frequent sequel of both diseases. Some useful differences between these diseases exist. Horses infected with Ehrlichia risticii can be febrile or have signs of colic several days before the onset of diarrhea, and often they have an absolute peripheral monocytosis. Although originally described as a disease of horses living near the Potomac River in Maryland, the disease has been confirmed serologically in several states, although a strong association remains with location near a river. The mode of transmission is unknown, although it does not appear to occur directly from horse to horse. An insect vector, as well as an intermediate host, is probably involved in the transmission of the disease.

The disposition of the infectious agent in recovered horses is unknown. Indeed, a few horses have had clinical relapses, responsive to tetracycline, 2 to 3 weeks following initial resolution of clinical signs.

Clostridium perfringens type A has been described as a cause of peracute toxemic colitis (colitis X), but the role of this organism in the initiation of acute diarrhea in the equine species has not been clearly defined.

Acute diarrhea in the horse has also been associated with the use of certain antibiotics, including lincomycin administered orally and tetracycline administered parenterally. These drugs have the potential to disrupt the normal cecal and colonic microflora. The pathophysiology of the resulting colitis and diarrhea can involve altered volatile fatty acid synthesis, colonization and invasion of the colon by pathogenic bacteria, and release of toxins by these bacteria. Salmonella, Clostridium perfringens, and Clostridium difficile have been implicated in such cases. The oral administration of trimethoprim-sulfa and penicillin has been associated with mild to moderate diarrhea in a small number of treated horses.

The excessive administration of NSAIDs has been associated with diarrhea secondary to the development of hypoproteinemia and cecal and colonic mucosal edema and ulceration. The inhibition of prostaglandin synthesis by NSAIDs disrupts mucosal blood flow and other cytopro-

tective mechanisms of the bowel. In addition to hypoproteinemia, these horses often have signs of severe septicemia. Many horses with diarrhea and septicemia secondary to excessive administration of NSAIDs are slow to respond to therapy and require long-term intensive care.

Acute diarrhea in the adult horse has also been associated with conditions such as granulomatous enteritis, intestinal lymphosarcoma, peritonitis, heavy metal intoxication, anaphylaxis, and stress.

Clinical Evaluation

A thorough physical examination should be done, paying particular attention to the hydration status (skin turgor, gum moisture, and capillary refill time), evidence of septicemia (injected sclera, conjunctiva, oral mucous membranes, mucous membrane color, capillary refill time), cardiovascular system (heart rate and rhythm, character of peripheral pulse, and capillary refill time) and signs of laminitis (lameness, digital pulse, and palpable temperature of hoof walls).

Horses with acute colitis are often moderately to severely dehydrated, with either purplish or brick-red mucous membranes. Purple mucous membranes reflect venous congestion and poor venous return, whereas brick-red color reflects arteriole-venule shunting and poor tissue oxygen exchange.

Laboratory tests that should be performed include complete blood count and fibrinogen to assess the horse's hydration status (packed cell volume), severity of sepsis (total white blood cell count, differential, and structure), and severity of inflammation (fibrinogen, total protein). Initially, in diarrhea resulting from Salmonella and other causes, the total white blood cell and neutrophil counts will be low because of bacterial endotoxins and the host's mediators of inflammation. The structure of the white blood cells reflects the severity of the inflammatory response and the degree of sepsis. Scalloped borders of the cell membrane and "toxic" changes, such as basophilia, granulation, and vacuolation of the cytoplasm, reflect not injury to the neutrophils by toxins, but rather the response to antigenic stimulation and the production of several chemicals by the neutrophils that are toxic to bacteria. The degree of these changes in circulating neutrophils can be used to assess the severity of sepsis and also the progress of the disease. Often, the first sign that a horse is improving is a decrease in the "toxic" appearance of the neutrophils. Horses with neutrophils having scalloped cell membranes adherent to red blood cells and with cytoplasmic vacuolation, granulation, and basophilia for more than 10 days have a poor prognosis.

Serum chemistry tests that should be performed include electrolytes (sodium, chloride, potassium, and calcium), serum urea nitrogen (SUN), creatinine, and total CO_2. Horses with acute diarrhea typically are hyponatremic, hypochloremic, and hypokalemic. With inappetance, hypocalcemia can occur.

The severity of these electrolyte disturbances should be monitored, often daily, to allow for appropriate therapy. Parameters of renal function, SUN and creatinine, are frequently increased in horses with diarrhea, for several reasons. Prerenal azotemia, caused by dehydration and decreased renal profusion, accounts for some of the increase in these parameters. Another factor causing an increase in SUN and creatinine is hyponatremia. Horses that are adequately hydrated yet moderately hyponatremic (serum sodium 120 to 128 mEq/L) will remain azotemic. The decrease in glomerular filtration rate secondary to hyponatremia results partly from increased renin and angiotensin and partly from a direct tubuloglomerular

response. Correction of the hyponatremia leads to correction of the azotemia.

The acid-base status can be evaluated by estimating serum bicarbonate based on the total CO_2, or directly from a venous or arterial blood gas analysis. Evaluation of a venous blood gas sample is also useful in septic patients. Venous P_{O_2} greater than 60 mm Hg (7.98 kPa) indicates poor capillary perfusion and oxygen delivery to the tissues.

Multiple fecal cultures for Salmonella should be performed on all horses with diarrhea. At least five fecal samples should be submitted for culture to enhance the chances of isolating Salmonella. Samples with little solid matter often yield negative culture results, even when the horse is infected with Salmonella. To ensure a positive culture from an infected horse, 5 to 10 g of feces should be submitted for culture in selective media such as tetrathionate or selenite broth and in brilliant green or Salmonella-Shigella agar. Culture of a rectal mucosal biopsy specimen will often identify positive Salmonella cases when fecal cultures have been negative.

In areas of the country where equine monocytic ehrlichiosis occurs, paired acute and convalescent blood samples of horses with diarrhea should be submitted for testing for antibodies to Ehrlichia risticii.

Treatment

Because the pathophysiology of equine colitis is complex, the treatment of these cases often incorporates several medications. For many of these treatments the benefit is well-documented; with others, the efficacy is based on empiric judgment only. Additionally, in many cases the factor limiting successful outcome is a complication of colitis, not a direct effect of colitis.

In cases of acute colitis, fluid administration remains the most important treatment.

Intravenous Fluid. Most cases will require intravenous administration of fluid, sodium, chloride, and potassium in the early stages of colitis. The current availability of several sterile commercial intravenous fluid products packaged in volumes suitable for use in adult horses is making intravenous fluid administration in the field a more common practice. Because under field conditions the exact acid-base and electrolyte status of most horses cannot be obtained quickly, fluid selection will be empiric; for most cases, lactated Ringer's solution or other multi-ionic solutions can be used without major risk. In severely hypokalemic horses, 20 to 40 mEq potassium chloride can be added to each liter of Ringer's or saline solutions. Often bicarbonate must be administered intravenously; the amount given is determined by measuring the base deficit, and multiplying by the factor of $0.5 \times$ body weight (kg).

The rate of fluid administration depends on the immediacy of the animal's fluid needs. In a severely dehydrated horse, fluids can be pumped intravenously at a rate of 1 L/minute. I have infused 30 L of lactated Ringer's solution intravenously in 30 minutes to severely dehydrated horses and improved intravascular volume tremendously. There were no apparent complications to this rapid fluid administration. In the absence of a pump system, two 5-L bags of fluids can be administered simultaneously through a two-lead arthroscopic irrigation set, with 10-gauge catheters in place in each jugular vein or lateral thoracic veins. As much as 20 L can be administered in 30 minutes with this method.

Which catheter system and which vein to use for fluid and medication delivery depends on several factors, including the volume and rate of fluid to be administered, the type of fluid administered, the potential for coagulopathies and venous thrombosis, and the duration of intravenous catheterization required. Polypropy-

lene catheters are available in sizes (10 and 12 gauge) that permit rapid administration of large volumes of fluid, but because of their size and material are highly thrombogenic and unsuitable for long-term catheterization in colitis. Teflon catheters (14 and 16 gauge) are less thrombogenic but can cause jugular thrombosis in septic patients. These catheters are also prone to forming kinks and cracks with constant use. Silicone elastomer and polyurethane catheters are the least thrombophilic and because they are quite flexible do not readily form permanent kinks. However, the largest size is limited to 16 gauge. These catheters are most appropriate for long-term use in horses with colitis and can be maintained in the jugular veins of septic patients, usually with minimal complications. Catheterization of the lateral thoracic vein is often preferable to catheterization of the jugular vein, because thrombosis of the jugular vein(s) can lead to severe swelling of the head.

Oral Fluid. Oral fluid administration is an effective adjunct to intravenous fluid administration. More highly concentrated solutions of electrolytes and bicarbonate can be administered by the oral route. The severely ill patient will not usually drink voluntarily, but once fluid and electrolyte deficits have been partially corrected intravenously, horses will often begin to drink. Diarrhea patients can be offered a "smorgasbord" of fluids—buckets containing fresh water, a commercial electrolyte solution, a solution of 60 to 80 g of potassium chloride or 120 to 140 g of "Lite Salt"/20 L water, and a solution of 100 to 200 g of bicarbonate/20 L of water. Horses often will select the solution containing the electrolyte in which they are deficient.

Plasma Therapy. Correction of other fluid deficits in horses with colitis might require plasma therapy. Most horses with colitis become hypoproteinemic secondary to protein leakage through the inflamed colon and catabolism of albumin secondary to negative energy balance. This hypoproteinemia frequently leads to edema in several areas of the body (see Chapter 11), including the intestinal tract, and can compromise the clinician's ability to keep the patient properly hydrated through fluid administration.

Albumin is the principal plasma protein that regulates plasma oncotic pressure. With colitis, albumin typically decreases to less than 2 g/dl (20 g/L), and as low as 1 g/dl (10 g/L). Equine plasma contains an average of 3 g albumin/dl (30 g/L). In normal horses with a plasma volume of 20 to 25 L, the intravascular albumin content is approximately 700 g. At a concentration of 1.5 g/dl (15 g/L), intravascular albumin content is in the range of 350 g. Therefore, approximately 10 L of plasma containing 3 g albumin/dl (30 g/L) is needed to significantly increase the plasma albumin concentration toward normal. Although this calculation is only approximate, because fluid and albumin shift between the extravascular and intravascular spaces and because it does not consider continued protein exudation through the inflamed intestine, it does indicate the magnitude of plasma volume that often must be administered to have an appreciable impact on plasma oncotic pressure. With the price of a 900-ml bag of commercial plasma running between $85.00 and $105.00, the cost of effective plasma therapy in adult horses is often prohibitive.

Plasma contains other proteins besides albumin, and its infusion thus can benefit the horse beyond improving plasma oncotic pressure. The role of nonspecific immunoglobulin in the treatment of colitis is unknown. Another factor present in plasma, fibronectin, is essential to the normal function of the monocyte-macrophage system in the processing of a variety of antigens. In septic humans, fibronectin can be severely diminished, and the administration of fibronectin-rich cryoprecipitate can be lifesaving. The presence and role of other proteins, such as elastase and proteinase inhibitors, complement inhibitors, antithrombin III, and other inhibitors of hypercoagulability in plasma of normal and septic equine patients has not been completely evaluated. These and other factors in plasma might offer further benefits to the septic equine patient.

Nutritional Supplementation. The nutritional needs of the septic colitis patient have generally been underemphasized. These horses are frequently anorectic, and the disruption of normal physiologic processes in the inflamed cecum and colon limits the effectiveness of these organs in the digestion and absorption of nutrients. Thus, even if the horse will eat, it probably will be in a severe caloric deficit for some time. Normally, an average horse requires 12,000 to 15,000 kcal/day. A septic horse might require 25,000 kcal/day. In a catabolic patient, muscle and fat tissue are mobilized and used in lieu of ingested nutrients. The plasma protein pool, including albumin and immunoglobulins, is also catabolized. In many cases of colitis, the decrease in plasma protein is due as much to catabolism as to leakage through the inflamed colon.

Principles of enteral supplementation in equine patients have been established, and principles of parenteral feeding are being developed. A variety of feeds can be employed for enteral feeding. The nutrients in these supplements must be digestible and absorbable within the small intestine, because the ability of the inflamed colon to digest or absorb nutrients is diminished. Calories, digestible protein, electrolytes, and vitamins should be provided.

The basic components of parenteral feeding solutions are balanced electrolyte and trace mineral solutions, dextrose, balanced amino acid solutions, lipid emulsions, and vitamin supplements. As an example, a 5-L solution containing 500 ml of a 20% lipid emulsion, 1000 ml of an 8.5%-balanced amino acid solution with electrolytes, 500 g dextrose (10% w/vol), and concentrated multivitamin solution, brought to the correct volume with lactated Ringer's solution, provides approximately 3000 kcal of usable energy. This solution is very hyperosmotic and should be infused relatively slowly (1 L/hour). The clinician should also be familiar with other considerations in the intravenous administration of parenteral nutrition solutions.

With this solution, it is possible to provide about 14,000 kcal/day to a horse. The septic horse's caloric needs are likely to be much greater than this, but providing this amount of calories and balanced amino acids can minimize the tremendous catabolism and body wastage that can occur rapidly in severely affected colitis patients. These solutions must be prepared as aseptically as possible and used immediately, because they are excellent media for the growth of bacteria. The cost of this therapy will vary with the products used, the provider, and the quantity purchased. In the example given, the daily cost of the solution, excluding materials (such as IV lines) and without retail mark-up, could range from $210 (discount price) to $550 (list price). Clearly, at the lower price, in the context of the overall cost of treating the intensive care colitis patient, parenteral nutritional therapy can be economically reasonable.

Other Medications. The use of NSAIDs is common in equine colitis patients. Flunixin meglumine, in particular, is appropriate in the context of equine endotoxemia. Several studies have demonstrated that *pretreatment* with flunixin meglumine prevents several of the pathophysiologic changes associated with the administration of sublethal doses of endotoxin in ponies.

A medication with potential anti-inflammatory benefit in colitis cases is dimethyl sulfoxide (DMSO). DMSO scavenges hydroxyl radicals produced by stimulated neutrophils. In the acute stages of equine colitis, frequently a pronounced neutrophilic invasion of the cecum and colon occurs, and in this context DMSO can be efficacious. A dosage of 100 to 300 mg/kg/day as a 10% solution intravenously is recommended.

The use of antibiotics in the treatment of colitis is controversial. In cases of diarrhea caused by Ehrlichia risticii, the efficacy of tetracycline, 6 to 11 mg/kg twice daily intravenously, is documented clinically and experimentally. In other cases of colitis, including Salmonella-induced colitis in which specific antibiotic sensitivities to the Salmonella have been established, the efficacy of antibiotic administration is less well documented. Many clinicians feel that the use of antibiotics for which the Salmonella has demonstrated sensitivity, such as chloramphenicol, trimethoprim-sulfa, gentamicin, and amikacin, does not significantly alter the course of the disease or hasten the elimination of the organism from the body. In septic, neutropenic patients, the use of broad-spectrum antibiotics is justified to prevent bacteremia or organ colonization by Salmonella and other enteric organisms.

Medications that could minimize or abolish colonic fluid secretion would be of tremendous benefit in the treatment of equine colitis. Medications such as kaolin, bismuth subsalicylate, and activated charcoal are frequently used in cases of colitis in adult horses, but their efficacy as antisecretory agents in this context has not been established. These medications are more effective in foals with diarrhea, probably because of an effect on the small intestine rather than the colon.

Several medications that demonstrate antisecretory activity have been examined in nonequine species, but their value in equine diarrhea is not established. These include NSAIDs, alpha-2 adrenergic agonists, and drugs that affect cellular calcium metabolism.

Unfortunately, at this time pharmacologic intervention is not able to minimize the fluid secretion that accompanies acute equine colitis. Additionally, antimicrobial therapy is ineffective in limiting colitis caused by Salmonella. Thus, treatment should be directed at replacing and anticipating deficits of fluid, electrolytes, plasma protein, and nutrients.

CHRONIC DIARRHEA

Chronic diarrhea is one of the most frustrating disorders encountered by equine practitioners, both in determining its cause and in its management. Chronic diarrhea has been defined several ways, but I prefer to consider it as persistent diarrhea of at least 1 month's duration. Using this definition, horses with severe septic colitis will not be included, because most of these cases do not survive longer than 1 month, even with intensive therapy.

Causes

While there are many causes of chronic diarrhea, cases can generally be divided into two groups: diarrhea resulting from a chronic inflammatory condition, and diarrhea resulting from a disruption in normal physiologic processes. With inflammatory conditions, inflammatory changes are evident histologically within the colon. With physiologic disorders, there are no morphologic changes in the colon, and diarrhea is presumed to result from abnormal volatile fatty acid synthesis, abnormal absorption, or both. A small percentage of horses with chronic diarrhea have a primary disorder of a system other than the intestinal tract.

Inflammatory disorders that can cause chronic diarrhea include disorders caused by infectious agents such as chronic salmonellosis; chronic parasitism with Strongylus vulgaris, Strongylus edentatus, and small strongyles; Rhodococcus equi infection of abdominal viscera; and in weanling foals, rotavirus. Noninfectious inflammatory causes include cellular infiltrative disorders such as granulomatous enteritis, granulomatous lymphosarcoma, and sand enteropathy. Sand causes diarrhea through continued irritation of the mucosal lining of the colon.

Noninflammatory chronic diarrhea of colonic origin is thought to be a result of abnormal fermentation of cellulose by the resident bacteria in the large intestine. In vitro fermentation of feces from normal horses and horses with chronic diarrhea revealed that feces from the diarrheic horses produced more gas, acetate, and propionate than feces from normal horses. Whether this difference reflects fermentative activity within the colon is not known, but an abnormal increase in acetate could lead to fluid retention within the colonic lumen, because acetate inhibits colonic absorption of sodium and water.

Disorders of systems outside of the gastrointestinal tract can cause chronic diarrhea. Congestive heart failure and secondary hepatic fibrosis can cause diarrhea secondary to increased hydrostatic pressure within the colonic microvasculature. Other forms of chronic liver disease can cause diarrhea. Chronic hepatopathies and cholelithiasis have been associated with chronic diarrhea.

Clinical Evaluation

The diagnostic approach to cases of chronic diarrhea should be based on attempting to differentiate inflammatory from physiologic causes. *The workup can be extensive, and expensive, and the client should be prepared for the cause of the diarrhea to remain undetermined!* If water consumption has matched water losses, horses with chronic diarrhea might be adequately hydrated. Often, though, such horses are mildly to moderately dehydrated. Moderate weight loss also has often occurred (see Chapter 2).

A complete blood count should be made to evaluate for signs of chronic inflammation. Such changes include a decrease in the red blood cell count and packed cell volume, owing to decreased erythrogenesis secondary to sequestration of iron by bone marrow macrophages (anemia of chronic inflammation). The white blood cell count can be normal or moderately increased. The fibrinogen will be normal or increased. Whether the white blood cell count and fibrinogen levels are increased is influenced by the degree of inflammation and whether the inflammatory response is localized. Thus, a normal complete blood cell count does not rule out an inflammatory cause of the chronic diarrhea. Serum chemistry values vary in horses with chronic diarrhea. Many cases are presented with severe hyponatremia, hypokalemia, hypochloremia, azotemia, and metabolic acidemia. Other horses with less severe chronic diarrhea have only mild serum chemistry abnormalities.

The total serum protein is usually decreased with a chronic inflammatory disorder of the colon, reflecting leakage of protein, particularly albumin, from the capillaries and disruption of the colonic mucosal integrity. With any chronic inflammatory process, the globulin fraction often increases. Hyperglobulinemia should be further characterized by a protein electrophoresis. An electrophoretogram can reveal increases in the alpha-, beta-, or gamma-globulin fractions. Specific disorders, particularly immune-mediated disorders such as granulomatous enteritis, can have a predominant increase in one protein fraction. Chronic parasitism can also be reflected by an increase in a single fraction, such as the beta fraction, IgGT, with Strongylus vulgaris infection.

Increases in serum bile acids and hepatic-associated enzymes, including sorbitol dehydrogenase, gammaglutamyltransferase, and aspartate aminotransferase, indicate the presence of hepatic disease, which might be the cause of the chronic diarrhea.

Peritoneal fluid analysis can reveal an increase in protein, the white blood cell count, or both, which indicates an inflammatory process within the peritoneal cavity. Often, though, colonic inflammation is not reflected by alterations in the peritoneal fluid.

Feces should be examined for parasite ova and should be cultured for Salmonella. Whereas in cases of acute diarrhea, five consecutive fecal samples should be cultured for Salmonella, in cases of chronic diarrhea, often many more are necessary. It is not unusual for 15 fecal cultures to be performed in order to get a positive Salmonella culture. Additionally, a rectal mucosal biopsy should be cultured. In weanlings, examination of the feces for rotavirus by transmission electronmicroscopy or enzyme-linked immunosorbent assay should be performed.

Far too often, the results of the previously mentioned diagnostic procedures do not define the cause of the chronic diarrhea. In such cases, an exploratory laparotomy is warranted. In addition to exploration of the abdomen for the presence of masses, abscesses, etc., the colon and cecum should be thoroughly examined. Biopsies from several sites of the colon, cecum, and mesenteric lymph nodes are submitted for histopathology and culture for Salmonella.

Treatment

Treatment of horses with chronic diarrhea is usually empiric. With inflammatory causes such as lymphosarcoma and granulomatous enteritis, the disease is often untreatable. Chronic salmonellosis does not lend itself to specific treatment, because antimicrobial therapy is generally unrewarding. Chronic parasitism might be resolved with appropriate anthel-mintic therapy, although damage to the mucosa might have become too extensive for normal absorption to be restored. The removal of sand from the colon can be facilitated through the administration of bulk laxatives (e.g., Metamucil). A precise dosage has not been determined, although 1 pound in the feed, two to three times weekly, has been effective.

Administration of products containing bismuth subsalicylate is effective in some cases. Bismuth subsalicylate acts by inhibiting prostaglandin synthesis, and possibly by other, undefined mechanisms. In full-sized horses, a large volume, 1 to 4 L/day, must be administered by stomach tube to be effective.

Iodochlorhydroxyquin is effective in managing some cases of chronic diarrhea caused by maldigestion of cellulose by colonic microorganisms. The actual mechanism of action of iodochlorhydroxyquin in resolving the diarrhea is not known. The drug was originally used because trichomonads were thought to be the cause of some chronic diarrheas. However iodochlorhydroxyquin has minimal effect on colonic protozoal populations. In cattle, iodochlorhydroxyquin depresses rumen production of acetate and propionate. The drug mildly suppressed the production of these volatile fatty acids in in vitro fermentation of feces from horses with chronic diarrhea. Thus, its effect might be the reduction of the concentration of volatile fatty acids in the colon, thereby removing an inhibition of colonic sodium and water absorption. Iodochlorhydroxyquin is not uniformly effective, and in many cases its effectiveness is only transient. Although initially feces become formed, the diarrhea often recurs within several days. An initial dose of 10 g is recommended for a 1000-pound (450-kg) horse. If diarrhea recurs, decreasing the dosage to 5 g/day is sometimes effective. If the medication is discontinued the diarrhea resumes.

Experience has shown that many horses with undiagnosed chronic diarrhea, particularly weanlings and yearlings, essentially "outgrow" the problem. These animals tend to have soft feces for many months but continue to grow and mature normally. Under these circumstances the diarrhea is more a "cosmetic" problem than a medical one. The owner's patience is the greatest problem in the management of such cases.

SUPPLEMENTAL READING

Argenzio, R.A., and Stevens, C.E.: Cyclic changes in ionic composition of digesta in the equine intestinal tract. Am. J. Physiol., *228*:1224–1230, 1975.

Argenzio, R.A., et al.: Interrelationship of Na, HCO_3, and volatile fatty acid transport by equine large intestine. Am. J. Physiol., *233*:469–E478, 1977.

Fantone, J.C., and Ward, P.A.: Role of oxygen-derived free radicals and metabolites in leukocyte dependent inflammatory reactions. Am. J. Pathol., *107*:397–418, 1982.

Granger, D.N., and Barrowman, J.A.: Microcirculation of the alimentary tract. I. Physiology of transcapillary fluid and solute exchange. Gastroenterology, *84*:846–867, 1983.

Palmer, J.E., Whitlock, R.H., and Benson, C.E.: Potomac Horse Fever. Diagnostic criteria and recognition of endemic areas. Abstr. Second Equine-Colic Res. Symp., Univ. Georgia 23, 1985.

Smith, B.P.: *Salmonella* infection in horses. Comp. Contin. Educ. *3*:S4–S13, 1981.

chapter 4

ACUTE ABDOMINAL PAIN

Warwick A. Arden

Abdominal pain, a common early manifestation of a number of diseases involving the abdominal organs, is detected by a pattern of behavioral and physiologic changes in the animal. Abdominal pain can be transient and largely inconsequential or it can be an early signal of a life-threatening disorder. The challenge for clinicians managing horses with acute abdominal pain is to integrate knowledge of the pathophysiology of the most common pain-producing abdominal disorders with a thorough structured clinical examination, in order to distinguish disorders requiring little or no treatment from those requiring more aggressive medical intervention, surgical intervention, or both. By defining the disease process as accurately as possible, the clinician can better establish a prognosis and make recommendations regarding future preventive measures. Prognosis is particularly important when economic factors limit therapeutic alternatives.

DEFINITION

The terms "abdominal pain," "acute abdomen," and "colic" are frequently used interchangeably. The term "acute abdominal crisis" (AAC) refers to a group of diseases whose common early outward manifestation is abdominal pain and whose progression leads to a rapid multisystem deterioration, most notably deterioration of cardiovascular homeostasis. Although the gastrointestinal tract is the most common site of primary involvement, "acute abdominal crisis" includes all abdominal tissues, that is, the urogenital tract, hepatobiliary system, spleen, pancreas, and peritoneum.

Abdominal pain originates from the viscus wall, the peritoneum (visceral and parietal), or both, and is initiated by two main categories of receptors, chemical and mechanical. Chemical receptors respond to mediators of the inflammatory process; mechanical receptors respond predominantly to stretch—to mural or parietal peritoneal tension caused by viscus distension, or to mesenteric traction caused by viscus displacement or an increase in viscus weight. Thus, diseases that produce abdominal pain do so by causing viscus distension, displacement, or weight gain; by producing parenchymal, intestinal, mural, or peritoneal inflammation; or by a combination of mechanisms.

Knowledge of pain mechanisms is useful in choosing analgesic strategies, be they physical or chemical. Examples of physical analgesia include gastric decompression by intubation, and percutaneous cecal and colonic decompression. Selection of a chemical analgesic can also be based on an assessment of the most likely pain mechanism. Nonsteroidal anti-inflammatory drugs (NSAIDs) are likely to be effective in pain of inflammatory origin (e.g., ischemic pain), whereas centrally acting analgesics such as xylazine and narcotics are best used to treat pain originating from distension or

traction. Management of pain is frequently necessary to prevent further patient trauma and to allow detailed physical examination. *However, analgesia should not be equated with treatment of the underlying disease process.*

Although in most instances the presence of abdominal pain will be obvious, frequently, characteristic behavioral patterns suggestive of pain are not present at initial examination. In these cases it is important to not simply accept the subjective evaluation of the owner, but rather to ask specific questions about what in the horse's behavior suggests pain—does the horse shift weight between limbs, look at the flanks, paw, kick, stretch, crouch, sink to the ground, or roll? Frequently physical signs such as hay or soil on the back, extensive sweat marks, or trauma to the head and distal limbs suggest past painful episodes, or the horse's environment will be disturbed. Conditions that owners frequently mistake for abdominal pain include laminitis, exertional myopathy, exhaustion, respiratory distress, urolithiasis, ataxia, fly worry, and parturition. Categorizing abdominal pain by duration, intensity, character, and progression is helpful to aid diagnosis and monitor progress (Table 4–2). Considerable variation exists among individual animals' tolerance and response to painful stimuli, however.

PATHOPHYSIOLOGY

Acute abdominal pain of gastrointestinal origin can come from one of four major sources: simple obstruction, strangulating obstruction, nonstrangulating infarction, and inflammation (Table 4–1).

SIMPLE OBSTRUCTION

Simple obstruction is characterized by obstruction of the digestive tract without significant compromise of vascular integ-

TABLE 4–1. PATHOPHYSIOLOGY OF ACUTE ABDOMINAL PAIN

Category	Lesion	Major Pathophysiologic Changes	Common Clinical Signs
Simple obstruction	Luminal obstruction without vascular compromise at onset Physical 　Luminal 　Mural 　Extramural 　Combined Functional 　Spasmodic 　Adynamic ileus 　Flatulent	Obstruction to aboral movement of ingesta, fluid, gas Luminal distension Activation of stretch pain receptors Increased motility early, decreased motility late Further intraluminal fluid accumulation due to 　Diminished absorption 　Stimulated secretion Further luminal distension and systemic dehydration Compromise of mucosal and perhaps mural circulation Dilated inactive bowel, systemic dehydration, mucosal disruption allowing endotoxin absorption, possible perforation or rupture	Varies with site, nature, and completeness of obstruction Physical obstructions: slow onset; mild to moderate pain; systemic dehydration and cardiovascular deterioration occur late; gastric reflux occurs if obstruction high or late, abdominocentesis is normal early, rectal examination is very important Functional obstructions: spasmodic, flatulent; moderate to severe pain early
Strangulating obstruction	Physical obstruction and extramural vascular compromise at onset	Effects of luminal obstruction for simple obstruction Activation of inflammatory pain receptors Vascular compromise Early—disruption of mucosal integrity 　Impaired absorption 　Transudation, exudation into lumen 　Access of bacterial toxin, particularly endotoxin to systemic circulation Late—transmural devitalization 　Release of tissue necrosis factors Perforation, peritoneal contamination, peritoneal toxin absorption	Rapid onset, moderate to severe pain, which may abate in late phase and depression predominate Rapid cardiovascular deterioration Gastric reflux if high obstruction, peritoneal fluid changes in many, rectal findings important

Nonstrangulating infarction Physical vascular obstruction (thromboembolic) Functional vascular obstruction (spastic, intestinal angina)	Vascular compromise without physical luminal obstruction at onset Rapid progression of functional obstruction	Endotoxemia Peripheral vascular failure: poorly controlled capacitance, increased vascular permeability, diminished cardiac return and cardiac output Intravascular coagulation Continued intravascular fluid loss, hypoperfusion of vital organs, diminished effective perfusion of viscera Pulmonary hypertension, vascular injury, deficient oxygen exchange Vicious cycle of falling venous return, falling cardiac output, hypoxemia, hypoperfusion, inadequate tissue oxygenation, and terminal central circulatory failure Essentially, as for strangulating obstruction	Clinical signs vary with location and extent of lesion, similar to strangulating obstruction Rectal examination may fail to identify evidence of physical bowel obstruction
Inflammation	Etiology Ischemic and/or septic Location Mucosal Mural Parenchymal (liver, kidney, spleen) Peritoneal	Mucosal inflammation Pain Disturbance of mucosal function—fluid, electrolyte abnormalities Disturbance of mucosal structure toxin absorption Motility abnormality Systemic circulatory disturbance, may follow Peritoneal inflammation Pain, peritoneal fluid/protein accumulation, peritoneal toxin absorption, intestinal motility abnormality, systemic circulatory disturbance	Varies greatly with location and nature of lesion; from minor intermittent pain with minimal systemic response to severe pain, rapid systemic response including cardiovascular deterioration

TABLE 4–2. CATEGORIZATION OF ABDOMINAL PAIN

Duration

Peracute:	<1 hr
Acute:	<24 hrs
Subacute:	24–72 hrs
Chronic:	>72 hrs

Intensity

Mild:	Horse paws lightly, occasionally looks at flanks, may stretch or circle. Sweating is not obvious.
Moderate:	Horse paws firmly, kicks at abdomen, looks at flanks, circles, crouches, and may lie quietly for brief periods. Sweating may be evident.
Severe:	Horse stamps feet or kicks, circles or crouches frequently, sinks or throws itself to ground, rolls. Sweating and flaring of nostrils is marked.

Character

Recurrent:	Days between painful episodes.
Occasional:	Painful episodes shorter than respites.
Intermittent:	Respites shorter than painful episodes.
Continuous:	Unabated pain.

Progression

Pain less obvious with time.
Pain unchanged.
Pain more obvious with time.

rity. The obstruction can be partial or complete, physical or functional.

Physical obstruction can be further categorized according to anatomic location, as intraluminal (e.g., fecalith, enterolith, foreign body, ascariasis), mural (e.g., abscess, neoplasm, hematoma), extramural (e.g., herniation with non-strangulating compression, displacement with compression by other organs, adhesion, pedunculated lipoma), or a combination of the above.

Functional obstruction results from failure of coordinated propulsive mechanical activity and can be secondary to a number of stimuli. Adynamic ileus, one example of functional obstruction, can result from diffuse mural or peritoneal inflammation, excessive bowel handling at laparotomy, and drug toxicity. "Spas-

modic colic," a poorly defined entity, is thought to produce pain by distension of bowel segments neighboring those undergoing intensive contraction. The pathogenesis of the spastic contraction is not known; however, psychogenic, neural, or transient ischemic mechanisms are often implicated. A third form of functional obstruction results from accumulation of intraluminal gas more quickly than it can be eliminated by progressive intestinal movements; the disorder is known as primary gastric dilation (or bloat) when it involves the stomach, and as cecal tympany or "flatulent colic" when it involves the colons. Although it is frequently initiated by the eating of fermentable feed, aberrant motility is often thought to play a role.

Prolonged or marked luminal distension resulting from physical obstruction can lead to reflex inhibition of motility and thus to functional obstruction. Similarly, prolonged functional obstruction can lead to physical obstruction by causing intraluminal accumulation of dried ingesta.

Untreated simple obstruction is usually subacute, beginning with occasional demonstrations of mild pain and progressing to continuous moderate to severe pain. The length of progression varies with the animal and particularly with the nature and site of obstruction. In general, physical obstructions of the stomach and small intestine have a shorter course than those involving the cecum and colons. Functional obstruction of the spastic type, or obstruction leading to rapid gas accumulation of both the small bowel and large bowel, tends to have a shorter course than physical obstruction or adynamic ileus. Simple obstruction, unlike strangulating obstruction, is not characterized by an early, rapid systemic deterioration. An exception occurs when the obstruction itself is functional and secondary to systemic disease, for example, ileus in association with severe peritonitis or anterior enteritis. However, prolonged simple obstruction can lead to eventual compromise of bowel integrity and predispose to systemic deterioration. Systemic deterioration is thought to occur predominantly by ischemic necrosis of the mucosa and eventually of the full thickness of the bowel wall from local circulatory insufficiency induced by prolonged high intraluminal pressures. If generalized, the mucosal damage is enough to allow systemic toxin absorption; if localized, full-thickness perforation leads to peritoneal contamination. Occasionally, bowel tearing can occur owing to acute excessive pressure without local vascular compromise.

STRANGULATING OBSTRUCTION

In strangulating obstruction, luminal obstruction is combined with variable but significant compromise of vascular integrity. The obstruction is predominantly physical and usually extraluminal, although theoretically a functional component exists owing to ischemic interruption of neuromuscular mechanisms. Both the physical luminal and vascular obstruction result from anatomic displacement, either by displacement of the bowel upon itself (intussusception, volvulus, torsion) or by bowel herniation through the mesentery or body wall. Compression of the bowel by nonintestinal tissue (lipoma, tumor, etc.) without primary bowel displacement occasionally leads to strangulation. The vascular interruption can be arterial, venous, or a variable combination. In practice, rarely does the affected bowel demonstrate the pallor and histologic findings suggestive of pure, early arterial occlusion, most commonly it is edematous, heavy, and red, purple, or black, suggesting hemorrhagic infarction or congestive vascular obstruction. These findings might be explained by the rela-

tive compressibility of the venous tree relative to the arterial tree and the extensive collateral circulation.

The rapid cardiovascular deterioration that accompanies strangulating obstruction is multifactorial. Certainly, intraluminal fluid accumulation depletes the patient of circulating intravascular volume. This accumulation occurs not only because of "passive" accumulation resulting from impaired absorption, but also because of "active" fluid accumulation resulting from increased secretion, transudation across an impaired mucosal microvasculature, and in some cases intraluminal hemorrhage. In cases of transmural damage, peritoneal fluid accumulation can add to intravascular volume depletion. The relative contribution of direct fluid losses to the overall cardiovascular deterioration varies with the site and extent of the ischemic lesion.

A second and perhaps more important mechanism of cardiovascular deterioration involves systemic accumulation of bacterial toxins, most notably the gram-negative cell wall fragment, endotoxin. The diverse biologic effects of endotoxin are beyond the scope of this chapter; however, their predominant effect in equine splanchnic ischemia is cardiovascular failure characterized by failure of peripheral vascular tone leading to pooling of blood, intravascular coagulation, increased vascular permeability, and eventually diminished cardiac return (and hence output) and hypoperfusion of vital organs. Experimentally, inhibition of the prostaglandin mediators of endotoxin by NSAIDs temporarily improves hemodynamic states in endotoxic shock. Cardiac depression resulting from release of myocardial depression factors might play a role in equine splanchnic ischemia, as in other species; however, this function has not been investigated. Lastly, neural mechanisms initiated by splanchnic pain might play a role but also have been largely uninvestigated.

Strangulating obstruction is usually characterized by a rapid onset of severe continuous abdominal pain. Most patients show early evidence of systemic response, that is, trembling, sweating, marked heart rate elevation, injected mucous membranes, and hemoconcentration. Occasionally, strangulated bowel is anatomically isolated, such as in a strangulating inguinal hernia, and the systemic reaction begins more slowly. Late in the disorder, pain can abate owing to destruction of neural receptors, and depression can predominate.

NONSTRANGULATING INFARCTION

Nonstrangulating infarction occurs when vascular compromise takes place without physical bowel obstruction. Most commonly, mesenteric thromboembolism, such as that resulting from parasitism, is blamed for the disorder; however, in some cases physical obstruction of the major mesenteric vessels is not apparent at necropsy, and some consider that a functional or spastic vascular obstruction can occur. In these cases parallels can be drawn with the syndrome of non-occlusive mesenteric infarction seen in humans.

The events following nonstrangulating infarction are similar to those following strangulating obstruction, as vascular compromise rapidly leads to functional bowel obstruction. Because large areas of the cecum and colon are frequently involved, pain is marked and systemic deterioration is usually rapid.

INFLAMMATION

Abdominal pain can result from primary mucosal, mural, or peritoneal inflammation, rather than being secondary to vascular compromise. Common examples include parenchymal abscess, localized peritonitis, and severe bowel inflammation, that is, enteritis and colitis, although with colitis, spastic contraction and functional obstruction also can play a role in pain production. The disease course varies greatly with the site and cause of inflammation; however, pain and systemic alterations are usually more pronounced with inflammatory bowel disease.

CLINICAL EVALUATION (Table 4–3)

For horses with acute abdominal pain, the initial decision-making process has two interrelated objectives—to accurately define the site, nature, and extent of the lesion(s), and to determine if surgical intervention is indicated. The two objectives are stated separately because, although the former can lead to the latter, frequently the clinician can determine the need for surgical exploration without

TABLE 4–3. CLINICAL EVALUATION

Patient History
Physical Examination
  *Pain assessment
  Bodily condition, injuries, concurrent conditions
  *Cardiovascular status
    Temperature; respiration, pulse rate, character,
     and strength; mucous membrane color and
     refill; skin temperature, turgor, PCV/TS
  Abdominal examination
    External abdomen
    External genitalia
    Auscultation
    *Nasogastric intubation
    *Rectal examination

Diagnostic Tests
  Complete blood count, fibrinogen
  Serum Na, K, Cl, osmolality, anion gap, Ca, urea
  Blood gas analysis
  *Peritoneal fluid examination
  Endoscopy
  Radiography
  Fecal examination; character, sand, parasites

---

* Indicates most important criteria.

first being able to define the exact site and nature of the lesion(s).

The diagnostic process for acute abdominal crisis unifies a sound knowledge of the pathophysiology of the most common diseases of the equine abdomen with a detailed history, meticulous physical examination, and appropriate use and interpretation of ancillary diagnostic tests to define the location, nature, and extent of the injury and to determine the requirement for early surgical exploration. All diagnostic criteria should be interpreted with regard to other criteria; over-reliance on a single factor usually results in misguided decisions. Of the factors discussed, four appear to deserve greater weight when early surgical intervention is considered—pain (intensity, duration, progression, responsiveness to analgesia), cardiovascular status, rectal examination findings, and positive abdominocentesis findings.

PATIENT HISTORY

The diagnostic process begins with an accurate patient history. As always, the clinician must take care to obtain observations and not the owner's interpretations. The clinician must note age, breed, sex, pregnancy, and parity. Exactly what behavior has the horse been demonstrating? What was the first change noticed and when did it occur? Has the horse a history of abdominal pain and, if so, were any diagnoses made? Has the horse been eating well recently? What has been the fecal frequency and consistency? Is the horse suffering from any concurrent disorder? Has the horse received any medications recently? Has the horse received any medications for the current condition? What, how, and when is the horse usually fed? Has there been any feeding changes? Have there been any other management or environmental changes?

PHYSICAL EXAMINATION

Physician examination should begin with observation of the animal's disposition, i.e., limb and body movements, presence of excess sweat, flared nostrils, character of respiration, and rectal or urinary straining; the clinician should note superficial injuries, especially to the head, hips, and limbs. By the time the history and initial observation are complete, the clinician should be able to categorize the pain by duration, intensity, character, and progression.

The first major system to be examined is the cardiovascular system. An early, rapid, and accurate assessment is critical. Such assessment can be made largely from simple physical examination and determination of hematocrit and total plasma solids. Heart rate will vary with age, excitement, and pain intensity, as well as with circulatory status; however, in an adequately restrained mature horse, mild elevation is 40 to 60 beats/minute, moderate elevation is 60 to 80 beats/minute, marked elevation is 80 to 100 beats/minute, and extreme elevation is 100+ beats/minute. The veterinarian should note the strength and character of the peripheral pulse, skin turgor, moisture and temperature, extremity temperature, eye position, mucous membrane color, and capillary refill time (CRT). Rarely in the acute abdominal crisis does the horse display the pale mucous membranes seen in hemorrhagic or traumatic shock. Rather, as circulatory embarrassment progresses, mucous membranes change from healthy light pink, to deep pink, to red (injected), to red/blue, to purple, with progressive slowing of capillary refill time from less than 2 seconds, to 6 seconds or longer. This rate is consistent with early peripheral vascular failure, as described above. As with heart rate, it is difficult to generalize about hematocrit elevations; however, in fit, mature horses, 45 to 50% (0.45 to 0.50 L/L) should be considered mild elevation, 50 to 60% (0.5 to 0.6 L/L), marked elevation, and greater than 60% (0.6 L/L), a very marked elevation.

At this stage of examination, the patient in advanced circulatory distress, i.e., with marked heart rate elevation, weak peripheral pulse, cool extremities, decreased skin elasticity, poor mucous membrane color, slow CRT, and marked hematocrit elevation, should receive immediate treatment aimed at cardiovascular restoration prior to further systems examination. Such treatment can include intravascular volume replacement, NSAIDs, and abdominal decompression, as indicated.

Physical examination of the abdomen, including the gastrointestinal system, has five phases: external examination of the abdomen, examination of the external genitalia, abdominal auscultation, nasogastric intubation, and rectal examination.

External abdominal examination includes observation of flank distension and external palpation of any distension to determine its consistency. Intraintestinal accumulation of gas rather than of fluid or fecal material is the most common cause of visible abdominal distension. In the adult, rarely does the distended small bowel exert enough pressure to distend the abdomen, and colonic distension is a more likely cause. Such is not the case for foals, however, who frequently exhibit abdominal distension with advanced small-bowel obstruction. The abdomen should also be examined for evidence of herniation or trauma. Ballottement of abdominal organs in horses is usually difficult and unrewarding.

Examination of the external genitalia is most important in the stallion and in the mare in advanced pregnancy. Stallions should undergo thorough palpation of the testicles, testicular cord, and inguinal regions for evidence of herniation or testicular torsion. Mares in advanced pregnancy should have a vaginal examination. Although the majority of uterine torsions in mares occur cranial to the cervix, occasionally one is detected caudal to the cervix by vaginal examination.

Abdominal auscultation should include the upper and lower left and right abdomen, with intensity, character, and duration recorded. In the mid-right flank, the characteristic ileocecal sound, a resonant fluid-into-gas high-pitch rumble, should be audible 1 to 3 times a minute. In the lower left abdomen the predominant sounds are intermittent low-pitch background fluid sounds from the small intestine (borborygmi). It is not possible to make specific diagnoses from abdominal auscultation alone, and frequently simply a record of the presence or absence of sounds is useful. With the exception of ileocecal sounds, which indicate a degree of progressive small-intestinal motility and terminal ileal patency, the majority of intestinal sounds indicate only local bowel activity. Similarly, lack of sounds, indicating a lack of bowel activity, can be a temporary result of physical or functional causes. Monitoring of intestinal sounds over time will usually produce a clearer picture of overall bowel activity.

Nasogastric intubation has four functions—diagnosis, analgesia, prevention of gastric rupture, and administration of medications. Examination of refluxed material for its quantity, character, and pH is helpful in diagnosis, although even a stomach moderately distended with fluid will not always show spontaneous reflux. The nasogastric tube must be primed with warm water, using a funnel, not a pump. Several funnels-full of water might have to be administered, with frequent repositioning of the tube, before reflux is initiated. Positive reflux is defined as return of a larger quantity of fluid than was administered. Positive reflux suggests diminished gastric emptying, intestinogastric reflux, or both. While positive reflux occurs most commonly with proximal bowel obstruction, other considerations include gastric outflow obstruction (e.g., gastroduodenal ulcer disease in foals), duodenal traction (secondary to large colon displacement), or long-standing distal bowel obstruction. Reflux of large volumes of fluid often provides significant analgesia. If significant reflux occurs or if the patient is being transported to a surgical facility, the nasogastric tube should be secured in place. While not foolproof, this measure will significantly decrease the incidence of gastric rupture. All too often, clinicians are tempted to administer medications by nasogastric tube, simply because the tube is already in place. Two rules should be followed: first, medications should not be administered by this route until the patient assessment is complete; second, medications should not be administered by this route if the horse has positive gastric reflux.

Rectal examination should be performed on all horses of reasonable size with acute abdominal pain. If excessive straining occurs, the examination can be facilitated by tranquilization with intrarectal lidocaine (2%) (30 to 50 cc), or, if necessary, by systemic administration of propantheline bromide (15 mg). Strong parasympatholytes such as atropine should not be used. Knowledge of the normal position, shape, dimension, and consistency of abdominal organs is essential. The clinician should identify the genital tract, inguinal canals, pelvic flexure, caudal spleen, nephrosphenic region, left kidney, cranial mesenteric artery, aorta and internal iliacs, cecum, small colon, and peritoneal character. The most common abnormal findings are viscus distension (by gas, fluid or feces), displacement, entrapment, or combinations of these. Although the small intestine can occasionally be felt in the normal horse, in general the finding of a palpably distended small intestine should be considered abnormal. Impactions present as firm, doughy ingesta, most commonly within the pelvic flexure, cecum, or ileum. Occasionally, small colon masses can be detected. Displacement can accompany impaction. Large-bowel displacement is usually detected by assessing the direction of colonic bands. Distension can accompany displacement. Entrapment (incarceration) is most commonly detected over the nephrosplenic ligament (left colon) or through the inguinal canal or broad ligament (small bowel). Epiploic, gastrosplenic, and mesenteric rent entrapments are frequently not detected on rectal examination. Uterine torsion is best diagnosed by rectal examination. The torsion can be palpated cranial to the cervix, and the broad ligament is felt to traverse the abdomen, being pulled tightly over the uterine body from one side and under from the other side.

LABORATORY TESTS

Ancillary examinations of the patient with acute abdominal pain can include complete blood count, serum electrolyte profile, blood gas analysis, peritoneal fluid examination, endoscopy, and radiography.

Complete Blood Count. A complete blood count is not essential on first examination, but in some cases it can aid the decision-making. Severe leukopenia caused by neutrophil margination, sequestration, and reticuloendothelial removal frequently accompanies endotoxemia in cases of strangulating obstruction and nonstrangulating infarction. If pain is severe, however, frequently the animal is presented prior to development of significant leukogram abnormalities. Patients with inflammatory mucosal disease (enteritis, colitis) frequently have marked neutropenia associated with endotoxemia, because the pain that precipitates examination often occurs later than the endotoxemia in the pathologic course. Marked leukocytosis is uncommon in horses with acute abdominal pain. A marked neutrophilia can suggest a localized inflammatory lesion such as renal, peritoneal, or bowel mural abscess, especially if neutrophilia is accompanied by elevated plasma fibrinogen concentration (>0.5 g/dl; 5.0 g/L); however, inflammatory processes unrelated to the abdominal pain, such as concurrent respiratory disease should not be overlooked. Eosinophilia has been reported in association with damage induced by parasitism. In my experience, however, this finding is uncommon.

Serum Electrolyte Profile. The majority of horses experiencing acute abdominal pain do not have marked serum electrolyte abnormalities. Sodium and chloride concentrations are usually well maintained, although potassium concentrations can vary slightly with acid-base status. In patients with marked circulatory disturbance, peripheral hypoperfusion and lactic acidosis can lead to mild serum potassium elevations associated with extracellular acid buffering. This effect is not marked, however, because unlike the intracellular buffering of inorganic acids, which requires cellular cation extrusion, organic acid intracellular buffering is frequently accompanied by intracellular movement of the conjugate base, obviating cation extrusion. Serum urea and creatinine levels are frequently elevated if dehydration accompanies abdominal pain. If azotemia persists along with reasonable hydration, renal mechanisms should be investigated in the usual manner (see Chapter 12).

Two major causes of abdominal pain appear to be associated with the most marked serum electrolyte abnormalities. First, primary mucosal inflammatory diseases, acute enteritis and colitis, frequently lead to severe sodium and chloride depletion, particularly if the primary pathogen causes hypersecretion by en-

dotoxin production or mucosal colonization and prostaglandin production. Salmonella colitis, for example, leads to a decreased mucosal sodium absorption and increased chloride secretion associated with mucosal cyclic adenosine monophosphate (cAMP) (see Chapter 3). Although total body potassium depletion can occur, frequently it is not reflected in serum potassium levels. Marked prerenal azotemia often accompanies dehydration in these cases. Second, major electrolyte abnormalities frequently accompany urinary-associated abdominal conditions, particularly uroperitoneum. Uroperitoneum is most common in foals with urinary bladder rupture. Typically such foals have severe hyperkalemia, hyponatremia, hypochloremia, azotemia, and metabolic acidosis. Similar abnormalities exist in adults with uroperitoneum; however, the hyperkalemia is often less marked because of a lower relative potassium intake.

Blood Gas Analysis. Blood gas analysis is frequently valuable in formulating initial fluid therapy. The majority of horses with acute abdominal pain and circulatory compromise present with a mild to moderate metabolic acidosis with partial respiratory compensation. Cases of severe colitis frequently present with severe metabolic acidosis associated with intestinal bicarbonate loss as well as peripheral hypoperfusion. Occasionally horses with severe pain without protracted circulatory compromise will present with an uncompensated respiratory alkalosis caused by hyperventilation. Horses developing abdominal pain associated with extensive aerobic exercise and exhaustion (e.g., endurance exercise) have been reported to present with metabolic alkalosis associated with extensive chloride losses in sweat. Metabolic alkalosis has also been reported in cases of high intestinal obstruction with prolonged gastric reflux.

Peritoneal Fluid Examination. The composition of the peritoneal fluid reflects the integrity of the visceral and parietal mesothelial surfaces. Although abdominocentesis and fluid examination are important in the decision-making process, significant interpretive limitations exist. Much can be determined from the gross appearance of peritoneal fluid. Normal peritoneal fluid is clear to light yellow with slight turbidity, and it might foam slightly when agitated. Excessive foaming suggests increased protein content. Sanguineous peritoneal fluids can be divided into two groups: fluids with clear supernatant when centrifuged (suggesting intact erythrocytes) and fluids with a red supernatant (suggesting erythrocyte lysis). Intact erythrocytes could result from contamination by puncture of abdominal wall vessels, splenic puncture, or diapedesis of intact erythrocytes from a reactive mesothelial surface surrounding damaged bowel. Contamination by puncture of abdominal wall vessels can be detected during abdominocentesis as clear fluid containing swirls of blood exiting from the abdominal cannula. Splenic puncture results in abdominal fluid with a high hematocrit ($\geq$30%; 0.3 L/L), while diapedesis from damaged bowel frequently yields a fluid of low hematocrit (2 to 10%, 0.02 to 0.1 L/L). Obviously, considerable overlap can exist, and frequently the erythrocyte source cannot be determined. Erythrocyte lysis is more commonly seen with advanced ischemic intestinal injury. A brown-green fluid indicates the presence of ingesta, suggesting either viscus rupture or viscus puncture with the instrument during abdominocentesis. Because most patients with a bowel rupture are euthanized, abdominocentesis must be repeated in at least two further sites, should such material be found. A typical history of sudden remission of severe abdominal pain associated with cardiovascular collapse and rectal examination

findings suggesting a large quantity of free abdominal fluid frequently accompany viscus rupture. The finding of grossly purulent abdominal fluid is extremely rare and is usually associated with localized peritonitis.

Laboratory assessment of abdominal fluid should include total solids (TS), total nucleated cell (TNC) count, nucleated cell differential count, particularly the percentage of polymorphonuclear cells (% PMN), cell character, and microscopic examination for bacteria and plant material.

Reports vary considerably regarding acceptable critical parameters for peritoneal evaluation. Reported critical limits vary from 3000 to 10,000 cells/μl (3×10^9 to 10×10^9L) TNC; from 72 to 78 (% PMN); and from 1 to 2.5 g/dl (10 to 25 g/L) (TS). In a recent prospective study conducted at the Veterinary Clinical Center, Michigan State University, where 74 consecutive abdominocenteses were performed on horses with acute abdominal pain, cellular indices (TNC $\geq$ 10,000/μl (10×10^9/L), %PMN $\geq$ 90) for predicting injured bowel requiring resection had very low sensitivity (21%) but high specificity (95%). Hence, of horses requiring immediate surgical intervention and intestinal resection, only one in five can be expected to demonstrate significantly abnormal cellular indices on peritoneal fluid examination. This differential is expected, because ischemic intestinal injury is first reflected at the mucosal level, and not until the pathologic process is advanced can one expect the inflammatory response to be manifest at the mesothelial level. Total solids elevation ($>$2.5 g/dl;25 g/L) demonstrated improved sensitivity for prediction of intestinal resection (63%); however, specificity fell to 70%. Red sample discoloration demonstrated similar sensitivity and specificity to total solids elevation for prediction of intestinal resection. Thus, a high rate of false-negative results (low sensitivity) is found, and in isolation, peritoneal fluid evaluation tends to underestimate the severity of intestinal lesions. Normality or minor change in peritoneal fluid should never be interpreted as evidence for lack of major intestinal damage.

Endoscopy. Fiberoptic endoscopy is occasionally used in the diagnosis of acute abdominal pain of gastric or duodenal origin. The most common condition thus diagnosed is gastric ulceration, although other pain-producing disorders such as gastric tumors and pyloric stenosis have been recognized. Most commonly, gastric ulceration is seen in adult horses treated with prolonged high-dose NSAIDs or in foals associated with stress or inappropriate NSAID usage. Unfortunately, adult horses often require a period of fasting (12 to 24 hours) for thorough endoscopic evaluation of the stomach, and the presence of gastric contents can limit the use of endoscopy for early diagnosis of gastric lesions causing acute pain.

Radiography. Because of the size of the equine abdomen, radiography has traditionally been used minimally in diagnosis of acute abdominal pain. Abdominal radiography is particularly rewarding, however, for foals and miniature horses. Foals can be radiographed either awake and standing or lightly sedated and placed on a small-animal radiology table. Contrast studies frequently add valuable information, particularly in cases of gastric outflow obstruction associated with gastroduodenal ulcer disease (GDUD). Miniature horses with acute abdominal pain appear to have a high incidence of gastric impaction, large-colon impaction, and small-colon fecaliths. These conditions are frequently diagnosed based on lateral radiographs taken with the horse standing. Sand accumulation in the large colon of adult full-sized horses can also be diagnosed on lateral radiographs of the ventral abdomen. In these cases, radiography is valuable for monitoring therapeutic progress.

TREATMENT (Table 4–4)

Medical management of the acute abdomen, either alone or as an adjunct to surgical intervention, has as its objective sedation or analgesia, normalization of intestinal motility and ingesta movement, inhibition of mucosal ulceration, restoration of cardiovascular function, and prevention of ischemic injury, sepsis, or adhesion formation.

SEDATION OR ANALGESIA

Drugs used to produce sedation and obstruct pain are categorized as narcotic analgesics, centrally acting non-narcotic analgesics, NSAIDs, hypnotics, sedatives, or psychogenics. Commonly used narcotic analgesics include morphine, meperidine, and butorphanol. Morphine is a good analgesic for equine abdominal pain but causes excitement if used alone. It is spasmogenic and can lead to decreased peristalsis. Meperidine, a slightly less effective analgesic, is hypotensive and spasmolytic. Both drugs are frequently used in combination with tranquilizers. Butorphanol, a morphine-like drug, has the advantage of not being a controlled narcotic drug. It is a good analgesic and sedative and, although it is commonly used in combination with xylazine, it does not appear to be as exitogenic as morphine and meperidine. In anesthetized ponies, butorphanol is a mild hypotensive and produces a mild decrease in intestinal blood flow, but does not alter intestinal vascular resistance or oxygen consumption.

Centrally acting non-narcotic analgesics include xylazine, pentazocine, and detomidine. Xylazine is widely used

TABLE 4–4. TREATMENT

Objectives
  Sedation, analgesia
  Cardiovascular restoration
  Normalization of
    Intestinal blood flow
    Motility
    Passage of ingesta
  Inhibition of
    Mucosal ulceration
    Ischemic injury
    Sepsis
    Adhesion formation

Therapeutic options
  Sedatives/analgesics
    Narcotic analgesics: morphine, meperidine, butorphanol
    Centrally acting non-narcotics: xylazine, pentazocine, detomidine
    Nonsteroidal anti-inflammatory drugs: flunixin, dipyrone, phenylbutazone
    Hypnotics/sedatives: chloral hydrate
    Psychotropics: acepromazine

  Laxatives/cathartics
    Contact: irritant—castor oil; surfactant—dioctyl sodium sulfosuccinate
    Bulk: bran, psyllium hydrophilic mucilloid
    Saline: $MgSO_4$
    Emollient: mineral oil
    Water: nasogastrically or intravenously

  Drugs directly altering autonomic control/motility
    Drugs that increase activity
      Parasympathomimetics: neostigmine, bethanecol
      Sympatholytics: adrenergic antagonists: propranolol, yohimbine
      Dopaminergic antagonists: metaclopromide
    Drugs that decrease activity
      Parasympatholytics: atropine, scopolamine, methylscopolamine, propantheline

  Drugs used in gastric ulcer disease
    Antacids: $AL(OH)_3$; $Mg(OH)_2$; $CaCO_3$
    Histamine-receptor antagonists: cimetidine, ranitidine
    Mucosal barrier drugs: sucralfate

  Cardiovascular restoration
    Intravascular fluids
      Crystalloid
      Colloid
      Plasma
    NSAID: Flunixin
    Corticosteroids: dexamethazone, prednisolone

  Antimicrobial agents: penicillins, aminoglycosides, sulfonamides, metronidazole

  Drugs used to optimize regional blood flow, prevent adhesions—heparin

  Drugs used to inhibit ischemic tissue injury
    Free-radical blockers: allopurinol, deferoxamine, catalase
    Free-radical scavengers: superoxide dismutase, dimethylsulfoxide, glycerol

for acute abdominal pain in the horse and is an excellent analgesic, sedative, and muscle relaxant. Because of the relatively short duration of its analgesic action, especially when it is used intravenously, it does not mask persistent pain for extended periods. If the patient is to be transported and sedation is needed, the intramuscular route might prolong analgesia and sedation. Xylazine has the disadvantage of decreasing systemic blood pressure and simultaneously increasing intestinal vascular resistance and intestinal activity, and therefore oxygen requirements. Large repeated doses should be avoided in patients with suspected ischemic intestinal disease. Pentazocine is a morphine-like non-narcotic with less analgesic effect than morphine but slightly more than meperidine. It is not sedative and produces hypotension of a similar degree and duration to morphine's. Its effect on the equine digestive tract are not well documented. Detomidine, an alpha-2 adrenoceptor agonist, is a potent analgesic and sedative currently being evaluated for clinical use in the horse.

Commonly employed NSAIDs include phenylbutazone, dipyrone, and flunixin. Although widely used as an analgesic in equine practice, phenylbutazone is infrequently used for acute abdominal pain. Dipyrone, although still a poor visceral analgesic, is better than phenylbutazone and is commonly used intravenously. Its supposed spasmolytic action is poorly documented. Flunixin meglumine is the most widely used NSAID for acute abdominal pain in the horse. It is an extremely effective antipyretic and analgesic, especially for pain of inflammatory origin such as that resulting from intestinal ischemia. Its efficacy in such cases has had the adverse effect of masking ischemic pain for long periods and improving the patient's disposition to such an extent that surgical intervention is often inappropriately delayed. Flunixin is also widely used for its ability to inhibit the prostanoid-mediated aspects of endotoxemia. The dosage required for such inhibition, however, is less than half the commonly employed analgesic dosages. In anesthetized healthy ponies, flunixin meglumine has been shown to increase systemic arterial pressure while causing a slight decrease in intestinal blood flow. It does not affect intestinal muscular activity and oxygen utilization. As with all NSAIDs, extreme caution should be taken not to exceed toxic limits. Mucosal ulceration and nephrosis are well documented complications of inappropriate NSAID usage in the horse.

Chloral hydrate is a hypnotic sedative that can be administered intravenously or orally in selected cases. It produces dose-dependent sedation, with recumbency and anesthesia at higher dosages. It is a poor analgesic and technically less convenient than the newer sedative/analgesics; however, it is relatively safe and dependable. The major psychotropic agent used is the phenothiazine derivative neuroleptic, acepromazine. While producing reasonable tranquilization for fractious patients, it produces significant hypotension and is not analgesic. It is therefore a poor drug for use in acute abdominal cases.

NORMALIZATION OF INTESTINAL MOTILITY AND MOVEMENT OF INGESTA

Laxatives and cathartics promote the aboral movement of ingesta and defecation. The most commonly used drugs are categorized as contact, bulk, saline, or emollient cathartics. Drugs that directly alter autonomic control of intestinal movements are discussed separately. Caster oil is an irritant contact cathartic that acts principally in the small bowel and, among other effects, reduces electrolyte and water absorption, increases secretion, and increases motility. It is occasionally used in constipated foals but is harsh and hence is not recommended.

Surface active or wetting agents such as dioctyl sodium sulfosuccinate (DSS) are contact cathartics. Their principal effect is to allow water and fat penetration of firm fecal masses. Surface active agents such as DSS are frequently used to treat colonic fecal impactions with variable success. Some authors caution combining surface active agents with emollients such as mineral oil (liquid petrolatum), as the emulsification, absorption, and foreign body reaction observed with the emollients is said to be increased.

Bulk laxatives such as bran and methylcellulose absorb intestinal water and secondarily stimulate motility. Neither is of great value for major colonic impaction, although they are used for treatment of colonic sand accumulation. Methylcellulose is best administered by stomach tube as a suspension in warm water. Magnesium sulfate (Epsom salts) is a commonly used saline cathartic of value in minor colonic impactions. Because it can produce systemic dehydration, it should be used only in well-hydrated, drinking patients.

Mineral oil is the most commonly used, even overused laxative in equine practice. It lubricates the surface of fecal masses, penetrates minor impactions, and can also interfere with water absorption. Unfortunately, it will not penetrate large or hard fecal masses. Although mineral oil is frequently used when mucosal irritation is suspected, there is little evidence for its use in motility disorders. Although limited absorption and foreign body reaction in the intestinal mucosa, mesenteric lymph nodes, liver, and spleen have been recorded in experimental animals, they are not recognized as clinical complications. In general, mineral oil should be limited to minor colonic impactions.

One of the most effective and overlooked cathartics is water. Extensive nonsurgical fecal impactions frequently respond well to nasogastric administration of 10 to 12 L of warm water every $1\frac{1}{2}$ to 2 hours (450-kg horse). The gastric tube can be secured to avoid repeated intubation. Administration should be discontinued if discomfort is increased or gastric reflux is noted. When intragastric administration is not possible and when cost permits, large-volume (15 to 20% body weight/24 hours) intravenous polyionic crystalloid solution administration is frequently effective in treatment of moderate colonic impaction. At this administration rate in otherwise healthy horses, intestinal transmucosal loss of excess fluid appears to occur without clinically recognized pulmonary complications.

Drugs that directly alter autonomic control of intestinal activity are parasympathomimetics, adrenergic blockade sympatholytics, dopamine antagonists, and parasympatholytics. The most commonly employed parasympathomimetic is the reversible anticholinesterase neostigmine. Little doubt exists that neostigmine increases jejunal muscular activity; however, considerable controversy surrounds its ability to initiate coordinated peristalsis and promote aboral movement of ingesta throughout the digestive tract. Neostigmine increases jejunal vascular resistance and oxygen requirements and is contraindicated when physical obstruction exists. Its use should be restricted to cases of functional obstruction such as ileus, preferably when laparotomy has confirmed the absence of intestinal vascular compromise or physical obstruction. Intense abdominal pain and bowel rupture are recorded complications. The muscarinic agonist bethanechol, the beta-1 and beta-2 adrenoceptor antagonist propranolol, and the alpha-2 adrenoceptor antagonist yohimbine have been evaluated in experimental ileus models with limited success. None of the above drugs are currently employed clinically. Metaclopramide, a dopamine receptor antagonist, has had limited clinical evaluation for postlaparotomy adynamic ileus and anterior enteritis syndrome. Parasympatholytics such as atropine, scopolamine, methylscopolamine, and propantheline are used occasionally when intestinal hyperactivity and spasm are thought to be present. Because the pathophysiology of such disorders is poorly documented and the risk of ileus high, such therapies are probably not indicated. Propantheline is occasionally used to produce colonic relaxation and facilitate rectal examination.

INHIBITION OF MUCOSAL ULCERATION

Drugs used to inhibit mucosal ulcer formation are antacids, histamine receptor antagonists, and ulcer adherent compounds. Antacids such as aluminum hydroxide, magnesium hydroxide, and calcium carbonate act locally to temporarily increase gastric pH and indirectly suppress peptic activity. With the exception of aluminum hydroxide, these drugs increase gastric motility by enhancing gastrin secretion. Aluminum hydroxide has been reported to delay gastric emptying in some species. The major controversy surrounding antacid use in animals is the acid rebound found to occur with calcium carbonate and to a lesser extent, with magnesium hydroxide and sodium bicarbonate. The efficacy of antacids or the occurrence of acid rebound in the horse has not been well documented, however, and antacids remain a popular treatment for gastric ulceration, particularly in foals. Cimetidine, an H_2-receptor antagonist, inhibits histamine-evoked gastric acid secretion and decreases gastrin/pentagastrin and

muscarine-stimulated acid secretion. Both cimetidine and a similar antagonist ranitidine have become widely used in the management of GDUD in foals and clinically appear to be effective. Sucralfate, a sulfate disaccharide aluminum complex, combines with mucosal proteins to form an ulcer adherent complex. The complex forms a barrier to gastric acid, bile salts, and pepsin penetration. Although used commonly, the compounds' efficacy remains largely unevaluated in equine models.

RESTORATION OF CARDIOVASCULAR FUNCTION

Intravascular crystalloid fluid therapy, the cornerstone of cardiovascular restoration in the acute abdominal crisis, will not be discussed in detail here. Choice of an appropriate fluid should be guided by serum electrolyte and acid-base status; however, balanced polyionic solutions such as lactated Ringer's solution are suitable in most cases. Notable exceptions include disease processes leading to excessive sodium, chloride, and bicarbonate loss (e.g., colitis), diseases producing alkalosis (e.g., anaerobic exercise exhaustion, pain-induced hyperventilation), or diseases producing hyperkalemia (e.g., urinary bladder rupture). In cases in which muscular weakness, persistent ileus, or synchronous diaphragmatic flutter is found, serum calcium concentrations should be monitored and adjusted appropriately by addition of calcium gluconate or calcium chloride to the regimen. When large quantities of intravascular protein are lost, that is, in mucosal or peritoneal inflammation or increased vascular permeability (endotoxemia), plasma or colloid therapy might be required to maintain intravascular oncotic pressure. This therapy is usually indicated if total serum solids fall to 3 g/dl (30 g/L). Other drugs used in the treatment of cardiovascular embarrassment in the acute abdominal patient include flunixin meglumine, as previously discussed, and corticosteroids. Although large systemic doses of corticosteroids have been shown to improve survival in traumatic shock in some species, considerable debate surrounds their use in septic shock conditions. Although some research data show temporary improvement in hematologic, coagulation, and blood gas data in experimental equine endotoxemia, improved survival, experimentally or clinically, has not been documented. Recent prospective studies of the use of steroids for treating human septic shock failed to show increased survival rates, and in some cases, increased complication rates resulted. Commonly employed dosages for acute abdominal shock in horses are considerably less than reported dosages for other species in shock and are probably not helpful.

PREVENTION OF ISCHEMIC INJURY, SEPSIS, OR ADHESION FORMATION

Dimethylsulfoxide (DMSO) has achieved considerable popularity in the treatment of the acute abdominal crises. It is administered intravenously at 0.25 to 1 g/kg body weight, diluted in saline. The rationale for its use stems from its well-documented ability to scavenge and inactivate oxygen-derived free radicals generated during tissue ischemia and inflammation. DMSO particularly scavenges the hydroxyl radical (OH), which is responsible for membrane lipid peroxidation and ground substance disruption. In experimental models of ischemia, free-radical scavenging and blocking agents such as allopurinol, superoxide dismutase (SOD), catalase, DMSO, deferoxamine, and protease inhibitors have been shown to improve postischemic structure and

function in intestine, heart, kidney, brain, and skeletal muscle. In a recent experimental evaluation in an equine model of ischemic intestinal injury, however, DMSO failed to significantly improve physiologic variables or preserve mucosal integrity. Further evaluation of DMSO and drugs of similar action is required before clinical usage can be recommended.

Antimicrobial therapy should be done perioperatively, especially when strangulating obstruction or nonstrangulating infarction is suspected. It should also be used in nonsurgical cases with evidence of peritoneal or visceral organ sepsis. The most common presurgical therapy is a combination of penicillin G and an aminoglycoside. If therapy is begun less than 2 hours prior to surgery, the penicillin should be given intravenously at 20,000 to 40,000 U/kg body weight and continued postsurgically intravenously or intramuscularly at the usual dosages. The most common aminoglycosides are gentamicin and amikacin. Care must be taken to avoid renal toxicity from aminoglycosides, particularly in dehydrated horses. Postoperative duration of therapy and choice of antimicrobial should be guided by intrasurgical findings, postsurgical physical status, sequential leukograms, abdominal fluid examination, culture, and microbial sensitivity. If used, abdominal drains can be cultured when removed. Considerable controversy surrounds the use of antimicrobial agents in nonsurgical inflammatory mucosal disorders (see Chapter 3).

Systemic sodium heparin is frequently used postlaparotomy with three therapeutic objectives: to aid intestinal blood flow where intravascular thrombosis is suspected, to limit peritoneal adhesion formation, and to minimize disseminated intravascular coagulation in endotoxemic patients. Unfortunately, data on heparin's effects on intestinal blood flow in the normal or diseased equine bowel is limited; however, evidence that heparin causes platelet aggregation and agglutination of equine erythrocytes suggests that heparin therapy could affect microvascular blood flow deleteriously. While recent studies indicate that systemic heparin usage might be indicated to minimize postsurgical visceral adhesion, experimental numbers are low and further investigation is required. The use of low-dose heparin to minimize endotoxin-induced coagulopathies is controversial. Inappropriate usage without awareness of the disorder's severity can exacerbate a consumptive coagulopathy.

SUMMARY

Deciding to explore the abdomen surgically and determining the appropriate medical regimen depend on a number of important criteria from each of the three phases of clinical evaluation discussed previously. For surgical exploration, the most important of these criteria are duration and intensity of pain, cardiovascular status, positive gastric reflux, rectal findings and peritoneal fluid changes. None of these criteria can be used in isolation to make such a decision. In some cases, evidence from two or three criteria immediately suggests a particular therapeutic course. In more difficult cases, additional criteria will need to be considered (Table 4–5). For example, acute bowel inflammatory lesions (anterior enteritis, colitis), which are generally considered to be nonsurgical conditions, can manifest as severe protracted pain accompanied by cardiovascular deterioration and gastric reflux. In such cases, added importance is given to rectal examination, quantitative peritoneal fluid analysis, and laboratory findings such as serum electrolyte and acid-base status. Similarly functional lesions such as ady-

namic ileus or colonic gas accumulation can present with protracted pain, gastric reflux, and distended bowel; however, close attention to the history (e.g., postlaparotomy, ingestion of excessive lush feed) and to cardiovascular, peritoneal fluid, and serum chemistry monitoring might suggest conservative management (analgesia, luminal decompression, and cardiovascular support).

In general, the clinician aims to evaluate as many of the criteria indicating surgery as is reasonably possible before subjecting the patient and client to the stress and expense of surgical exploration. This process should be tempered, however, by several suggestions: 1) Despite the frequent temptation to look for one, a simple and uniformly applicable physical or laboratory criterion does not exist. 2) A good clinical diagnosis should not be dismissed on the basis of incomplete compatibility of laboratory data. 3) The diagnostic return from increasing numbers of criteria is not proportional; that is, the return from 15 to 20 criteria may not add considerably to the insight gained from 5 to 8 criteria. 4) With improved anesthetic and surgical techniques, the risk incurred by exploratory laparotomy has become reduced. In diagnostically difficult cases, when economic considerations permit, early exploration might be superior to waiting until all surgical criteria are met.

If surgical intervention is selected, accompanying medical therapy should include normalization of circulating fluid volume, intravascular oncotic pressure, and electrolyte and acid-base status; appropriate use of analgesics; and broad-spectrum antimicrobial prophylaxis. If medical therapy alone is indicated, objectives include analgesia; normalization of cardiovascular status; intestinal motility and ingesta movement; minimization of mucosal ischemia, inflammation, and ulceration; and elimination of intra-abdominal sepsis.

TABLE 4–5. SURGICAL CRITERIA

Clinical Criteria	Generalization	Noted Exceptions
Severe, protracted pain (>6 hrs)	Most commonly seen with physical obstruction, with displacement causing continued mesenteric traction, or where vascular integrity is compromised	Functional obstructions, e.g., adynamic ileus Primary inflammatory disorders, e.g., gastric ulceration, anterior enteritis, colitis Mesenteric traction amenable to conservative management, e.g., some displacement, broad ligament hemorrhage
Abdominal pain and progressive cardiovascular deterioration	Commonly associated with splanchnic ischemia and subsequent systemic liberation of circulatory toxins	Any intra-abdominal inflammatory process leading to pain and systemic toxin accumulation, e.g., enteritis, colitis, grain engorgement, peritonitis, septic metritis
Positive gastric reflux	Commonly associated with gastric outflow obstruction, small-bowel physical obstruction, long-standing large-bowel obstruction	Adynamic ileus of any cause Inflammatory lesions of the proximal small intestine (anterior enteritis) Colonic distension or displacement causing duodenal traction
Rectal finding of bowel distension (fluid, feces, gas), displacement, or entrapment	Usually associated with physical bowel obstruction	Functional obstructions, i.e., adynamic ileus, flatulent colic Minor obstructions (impaction) and displacements amenable to medical therapy
Peritoneal fluid composition changes	Marked cellular and protein elevations frequently indicative of transmural intestinal disease	False negatives more common than false positives Marked protein elevations accompanying primary bowel inflammatory disease Marked cellular elevations associated with localized peritoneal disease

SUPPLEMENTAL READING

Adams, S.B., and McIlwraith, C.W.: Abdominal crisis in the horse: A comparison of pre-surgical evaluation with surgical findings and results. Vet. Surg., 3:63–69, 1978.

Adams, S.B., Fessler, J.F., and Rebar, A.H.: Cytologic interpretation of peritoneal fluid in the evaluation of abdominal crises. Cornell Vet., 70:232, 1980.

Bach, L.G., and Rickettes, J.W.: Paracentesis as an aid to the diagnosis of abdominal disease in the horse. Equine Vet. J., 6(3):116–121, 1974.

Burrows, G.E.: Endotoxemia in the horse. Equine Vet. J. 13:89–94, 1981.

Colahan, P.T.: Evaluation of horses with colic and selection of surgical treatment. Compend. Contin. Educ. 17:141–149, 1985.

Ducharme, N.G, et al.: Positive predictive value of clinical examination in selecting medical or surgical treatment for horses with abdominal pain. *In* Colic Research; Proceedings of the Second Symposium of the University of Georgia. Edited by J.N. Moore, N.A. White, and J.L. Becht. Lawrenceville, Veterinary Learning Systems, 1986, pp. 200–203.

Greatorex, J.C.: Rectal exploration as an aid to the diagnosis of some medical conditions in the horse. Equine Vet. J. 1:26–30, 1968.

McIlwraith, C.W.: Equine digestive system. *In* The Practice of Large Animal Surgery. Edited by P.B. Jennings, Philadelphia, WB Saunders, 1984, pp. 554–663.

Moore, J.M., Gaines, H.E., Shapland, J.E., and Schaub, R.E.: Equine endotoxemia: an insight into cause and treatment. J. Am. Vet. Med. Assoc., 179(5):473–477, 1981.

Morris, D.D., and Johnston, J.K.: Peritoneal fluid constituents in horses with colic due to small intestinal disease. *In* Colic Research; Proceedings of the Second Symposium of the University of Georgia. Edited by J.N. Moore, N.A. White, and J.L. Becht. Lawrenceville, Veterinary Learning Systems, 1986, pp. 134–142.

Parry, B.W., Anderson, G.A., and Gay, C.C.: Prognosis in equine colic: A study of individual variables in case assessment. Equine Vet. J. 15:337–344, 1983.

Parry, B.W., Gay, C.C., and Anderson, G.A.: Assessment of the necessity for surgical intervention in cases of equine colic: A retrospective study. Equine Vet. J. 15:216–221, 1983.

Pascoe, P.J.: Accuracy of clinical examination in the prognosis of abdominal pain in the horse. *In* Colic Research; Proceedings of the Second Symposium of the University of Georgia. Edited by J.N. Moore, N.A. White, and J.L. Becht. Lawrenceville, Veterinary Learning Systems, 1986, pp. 149–152.

Stick, J.A., Chou, C.C., Derksen, F.J., and Arden, W.A.: Effects of xylazine on equine intestinal vascular resistance, motility, compliance and oxygen consumption. Am. J. Vet. Res., 48:198–203, 1987.

White, N.A.: Equine Acute Abdomen, Philadelphia, Lea & Febiger, 1989.

White, N.A., Tyler, D.E., Blackwell, R.B., and Allen, D.: Hemorrhagic fibrinonecrotic duodenitis-proximal jejunitis in horses: 20 cases (1977–1984). J. Am. Vet. Med. Assoc., 190(3):311–315, 1987.

chapter 5

CHRONIC OR RECURRENT ABDOMINAL PAIN

Warwick A. Arden

PATHOPHYSIOLOGY (Table 5–1)

Chronic or recurrent abdominal pain in an individual patient may affect a number of animals on a particular farm or in a specific location. The diagnosis of specific causes of chronic abdominal pain can be difficult and unrewarding. Frequently, the horse's owner is disturbed enough to request exploratory laparotomy, even when no immediate life-threatening condition is apparent. In cases of recurrent abdominal pain, the diagnosis is frequently undetermined even after surgical exploration. The following possible causes of chronic and recurrent abdominal pain are not complete, but rather alert the clinician to the major diagnostic possibilities.

Assuming that most abdominal pain relates to activation of mechanical stretch receptors or release of inflammatory mediators (see Chapter 4), potential causes of chronic or recurrent pain can be categorized as those conditions causing bowel wall (mural) stretch; mesenteric traction; or mucosal, parenchymal, or peritoneal inflammation.

BOWEL WALL STRETCH

The majority of conditions causing bowel wall stretch and chronic pain are forms of simple obstruction, because strangulating or infarctive conditions are unlikely to lead to prolonged or recurrent pain. Such simple obstruction can be physical or functional and is incomplete or at least transient.

Physical Obstruction

Physical intestinal obstructions can further be divided into congenital and acquired lesions. An example of a congenital lesion causing recurrent pain is pyloric stenosis. The condition is en-

TABLE 5–1. POTENTIAL CAUSES OF CHRONIC AND RECURRENT ABDOMINAL PAIN

Pain caused by bowel wall stretch
  Physical obstruction—usually simple and
  incomplete or transient
    Congenital—pyloric stenosis
    Acquired
      Pyloric/duodenal lesions associated with GDUD
      Gastric tumors
      Ileal hypertrophy and parasitism
      Chronic intussusception
      Recurrent fecal impaction
      Enterolith formation
      Foreign material accumulation
  Functional obstruction
    Gastric or colonic gas accumulation
    Intestinal spasm

Pain caused by mesenteric traction
  Chronic impactions
  Tumors
  Splenomegaly

Pain caused by inflammatory lesions
  Mucosal lesions
    Ulceration
    Sand irritation
  Parenchymal abscess
    Liver, kidney, spleen
  Tumors
  Localized peritonitis

Other
  Cholelithiasis

countered most commonly in foals when solid food becomes a substantial proportion of the diet, and diagnosis can be based on history (pain related to feeding), gastroscopy, and contrast radiographic studies.

Acquired obstructive lesions, more common, include gastric outflow obstruction secondary to gastric duodenal ulcer disease (GDUD) in foals, gastric tumors in adults, ileal hypertrophy and parasitism, chronic intussusception (jejunojejunal, jejunocecal, or cecocolic), recurrent fecal impaction, enterolith formation, and foreign body retention. Gastric outflow obstruction associated with GDUD can occur in association with severe pyloric and proximal duodenal inflammation, pyloric spasm, or pyloric abscess and adhesion. A suggestive history includes moderate to severe abdominal pain associated with eating, superimposed on a history of chronic or intermittent pain, bruxism, ptyalism, and frequently an accompanying primary condition causing stress. Reflux of milk or feed material can occur with nasogastric intubation. Endoscopy may be helpful if the stomach can be evacuated. Plain abdominal radiographs show gastric enlargement and contrast films show delayed gastric emptying of barium sulfate. Many foals with duodenal lesions secondary to GDUD can be managed medically with antacids, histamine antagonists, sucralfate, low-dose anti-inflammatories, systemic antimicrobials, fluid replacement, and frequent small-volume feedings. Successful management with surgery has also been reported.

Gastric tumors are rare; the most common, squamous cell carcinoma, presents with inappetence, weight loss, anemia, and occasionally melena. Some horses also have mild intermittent abdominal pain that might be related to feeding. A space-occupying lesion on contrast radiographs is suggestive of gastric tumors, while gastroscopy and endoscopic biopsy are diagnostic.

Ileal hypertrophy, parasitism (Anaplocephala), or both can present with low-grade recurrent pain, but most commonly they are diagnosed at exploratory laparotomy, which is done when obstruction becomes almost complete and the patient presents with moderate to severe acute abdominal pain. Occasionally a diagnosis can be made presurgically by careful rectal examination.

Chronic intussusception is rare but has been recorded in foals. A history of depression, anorexia, mild intermittent pain, and intermittent melena can accompany the condition. Abdominal paracentesis and abdominal radiographs are valuable in guiding the clinician to surgical exploration and treatment.

Recurrent fecal impaction is diagnosed predominantly by rectal examination and is most common in older horses. Although perhaps aberrant colonic motility plays a role, many cases can be traced to poor dental condition or inadequate access to fresh water.

Colonic enterolith formation frequently has a specific geographic distribution. Feed and water mineral composition are thought to play a role. Enteroliths develop over a long period, frequently around a foreign body nidus, and can cause abdominal pain or discomfort by mesenteric traction owing to the weight of the enterolith, or by intermittently moving toward a narrow area of the colon, e.g., right dorsal to transverse colon and causing an obstruction. Enteroliths can be diagnosed by rectal examination or occasionally by abdominal radiographs. Definitive diagnosis is frequently made at surgical exploration when the mass has caused complete obstruction.

Foreign materials reported to accumulate in the equine colon and cause recurrent abdominal pain include twine from hay bales, sand, and rubber and nylon. Rubber-nylon strip fencing produced from old conveyer belts is the most common source of this material. Frequently rubber-nylon and twine act as a nidus for fecolith formation, and diagnosis is often made at laparotomy when complete obstruction has occurred. Sand can produce abdominal pain by visceral traction (especially cecal accumulation), luminal obstruction (especially pelvic flexure and dorsal large colon), or mucosal irritation. Diagnosis is based on a history of pasturing in a sandy area, rectal examination, abdominal radiographs, and the presence of sand in fecal washings. Mild to moderate sand accumulation responds well to medical management with laxatives and cathartics; severe accumulations are best treated by laparotomy and colotomy or cecotomy.

Functional Obstruction

Functional obstructions that can cause recurrent abdominal pain include gastric and colonic gas accumulation and intestinal spasm. Primary gastric dilation, an uncommon condition, is frequently related to wind-sucking. Gastritis might accompany the condition. Colonic dilation (flatulent colic) is more common and is usually related to excessive ingestion of easily fermentable green feed. Gastric dilation can be relieved by nasogastric intubation, while colonic dilation can be treated by percutaneous colonic and cecal decompression. In severe cases and those in which colonic displacement cannot be excluded, laparotomy should be performed.

Spasmodic colic is a poorly defined entity recognized frequently in young nervous horses by an acute onset of severe abdominal pain, which passes quickly, frequently without treatment. Cardiovascular and abdominal examinations are usually unremarkable, except that small-intestinal sounds are frequently loud and irregular. A history of pain might be associated with feeding. The pathogenesis of this syndrome is poorly defined; mucosal irritant, psychogenic, and ischemic hypotheses have been suggested. If a distinct correlation with feeding and mesenteric thrombosis can be identified, relative intestinal ischemia (demand exceeding availability) might be a plausible explanation, as marginal ischemic states are known to induce intense intestinal contraction. Frequent feeding of small quantities of low-concentrate feed and a vigorous anthelmintic program might be indicated in such cases.

MESENTERIC TRACTION

Conditions causing pain by mesenteric traction include chronic impactions, tumors, and splenomegaly. Chronic impactions have been discussed above. Ovarian tumors are well recorded in the horse and occasionally are large enough to lead to abdominal discomfort, either with exercise or at rest. Diagnosis is based on a history of behavioral change in some horses and on careful rectal examination to identify the lesion and rule out other conditions. Ovarian removal via laparotomy might be indicated. Occasionally, young mares show recurrent abdominal pain that appears to be related to the reproductive cycle. Episodes are most evident at ovulation. The pathogenesis of pain production in such cases is unclear. Splenomegaly is an uncommon cause of chronic and recurrent abdominal pain. Pain is thought to originate from traction of the nephrosplenic mesentery. Physical and laboratory examination is usually unrewarding, except for rectal findings. A greatly enlarged spleen, which bulges from the left abdominal wall and can extend almost to the pelvic inlet, might be identified. In most cases, the etiology of splenic enlargement is unknown, and splenotomy has been known to alleviate the pain in refractory cases.

INFLAMMATORY LESIONS

Inflammatory lesions as a source of recurrent or chronic pain include mucosal lesions (ulceration, sand irritation), visceral (parenchymal) abscesses, tumors, and peritonitis. With the exception of gastric ulceration, which can present in foals with severe abdominal pain, and sand irritation, which can also cause pain by viscus obstruction and distension, the majority of inflammatory lesions lead to dull, chronic pain, manifest more by an arched back and a stiff walk than by the more typical colic symptoms discussed in Chapter 4. Diagnosis and treatment of gastric ulceration and sand accumulation have been discussed (see Chapter 4.) Hepatic, splenic, and renal abscesses are uncommon but recorded causes of abdominal pain. Diagnosis, which can be difficult, is aided by peripheral leukogram and fibrinogen concentration, peritoneal fluid examination, rectal examination, and urinalysis. Transrectal and transabdominal ultrasonography have proven to be extremely valuable in localization of splenic and renal lesions. The most common abdominal tumors causing low-grade pain are gastric and ovarian and have been discussed in previous sections of this chapter. Localized peritonitis is diagnosed by rectal examination, abdominocentesis, and transabdominal ultrasonography. Treatment consists of microbial identification and sensitivity testing, and appropriate long-term parenteral antimicrobial therapy.

MISCELLANEOUS

Cholelithiasis is an infrequent cause of chronic or recurrent abdominal pain in the horse. Pain is thought to arise from activation of both mechanosensitive and chemosensitive receptors and to be transmitted by sympathetic afferents. The diagnosis is based on finding obstructive jaundice in horses with recurrent pain and ultrasonic identification of the mineralized density.

INVESTIGATING THE PROBLEM FARM (Table 5–2)

Frequently, chronic or recurrent abdominal pain in an individual horse and acute or recurrent pain in a group of horses can be traced to environmental and management factors. Factors that feature heavily in the investigation include feeding management, water access and quality, stall environment, pasture environment, dental care, antiparasitic practices, transportation practices, and routine neonate management. It is important not merely to discuss management techniques in an office situation, but to make a site visit. Prior to visiting, the clinician should review the medical records of as many of the affected cases as possible, including surgical and necropsy reports, to form an impression of common pathologic factors.

Frequently, causative factors might not be obvious at the first visit, and clinicians should be encouraged to develop a cooperative approach to investigation, including consultation with other veterinarians who service nearby establishments, acute abdomen referral centers to establish regional incidences, field officers from the Departments of Agriculture and Natural Resources, and extension officers at the state colleges. With growing intensification of the equine industry, collaborative investigation and preventive medical intervention are likely to become increasingly important in clinical practice.

FEEDING MANAGEMENT

Investigation of feeding management should include observation of the com-

TABLE 5–2. INVESTIGATING THE PROBLEM FARM

Step 1: Medical records
        Necropsy reports
Step 2: Discussion of facilities, management
        practices, and techniques with farm
        managers
Step 3: On-site visitation
    Feeding management
        Composition and quality
        Timing and regularity
        Placement
        Competition
    Water
        Quality
        Quantity
        Access/competition
        Temperature
    Stall environment
        Bedding
        Wall construction
        Feeder and waterer construction
        Ventilation
        Crib biting/wind-sucking
        Stress from surroundings
        Chemicals used in barn
    Pasture environment
        Pasture composition
        Ground cover, soil character
        Feeders, waterers
        Fencing construction
        Shade, shelter
        Fertilizers, weedicides, pesticides
        Neighboring industrial complexes
        Stress from surroundings
        Free water
    Other management
        Parasitic
            Anthelmintic regimen
            Pasture hygiene
            Fecal examination
        Dental
        Transportation
            Facilities and techniques
            Examination of other frequented sites
        Neonate management
        Routine medications
Step 4: Ancillary examination
    Feed analysis
    Water analysis
    Fecal examination
    Toxicologic serum chemistry
Step 5: Consultation
    Local veterinary practitioners
    Local referral centers
    Departments of Agriculture, Natural
        Resources, University Extension

position and quality of feed, timing of feeding, regularity of feeding and placement of feed. Excessive poor-quality roughage can predispose to simple colonic impactions, particularly in older horses with poor teeth and in the summer or winter, when water can be limited. Rations excessively high in carbohydrate can predispose to development of an atypical luminal bacterial population and hence to diarrhea, excessive gas production, or both.

Perhaps more important than feed composition are sudden changes in the feeding pattern. Any changing of rations should occur over 7 to 10 days. Timing and regularity of feeding are important, and problems can occur if horses are worked heavily after large carbohydrate meals or if feed times are suddenly changed. Any recent changes in stable or farm personnel should be noted. On larger establishments the veterinarian should question the staff rather than just the management about the details of feeding procedures.

Placement of feed is important from two perspectives. First, horses fed as a large group tend to develop more problems than horses fed separately because of competition for feed. Less competitive horses might not eat enough, or if one or two horses are inappetent, the potential for excessive feed ingestion by others is increased. Second, horses should be fed from an elevated clean surface (e.g., manger) to avoid excessive ingestion of foreign material from the ground. This placement of feed is particularly important for horses on sandy lots or horses bedded on wood chips or shavings.

WATER

Water access and quality should be monitored, particularly in very hot and very cold climates. A healthy, 450 kg horse in a temperate environment and not performing heavy work will drink up to 30 L/day, and an excess of this amount should be provided. Water quality testing is frequently available from commercial and, on occasion, state laboratories. If horses are watered from individual buckets, the buckets should be filled regularly. Constantly empty buckets usually means inadequate access. Automatic waterers should be checked for function. In cold climates, freezing of waterers can limit access for long periods. Because horses are less likely to drink adequate quantities of water that is of extreme temperatures, water sources should be shaded in summer and perhaps heated in winter. The provision of salt blocks will usually increase water intake if adequate access but inadequate ingestion is occurring. When horses are watered as a group, one or two dominant horses must not be allowed to limit water access for the others.

ENVIRONMENT

The horse's stall should be examined for bedding character, quantity, and quality; wall and door construction; feed and waterer construction; and ventilation. Is there any evidence of crib biting? Is the horse comfortable in its environment or stressed by neighboring animals or proximity to human activity? Any chemicals used in the barn (disinfectants, cleaning agents, pesticides, etc.) should be documented. Similarly, pasture environment should be examined for soil character, pasture composition and ground cover, placement and type of feeders and waterers, fencing construction and topical fencing treatments, shade, and shelter. The horses should be observed for comfort in the pasture, particularly for freedom from harassment by other horses, dogs, people, or traffic. Any treatments of that or neighboring pastures (fertilizers, weedicides, pesticides) and proximity to industrial complexes should be noted. Any free water running through the pasture should be examined and its source determined. If water or pasture contamination is suspected, assistance from state and federal agencies should be considered.

OTHER MANAGEMENT

Measures to control internal parasites should be noted, including anthelmintic regimen, pasture, and feed hygiene. If doubts exist, fecal egg characterization and quantitation should be performed on a sample of horses. This testing might have to be repeated serially, particularly pre- and postanthelmintics, to test for drug and administration efficacy. Dental care can be monitored by oral inspection of a number of horses, particularly the older horses. If horses are being transported to and from the property frequently, transportation practices (feed, water, trailer, rest) should be examined. Similarly, if horses are regularly transported to a limited number of destinations (for showing, training, racing, etc.), these premises might also require inspection. For breeding establishments with recurrent gastrointestinal problems in foals, routine neonatal management should be critically evaluated. If horse establishment carries diverse prescription and nonprescription medications, these should be noted and the staff questioned regarding routine dosages. This questioning is particularly important for nonsteroidal anti-inflammatory drugs (NSAIDs), which tend to be used liberally.

PREVENTIVE MEASURES

Numerous routine procedures can minimize the incidence of colic at horse establishments. Among the most important are regular and preferably individual feeding of a balanced ration and provision of adequate fresh water. High-concentrate feeds should not be fed immediately following strenuous exercise. Horses kept on sandy lots should always be fed from elevated clean surfaces. If horses still consume moderate quantities of sand while foraging in such lots, bulk laxatives such as bran or methylcellulose can be added to the diet. If substantial quantities of bran are added, the calcium and phosphorus balance of the ration must be adjusted.

Perhaps the next most important preventive measure is adequate parasitic control by environmental hygiene, pasture rotation, and an effective anthelmintic program. Manual removal of feces from yards and small pastures is an effective means of limiting infective stages of intestinal parasites. For larger areas, harrowing or, more effectively, pasture vacuuming are efficient control measures. When availability of land permits, rotation of pastures among horses of different ages or among horses and other species can be practiced.

Anthelmintics can be administered by either nasogastric intubation or use of an oral paste at 6- to 12-week intervals. In warm climates where horses are pastured in groups, administration at 4-week intervals has been recommended. Efficiency of an anthelmintic program can be monitored by fecal examination pre- and postanthelmintic administration. Therapeutic failure is most commonly related to ineffective technique of administration or to drug resistance. Rotation of anthelmintics is frequently advocated to minimize the development of such resistance.

Other routine procedures that can minimize the incidence of abdominal complaints include regular dental care; monitoring of fecal consistency and frequency, particularly in neonates; close attention to removal of foreign material (e.g., twine, plastics, rubber) from the feed and environment; and adequate rest during long-distance transportation.

SUPPLEMENTAL READING

Gay, C.C., et al.: Foreign body obstruction of the small colon in six horses. Equine Vet. J., *11*:60–63, 1979.

Greatorex, J.C.: Rectal exploration as an aid to the diagnosis of some medical conditions in the horse. Equine Vet. J., *1*:26–30, 1968.

Pearson, H., Pinsent, P.J.N., Denny, H.R., and Waterman, A.: The indications for equine laparotomy—an analysis of 140 cases. Equine Vet. J., *7*:131–136, 1975.

Taylor, T.S., Martin, M.T., and McMullan, W.C.: Bypass surgery for intestinal occluding abscesses in the equine: A report of 2 cases. Vet. Surg., *3*:136–138, 1981.

White, N.A., Moore, J.N., Cowgil, L.M., and Brown, J.: Epizootology and risk factors in equine colic at university hospitals. *In* Colic Research; Proceedings of the Second Symposium of the University of Georgia. Edited by J.N. Moore, N.A. White, and J.L. Becht. Lawrenceville, Veterinary Learning Systems, 1986, pp. 26–29.

Wilson, J.H.: Gastric and duodenal ulcers in foals: A retrospective study. *In* Moore J.N., White N.A., Becht J.L. (ed), Colic Research; Proceedings of the Second Symposium of the University of Georgia. Edited by J.N. Moore, N.A. White, and J.L. Becht, Lawrenceville, Veterinary Learning Systems, 1986, pp. 126–129.

See Also Chapter 4.

chapter 6

DYSPHAGIA AND CHOKE

Pamela C. Wagner

DYSPHAGIA

Dysphagia means difficulty in eating, swallowing, or both. It is used to define the clinical sign of *inability* to eat rather than *unwillingness* to eat. Dysphagia can be characteristic of many syndromes, the degree depending on the underlying cause. To eat properly, the horse must adequately prehend, masticate, and swallow the food. The following section describes the mechanisms necessary to these functions. Alteration of the normal function will be related to specific causes of disfunction.

"Choke," or esophageal obstruction, can be either an anatomic or a functional problem. To deliver swallowed food to the stomach the esophagus must be unobstructed and able to function in an organized manner. Abnormalities of the esophagus resulting in functional or anatomic obstruction will be described and management techniques noted.

PATHOPHYSIOLOGY

Physiology of Prehension

The lips are the major organ of prehension in the horse. They are used to grasp plant material, which is then severed by the incisor teeth. The lips are two musculomembranous folds that surround the orifice of the mouth. They are highly vascular and well-innervated, and they move almost constantly. The motor functions of the major muscle groups involved in food-gathering are controlled by the buccal branch of the facial nerve (cranial nerve VII). Sensory input through the lips occurs through the trigeminal nerve (cranial nerve V).

The voluntary effort of prehension is controlled centrally in the cerebral motor cortex and basal nuclei. The medulla contains the nuclei of the cranial nerves involved in prehension control. Therefore, the inability to prehend food might be due to damage in the forebrain, the medulla, and cranial nerves V and VII, as well as to damage to the various muscles affected by these nervous structures.

The terminal event of prehension is severing of the material by the incisors. The horse has six incisors in the mandible and six opposing in the maxilla. Central deciduous incisor teeth erupt at approximately 6 days after birth, lateral teeth at 6 weeks, and corner teeth at 6 months. These deciduous incisor teeth are shed and replaced by adult incisors in the same order at $2\frac{1}{2}$, $3\frac{1}{2}$, and $4\frac{1}{2}$ years, respectively. Primary incisor disorders such as loose or fractured teeth as well as inability to close the incisors properly, as occurs in fracture of the jaw or loss of muscle control of the jaw, can result in dysphagia.

Abnormality. Dysphagia caused by prehension problems can involve obvious anatomic abnormalities such as lacerations to the lips or to the muscles of the buccal walls. If these muscles are paralyzed, rather than mechanically interrupted, the horse might attempt prehension by grasping feed with the teeth and vigorously tossing its head to move the feed into the mouth. Excess salivation and escape of saliva from the lip commissures are common. When drinking the horse will submerge the nose to the level of the pharynx.

Causes. Lacerations and ulceration of the lips cause temporary prehensile dysphagia. The laceration can be accompanied by direct trauma to nerves in the area or by neuropraxia caused by inflammation in the area of the wound. Wounds that involve the mucocutaneous border of the lips are most difficult to heal because of constant movement; however, even severe lacerations of the lips with obvious peripheral nerve involvement respond to therapy. Depending on the temperament of the horse, debridement, cleaning, and surgical reappositioning of the tissues can be done with the horse standing or under anesthesia. Rough feed should be withheld for several days and copious flushing of the mouth repeated after meals of soft feed.

Malocclusion of the jaws or teeth can be determined by oral examination and often is secondary to jaw fracture. If the premaxilla is fractured and nondisplaced, fixation of the fracture is not needed, and often soft feed for 3 to 4 weeks will suffice. Unilateral fracture of the mandible can also be treated conservatively, although any displacement of the incisors in the lower jaw indicates bilateral rami fracture, which often requires stabilization for proper healing. Many methods of stabilization are available, but often stability can be achieved using wires around the base of the teeth in addition to Steinmann's pins or lag screws across the fracture.

Nerve abnormalities leading to prehension difficulties include central and peripheral disorders. Yellow star thistle and Russian knapweed poisoning cause irreversible lesions of the basal nuclei. The horse is unable to prehend food and move it aborally, but can swallow if food is placed in the pharynx. There is no therapy.

Damage to the facial nerve causes the lower lip to droop on the affected side. If the nerve is affected bilaterally the lower lip is nonfunctional, and because the buccinator muscle is also affected, all food accumulates in the buccal cavities. Damage to the trigeminal nerve causes loss of sensation of the lips and can alter feeding habits and attitude. If peripheral neuropathies are due to inflammation of tissues around the nerve, anti-inflammatory drugs such as phenylbutazone or flunixin meglumine are indicated. Central brain lesions resulting in damage to the nuclei of cranial nerve V or VII are often infectious or neoplastic and might not be amenable to treatment.

Mastication

The chewing of feed material after prehension and before swallowing requires the use of the premolar and molar teeth and the muscles of mastication, which are controlled by cranial nerves V and VII. The process is abetted by the buccinator muscle, which keeps food from accumulating in the buccal pouches, and the salivary glands, which supply saliva for softening and initial digestion of masticated feed.

Mastication in the horse is crucial, as the bulk of the diet is rough herbage and requires mechanical breakdown and mixture with saliva prior to deglutition. The salivary glands secrete saliva in response to the rhythmic motions of the mandible during mastication. The rhythmic motions are reflex; however, they are under voluntary control and can be interrupted intentionally.

Difficulty in mastication can result from neurologic or muscular deficits that inhibit normal occlusion and grinding movements of the mandibular and maxillary teeth. Pain resulting from abnormality of the teeth, bone, or muscles involved in mastication can cause the horse to limit or halt the processing of food voluntarily.

Abnormality. Clinical signs vary from prehension with no attempts to chew to refusal to open the mouth. The horse is interested in food when it is offered but hesitates after prehension and allows food to fall from its mouth. The horse might stand near a feed tub but not eat. There may be continual or excessive salivation and, in some cases, a fetid odor to the breath.

Causes and Treatment. Causes of problems with mastication are related to the teeth, tongue, jaws, and temporomandibular joints. The most common cause of difficulty resides with the teeth. Sharp points on the outside of the upper molars and the inside of the lower molars can lacerate the buccal surface of the cheeks and the tongue. Pain from these abrasions makes the horse unwilling to chew. When points are removed by the use of a tooth float (rasp), the wounds to the mucous membranes heal quickly. Severe ulceration or stomatitis caused by rough feed can cause similar signs.

Decay of the teeth is secondary to communication of the infundibulum with the pulp cavity of the tooth. Feed contamination with subsequent infection and toothroot abscessation can cause enough pain to inhibit mastication. When abscessation is present in the lower arcade, an obvious swelling and often a draining tract will be present. When the tooth is in the upper arcade it can abscess into the sinus, causing a nasal discharge. Radiography confirms the presence of an abscessed tooth root and the degree of alveolar bone involvement. Removal of the affected tooth, treatment of the sinusitis or osteomyelitis, and antibiotic therapy are indicated.

Severe lacerations of the tongue or foreign body entrapment in the oral cavity can be determined during the oral examination. A horse can lose up to one third of the distal end of the tongue without permanent impairment of mastication; however, lacerations farther back should be sutured. A general anesthetic might be required. Absorbable sutures should be placed in the parenchyma of the tongue and nonabsorbable sutures on the mucosal surface. Large tension-relieving sutures should span the mucosal suture line to protect it during movement of the tongue.

Foreign bodies can penetrate under the tongue, causing swelling and pain, or can wedge between the upper arcades, preventing the tongue from moving the food bolus aborally. If the foreign body is obvious it can be removed with the horse tranquilized. If it is embedded in soft tissues, general anesthesia and exploratory surgery might be needed.

Fractures of the jaw or the temporomandibular joint can be diagnosed using radiography. Pain in the temporomandibular joint makes the horse unwilling to open the jaws at all, and feeding behavior is reduced to nibbling and dropping of feed. If the temporomandibular joint pain is due to osteoarthritis, steroid injections into that joint might give some measure of relief.

Other causes of inability to masticate include atrophy of the muscles of mastication secondary to cauda equina neuritis (polyneuritis equi) and tetanus infections. Other clinical signs of cauda equina neuritis in the horse include rear limb ataxia and gluteal muscle wastage. Tetanic horses often show more severe signs than failure to eat, such as limb rigidity, elevation of the tail, tetanic muscle tremors, and respiratory difficulty. Cauda equina neuritis has no treatment; therapy for tetanus includes tranquilization antibiotics, antitoxin, and nursing care.

Deglutition

Deglutition, or the act of swallowing, is initiated by the presence of material delivered into the pharynx.

Swallowing is divided into several stages. In the first or oral phase, a bolus of food is formed in the oropharynx. Sweeping motions of the tongue move the bolus aborally. In the pharyngeal phase, the bolus is moved through the pharynx, respiration ceases, and the larynx and nasopharynx close. The soft palate seals off the nasopharynx, preventing nasal reflux, and the epiglottis and arytenoid cartilages protect the entry of the bolus into the larynx. The third or cricopharyngeal stage is initiated by constriction of the caudal musculature of the pharynx. The paired cricopharyngeal muscles relax to accommodate the bolus and then contract behind the bolus to prevent its return to the pharynx.

The pharyngeal and cricopharyngeal stages of swallowing are controlled by the glossopharyngeal nerve (CN IX) and the vagus nerve (CN X). The motor nucleus governing these activities is the nucleus ambiguus; however, coordination by higher centers is also required.

Abnormality. Most cases of inability to swallow begin gradually over hours or days. At first, the horse might attempt to eat or drink. Gagging and paroxysms of coughing occur when the food reaches the pharynx but cannot be swallowed. Feed and saliva or lumps of masticated feed will fall from the mouth. Salivation may increase, or appear to increase, when saliva is expelled instead of swallowed. In many cases the inability to swallow is accompanied by inability to close the nasopharynx, and reflux from the nose is common. If feed becomes impacted within the pharynx, respiratory stridor with intermittent forceful expulsion of feed occurs. In most chronic cases oral fetor and some degree of weight loss is seen. In diseases such as rabies and other encephalides involving the central nervous system, depression or abnormal behavior accompany the signs of dysphagia.

In a horse that cannot swallow, particularly if the condition is of recent onset, rabies should be suspected and human handlers protected. Avoiding saliva, wearing gloves to handle the animal, and proper restraint techniques can minimize exposure.

Causes and Treatment. The numerous causes of inability to swallow can be neurologic, mechanical, or iatrogenic. Neurologic disorders of the central nervous system include viral encephalomyelitis, botulism, brain stem masses, and rabies.

Viral encephalomyelitis (Western, Eastern, and Venezuelan equine encephalomyelitis) is caused by viruses that usually are confined to mosquito vectors and avian reservoirs. Occasionally, horses are infected by the insect vector carrying the virus from birds to horses. The affected horse shows a generalized febrile response, anorexia, depression, and a profound leukopenia. Encephalomyelitis follows, causing behavior changes, one of which involves an apparent dysphagia caused by pharyngeal paresis. The animal is also ataxic and weak and acts as if blind. Diagnosis can be confirmed by analysis of the cerebrospinal fluid or blood for antibodies. The horse can become recumbent and convulsive, and more than 50% die. Supportive treatment includes comfortable bedding, maintenance of hydration via intravenous fluids, and an indwelling nasogastric tube. Convulsions are controlled by muscle relaxants or barbiturates. Vaccination to protect against these encephalomyelites are effective for 6 months and should be given before the insect vectors are active.

Horses with infection of the brain stem in the area of the nuclei that coordinate swallowing show similar signs of feed and water regurgitation. A brain abscess can be suspected when the horse has an elevated white cell count and plasma protein and when other functions controlled by nuclei in this area are affected, leading to such signs as head tilt and circling. In addition the horse can have fever and hematologic findings consistent with bacterial infection. The cerebrospinal fluid can also reflect the inflammatory process, and culture might indicate the causative organism. Treatment is not usually successful.

Inability to swallow is one characteristic of rabies in horses. Other symptoms include abnormal vocalization, depression, ataxia, and progressive posterior paresis. In any case of suspected rabies, contact with the saliva must be avoided. Rabid horses die or are killed because of the severity of their clinical signs. The horse's brain should be submitted to state laboratories for examination for Negri bodies in the cytoplasm of the neurons.

Peripheral neuropathies affecting the glossopharyngeal, hypoglossal, and vagus nerves can lead to pharyngeal paresis or paralysis. The most common causes of neuropathy are guttural pouch mycoses, empyema, fracture of the stylohyoid bone, chronic lead poisoning, or, as sequals to chronic otitis media, fracture of the temporal bone.

In the guttural pouch the vagus hypoglossal, and glossopharyngeal nerves, all involved in swallowing, cross the dorsal medial compartment. Mycotic infections, with a predilection for this site, can damage the nerves and cause inability to swallow. Mycotic lesions can be diagnosed by endoscopic examination of the guttural pouch or by visualization of mycotic spores in lavage of the pouch. When the infection has invaded the nerves sufficiently to cause dysphagia, the prognosis for recovery is grave. Infiltration of mycelia into the nerves has been demonstrated. Fatal epistaxis often accompanies the dysphagia when the carotid artery is eroded. Treatment with systemic antifungal agents has not been successful.

Severe empyema of the guttural pouch can damage the nerves involved in swallowing but more often hinders deglutition by distending the guttural pouch. Drainage of purulent material and use of indwelling catheters for lavage, coupled with appropriate antibiotic therapy, might resolve the dysphagia.

Tympany of the guttural pouch is usually seen only in young horses. The pharyngeal opening of the pouch works as a one-way valve in affected horses, allowing air to enter but not exit. Extreme distension of the pouch applies pressure to the pharynx and causes dysphagia. The condition can be corrected by surgical removal of the flap through a ventral surgical approach to the guttural pouch.

Fracture of the stylohyoid bone can occur secondary to direct trauma or to a chronic guttural pouch empyema. Although it can be diagnosed readily by radiography, treatment is limited to anti-inflammatory drugs and management of the empyema.

Chronic otitis media causes fusion of the stylohyoid and temporal bones at their junction. Early signs include head shaking and head tilting. Sudden movements of the tongue can cause the temporal bone to fracture as the bone absorbs forces generated along the hyoid bone. Fracture is manifest by the acute onset of signs of pharyngeal paresis, head tilt, and hypoglossal nerve involvement in a horse that previously demonstrated head shaking. The abnormality can be revealed by ventrodorsal radiographs in the recumbent horse. Therapy is limited to anti-inflammatory and antibiotic therapy for long periods of time. The horse is often left with permanent deficits.

Heavy metal intoxications, particularly with lead, can cause cranial nerve dysfunction and dysphagia. However, bilateral laryngeal paralysis is usually also present, and the clinical signs of dyspnea and cough secondary to food aspiration are more prominent clinical signs.

Leukoencephalomalacia ("moldy corn poisoning") also can lead to pharyngeal paralysis and dysphagia, but again other clinical signs usually predominate. These include depression, head pressing, aimless wandering, hyperreactivity, and incoordination. There is no effective treatment.

Botulism can occur in adult horses, usually following ingestion of preformed toxin in silage. Clinical signs include weakness and dysphagia. Endoscopic examination often demonstrates displaced soft palate. With strenuous exercise these horses may collapse. The disease has a rapid course, with death in 24 to 48 hours in many cases.

Treatment of these syndromes is symptomatic, and other factors in the patient history are instrumental in determining the diagnosis. Specific antisera are available in a few referral centers.

Mechanical causes of abnormalities of deglutition include pharyngeal masses, congenital defects, and inflammatory reactions of the pharyngeal area.

Masses in the throat are not common and are usually due to enlarged lymph nodes, retropharyngeal abscesses, or neoplasia. Infection of the young horse with Streptococcus equi ("strangles") can cause enlargement of lymph nodes caudal to the pharynx and impingment on the esophageal opening (Fig. 6—1). Trauma to the caudal portion of the pharynx with a balling gun or nasogastric tube can introduce bacteria beneath the mucosa, resulting in local abscessation. The most common neoplasia is squamous cell carcinoma, but even this is rare. Masses can be evaluated by endoscopy and the extent of the mass sometimes determined by radiography. Drainage of abscessed areas can be indicated, but because of the multiple nervous and vascular structures in the area,

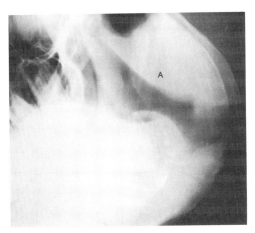

Fig. 6–1. Lateral radiograph of the pharynx of a horse with a retropharyngeal abscess (A). Notice the marked narrowing of the pharyngeal lumen (compare with Fig. 6–2).

Vesicular stomatitis can cause erosions and vesicles on the lips and tongue, but it rarely causes enough inflammation in the pharynx to impair swallowing. Stomatitis in immunodeficient or immunosuppressed animals can be caused by adenoviruses and fungal infections. Ulcerations of the mucosal surfaces have been in association with renal disease in severely dehydrated horses and in overdosage with nonsteroidal anti-inflammatory drugs. Such oral lesions are treated symptomatically with frequent flushing of the mouth with dilute povidone iodine solutions and topical or systemic anti-inflammatory preparations. Oral lesions and swellings resolve quickly if the related primary disorders can be corrected.

drainage can be difficult. Squamous cell carcinoma of the pharyngeal area has not been successfully treated.

Congenital defects that can cause dysphagia include cysts in the pharyngeal region and cleft palates. Cysts are most often subepiglottal and represent remnants of the thyroglossal duct. Dorsal pharyngeal cysts have also been seen but do not significantly interfere with swallowing. Subepiglottal cysts can be visualized endoscopically as masses of tissue obscuring the normal epiglottal architecture. The shape of the epiglottis can be visualized radiographically to help determine if the epiglottis is itself defective. If it is not, subepiglottal cysts can be removed surgically, allowing a good prognosis.

Cleft palate can cause regurgitation of milk in the young foal. The cleft most often involves the soft portion of the palate only. Diagnosis can be made by endoscopic examination, which shows the epiglottis dropping into the oral cavity instead of lying on top of the soft palate, or by manual exploration of the oral cavity. Repair of cleft palates has been reported, although the surgical complication rate is high.

Inflammatory lesions of the pharynx causing dysphagia are rarely primary.

CLINICAL EVALUATION

An accurate history can eliminate or indicate several differential diagnoses in the horse with dysphagia. A thorough clinical examination including physical examination of the head in general and the throatlatch area and an oral examination can help to confirm the diagnosis. The horse should be offered food and carefully observed. Confirming the cause of the dysphagia might require neurologic examination (especially examination of the cranial nerves), endoscopic evaluation of the pharynx and guttural pouches, and radiography.

The neurologic examination is described in Chapter 16. Of particular interest in the dysphagic horse are CN V, VII, IX, X, and XII, all of which are involved in eating and swallowing.

Endoscopic examination is most useful in horses with problems of deglutition; if the endoscope is longer than 1.5, it might be useful in diagnosis of esophageal obstructions. The endoscope can be used to evaluate the condition of the pharynx, guttural pouches, soft palate, and epiglottis in the standing, restrained horse.

Radiography of the throatlatch area can be done on the standing or recumbent animal. The air-filled paranasal sinuses, guttural pouches, and nasopharynx provide contrast for the soft-tissue structures of the larynx, soft palate, and nasopharyngeal walls. A lateral radiograph of this area can demonstrate the length and position of the soft palate and epiglottis and determine if the epiglottis is properly situated above the soft palate (Fig. 6–2). The radiograph shows the thickness of the walls and presence of fluid within the guttural pouches. If extreme thickening of these structures obliterates the definition of the borders of the tissues, a barium swallow can be used to outline the anatomy (Fig. 6–3).

Examination should attribute the cause of the dysphagia to difficulties in prehension, mastication, or deglutition,

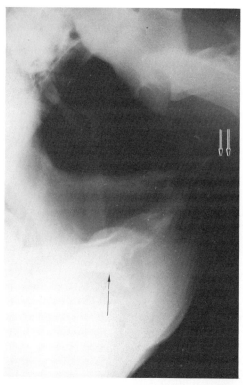

Fig. 6–3. Lateral radiograph of the pharyngeal region of a normal horse taken following the swallow of barium sulfate paste. Note the pooling of contrast ventral to the soft palate (arrow), and also contrast in the initial part of the esophagus (double arrows).

both functional and structural (Fig. 6–4). In general, functional problems include those of neurologic, neuromuscular, or muscular origin, whereas structural problems include malformations, trauma, and agents causing inflammation, which causes distortion.

ESOPHAGEAL OBSTRUCTION (CHOKE)

Normal esophageal function can be disrupted by structural or physiologic disorders. Structural disorders mechanically prevent the passage of ingesta from pharynx to stomach; physiologic abnormalities cause obstruction primarily by causing motor dysfunction. The result is

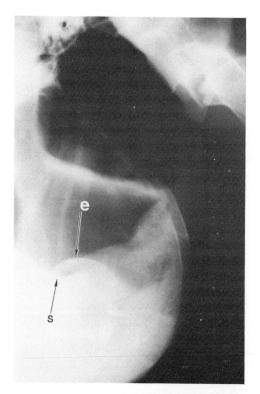

Fig. 6–2. Lateral radiograph of the pharyngeal region of a normal horse. Note the position of the epiglottis (e) situated dorsal to the soft palate (s).

the same—the horse exhibits signs of esophageal obstruction.

NORMAL ESOPHAGEAL FUNCTION

Lying between the longus colli muscle and the trachea, the esophagus courses from the pharynx to the thoracic inlet on the midline in the upper third of the neck and slightly to the left in the lower portion of the cervical area. At the thoracic inlet, it moves slightly to the right of midline; as it passes through the hiatus esophagus of the diaphragm, the angle of passage is slightly to the left.

The upper two thirds of the esophagus are composed of striated muscles, while the distal one third is smooth. At the pharyngeal opening, the upper esophageal sphincter is formed by the esophageal striated muscles and the cricopharyngeus muscle. The lower esophageal sphincter is functional and is represented by a thickening of the smooth muscle at the gastroesophageal junction. The layers of the esophagus from inside to outside include a mucosa of stratified squamous epithelium, a submucosal layer, the muscular layers, and a loose tunica adventitia. A serosal surface is found only on the short abdominal portion of the esophagus. The diameter of the lumen of the esophagus varies considerably along its course. The narrowest portions are located at the post-pharyngeal region, the thoracic inlet, the base of the heart, and the cardia of the stomach. The widest lumen diameters are at the caudal cervical area and within the thoracic region.

Innervation of the esophagus includes mesenteric ganglion cells of the muscle layers, the sympathetic trunk, and the glossopharyngeal and vagus nerves. Deglutition, which initiates esophageal peristalsis, is voluntary and controlled in the medulla. Vagal fibers, which are responsible for the propagation of the peristaltic wave, originate in the nucleus

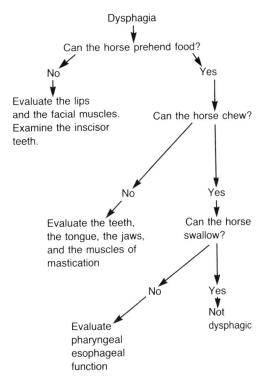

Fig. 6–4. Clinical evaluation of dysphagia.

ambiguus. If damaged, these two areas of the brain stem can affect transport.

The esophagus transports the food bolus from the pharynx to the stomach. Two peristaltic waves are involved in this transport. The primary wave begins at the pharynx and passes distally. If the wave diminishes, the bolus of food remains in the esophageal lumen until moved by another primary peristaltic wave or by a secondary peristaltic wave, which originates at the site of the bolus in mid-esophagus. The primary waves are an extension of pharyngeal contraction, while secondary waves begin at the location of the bolus.

When the bolus arrives at the caudal sphincter, the sphincter relaxes, allows bolus to pass, and then closes.

Very few drugs significantly affect the function of the esophagus. Atropine decreases the amplitude of peristalsis in the smooth muscle portion but not within the striated area. General anesthesia de-

Fig. 6–5. Lateral radiograph of the upper cervical esophagus in a horse with a foreign body (FB) lodged in the lumen of the esophagus. A stomach tube (T) has been passed beyond the obstruction. Note the compression of the trachea by the foreign body in the esophagus (arrow).

presses motor function of the entire esophagus.

PATHOPHYSIOLOGY AND TREATMENT

Inability to move ingesta to the stomach can result from partial or complete obstruction of the lumen of the esophagus. The anatomy of the horse predisposes to obstruction in four places in the esophagus: the postpharyngeal area, the thoracic inlet, the base of the heart, and the cardia of the stomach. If the obstruction is complete, the area can be located by passage of a nasogastric tube; if it is partial it can be detected only as an area causing difficulty to passage of a stomach tube. Radiographs of the area can be used to confirm the diagnosis (Fig. 6–5).

Any damage to the mucosal lining of the esophagus is serious because of the tendency of the esophagus to repair by forming scar tissue. Fibrous tissue forms as the injury heals, and as the scar contracts a stricture of the lumen results. The prognosis on any case of choke that has persisted for more than 12 hours must be guarded for this reason.

The most common type of obstruction is feed material, such as alfalfa cube, sugar beet pulp, and carrots. Obstruction by medicinal boluses, pieces of wood, and metal foreign bodies has also been seen.

Treatment is aimed at removing the obstruction as atraumatically and rapidly as possible to prevent mucosal damage. In some cases, simply calming the horse and relaxing the muscles surrounding the esophagus can be adequate to remove the material.

When the animal is first seen, if the choke is less than 4 hours' duration, tranquilization with acepromazine and xylazine will calm the horse, cause it to lower its head, and provide some analgesia. If the blocked material does not pass on its own after 1 to 2 hours, a large-bore nasogastric tube can be advanced to the bolus, air blown in, and gentle advancement performed. If this technique is unsuccessful, warm water can be pumped gently into the esophagus. The horse must be tranquilized to keep the head low and prevent aspiration. Excess fluid can be resuctioned if the bolus does not move or break up.

Some feed boluses are firmly impacted and dry, and painful spasms of the esophagus prevent any further movement. In such cases, before more aggressive treatment is begun, a mixture of 15 cc of 2% lidocaine, 15 cc of 5% dioctyl sodium sulfosuccinate (DSS), and 30 cc of water can be deposited on top of the obstruction using the stomach tube. The lidocaine relieves pain and the DSS wets the dry feed material. After 15 to 30 minutes, another attempt to dislodge the bolus using warm water can be made.

If all these attempts fail, lavage or surgical removal can be performed under general anesthesia. Surgery of the esophagus in the cervical region is not difficult to perform, but various healing problems are encountered. Lacking a serosa, the esophagus does not hold sutures well. Dehiscence and infection are common postsurgical complications in the first 2 weeks after surgery. Stricture formation at the surgery site can occur from 1 to 6 months after surgery.

OTHER CAUSES

Although regurgitation of feed and water through the nostrils, coughing when trying to swallow, and distress are most commonly associated with esophageal lumen obstruction, the same clinical signs can have a variety of causes. Differentiating the conditions that cause these signs allows the veterinarian to formulate a prognosis as well as a rational approach to therapy, if required.

Esophageal Stricture

Damage to the esophageal muscles and mucosa can result in constricting fibrosis. This can be diagnosed by passage of a nasogastric tube to the affected area, by passage of an endoscope into the esophageal lumen and visualization of the stricture, or by barium swallow. The causes of stricture include any insult to the esophageal wall, including severe esophagitis; trauma to the neck by kicks or blows; and trauma by nasogastric tube passage, or rarely, by tumor encroachment on the lumen. In most cases the strictures occur gradually and are manifest as recurrent mild bouts of choke. If the stricture occurs in the cervical area, it is accessible for treatment.

Involvement of the esophageal mucosa can be determined from the endoscopic or barium study. If the mucosa is not involved, usually the stricture is due to extraluminal scarring, and the outlook for surgical therapy is more optimistic. If the mucosa is scarred, that section must be removed. Resection and anastomosis of up to 2 cm of esophagus has been done successfully, but complications, resulting from infection and dehiscence, are frequent. A patch of sternocephalicus muscle can be used to widen the esophageal lumen without requiring resection of a circumferential piece. If the mucosa is not involved, the muscle that is scarred can be removed, allowing the mucosa to expand in the strictured area. At least half of the circumference of muscle tissue should be removed to prevent restricturing. The horse should be returned to dry feed gradually. Some horses with esophageal strictures can be managed conservatively. If they are fed a semisolid diet for several months, the esophageal stricture can be gradually stretched and a normal diameter achieved. This is the only conservative approach that can be used for intrathoracic strictures. Suitable diets can be made by thoroughly soaking pellets of complete horse feed in water.

Dilation

The esophagus can dilate secondary to a more distal stricture, owing to failure of the lower esophageal sphincter to relax or owing to generalized neuromuscular disorders.

An idiopathic condition known as megaesophagus is seen in young horses when solid food is first introduced into the diet. The cervical esophagus fills and the neck feels doughy. Radiographs show ingesta in an enlarged esophagus. Whereas in adults a discrete stricture distal to the dilation can be identified postmortem, in the young such an area is not seen.

Dilation secondary to stricture can improve if the stricture is corrected. The prognosis for idiopathic megaesophagus is poor.

Diverticula

Two types of esophageal diverticula have been described: pulsion and traction. Herniation of the esophageal mucosa through the muscular wall of the esophagus and formation of a sac that entraps feed material is a pulsion diverticulum. It can be congenital or can be acquired following trauma to the cervical region. Filling occurs intermittently and is seen most commonly as a bulge in the lower third of the neck after feeding. Even when filled, the mass is not painful, but if the feed is coarse, obstruction of the entire esophagus can occur.

A traction diverticulum involves the entire wall of the esophagus and represents adhesions of the wall in surrounding cervical musculature. It usually occurs after lacerating trauma to the esophagus or an inflammation adjacent to the esophagus.

Endoscopy and contrast radiography are used to confirm the diagnosis of diverticula. In many cases the intermittent filling of the sac is more a cosmetic anomaly than a cause for obstruction. If obstruction occurs repeatedly, especially with pulsion diverticula, surgical reduction of the hernia and oversewing of the muscular layers is advised.

Hypertrophy of the Esophageal Musculature

The cause of hypertrophy of the esophageal musculature is unknown, but the defect is assumed to be congenital. Although the mucosa is normal, the muscle is hypertrophied, making the passage of ingesta abnormal. Diagnosis of a functional stricture can be made by passage of a nasogastric tube or by barium swallow. Onset of severe symptoms occurs when the foal begins to ingest mostly solid food material.

Esophageal Cysts

These fluid-filled sacs within the esophageal musculature are assumed to be embryonic remnants of bronchogenic cysts. They cause intermittent obstruction in the young horse in the cranial third of the esophagus. They are identified on lateral radiographs as soft-tissue masses outlined by air within the esophagus and can be surgically removed.

Neoplasia

The most common tumor causing obstruction is an extended squamous cell carcinoma from the stomach; more rarely, fibromas and melanomas are seen. The smell from the nasogastric tube is usually fetid, and the horse can exhibit overall cachexia if the obstruction has persisted for an extended period. Endoscopy and biopsy are possible to confirm the diagnosis, but the prognosis for survival is poor.

CLINICAL EVALUATION

The signs of choke reflect the anxiety and pain the animal feels as well as the physical obstruction to food, water, and saliva. Saliva, food, and, later, mucus flow from the nostrils, and the horse stretches its neck and makes wretching sounds. The animal becomes restless and might repeatedly attempt to swallow water, which flows back out of the nostrils. Coughing and gagging occur if material is inadvertently inhaled.

A large mass of material caught in the cervical area can be palpated in the area of the left jugular furrow. If the obstruction remains, the horse gradually quiets, stops drinking, and becomes dehydrated and depressed. Saliva drains from the mouth in copious amounts, leading to weakness and electrolyte imbalances, particularly hyponatremia and hypokalemia. Aspiration pneumonia can occur within the first day.

Because of its superficial location in the cervical region of the horse, esophageal distension can be palpated from pharynx to thoracic inlet. Other areas of obstruction, and obstructions caused by nondistending lesions, must be located by other means.

Passage of a nasogastric tube can locate the area of obstruction. Endoscopy can allow visualization of the obstruction. In most horses the endoscope must be at least 2 m long to reach the cardia of the stomach, but shorter endoscopes can be used to view the cervical region. The endoscope is introduced like a nasogastric tube, the esophagus is ballooned with air, and the endoscope is gradually withdrawn to observe the lumen. Both nasogastric tube and endoscope must be passed with care in cases of obstruction because the esophageal walls might be friable and liable to rupture. The site of obstruction might not be immediately located by nasal intubation or endoscopy, as food can become impacted cranial to the obstruction and prevent the tube with endoscope from reaching the level of the obstruction. In these cases lavage of the esophagus might be necessary to remove the impacted food and expose the obstruction.

Radiography (plain, contrast, and fluoroscope) can be used to demonstrate

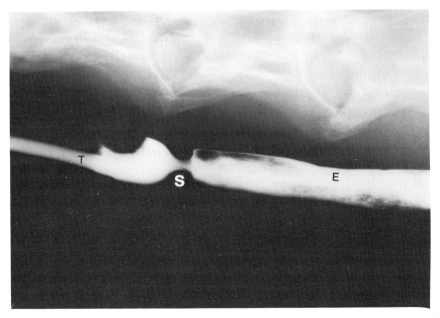

Fig. 6–6. A positive-pressure contrast cervical esophagram produced by injecting contrast through a cuffed tube (T) into the esophagus. The esophagus distal to the tube is well demonstrated (E). The apparent stricture (S) is a peristaltic contraction, and should be kept in mind when interpreting these studies.

and define the area of obstruction. After a nasogastric tube is passed to the obstructed area, the location is radiographed. Radiopaque foreign bodies, ingested material, gas shadows, and sharp-sided objects, as well as tracheal and soft-tissue displacements, can be visualized on plain films. Positive-contrast radiographs are made by administering by mouth or by nasogastric tube a substantial (50 to 100 ml) amount of contrast media. If the obstruction is high, less contrast media is used to avoid aspiration in case the material is not transported distally in the esophagus. A stomach tube with a cuffed distal end can be used to prevent leakage of contrast medium back up the esophagus, and to allow a positive-pressure esophagram to be obtained (Fig. 6–6).

SUPPLEMENTAL READING

Baker, G.J.: Diseases of the teeth and paranasal sinuses; Koch, D.B.: The oral cavity, oropharynx and salivary glands; Freeman, D.E.: The esophagus. *In* Equine Medicine and Surgery. Edited by R.A. Mansmann, and E.S. McAllister. Santa Barbara, American Veterinary Publications, 1982.

Bowman, K.F., et al.: Megaesophagus in a colt. J. Am. Vet. Med. Assoc., 172:334–337, 1978.

Greet, T.: Observations on the potential role of oesophageal radiography in the horse. Equine Vet. J., 14:73–79, 1982.

Greet, T.: Differential diagnosis of nasal discharge in the horse. In Practice, 8:49–57, 1986.

Jennings, P.B.: The Practice of Large Animal Surgery. Philadelphia, W.B. Saunders, 1984.

Meagher, D.M., and Trout, D.R.: Fractures of the mandible and premaxilla in the horse. 26th Proc. Am. Assoc. Eq. Practitioners, 1980, pp. 181–191.

Scott, E.A., et al.: Intramural esophageal cyst in a horse. J. Am. Vet. Med. Assoc., 171:652–654, 1977.

Stick, J.A.: Surgery of the esophagus. Vet. Clin. N. Am. Large Anim. Pract., 4:33–59, 1982.

Wagner, P.C., Rantanen, N.W., and Grand, B.D.: Differential diagnosis of dysphagia in the horse. Mod. Vet. Pract., 60:1029–1033, 1979.

Watrous, B.J.: Dysphagia and regurgitation. *In* Veterinary Gastroenterology. 2nd Ed. Edited by N.V. Anderson. Philadelphia, Lea & Febiger, 1989.

chapter 7

COUGHING AND LABORED BREATHING

Christopher M. Brown

DEFINITIONS

COUGHING

Coughing, one of the defense mechanisms of the respiratory system, is designed to forcefully eliminate unwanted material and protect the lower respiratory tract. A reflex activity, coughing is initiated by stimulation of receptors within the pharynx, larynx, trachea, and bronchi that respond to both mechanical and chemical stimuli. In horses, sensitivity to mechanical stimuli varies along the airway. Frequently a stomach tube passed through the nostril can enter the trachea and not induce coughing until the tip reaches the bifurcation. Although the significance of this observation is not clear, commonly a large pool of mucoid material is encountered in the trachea of a horse with little or no history of coughing.

LABORED BREATHING

Increased respiratory effort can be induced by a variety of pathologic processes. Normal respiratory rate and patterns are maintained by central and peripheral monitoring of blood gas status, with reflex adjustments made to maintain CO_2 and O_2 within a fairly narrow range. Any problem that interferes with the movement of air to and from the lungs, its distribution within the lungs, the exchange of gases within the lungs, or the transportation of the gases once exchanged can stimulate an alteration in the rate, depth, or effort of breathing. Hence, lesions from the nostril to the alveolus can be involved, in addition to those including the transportation system, that is, the blood and cardiovascular system.

CLINICAL EVALUATION

If coughing is the only or main clinical sign, the veterinarian must determine which receptor site, or sites, are being stimulated, and what is the cause of that stimulation. This information can sometimes be obtained by a thorough and logical evaluation of the respiratory system (Fig. 7–1). Not all steps will be necessary in all horses; the cause of the problem might become obvious early in the physical examination or even during the history-taking. Additional tests might be indicated only to confirm a diagnosis or rule out additional diseases.

As always, an accurate thorough patient history is the foundation of diagnosis (Fig. 7–2). The accuracy and thoroughness depends not only on the veterinarian's skills, but also on the owner's knowledge and honesty. Figure 7–2 emphasizes the major aspects of the history that might indicate possible causes and further investigations.

Thoracic auscultation is vital in the evaluation of a coughing horse. Equine lungs at rest are normally quiet and difficult to hear, particularly if the horse is fat. Most stables and barns are noisy, and finding a quiet area to auscultate the chest is often difficult. Removing the horse from the stall to a

quiet unbedded area is worthwhile. Respiratory rate and depth can be increased by exercise or by using a "rebreathing bag," a large plastic bag placed over the muzzle with sufficient space around the edges to allow some air to enter and leave. Because the horse is rebreathing some of its exhaled air, presumably the Pa_{CO_2} is raised, increasing respiratory drive. This simple but effective technique increases the depth of respiration and accentuates lung sounds, often uncovering abnormalities not heard initially.

Thoracic percussion is not widely practiced because technology has advanced, although it is simple, noninvasive, cheap, and often helpful. With practice, the veterinarian can determine areas of dullness caused by lesions such as pulmonary abscess or pleural effusion, and can determine the normal limits of the processable lung field.

In many simple cases laboratory data are not needed in the initial stages. However, hematology is indicated in chronic infections, if an inflammatory process is suspected at the outset, or if severe tachypnea is thought to be due to anemia.

Endoscopy of the airways is extremely valuable in the evaluation of many coughing or dyspneic horses, as it allows for rapid and accurate localization of the possible causes. Frequently, further diagnostic investigations are not necessary.

Transtracheal aspiration should be performed prior to endoscopy if lower airway infection or inflammation is suspected from the presence of exudate coming through the larynx; endoscopes are not sterile after passage through the upper airways, and if they are passed into the trachea, contaminants will be carried into the tracheal lumen. Thus, transtracheal aspiration and culture is more difficult to interpret following tracheal endoscopy than before endoscopy. Protected, double-sheathed catheters have been developed for the collection of uncontaminated airway secretions and cells via

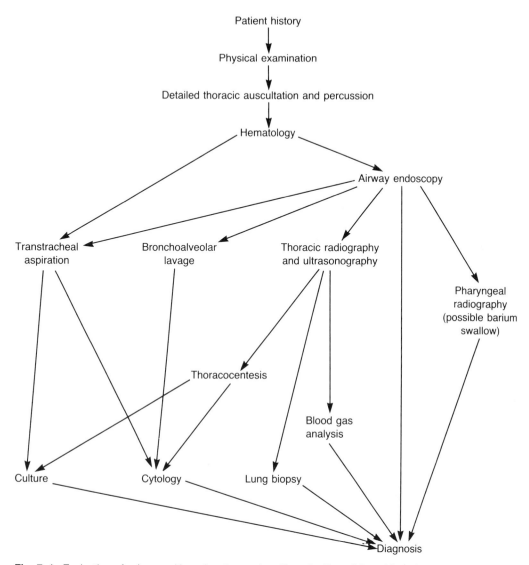

Fig. 7–1. Evaluation of a horse with a chronic cough, with and without labored breathing.

the endoscope in human medicine. It is hoped that these catheters will prove to be equally useful in equine medicine and allow for the collection of uncontaminated samples from equine airways.

Bronchoalveolar lavage provides more information about the cells of the distal airways than the transtracheal aspirate does. The technique is not yet widely practiced in horses, however, and is valuable only in diffuse pulmonary disease. A long endoscope or plastic tube about 1 cm in diameter is introduced into the trachea via a nostril and advanced until it is wedged in a bronchus. Coughing can be reduced by spraying the area with 2% lidocaine through the tube or endoscope biopsy channel. Three 100-ml aliquots of buffered saline are sequentially flushed into the bronchus through the tube or endoscope biopsy channel. After each irrigation, as much of the fluid as possible is aspirated. The aspirates are pooled and submitted for cytology. The cellular population of

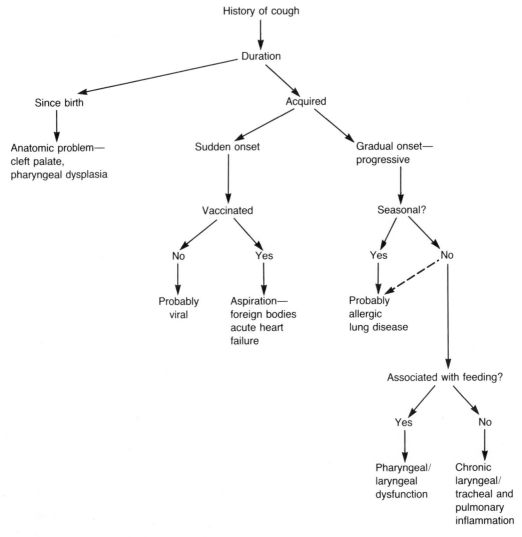

Fig. 7–2. History of a horse with a cough.

normal equine bronchoalveolar fluid consists of less than 10% neutrophils, mast cells, and epithelial cells combined, and less than 1% eosinophils. Usually, macrophages and lymphocytes constitute over 90% of the cell population. This ratio contrasts with the main cell types in the transtracheal aspirate fluid of normal horses, which are neutrophils and epithelial cells. In both normal and diseased horses, no correlation exists between the cell populations within the trachea and the distal airways, based on a comparison of these two techniques. Bronchoalveolar lavage might be more useful than transtracheal aspiration for the evaluation of diffuse small airways disease, which is common in horses. Bronchoalveolar lavage fluid cannot be collected without being contaminated and hence is not suitable for culture.

Radiography can be useful for the evaluation of the equine respiratory system but should be used only as an adjunct to other tests and follow a thorough physical and endoscopic examination. Thoracic radiography of adult horses is not usually possible in most equine practices; it is used predominantly in referral centers. Only standing lateral views can be obtained, and much of the lung field is obscured by the dome of the diaphragm and heart. Only fairly marked changes can be diagnosed with confidence; subtle increases in interstitial density, airway diameter, or lung volume cannot be determined. However, thoracic radiography is invaluable for some horses with severe thoracic diseases, both for diagnosis and for monitoring progress. Radiography of the head and neck can also be valuable in confirming or refining a diagnosis made on palpation or endoscopy. Lesions such as retropharyngeal abscesses and laryngeal calcification can be seen. In addition, radiographs taken following a barium sulfate swallow might confirm a suspected pharyngeal/laryngeal dysfunction as the cause of aspiration and coughing.

Thoracic and ultrasonographic evaluation can be invaluable in the evaluation of pleural effusion, thoracic masses, and cardiac structure and function.

CAUSES

Coughing can be acute or chronic, productive or nonproductive, dry or moist, or occasional or frequent, but all types result from stimulation of receptors within the respiratory tract, located just beneath or within the epithelium of the airways. Diseases that can lead to this stimulation are outlined in Figure 7–3.

COUGHING WITHOUT LABORED BREATHING

Acute

The majority of horses that suddenly start coughing are suffering from an upper-respiratory viral infection.

Although many horses are routinely vaccinated against influenza and rhinopneu-

monitis, probably many other viral respiratory pathogens infect horses and cause coughing. A viral cause should not be discounted in a vaccinated horse. In addition to a cough, these horses can have serous to purulent nasal and occular discharges. They can be febrile, anorexic, and depressed. Additional investigation of these horses is not usually needed, and therapy is not required as long as food and water intake are adequate. Antibiotic therapy and nonsteroidal anti-inflammatory drugs (NSAIDs) might be indicated if bacterial infection is suspected, or if a high fever is associated with severe anorexia. Most horses require only 6 to 10 days of rest and general care.

Other possible causes of sudden onset of cough include traumatic pharyngitis and laryngitis caused by stomach tubing, and aspiration into the larynx and trachea of food material or other foreign bodies. Foreign bodies such as twigs are rarely a cause of sudden onset coughing. Aspiration of food and saliva occurs most frequently following esophageal obstruction (Chapter 6) but can also follow the sudden onset of laryngeal or pharyngeal dysfunction. This dysfunction can result from cranial nerve damage secondary to either cranial trauma or another acute neurologic problem, such as rabies and migrating parasites. Endoscopic and radiographic findings assist in a diagnosis. Management depends on the cause. Choke should be relieved and other foreign bodies removed. If pharyngeal or laryngeal paralysis is present, nasogastric intubation, endotracheal intubation, or both might be indicated to feed the horse and to assure ventilation. In cases of aspiration, broad-spectrum antibiotics should be administered to reduce the possibility of bacterial infection.

Chronic

Though arbitrary, the definition of chronic cough is considered here as cough present for at least 3 weeks.

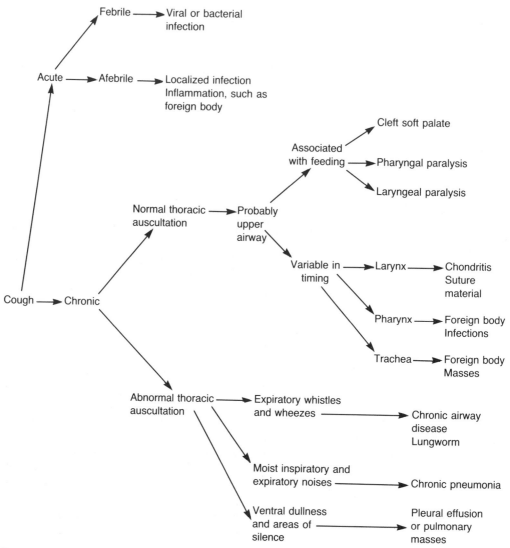

Fig. 7–3. Findings and causes for coughing in horses.

Possible causes and diagnostic features are given in Figure 7–3. Cough without labored breathing is emphasized here, although some problems considered here, such as chronic small-airways disease, can be progressive and result in labored breathing.

Horses with chronic coughs can be divided into two groups, those with no abnormal findings on thoracic auscultation, and those with abnormal findings. Those with normal auscultation are more likely to have upper airway problems, those with abnormal findings to have some form of pulmonary disease. However, some horses with upper airway problems, such as pharyngeal paralysis, can have aspiration pneumonia and hence abnormal auscultatory findings. Similarly, a horse with a deep-seated pulmonary abscess pressing on a bronchus can have normal auscultory findings. For the sake of this discussion, these horses will be considered in sepa-ate groups based on auscultation, but they should not be regarded as mutually exclusive.

Chronic Cough with Normal Thoracic Auscultation. Horses with chronic cough with normal thoracic auscultation usually have some form of upper airway problem. In horses that cough when eating or drinking, pharyngeal or laryngeal dysfunction should be suspected. Such dysfunction can be due to neurologic damage, such as guttural pouch mycosis involving the cranial nerves, pharyngeal masses, or retropharyngeal masses (e.g., tumors and abscesses). In these horses, food and water is aspirated into the larynx and trachea, causing paroxysms of coughing. Food can be ejected into the nasal cavity, and the horse can have a green-brown nasal discharge, a mixture of food, saliva, and mucus. A similar, less severe problem occurs in some horses that have had laryngeal surgery, usually for the treatment of hemiparesis ("roaring"). If the problem has been present since birth, cleft soft palate or some form of pharyngeal dysplasia should be suspected. Diagnosis can be confirmed by endoscopy of the airway and of the guttural pouch, if indicated. Radiography, possibly with barium sulfate swallow, might demonstrate a functional lesion not obvious endoscopically. Few of the chronic problems causing this problem can be managed or cured successfully. Retropharyngeal abscesses might respond to long-term antibiotic therapy. Because streptococci are most commonly involved, procaine penicillin G at 20,000 U/kg twice daily intramuscularly for 2 to 4 weeks is probably a good empiric choice. Most neurologic problems do not resolve spontaneously or respond to various therapeutic regimens, including anti-inflammatory agents.

Other horses in this group with normal-sounding lungs may cough spontaneously at any time. These usually have chronic inflammatory conditions of the larynx, pharynx, or trachea. Pharyngeal conditions include polyps and foreign bodies, both uncommon. In the larynx, chronic chondritis can be associated with chronic coughing. This disease can be spontaneous disease or can follow laryngeal surgery. Postoperative coughing can also occur if suture material protrudes into the lumen of the airway. Some horses with entrapment of the epiglottis by the aryepiglottic fold can have spontaneous chronic coughs. Coughing usually occurs when the entrapping tissue becomes thickened, ulcerated, and granulomatous.

Though uncommon, tracheal foreign bodies can cause chronic coughing with little change in lung sounds. Tracheal masses are rare, but granulation tissue can develop at the site at which a transtracheal aspiration was performed or at a previous tracheostomy site. A history of airway surgery is therefore important when evaluating a chronically coughing horse.

Again, endoscopy and radiography are invaluable diagnostic aids. Management depends on the cause. Foreign bodies, including suture material, should be removed. Laryngeal chondritis might best be treated by resection of the affected cartilage. Tracheal masses are difficult to remove because anastomosis is difficult, but removal is probably the best approach.

Chronic Cough with Abnormal Thoracic Auscultation. Horses with chronic cough and abnormal thoracic auscultation fit into one of three main groups (Fig. 7–3).

Expiratory Wheezes and Whistles. In this group, the abnormal auscultatory findings are due to chronic small-airways disease, with expiratory whistles and wheezes. These horses are in the early stages of heaves (see below) but have not yet developed enough obstruction to have labored breathing. Their major problem is usually exercise intolerance

(Chapter 17), and they often cough at the beginning of work. A purulent intermittent bilateral nasal discharge might occur. The animals are afebrile and otherwise well. The disease is probably due to sensitivity to fungal spores inhaled from hay and straw, and hence is most common in stabled horses and also in winter. In some warm areas a similar disease occurs in pastured horses in summer, presumably because of sensitivity to airborne plant materials, probably pollens. These two sensitivity syndromes can progress to a more severe respiratory problem (see later).

Horses infected with the lungworms Dictyocaulus arnfieldi also have chronic coughs, often with abnormal auscultatory findings, although some can sound normal. Horses with lungworm infections usually have been pastured with donkeys, who are the primary asymptomatic host for the parasite.

Diagnosis of chronic airway inflammation as a cause of chronic cough is based on auscultatory findings and endoscopic evaluation of upper airway and trachea. The upper airway is usually normal anatomically, although mucoid material can be present in the pharynx. The trachea usually contains mucopurulent material. Rarely is there a bacterial infection; therefore, culture of tracheal aspirates is of little value. Bronchoalveolar lavage fluid is often high in neutrophils, over 50% of the cell population. Eosinophils might be more frequent in horses with lungworm infection, and occasionally, intact parasites are lavaged from the lung. Lungworm infections are rarely patent in horses, and fecal examinations for larvae hence are unrewarding.

Management of horses with chronic airway disease is designed primarily to eliminate exposure to the inciting agent. The protocol is the same as that for the more severely affected horses with heaves, discussed in the next section, except that medication, in addition to environmental management, is rarely needed in these mildly affected horses. If lungworms are considered to be involved, a single oral dosage of ivermectin at 200 μg/kg should resolve the problem. Affected horses often cough more frequently after anthelmintic treatment, presumably related to the death and removal of lungworms.

Moist Inspiratory and Expiratory Noises. Moist abnormal lung sounds with both inspiratory and expiratory components reflect diffuse pulmonary inflammation and airway exudation, probably caused by chronic pneumonia. This disease is fairly uncommon in adult horses, more frequent in foals and weanlings. In adults, diffuse problems occasionally develop when an abscess ruptures and exudate is spread through the lung. In addition, widespread but predominantly ventral pneumonia can develop following aspiration of food, such as following choke, or if fluid is inadvertently delivered into the lung instead of the stomach during nasogastric intubation. The horse can have mild to moderate fever, and laboratory data are consistent with chronic inflammation. Diagnosis is based on clinical signs and transtracheal aspiration with culture. Endoscopy usually shows mucopurulent material in the trachea, and thoracic radiography might define the extent and severity of the problem. Therapy depends on the etiologic agents isolated, but usually 10 to 14 days of antibiotic therapy are necessary, together with rest.

Unlike in humans and dogs, chronic cardiac disease is a very uncommon cause of chronic coughing in horses. Occasionally, horses with severe valvular disease, usually mitral incompetence, develop heart failure and pulmonary edema. These animals have chronic coughs. Clinical findings are consistent with heart failure, with a loud, widely radiating murmur audible in the left side.

The diagnosis can be confirmed by echocardiography. Medical management can be considered, but the horse cannot be salvaged as an athlete (Chapter 10).

Ventral Dullness and Areas of Silence. In other horses with chronic coughs, the abnormal auscultatory findings are characterized by ventral dullness or silence, or by discrete areas of silence. On percussion these quiet areas have no resonance. The underlying disorder can represent pleural effusion, pleuritis, pulmonary abscess or other masses, or a combination of these. Pleural infections can be primary but often follow rupture of a pulmonary abscess. The right side is frequently affected more than the left, although the disease is often bilateral. Pleural effusion can result from intrathoracic neoplasia such as primary mediastinal lymphosarcoma, or from metastases from elsewhere, such as squamous cell carcinoma of the stomach. Neoplastic conditions are more likely to cause dyspnea than cough, unless they involve the airways or are associated with severe necrosis or infection.

Pulmonary abscesses are not associated with coughing unless the abscess ruptures into the airways or applies direct pressure onto a bronchus. Primary lung tumors are rare in horses and not a major cause of chronic coughing.

Clinically, horses with chronic pleuritis or pulmonary abscessation are usually partially anorexic, have low-grade fevers, and lose weight. Some have foul breath. Severe cases are often very dyspneic. Laboratory data are consistent with chronic infection. Diagnosis is based on clinical signs, culture of tracheal exudate, thoracic ultrasonography, radiography, and thoracic fluid cytology and culture. Therapy depends on the cause; neoplastic conditions are generally untreatable. Severe chronic infections do not respond well to therapy, which is often expensive. The approach

to managing chronic infections of the chest is discussed in the next section.

LABORED BREATHING WITH COUGHING

Although many of the conditions already discussed can progress so that the animal develops labored breathing, additional conditions should be considered in a horse with a cough and dyspnea. Possible causes are given in Fig. 7–4.

Cough With Inspiratory Effort

Marked inspiratory effort usually indicates obstruction of the upper airway, that is, the nasal passages, pharynx, larynx, or trachea. Cough as well usually indicates involvement of the pharynx, larynx, or trachea, because simple nasal obstruction is not usually associated with a cough.

Pharyngeal conditions causing labored breathing and cough include pharyngeal paralysis, pharyngeal masses, and retropharyngeal masses. Pharyngeal paralysis can be secondary cranial nerve lesions and associated with dysphagia (Chapter 6). The respiratory obstruction can result from collapse of the pharyngeal walls during inspiration, and the cough can be due to aspiration into the larynx and trachea of unswallowed food and saliva. The problem can develop slowly, as in guttural pouch infections involving cranial nerves IX and X, or suddenly, as in head trauma or botulism. In chronic cases, auscultation of the lungs will suggest aspiration pneumonia, in which case the cough might result from both laryngeal/tracheal irritation and lower airway irritation. Food and water can be expelled down the nose. Diagnosis is based on physical findings and endoscopy. Caution should be used when performing endoscopy on these patients; they are easily stressed, and if airway

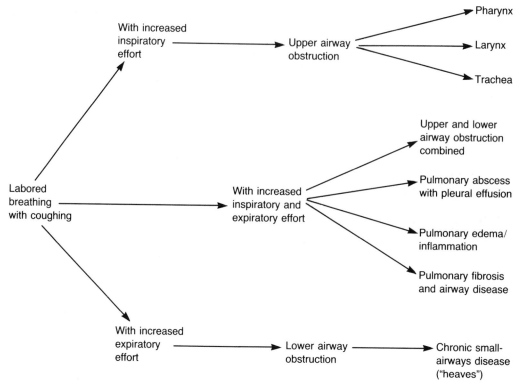

Fig. 7–4. Findings and causes for cough with labored breathing in horses.

obstruction is severe, asphyxia is possible. In addition, tranquilization, particularly using xylazine, should be used carefully; xylazine causes pharyngeal relaxation and can exacerbate a partial paralysis and further compromise the horse. Direct observation of pharyngeal function and structure is often diagnostic. If guttural pouch infection is suspected as a cause of dysfunction, the pouch should be examined endoscopically. Pharyngeal radiographs can be helpful, particularly after a barium sulfate paste swallow.

Pharyngeal paralysis caused by cranial nerve damage carries a poor prognosis. Horses with botulism might recover if treated early in the disease with polyvalent equine antitoxin; this drug, however, is not widely available. Management of all patients with pharyngeal paralysis might also include alimentation through

nasogastric intubation and broad-spectrum antibiotic therapy if aspiration pneumonia is present or likely. In severely dyspneic patients, a tracheotomy and intubation may be necessary and should be maintained until the airway resistance is reduced to tolerable levels.

Pharyngeal masses are uncommon causes of chronic cough and labored breathing, although occasional foreign bodies can lodge in the pharynx. Sporadic cases of pharyngeal neoplasia are encountered. These are readily diagnosed with endoscopy and radiography.

Retropharyngeal problems, usually a retropharyngeal abscess, are common causes of labored breathing and cough. Abscesses can develop in primary diseases such as "strangles" (Streptococcus equi), or secondary to pharyngeal trauma and perforation, such as following gastric intubation. Depending on the cause, the problem can begin suddenly or gradually. The mass presses down, reducing the pharyngeal lumen and causing inspiratory resistance. Coughing, usually related to dysphagia, is more severe when the horse eats and drinks, but is always present intermittently because saliva is aspirated continuously. A nasal discharge of pus, food, and saliva is often present, and the breath is foul-smelling.

Diagnosis is based on clinical, laboratory, radiographic, and endoscopic findings. Management depends on the cause, but nasogastric intubation for alimentation, and tracheotomy and intubation might be necessary for life support in severe cases. Appropriate antibiotic therapy for the primary problem, if it is an abscess, and the secondary aspiration pneumonia might be indicated. As streptococci are one of the most likely pathogens, this regimen should include procaine penicillin G at 20,000 μ/kg twice daily intramuscularly, usually for 2 to 3 weeks. Some horses with severe cases will do remarkably well with this therapy; some might have some residual pharyngeal dysfunction.

Laryngeal disease as a cause of coughing and inspiratory dyspnea is rare. Bilateral laryngeal paralysis can occur idiopathically or in some horses exposed to organophosphates or lead. In chronic lead poisoning the cough is probably also caused by pharyngeal dysfunction, dysphagia, and aspiration. Subepiglottic cysts can also cause varying degrees of upper-airway obstruction, dysphagia, and cough. Occasionally, large granulomas develop within the larynx, either spontaneously or following surgery. These cause irritation and cough as well as increased respiratory resistance. Clinical signs, endoscopy, and radiographic findings are diagnostic of the problem. Confirmation of chronic lead poisoning requires tissue concentration measurement because serum lead concentrations can be normal. A rise in urinary lead concentrations following the administration of calcium versenate also suggests a diagnosis of chronic lead poisoning.

Therapy depends on the cause. Dysfunction caused by chronic lead poisoning is probably irreversible, and the prognosis is poor. Subepiglottic cysts should be treated by surgical excision, as should other space-occupying lesions of the larynx.

Tracheal disease as a cause of inspiratory effort, and chronic cough is uncommon. Granulomas can develop at previous surgical sites and become large enough to cause cough and dyspnea. Diagnosis is based on endoscopic findings. Surgical excision should be considered, although it is complicated.

Cough With Inspiratory and Expiratory Effort

Cough with inspiratory and expiratory effort can result from a combination of upper- and lower-airway disease, such as in a horse with tracheal stenosis and heaves. These combinations are rare, however, and initially a single cause for the problem should be sought (Fig. 7–4).

Horses with pulmonary abscesses often present with a cough and other signs of bacterial infections. Labored breathing develops only when extensive amounts of lung tissue are involved, or when pulmonary expansion is compromised by pleural effusion, often following rupture of an abscess into the pleural space. The history often indicates that the horse was transported for over 8 hours prior to becoming ill. Signs usually develop insidiously over several days to weeks, with anorexia, fever, depression, and a "guarded" gait. Thoracic auscultation and percussion demonstrate ventral dullness, with pain on firm pressure on the chest wall. Breathing may be rapid and shallow or slow and deliberate. Leukocytosis, hyperfibrinogenemia, hyperglobulinemia, and often a mild anemia are consistent with chronic inflammation. Thoracic radiography and ultrasonography are useful to define the extent of the lesions and the degree of pleural reaction, and to determine whether the infection is compartmentalized. Thoracocentesis can be used to obtain fluid for cytology and culture and for therapeutic drainage. In severe cases, up to 50 L of fluid might be removed. Indwelling drainage tubes can be placed for continuous drainage over several days. Transtracheal aspiration and culture is indicated in most cases. Infections are often mixed, and all fluids should be cultured aerobically and anaerobically. The greater the number of bacterial species isolated, the graver the prognosis. Broad-spectrum antibiotic therapy is indicated; frequently gentamicin is administered at 2 mg/kg twice daily and penicillin G at 20,000 µ/kg three times daily in combination, together with metronidazole 7.5 mg/kg orally four times daily. Subsequent culture results might dictate a change in therapy. In severe well-established cases, therapy can last 30 or more days, which is expensive. Although single localized abscesses or infections caused by a single bacterial species such as a streptococcus might respond well to aggressive therapy, and the horse restored to useful work, economic considerations may override medical possibilities.

Pure pulmonary edema, in the absence of infection, is uncommon as a cause of cough and labored breathing in horses. Acute allergic reaction can cause cough and labored breathing if the horse sensitized to an agent systemically is then exposed to the agent through the airways. This situation apparently occurs uncommonly. Anecdotal reports suggest that horses can develop acute pulmonary changes as a part of acute allergic reactions, but cough is not usually present. Chronic coughing and dyspnea can develop in the rare case of heart failure seen in horses. A clearly defined small group of horses with this problem are horses

with rupture of the mitral chordae tendineae. When the chorda ruptures, acute pulmonary edema occurs, often with coughing and labored breathing. Some horses die at this stage. Others survive with varying degrees of dyspnea and coughing. Auscultation reveals moist to wet lung sounds and a loud pansystolic murmur. Some of these animals develop atrial fibrillation. History and clinical signs arouse suspicion, and echocardiography can confirm the diagnosis. Prognosis is poor, although empiric medical therapy to reduce the edema, such as furosemide, can give temporary relief. In addition, other heart diseases occasionally lead to heart disease, pulmonary edema, dyspnea, and cough (Chapter 10).

Restrictive lung disease is uncommon in horses. Occasional cases of marked interstitial fibrosis are seen, and pulmonary silicosis has been reported in an area of California. In these conditions, the lung becomes stiff and causes breathing to be labored. Coughing can be due to increased mucus production. The lungs are often remarkably quiet given the degree of dyspnea. Endoscopically increased tracheal mucus might be seen, and radiographically a prominent interstitial pattern, much more dense than that seen in a typical "heavey" horse, might be present. A definitive diagnosis might require a lung biopsy, a technique for the specialist. The chronic severe fibrosing nature of this condition precludes its resolution by medication or management.

Cough With Expiratory Effort

The most common cause of labored breathing and coughing in horses is chronic small-airways disease (bronchiolitis). The exact incidence of this problem is not known, nor is the cause. Although labored expiration and coughing is considered to be one problem given many names, it might in fact be a number of different diseases, although these have not been characterized.

The severity of the problem varies from causing reduced athletic performance (Chapter 17), to causing mild intermittent cough, to causing severe expiratory dyspnea and chronic productive coughing.

Expiratory dyspnea and chronic productive coughing is the classic heaves disorder. Although not proven, this chronic bronchiolitis with bronchoconstriction is probably allergic in origin. The inciting agents are most likely the fungal spores found in hay and straw. This theory is supported somewhat by experimental and epidemiologic data; the disease is more common in older stabled horses, and the signs are often reduced or abolished when the horses are permanently put out onto fresh pasture.

Typically the disease is insidious and progressive, severity increasing year by year, with signs most severe in the winter, when horses are stabled. A horse with well-established chronic small-airways disease will have a marked expiratory effort, hypertrophy of the abdominal musculature giving an obvious "heave-line" along the flank. Athletic performance is markedly reduced and often weight is lost. Cough is intermittent and productive, with a white bilateral nasal discharge. Auscultation reveals increased inspiratory and particularly expiratory sounds, with whistles, wheezes, snaps, crackles and pops. Endoscopy reveals increased intratracheal mucus, and affected horses cough more than normal horses during endoscopy.

Laboratory data are not dramatic. Bacteria might be seen in the tracheal aspirate fluid but are not usually indicative of a chronic infection. The cytology is compatible with chronic inflammation. Bronchoalveolar lavage fluid is high in neutrophils (greater than 50%), and examination of this fluid might be a more useful diagnostic technique than transtracheal aspiration. Horses in remission often yield fluid with a cell population in the normal range. On arterial blood gas analysis, PaO_2 is below 80 mm Hg (10.6 Kpa), often down to 50 mm Hg

(6.7 Kpa). Carbon dioxide concentration is usually normal. Some centers attempt to identify the specific etiologic agent(s) using intradermal testing with potential allergens. The technique is not very precise because many nonspecific reactors exist within the equine population, but evidently, heavey horses do have a higher reaction rate to a variety of allergens, particularly fungal spores. Thoracic radiographs might demonstrate an overall increase in interstitial density with bronchial thickening. However, diagnosis on clinical grounds is for the most part straightforward, and laboratory and other tests are not usually needed.

In addition to the classic "winter heaves" of stabled horses bedded with hay and straw, a "summer heaves" is recognized in some southern areas. These horses are normal in the winter, but develop signs similar to those described above in the summer months. Presumably they are sensitive to some airborne agent, probably of plant origin.

Treatment of heaves is geared toward control, and complete cures are unlikely; the sensitivity tends to be lifelong. The most sensible and often beneficial approach is based on environmental management, with the goal of eliminating airway exposure to the agents responsible for the reaction. Stabled horses should be turned outside onto grass pasture during the summer. In the winter they should also be outside, with open-sided shelter if necessary. In the winter the feed should be pelleted or cubed hay and grain, or soaking-wet hay. If turning the horse out is not possible, all attempts should be made to reduce exposure to hay and straw dust. The horse should be kept in a well-ventilated stall, preferably near the barn door, which should be open at all times. Bedding should be shavings, sawdust, peat moss, or some other nonhay/nonstraw material. Hay should be placed in a large net into a 50-gallon drum of water and soaked until bubbles stop rising. Generally, an inside environment cannot be improved sufficiently to reduce the exposure to dust.

Owner compliance is a problem. Many will keep the horse outside 70 to 80% of the time, bringing in the horse in the evening or at feeding time. For many heavey horses, 1 to 2 hours of exposure to dust per day is enough to keep the problem active. Noncompliance with the "fresh-air" regimen is the main reason for failure of management protocols.

For horses with "summer heaves," the opposite protocol applies. These horses appear to improve when housed inside in the summer, presumably because doing so reduces their exposure to the inciting agent.

Horses with severe problems or acute exacerbations of chronic ones might benefit from a short course of medication to alleviate the clinical signs, while environmental improvements are taking effect. Corticosteroids have a wide range of actions and are helpful to many horses with chronic small-airways disease. They should be used with care, however, because of potential side effects, including immune suppression, iatrogenic Cushing's syndrome, and with some horses, laminitis. Most widely used are prednisolone and dexamethazone. Prednisolone can be given initially at 1 to 2 mg/kg once daily in the morning, either orally or intramuscularly. This dosage is given for 5 to 6 days, then changed to every other day. At the end of 2 weeks of therapy, if the horse's condition has improved, the dosage can be gradually reduced over the next 2 to 3 weeks. This therapy must be used with environmental improvement, and the administration schedule can be shortened if a rapid response occurs. A similar regimen is used with dexamethazone, starting at a dosage of 0.1 mg to 0.2 mg/kg. Laminitis seems to be more likely with dexamethazone usage.

Many of the bronchodilators used in human medicine have been used empirically in horses, although few have been evaluated for efficacy and dosage. In many countries the beta-2 agonist clenbuterol is licensed for use in horses. Well-controlled studies are few, but some evidence suggests that a dosage of 0.8 μg/kg twice daily helps some affected animals. Terbutaline, another beta-2 agonist, used empirically at a dosage of 0.07 mg/kg orally four times daily, appears to help some horses. Sodium cromoglycate, which inhibits immediate and delayed hypersensitivity reactions in human patients with asthma, has been shown to be beneficial in some horses with chronic small-airways disease. The drug is administered by inhalation as a single daily 80-mg dose. Horses remain unresponsive to challenge for up to 3 weeks, depending on the number of days of treatment they receive prior to challenge. Sodium cromoglycate can be useful for horses that must be brought inside for limited periods. In some countries, but not the U.S., a face mask and administration unit are sold for administration of this drug.

Expectorants of various types are also used to clear out the excessive mucus produced in chronic small-airways disease. These include glycerol guaiacolate and various iodides. Evidence for their effectiveness is lacking, and because mucus hypersecton is a result of continuous stimulation, the most effective way to clear out the lung is to clean up the inhaled air.

In conclusion, the management of chronic small-airways disease pivots on the reduction of dust exposure; all other therapies are adjuncts and should be used only for short-term support while environment changes are being made and beginning to take effect.

LABORED BREATHING WITHOUT COUGH

Horses are not commonly presented for the assessment of this problem. When the only major sign is inspiratory effort, upper-airway lesions are most likely. If the horse has no cough, the lesion is often rostral to the pharynx, that is, in the nasal cavity. Obstructive lesions of the nose can be due to infectious and noninfectious processes. They can result from proliferative lesions within the nasal cavity, or those expanding into the cavity from adjacent structures, such as the paranasal sinuses. If only one nasal passage is obstructed, breathing can appear normal at rest, although the horse can have exercise intolerance.

Chronic granulomatous lesions develop from a variety of infections, such as with Cryptococcus neoformans. Primary nasal neoplasms are rare and grow slowly, occluding first one, then the other nostril. Similarly, lesions of the paranasal sinuses, such as neoplasms and cysts, can push the medial wall of the maxillary sinus outward to obstruct the nasal passages. This obstruction can extend to deviate the septum, hence obstructing the opposite side also. The septum and other structures can be destroyed as the tumor expands and occludes airflow. In addition to reduced airflow and inspiratory dyspnea, affected horses often have bilateral or unilateral nasal discharges, which are purulent, often foul-smelling, and hemorrhagic. With proliferative lesions, facial deformity can occur.

Another occasional nasal lesion leading to obstruction and labored breathing is a hematoma of the rostral end of the nasal septum, a slowly progressive lesion causing bilateral obstruction. The cause is unknown. The condition is most easily diagnosed by digital examination of the rostral septum.

Diagnosis of other nasal obstructive lesions is based on clinical examination, endoscopy, and in some cases radiography. Biopsy of some lesions for histology, culture, or both might be useful.

Therapy for most lesions is unrewarding. Neoplasms are usually too well established and are inoperable. Sinus lesions such as cysts can be removed, but to re-establish an airway, extensive amounts of the nasal turbinates might have to be removed. Hemorrhage is often severe and can be life-threatening in these operations. Equally, septal hematomas are difficult to remove. Cost and a poor prognosis can preclude therapeutic intervention.

Obstructive lesions of the pharynx, larynx, and trachea that cause inspiratory dyspnea but not cough are uncommon. Bilateral laryngeal paralysis has been seen following ingestion of organophosphates in a few horses. These animals had varying degrees of dyspnea and exercise intolerance but no cough. Diagnosis is made endoscopically.

If labored breathing without a cough has both inspiratory and expiratory components or is characterized by rapid, short, distressed breathing, severe thoracic disease should be considered. If the onset is sudden, pneumothorax or ruptured diaphragm might be considered. Pneumothorax and ruptured diaphragm are rare in horses and usually follow trauma. Their diagnosis is not always easy, particularly because they are unexpected; lung sounds might be inaudible in both cases, and in diaphragmatic hernia gut sounds or splashing sounds might be heard within the thorax. Radiography, if available, is invaluable.

Successful treatment of diaphragmatic hernias in horses is reported infrequently. Treatment of pneumothorax by closure of the chest wall defect and evacuation of the air from the pleural space is justified only if the pneumothorax is severe and due to an obvious penetrating wound. If the condition is secondary to lung tearing or rupture, leaving the lung in partially collapsed position might be advisable so that the tear can seal. The air will be resorbed in time, and the lung re-expanded.

Labored breathing is also seen in very severe anemias. Respiratory signs often do not develop until the packed cell volume is between 8 and 10% (0.08 to 0.1 L/L). The causes, clinical signs, and clinicopathologic data for anemia in horses is discussed in Chapter 13.

SUPPLEMENTAL READING

Britt, D.P., and Preston, J.M.: Efficacy of ivermectin against *Dictycaulus arnfeldi* in ponies. Vet. Rec. 116:343–345, 1985.

Brown, C.M., Bell, T.G., Paradis, M.R., and Breeze, R.G.: Rupture of the mitral chordae tendineae in two horses. J. Am. Vet. Med. Assoc., 182:281–283, 1983.

Clark, A.F, Madelin, T.M., and Allpress, R.G.: The relationship of air hygiene in stables to lower airway disease and pharyngeal lymphoid hyperplasia in two groups of Thoroughbred horses. Equine Vet. J., 19:524–530, 1987.

Corrier, D.E., Wilson, S.R., and Scrutchfield, W.L.: Equine cryptococcal rhinitis. Compend. Contin. Educ. 6:S556–558, 1984.

Derksen, F.J., et al.: Bronchoalveolar lavage in ponies with recurrent airway obstruction (heaves). Am. Rev. Resp. Dis., 132:1006–1070, 1985.

Derksen, F.J., et al.: Chronic restrictive pulmonary disease in a mare. J. Am. Vet. Med. Assoc., 180:887–889, 1982.

Duncan, I.D., and Brook, D.: Bilateral laryngeal paralysis in the horse. Eq. Vet. J., 17:228–233, 1985.

Freeman, D.E.: Diagnosis and treatment of diseases of the guttural pouch. Compend. Contin. Educ., 2:S3–S11, 1980.

Raphel, C.F., and Beech, J.: Pleuritis secondary to pneumonia or lung abscessation in 90 horses. J. Am. Vet. Med. Assoc., 181:808–810, 1982.

Raphel, C.F., and Gunson, D.E.: Percutaneous lung biopsy in the horse. Cornell Vet., 71:439–448, 1981.

Thompson, J.R., and McPherson, E.A.: Chronic obstructive pulmonary disease in the horse 2: Therapy. Equine Vet. J., 15:207–210, 1983.

Thompson, J.R., and McPherson, E.A.: Effects of environmental control on pulmonary function of horses affected with chronic obstructive pulmonary disease. Equine Vet. J. 16:35–38, 1984.

Todhunter, R.J., Brown, C.M., and Stickle, R.: Retropharyngeal infections in five horses. J. Am. Vet. Med. Assoc., 187:660–604, 1985.

chapter 8

PURULENT NASAL DISCHARGE

Christopher M. Brown

Many of the problems discussed in Chapter 7 on cough and labored breathing also are associated with nasal discharge. However, in several other problems, nasal discharge is present but cough and dyspnea are not always a feature.

Nasal discharge can arise from primary lesions within the nasal cavities, paranasal sinuses, guttural pouches, larynx, trachea, bronchi, bronchioles, and pulmonary parenchyma. In addition, pharyngeal and esophageal disorders can lead to the discharge of exudate, food, and saliva from the nose. Hence, the evaluation of a horse with a purulent nasal discharge should include a detailed examination from nostril to alveolus or stomach.

The patient history can be valuable. Sudden-onset conditions are usually due to acute infections, trauma, or obstructions. The insidious, chronic conditions are caused by chronic infections, neoplasms, or progressive neurologic disease.

Nasal discharge can be acute or chronic, bilateral or unilateral. It can vary from serous to purulent to hemorrhagic. Some of the features that distinguish these causes are shown in Figure 8–1.

The initial physical examination should concentrate on the head. The symmetry of airflow out of the nostrils should be determined by holding the palms of the hands about 2 inches in front of the nares. The odor of the breath should be noted. Facial swelling, particularly over the paranasal sinuses, should be evaluated. The sinuses can be percussed to determine if they contain fluid or other material. If sinus involvement is suspected, a

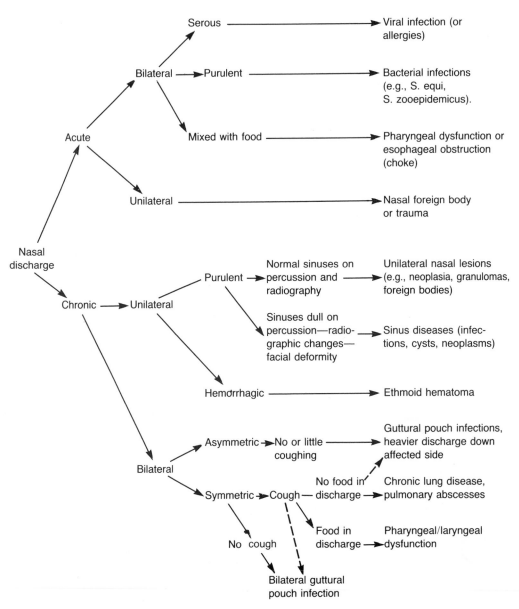

Fig. 8–1. Causes of nasal discharge.

detailed dental examination is indicated. Particular attention should be paid to palpation of lymph nodes in the inter-mandibular space and to the parotid region. In addition, a detailed auscultation of the thorax is essential (Chapter 7).

Often the most rapid and accurate way to locate the source of a nasal discharge is endoscopy. This technique can provide the definitive diagnosis (e.g., of ethmoid hematoma) or indicate where further investigations should be concentrated (e.g., excessive tracheal mucous indicates lung disease). These further investigations include radiography, biopsy, transtracheal aspiration for culture and cytology, and bronchoalveolar lavage (Chapter 7). In addition, routine biochemistry and hematology might be indicated in some cases.

ACUTE NASAL DISCHARGE

UNILATERAL DISCHARGE

Acute unilateral nasal discharge is uncommon. Probable causes include foreign bodies and trauma, such as following nasogastric intubation or endoscopy. Hemorrhage is also usually present. Diagnosis is based on history and endoscopic findings, and management depends on the cause. Foreign bodies should be removed, and most traumatic lesions resolve with rest.

BILATERAL DISCHARGE

Bilateral acute nasal discharge indicates disease caudal to the internal nares or a diffuse disease affecting both of the nasal cavities and related structures.

Acute Viral Respiratory Infections

Acute viral respiratory infections are extremely common causes of bilateral nasal discharge. Discharge can initially be serous and often becomes purulent. Pos-sible agents include influenza viruses, rhinopneumonitis virus (herpes type 1), rhinovirus, and equine arteritis virus). Additional clinical signs vary but include anorexia, depression, cough, ocular discharge, and, with arteritis, limb and ventral edema. Frequently several, and often all, horses in a group are affected, usually within 7 to 10 days. Culture and sensitivity testing might be indicated if secondary bacterial infections develop. Some infective agents can be confirmed if both acute and convalescent sera are submitted for antibody titres. These data are of little value for the management of the acute problem, however.

Treatment is not usually needed. Stall rest for at least 7 days after the end of the febrile period is necessary. Many horses are returned to full work far too soon after a bout of viral respiratory infection. The consequences probably include poor performance and chronic lung disease. Animals with high fevers and reduced food and water intake might benefit from nonsteroidal anti-inflammatory drugs (NSAIDs) for 1 to 2 days. By reducing fever, however, NSAIDs can mask a developing bacterial infection or an unresolving problem. Antibiotic therapy is not needed unless secondary bacterial infections are confirmed or suspected.

Vaccination programs can reduce the severity of the problem on farms, but because vaccines are available for only three strains of influenza and one strain of rhinopneumonitis, the protection induced can be incomplete and short-lived. Many other respiratory pathogens for which vaccines are not available can cause fever, cough, and nasal discharge (Chapter 15). Therefore, even in routinely vaccinated horses, outbreaks of "flu" and "rhino" occur.

Bacterial Infections

Acute purulent bilateral nasal discharge, occurring with viral infections, often indicates a secondary bacterial infection or a primary bacterial infection, such as with Streptococcus equi. Acute pneumonia, uncommon in adult horses, can also be associated with cough and bilateral purulent nasal discharge, as can acute guttural pouch infections. Additional signs include fever, anorexia, and altered lung sounds. In classic S. equi infections ("strangles"), marked lymphadenopathy occurs, often with abscessation and rupture. The disease is characterized by an initial 2- to 4-day period of serous to purulent nasal discharge followed by lymphadenopathy with abscessation and rupture about 7 to 10 days after the onset of signs. Although S. equi is the most common cause of this disease, S. zooepidemicus is also occasionally isolated.

Diagnosis of these conditions can usually be made on clinical signs, but for horses with acute pneumonia, a culture is indicated. Treatment of acute bacterial respiratory infection is usually empiric, and at times is controversial. Many veterinarians do not treat strangles with antibiotics, believing antibiotics only prolong the problem. In addition, they believe that treated horses are more likely to develop internal abscesses. However, most horses treated with appropriate dosages of penicillin for a long enough period, such as procaine penicillin G intramuscularly at 20,000 μ/kg for 10 to 15 days, will be cured. Experience has shown that if all horses in an affected group are treated this way, the outbreak might be controlled and often new cases prevented. The decision to treat or not to treat depends on the clinical signs of not only a particular horse, but also the others at risk, and on the ability of the owners to administer the medication. Vaccination is helpful on some farms.

Penicillin is a good empiric choice whenever acute bacterial infections are suspected. If culture indicates a different choice, or if the condition is unresponsive, other agents, such as trimethoprim-sulfa combinations or ampicillin, can be selected.

Choke and Pharyngeal Dysfunction

If an acute bilateral nasal discharge contains food material and is associated with coughing, the veterinarian should consider acute pharyngeal dysfunction or acute esophageal obstruction (choke) (Chapter 6). Choke is usually associated with the lodging of a piece of food, such as a carrot, hay cube, or sugar beet pulp, in the esophagus, with subsequent filling proximal to the obstruction. Diagnosis is based on clinical signs, and the impacted esophagus can often be felt on the left side of the neck. A stomach tube cannot be passed, and the diagnosis can be confirmed endoscopically and radiographically. Choke is relieved by lavage, often under general anesthesia.

Acute pharyngeal dysfunction can develop following pharyngeal trauma, such as following attempts at nasogastric intubation, during the course of some diseases, such as rabies and botulism, or following cranial nerve damage, such as occurs with skull fractures. In addition to having cough and a nasal discharge containing food, these animals are usually dysphagic (Chapter 6). Diagnosis is based on clinical signs and endoscopy. Radiographs, both plain and contrast, can be helpful. Therapy depends on the cause. Because rabies is a possible cause, the veterinarian must be careful when examining these horses.

CHRONIC NASAL DISCHARGE

UNILATERAL DISCHARGE

Chronic unilateral nasal discharge can be purulent or hemorrhagic.

Purulent

Purulent unilateral discharges arise from chronic conditions of the paranasal sinuses or from chronic unilateral nasal lesions such as neoplasms and granulomas. Occasionally chronic guttural pouch infections produce unilateral discharges, but more frequently the discharge is bilaterally asymmetric in these cases. The initial diagnostic approach is to evaluate the maxillary and frontal sinuses for evidence of disease; if they are found to be normal, an alternative source of the discharge should be sought.

Sinus percussion is simple and useful. Space-occupying lesions, either fluid or solid, reduce the resonance, and in over half of affected horses the dullness on percussion can be detected by comparing the normal and abnormal sides.

In addition, some horses with sinus lesions can have facial swelling and distortion over the area of the sinus. Epiphora can result from obstruction of the nasolacrimal duct. However, normal facial contour and normal percussion do not rule out sinus disease as a cause of unilateral chronic nasal discharge.

The next diagnostic step is endoscopy of the nasal cavities. The nasomaxillary opening is into the middle meatus, and nasal discharge originating from the sinuses can be seen emerging into the middle meatus between the dorsal and ventral conchae (turbinates). If no discharge drains into the middle meatus, an alternative source might be found, such as a neoplasm, foreign body, or granuloma.

Sinusitis. Additional investigations can refine and confirm a diagnosis of suspected sinusitis. Lateral radiographs of the head can show filling of the sinuses, or fluid lines within them. In addition, because the roots of the cheek teeth are often involved, oblique views of the affected side place the teeth in profile.

Dorsoventral views are also useful to compare normal and abnormal sides, although these are not always easily obtained in the standing horse.

Aspiration of sinus contents through a trephine hole can provide useful diagnostic material. This procedure is safe and simple. Initially, the rostral maxillary sinus is tapped just dorsal to the rostral end of the facial crest. A small area of the skin is clipped and the area anesthetized by infiltration of 2% lidocaine solution. The sinus is penetrated using a Steinmann's bone pin held in a Jacob's chuck. The hole is made by a to-and-fro rotation using firm pressure. The pin should be large enough to make a hole through which an 18-gauge, 2-inch hypodermic needle can be passed. Once the hole is made, the needle is inserted and the contents are aspirated. If no fluid is withdrawn, 20 cc of sterile saline can be instilled into the sinus and the aspiration repeated. The fluid obtained should be examined both cytologically and microbiologically.

Primary septic sinusitis, though uncommon, can develop following acute respiratory infection. Diagnosis is based on clinical signs, lack of involvement of the teeth, and culture results. Treatment usually requires surgical drainage and lavage, together with appropriate systemic antibiotic therapy. Antibiotic therapy alone is not usually successful in resolving the problem; though the horse improves temporarily, the problem recurs shortly after the end of the therapy.

More commonly, sinusitis is secondary to dental disease, particularly patent infundibulae of the molars, especially the first molar. The disease is most common in 4- to 10-year-old horses. Clinical signs vary in severity, but in addition to a purulent, often foul-smelling nasal discharge, the horse can have facial deformity, epiphora, and signs of dental disease. Diagnosis is based on clinical signs, endoscopy, and radiography. Treatment requires surgical drainage, lavage, and removal of the affected tooth or teeth. Surgical management of dentally related sinusitis in horses can be successful. However, the client must be aware of the long-term postoperative management problems, including frequent dental care, and the cost.

Cystlike lesions in paranasal sinuses are of unknown cause; they can be congenital or can develop after submucosal hemorrhage. Signs do not usually develop until the horse is 2 to 3 years old. The slow-growing lesions lead to facial deformity, and in some horses to a chronic purulent unilateral nasal discharge. A thick yellow fluid is obtained with trephination and aspiration. It is not highly cellular and contains no bacteria, unlike the pus obtained in cases of septic sinusitis. Deformation of the ventral concha (turbinate) due to pressure from within the maxillary sinus can be seen endoscopically. Treatment is surgical, with a bone flap approach to the sinus and removal of the entire cyst.

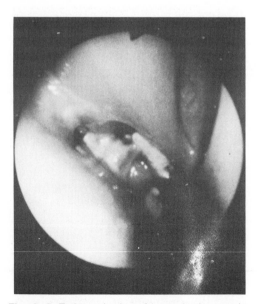

Fig. 8–2. Endoscopic view of a neoplastic mass in the internal nares of a horse with chronic unilateral nasal discharge.

Other, rare lesions of the paranasal sinuses include neoplasms, hematomas, and granulomas. Diagnosis is based on elimination of other causes, and possibly surgical exploration.

Intranasal Lesions. If the sinuses are normal, the cause of a chronic unilateral purulent nasal discharge is usually an intranasal lesion. Such lesions are fairly uncommon and are most readily diagnosed by endoscopic examination (Fig. 8–2). Airflow on the affected side can be reduced, and the breath can be foul-smelling. Lesions include neoplasms (such as adenocarcinomas), granulomatous infections (such as Cryptococcus neoformans), foreign bodies, and polyps. Biopsy, taken through the endoscope, might help in the diagnosis of proliferative lesions. The surface material obtained might consist entirely of inflammatory exudate, however. Radiographs might help to define the limits of the lesion, and also the involvement of adjacent structures.

Some of these unilateral nasal lesions are treatable. Foreign bodies can be withdrawn through the nostrils. Polyps can be excised surgically, using either rhinotomy or a thermocautery snare through the endoscope. Rhinotomy is more radical, risky, and expensive. Granulomatous lesions are more difficult to treat. Cryptococcal infections are potentially zoonotic, and therapy might be unwise. Most attempts at therapy using amphoteracin B, iodides, and surgical excision have been unsuccessful. Occasional cases regress for months to years after therapy, but they recur.

Hemorrhagic

Although the unilateral purulent nasal discharge from foreign bodies and neoplasms can contain some blood, the most likely cause of chronic unilateral hemorrhagic nasal discharge in a horse is a progressive ethmoid hematoma. These lesions are of unknown cause, but might develop following repeated bouts of submucosal hemorrhage in the ethmoid region. Occasional lesions involve the paranasal sinuses. Clinical signs include an intermittent unilateral sanguinous nasal discharge, and, if the lesion is large enough, reduced airflow. The endoscopic appearance is fairly characteristic—a green-black mass in the area of the ethmoids (Fig. 8–3). The mass bleeds easily when probed. Dorsoventral and lateral radiographs define the size and location of the mass. If the lesion is causing a significant problem, surgical removal should be considered. Lesions involving the sinus are removed using a flap approach; those confined to the ethmoid are approached through the frontal sinus. Hemorrhage can be profuse, and the surgery is not without risk. Small lesions, with a narrow base, can be removed using an electrocautery snare through the endoscope. Recurrence following removal is common.

ASYMMETRIC DISCHARGE

Chronic guttural pouch infections can arise following acute upper respiratory infections or after the rupture of retropharyngeal abscesses into the pouch. The consistency of the exudate can vary from a thin fluid to thick viscid pus, which can become inspissated and form discrete concretions (chondroids).

If the exudate is fairly thin, the history often indicates an increased asymmetric nasal discharge when the horse puts its head down to eat or drink. This discharge pattern occurs because in the normal upright position, the exit from the pouch, the pharyngeal orifice, is dorsal to much of the pouch. Fluid can accumulate and not drain. When the head is lowered the fluid flows forward and up to the exit.

When the horse swallows, the opening to the pouch is expanded, and exudate drains out.

In addition to nasal discharge, horses with chronic guttural pouch infections can have local lymphadenopathy, swelling in the parotid region, and, if cranial nerves are involved, dysphagia, dyspnea, and Horner's syndrome.

The two most valuable diagnostic aids are endoscopy and radiography. Endoscopically, exudate can be seen draining from the pharyngeal orifice (Fig. 8–4). The mere presence of mucus in the region of the orifice should not be taken as evidence of pouch infection. Frequently, in horses with lower airway disease, tags of mucopurulent material adhere to the area in which material is coughed into the pharynx from the trachea. Drainage can be confirmed by making the horse swallow and observing the orifices at the same time. Swallowing can be induced by spraying the pharynx with water using the endoscope. Pouch infection can be confirmed absolutely by passing the endoscope into the

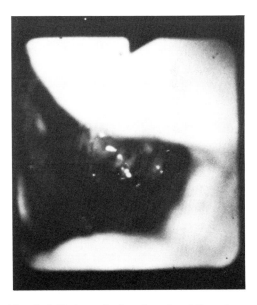

Fig. 8–3. Endoscopic view of an ethmoid hematoma in a horse with an intermittent sanguinous purulent unilateral nasal discharge.

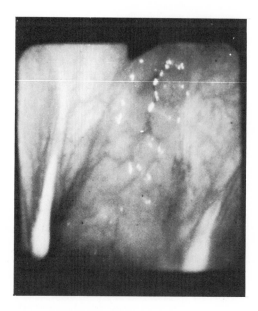

Fig. 8–4. Endoscopic view of the pharynx of a horse with purulent material draining through the orifices of both auditory tubes.

pouch. Most endoscopes of 1 cm in diameter or less can be passed into the pouches of most 400-kg horses. Larger endoscopes or smaller horses present more difficulty. Smaller endoscopes, such as human bronchoscopes, are more easily passed, but are not widely used by equine practitioners. Passage of the endoscope is aided by one of two techniques. In one method, the veterinarian passes a rigid catheter with a curved tip (e.g., Chamber's) through the ventral meatus into the pharynx. Then, while observing with the endoscope, the veterinarian passes the tip under the flap of the orifice and advances the catheter into the pouch. The catheter is then used to hold the flap of the orifice open while the endoscope is advanced into the pouch (Fig. 8–5). As the endoscope is advanced, the catheter is withdrawn. The other method passes a flexible guide, such as the endoscope biopsy instrument, down the biopsy channel of the endoscope and out into the pharynx. The tip is manipulated, under direct visualization, into the orifice and 5 to 10 cm advanced into the pouch. The endoscope

is advanced and guided into the pouch, following the guide. The endoscope usually has to be rotated as it is advanced to push the flap of the orifice to one side.

Clear visualization of the structures might be impossible if a large amount of viscid exudate is present in the pouch. In other pouches the exudate can be seen on the ventral floor of the compartment.

There is no reliable way of obtaining an uncontaminated sample of fluid for culture from the guttural pouch. A "clean" sample can be taken using the endoscope, but the interpretation of the culture results should include the possibility of contamination. A heavy growth of a well-recognized pathogen is significant. A mixed growth of pathogens and nonpathogenic bacteria is difficult to interpret.

Lateral radiographs of the pouches are particularly valuable in determining the extent and nature of some infections. Horizontal fluid lines suggest thin fluid, whereas irregular masses suggest inspissated pus or, more rarely, neoplasia. In addition, these views can show retro-

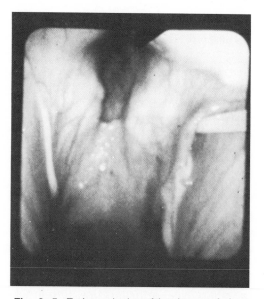

Fig. 8–5. Endoscopic view of the pharynx of a horse with a catheter entering the orifice of the auditive tube. This catheter is used to elevate the cartilaginous flap of the orifice to assist entry of the endoscope tip.

pharyngeal lymphadenopathy or abscessation. Radiographic changes are often not present in early mycotic infections, although in some bony changes can occur in both the hyoid and the skull.

Therapy depends on the cause and the stage of the problem. If there is a bacterial infection and the pus is fairly fluid, systemic antibiotics and pouch lavage might be adequate. Choice of antibiotics depends on culture results, but in most cases penicillin is a good empiric choice. The most efficient way to lavage the pouch is to place an indwelling catheter through the nostril. The catheter can be made from a No. 8 French polypropylene dog urinary catheter, about 60 cm long. A 70-cm-long piece of fairly stiff wire is passed down the lumen of the catheter to the end. The distal 10 cm of the catheter is wound into a coil about 1.5 cm in diameter. This coiled tip is placed in boiling water for 5 minutes, then cooled. The coil is unwound and the catheter straightened. The wire is left in place. Under endoscopic visualization, this catheter is passed up the nostril, and the tip is advanced into the pouch for about 15 cm. The catheter is held firmly, and the wire stylet pulled out. The end of the catheter in the pouch will coil back into a spiral and becomes self-retaining (Fig. 8–6). The open end of the catheter protrudes 2 to 3 cm from the nostril.

The pouch can be irrigated twice daily through this catheter. To facilitate good drainage the horse should be sedated with xylazine, which will cause it to lower its head. About 3 L of sterile electrolyte solution should be infused twice daily. No disinfecting or other agents must be added to the solution. The objective is to flush out the exudate. Systemic therapy is directed against the infection. Gravity flow is often adequate, but more aggressive irrigation can be obtained using an infusion pump or pressure apparatus.

Initially, irrigation will produce a fairly heavy flow of exudate, but over several days the volume should decline. The irrigation should be performed for at least 3 days, and some horses require treatment for 6 to 7 days. If catheters are left in too long, erosion of the cartilage of the orifice can occur, with subsequent scarring. If the exudate is very viscous or chondroids have developed, surgical opening and drainage of the pouch are indicated.

Mycotic infections of the guttural pouch are usually situated dorsally in the medial compartment and can also involve signs of chronic purulent nasal discharge. More frequently, however, they involve more prominent signs such as epistaxis owing to internal carotid artery rupture (Chapter 9) or dysphagia and dyspnea owing to cranial nerve involvement (Chapters 6 and 7). Angiography might be indicated if the mycotic infection involves the internal carotid artery.

Mycotic infections are more difficult to treat, and therapy is not always successful. A variety of regimens have been tried, usually involving ligation of the internal carotid artery at its origin to stop or

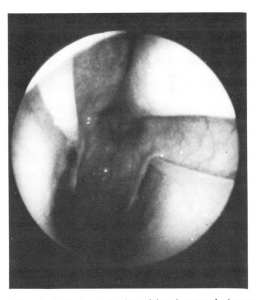

Fig. 8–6. Endoscopic view of the pharynx of a horse with bilateral guttural pouch infections. A self-retaining catheter is in position in each pouch for repeated irrigation.

prevent hemorrhage arising from erosion and rupture of the artery in the pouch. The mycelium can also be removed at surgery. In addition, various systemic or local therapies are directed against the fungal infection. These include topical nystatin. Thiabenzadole and abendazole have both been used orally. The length of therapy and dosages depend on the endoscopic appearance and resolution of the lesion. About 40 to 50% of horses treated by various combinations of these methods show complete or partial recovery.

SYMMETRIC DISCHARGE

Bilateral guttural pouch infections are an uncommon cause of chronic bilateral symmetric nasal discharges. Cough is often not a feature. Diagnosis and treatment are the same as for unilateral infections.

Bilateral chronic nasal discharges that are symmetric and associated with coughing are due to two main problems. Horses with a cough and food in the discharge often have pharyngeal, laryngeal, or esophageal dysfunctions. Horses with cough and no food in the nasal discharge have chronic pulmonary problems, such as heaves or pulmonary abscesses. Diagnosis and differentiation of these problems is based on clinical signs, endoscopic findings, radiographic findings, and culture and sensitivity, where indicated. Evaluation and management of these coughing horses is discussed in detail in Chapter 7.

SUPPLEMENTAL READING

Carrier, D.E., Wilson, S.R., and Scrutchfield, W.L.: Equine cryptococcal rhinitis. Compend. Contin. Educ., 6:S556–S558, 1984.

Church, S., Wyn-Jones, G., Parks, A.H., and Ritchie, H.E.: Treatment of guttural pouch mycosis. Equine Vet. J., 18:362–365, 1986.

Freeman, D.E.: Diagnosis and treatment of diseases of the guttural pouches. Compend. Contin. Educ., 2:S3–S11, 1980.

Lane, J.G., Longstaffe, J.A., and Gibbs, C.: Equine paranasal sinus cysts: A report of 15 cases. Equine Vet. J., 19:537–544, 1987.

Mason, B.J.E.: Empyema of the equine paranasal sinuses. J. Am. Vet. Med. Assoc., 167:727–731, 1975.

Todhunter, R.J., Brown, C.M., and Stickle, R.: Retropharyngeal infections in five horses. J. Am. Vet. Med. Assoc., 187:600–604, 1985.

chapter 9

BLEEDING FROM THE NOSE

Michael W. O'Callaghan

Bleeding from the nose (epistaxis), whether simply a mild serosanguinous discharge or a profuse, life-threatening hemorrhage, is a dramatic sign for the horse owner, who generally seeks veterinary attention promptly. The response of owners and trainers of racehorses is more complex, often influenced by the local racing authority's regulations on exercise-induced pulmonary hemorrhage (EIPH). When prophylactic furosemide administration is permitted prior to racing, most owners and trainers are eager to register "bleeders," in order to have their horses race using the drug. Where horses with EIPH are not allowed to race, owners and trainers are often reluctant to report cases of epistaxis, whatever the cause, for fear of having the horse withdrawn from racing.

For the veterinarian, the often transient and episodic nature of nosebleeding makes detecting the source of bleeding difficult, even when the horse is examined promptly. The reluctance of some owners or trainers to provide a satisfactory history should also be taken into account by the examining veterinarian.

SITES AND CAUSES (Fig. 9–1).

Blood emerging at the nares can originate from any space or organ normally communicating with the respiratory tract, including the mouth or the esophagus. In addition, certain disease processes such as trauma, sepsis, and tumors can provide routes for hemorrhage from areas not normally in contact with the respiratory tract.

NASAL CAVITY

The nasal cavity structures are highly vascular and, by their position, susceptible to injury and lesions leading to hemorrhage. Bleeding can be caused by foreign bodies, tumors, or other masses impinging on the highly vascular turbinate structures. The most common cause of nosebleed from the nasal cavity is trauma induced by passage of a nasogastric tube or endoscope. Ulcerative lesions or direct infection of the mucosa caused by these tubes are common sources of hemorrhage.

Progressive ethmoid hematomas arising from the ethmoid labyrinth initially invade the caudoventral maxillary sinus and later protrude into the nasal cavity. These hematomas cause serosanguinous discharge.

Hemorrhage resulting from fractures of the nasal bones and skull is relatively common, though not always reported in the literature, because in many cases the cause is obvious and the symptoms transient. However, fractures associated with the basisphenoid bone often produce fatal hemorrhage. Neoplasia and fungal granulomas are less common, but should be considered.

PARANASAL SINUSES

The paranasal sinuses are also a source of hemorrhage (Fig. 9–2). Serosanguinous discharge, often unilateral, following from a mucopurulent nasal discharge indicates conditions such as progressive ethmoid hematomas, cystic lesions, severe sinusitis with ulceration, or dental disease affecting the molar teeth that project into the maxillary sinuses. Fractures involving the bones bounding the sinuses are also a possible cause of hemorrhage.

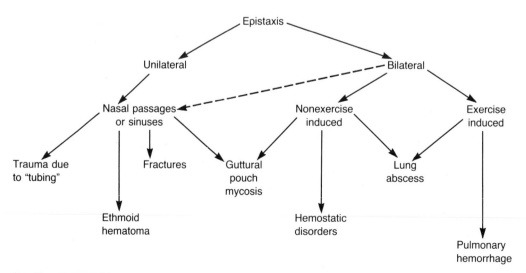

Fig. 9–1. Causes of equine epistaxis.

GUTTURAL POUCH

Lesions of the guttural pouch (auditory tube diverticulum) are an important consideration in any examination for epistaxis, particularly in abrupt massive hemorrhage in a resting horse (Fig. 9–2). The main lesion to consider is mycotic infection, which causes erosive plaques to form over the internal carotid artery, resulting in acute, episodic, and often fatal hemorrhage. Bacterial infections of the guttural pouch also can induce erosions and hemorrhage, although a more common outcome of bacterial infection is empyema, and in the long term, formation of chondroids. Strangles, abscesses rupturing into the guttural pouch, are a less common cause of nosebleed.

PHARYNX, LARYNX, OR MOUTH

Bleeding from structures in the pharynx occurs less commonly than bleeding from the nasal cavity and paranasal sinuses. A wide variety of lesions potentially cause minor hemorrhage. These include erosions associated with epiglottic entrapment, dental lesions in the molar region, foreign bodies wedged in the mouth, and abscesses from strangles lesions. Hemorrhage noted in the trachea or larynx is nearly always of pulmonary origin.

LUNG

The lung is a major source of hemorrhage, particularly if the signs occur during or immediately following exercise (Fig. 9–3). EIPH occurs in 40 to 75% of racing horses, with the highest prevalence noted in Thoroughbreds.

Most cases of EIPH, however, do not result in bleeding from the nose. Several surveys suggest that approximately 2 to 5% of racing Thoroughbreds bleed from the nose. Overt bleeding from the nose

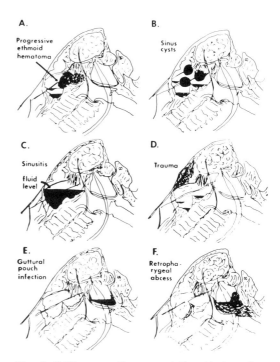

Fig. 9–2. Diagrammatic representation of lesions affecting the paranasal sinuses and guttural pouch often associated with nosebleeding (as viewed radiographically). *A,* Nodular masses of progressive ethmoid hematoma accompanied by fluid-gas interfaces resulting from accumulated blood or serosanguinous discharge. *B,* Multiple cystic structures with accompanying fluid accumulation. *C,* Large accumulation of mucopurulent material in the maxillary sinus associated with chronic sinusitis. *D,* Thickening and irregular opacification of bone overlying the sinuses as a result of trauma. *E,* Moderate fluid accumulation in the guttural pouch associated with mild empyema or occasionally with guttural pouch mycosis. *F,* Severe retropharyngeal infection (often from strangles) with enlarged or abscessed lymph nodes and associated thickening of the floor of the guttural pouch that impinges on the nasopharynx.

occurs in only a small proportion of horses with endoscopically confirmed EIPH. Even though so few cases of EIPH present with epistaxis, EIPH occurs so commonly that it is the most likely cause of epistaxis.

In most cases, bleeding varies from mild rose-colored staining of the serous nasal discharge to a constant trickle of fresh blood that can last for several hours. Distress is uncommon, most horses demonstrating only a slower-than-usual return

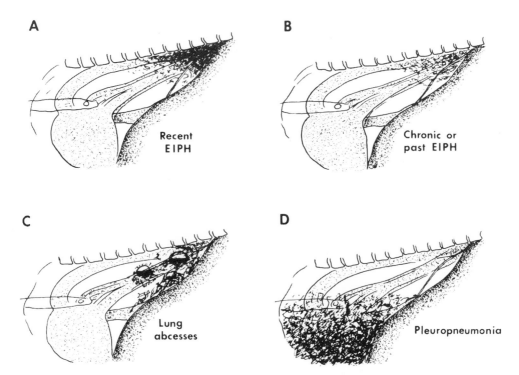

Fig. 9–3. Diagrams of radiographic changes seen in some lung lesions associated with bleeding. *A,* Air space (alveolar) opacity seen in the dorsocaudal lung field in a small proportion of acute EIPH cases. *B,* Mild or vague bronchointerstitial pattern in the dorsocaudal lung angle, often detected in cases of EIPH, but of uncertain significance in many cases. *C,* Multiple mature abscesses with fluid levels. Abscesses are usually associated with surrounding diffuse interstitial and alveolar opacification indicative of pneumonia. *D,* Severe pleuropneumonia with dense opacification of the ventral lung fields as a result of pleural effusion and ventral bronchopneumonia. Radiographically, pleural effusion and ventral lung consolidation are difficult to distinguish, often requiring ultrasonography for more precise characterization.

to normal respiratory rates following racing or no respiratory symptoms other than the hemorrhage. Autopsy examinations have shown the lesions to be confined mostly to the dorsocaudal lung field. The major findings consist of intense hemosiderin staining, diffuse small-airways disease, and intense proliferation of the bronchial arterial vasculature in affected areas of the lung. Fatal massive epistaxis is a much less frequent consequence of exercise. Autopsy evidence suggests that cases of fatal hemorrhage result from tearing of the lung in association with pleural adhesions or focal shear stress.

Another important differential diagnosis of pulmonary hemorrhage is lung abscess, often also manifest after exercise and not readily separated from EIPH on clinical grounds, although animals with lung abscesses may have a fetid odor to their breath. Other, less frequent conditions are bleeding secondary to bronchopneumonia, corynebacterial abscesses in young horses, and severe heaves in older horses. In the terminal stages of severe left heart failure with pulmonary edema, serous discharge from the nares can become serosanguinous.

GENERALIZED CONDITIONS

Some conditions have generalized hemorrhagic effects on various mucosae, including the respiratory tract. These conditions include purpura hemorrhagica (often initiated by lung infections), disseminated intravascular coagulation (DIC), thrombocytopenia (sometimes immune-mediated), and warfarin or other anticoagulant therapy.

CLINICAL EVALUATION

PATIENT HISTORY

Epistaxis Associated with Exercise

The high incidence of EIPH among horses that compete makes determining whether the bleeding is associated with exercise important. If bleeding is associated with exercise, the veterinarian should determine if signs of respiratory disease such as coughing, serous nasal discharge, or dyspnea were noted prior to the current episode. Apparently, small-airways disease, in many cases subclinical, is important in the pathogenesis of EIPH. A history of a previous "cold" or serous nasal discharge in association with bleeding at exercise could therefore indicate EIPH or the possibility of lung abscesses, a condition with similar presenting signs (Fig. 9–1). EIPH signs vary from the most minor of rose-colored tinging of the nasal mucus in the first 1 to 2 hours following exercise to acute, massive, and fatal hemorrhage during a race. In the latter cases, autopsy examination demonstrates either massive intraparenchymal hemorrhage or rents in the side of the lung with massive hemothorax.

Epistaxis Not Associated with Exercise

Nosebleeding in the absence of exercise involves a large list of differential diagnoses. The nature of the hemorrhage, its physical appearance, its volume, and the period over which it occurred need to be determined.

Profuse intermittent hemorrhage of pure red blood indicates hemorrhage from a large artery. Mycotic infections of the guttural pouch with erosion of the internal carotid artery wall induce such episodes, the most common pattern being two or three irregularly repeated episodes, followed, in the absence of treatment, by fatal exsanguination. Severe head trauma and fracture of the basisphenoid bone from rearing over backward also causes similarly profuse and often fatal hemorrhage, frequently with severe neurologic signs. Profuse hemorrhage is also possible from other forms of skull fracture and from gunshot wounds.

Intermittent streaky hemorrhage superimposed on a mucopurulent nasal discharge indicates lesions associated with septic processes such as nasal cavity masses, foreign bodies, or ulcerative lesions; paranasal sinus lesions such as sinusitis, periapical tooth-root infections, cysts, or progressive ethmoid hematomas; and strangles abscesses or empyema of the guttural pouches. Lung conditions such as abscesses, bronchopneumonia, bronchitis/bronchiolitis, and infectious pleuropneumonia can produce similar findings.

Serosanguinous nasal discharge is a feature of nonseptic paranasal sinus lesions, particularly sinus cysts, progressive ethmoid hematomas, or granulomatous masses. Generalized conditions such as warfarin toxicity, viral arteritis in the early stages, DIC, thrombocytopenia with hemorrhage, EIPH, and pulmonary edema from left heart failure also cause serosanguinous discharge. Snakebites also cause serous oozing and if associated with hemorrhage will produce a similar discharge.

PHYSICAL EXAMINATION AND SPECIAL TESTS

Approach

Examination should initially be aimed at ruling out generalized conditions of which bleeding at the nose is simply one manifestation. In resting horses the body temperature, respiratory rate, and heart rate can indicate conditions such as viral arteritis, bronchopneumonia, lung abscesses, and pleuropneumonia.

Following initial physical examination, the evaluation should concentrate on the respiratory system. The most productive step is an endoscopic examination of the airways and guttural pouches, unless the primary lesion is thought to be in the paranasal sinuses, in which case a radiographic examination of the skull is indicated.

If hemorrhage is not related to exercise, the examination should initially be directed to the upper airways, a more likely source of hemorrhage than the lungs. If hemorrhage is related to exercise, the veterinarian should try to perform an endoscopic examination of the larynx and trachea while the bleeding is occurring or at least within 2 hours of exercise. Observation of blood in the trachea, varying from a few flecks to a constant stream in the midventral lumen, indicates pulmonary hemorrhage. In this case, further diagnostic efforts should be concentrated on the lung, including percussion, radiography, and in some cases, pulmonary function testing and lung scintigraphy to localize lesions and to characterize ventilation/perfusion efficiency and regional lung function.

Thorough investigation of epistaxis requires an endoscope, preferably a flexible fiberoptic type. Most fiberoptic or other forms of flexible endoscope allow examination of the airways to the level of the proximal trachea. Longer endoscopes (at least 180 cm) extend this zone to beyond the bifurcation of the trachea. Rigid endoscopes equipped with an angled tip are suitable for examining the respiratory system only to the level of the arytenoid cartilages of the larynx; they are more suitable for examining the guttural pouches.

In addition to endoscopy, a satisfactory radiograph of the head, pharynx, and lung fields are extremely valuable.

Head

The nasal bones and flat bones overlying the maxillary and frontal sinuses should be inspected carefully for any sign of asymmetry. This examination should also include careful palpation, particularly to look for soft areas or bulges. Masses within the paranasal sinuses often cause pressure necrosis of the overlying bone. Although pressure necrosis is readily detected on careful palpation, it is often overlooked until bulging is noticed by the client. Exophthalmos indicates periocular extension of sinus involvement. Epiphora from the pressure of masses on the nasolacrimal duct can accompany these deformities or can be the only external sign of a paranasal sinus mass. Also, the symmetry of airflow from the nares should be tested. Unilateral reduction of flow is commonly encountered with mass lesions or inflammatory swelling of the mucosa in one of the nasal cavities. Progressive ethmoid hematomas should be considered, particularly in the later stages when the expanding mass has extended into the turbinates. Percussion of the sinuses is also indicated. Dullness can indicate fluid or masses. Many horses, however, have no external signs of sinus involvement apart from mucopurulent or serosanguinous nasal discharge, often unilateral.

Nasal Cavity

Endoscopic examination of the nasal cavity can reveal erosive lesions, polyps, or other small masses. Purulent or sanguinous discharge arising from the paranasal sinuses might also be seen emerging from the caudal portion of the middle meatus below the caudal conchal sinus. In cases of progressive ethmoid hematoma, part or all of the nasal airway might be filled, with the mass extending from the paranasal sinuses. Progressive ethmoid hematoma tissue is readily identified as an irregular, grayish, soft mass projecting into the middle meatus, sometimes with associated mucosal erosion and local hemorrhage around its margins. Other mass lesions causing hemorrhage are much less common. Coccidial granulomas, polyps, and masses of granulation tissue from foreign body reactions might also be detected, as might erosive lesions of the mucosa. In the caudal nasal cavity leading to the nasopharynx, the slitlike openings of the auditory (eustachian) tubes should be examined. Purulent or serosanguinous material emerging from the opening can indicate guttural pouch empyema or mycotic infection.

Paranasal Sinuses

The paranasal sinuses are inaccessible to the endoscope, but they are particularly amenable to radiographic examination because of the inherent contrast provided by contained air. A standing lateral projection is the best view for general study, because it demonstrates the fluid-air interfaces that are commonly present with many conditions such as sinusitis, dental lesions, mass lesions, cysts, and progressive ethmoid hematomas. Dorsoventral views can be obtained if horses are heavily sedated with xylazine to lower their heads. For a dorsoventral view, the cassette, preferably with grid, is positioned beneath the lower jaw against the throat, and the beam is directed in a rostrocaudal direction. This view requires a relatively high kilovoltage and milliampere-seconds compared to the lateral view, thus requiring a higher-powered machine. The dorsoventral view often demonstrates increased opacification of one maxillary sinus, thus identifying the affected side when the lesion is unilateral. This information is not readily appreciated from the lateral view.

The most widely reported paranasal sinus lesions leading to hemorrhagic nasal discharge are progressive ethmoid hematoma, cystic lesions (often multiple and of uncertain origin), and inflammatory sinusitis, which only occasionally causes epistaxis (Fig. 9–2). Fractures of the nasal and frontal bones impinging on the sinuses can also cause bleeding.

Progressive ethmoid hematomas produce a characteristic radiographic pattern. Single or multilobular rounded opacities are usually visible in the ventral aspect of the caudal maxillary sinus, partially superimposed on the ethmoid turbinates. In some cases the mass can extend dorsally into the frontal sinus separated from the ethmoid turbinate. The shadow produced by the ocular globes lies in approximately the same position as a lesion and should not be mistaken for a lesion. If the image is doubtful, a metallic marker ring should be placed over the horse's eye and the radiograph repeated. If the above radiographic signs are accompanied by an endoscopic finding of a grayish mass protruding into the nasal cavity, the diagnosis is almost certain.

Cystic structures are commonly multiple, well-circumscribed opacities widely dispersed in the paranasal sinuses. These and other mass lesions can cause fluid in the ventral recesses of the maxillary sinus.

In sinusitis, mass lesions are not seen. The most prominent sign of sinusitis is a variable amount of fluid in the paranasal sinuses, with a single or with multiple horizontal fluid-air interfaces.

Recent fractures of the nasal bones leading to nosebleed can be manifest by soft-tissue thickening beneath the dorsal bony margins of the sinus as a result of hematoma formation. In some cases, inward displacement of the nasal bones can be detected. If fractures are suspected, further oblique films might be needed to highlight subtle bony changes. Trauma to the nasal bones leading to fracture is relatively common, and a deviation from normal might represent an unrelated previous injury. Identification of remodeled new bone suggests an older lesion, less likely to be the cause of hemorrhage.

Guttural Pouch

Guttural pouch lesions often cause no clinical signs other than hemorrhage. Some horses might have minor swelling in Viborg's triangle from fluid accumulation in the pouch, caudal and ventral to the angle of the jaw. Pain might also be elicited by digital pressure at the base of the conchal cartilage on the affected side. A variety of neurologic signs result from effects on the cranial nerves. The most common signs are dysphagia and pharyngeal paralysis from damage to cranial nerves IX, X, and XI (Chapter 6) and Horner's syndrome, indicating damage to the sympathetic supply as it traverses the guttural pouch. Laryngeal paralysis and abdominal pain resulting from damage to the vagus also can occur. Other signs indicating damage to cranial nerves VII (unilateral facial paralysis), V (corneal opacity), and VIII (head tilt, nystagmus, and ataxia) are reported less commonly. The most likely cause is mycotic infection with plaques on the roof of the medial compartment of the guttural pouch overlying the tympanic bulla. Lymph node enlargement (parotid or submandibular) can be associated with infections of the guttural pouch or other infections of the buccal cavity, paranasal sinuses, or pharynx.

Radiography is a valuable diagnostic aid, if guttural pouch lesions are suspected. In general, only lateral views are used routinely. In cases of severe nosebleed from suspected mycotic erosions of a major artery, the affected guttural pouch can demonstrate a fluid-air interface that cannot be distinguished from other causes such as empyema. Another important feature is evidence of nodular masses in-

denting the caudal margins of the pouch. These represent enlarged retropharyngeal lymph nodes or abscesses. The floor of the guttural pouch, which also forms the roof of the nasopharynx, is sometimes markedly thickened in cases of empyema, causing reduction in the size of the guttural pouch and nasopharynx. New bone formation and sclerosis associated with mycotic infections can also be visible at the junction of the stylohyoid bone with the petrous temporal bone.

Endoscopy is indicated for examining the guttural pouch following nasal hemorrhage. If the hemorrhage has been severe, examination should be delayed for a few days to allow at least partial clearance of blood from the guttural pouch. A small-diameter flexible or rigid endoscope can be used. The rigid endoscope allows the veterinarian to enter the auditory tube working "blind." Flexible endoscopes can be placed in the auditory tube entrance by initial insertion of a flexible probe from the biopsy port of the endoscope. The endoscope is then advanced over the guide into the pouch.

Lesions of guttural pouch mycosis are characteristic grayish white, roughened, diphtheritic plaques usually on the dorsal walls of the medial compartment, often overlying the distal section of the internal carotid artery and occasionally lying laterally over the external carotid artery or caudal auricular artery. Suction biopsy of the plaque and examination of the material by microscope will usually reveal mycelia. Other possible findings are ulcerated mass lesions from lymph node enlargement or low-grade inflammation of the mucosa. Mucopurulent material usually accompanies these bacterial infections. In cases of true empyema, the pouch is filled with purulent material, often rendering endoscopic examination impossible.

If endoscopy reveals a mycotic lesion, an angiographic contrast study is recommended to determine if an aneurysm has developed in any of the large arteries underlying the lesion. If an aneurysm is confirmed, the affected artery should be surgically ligated while the horse is still under anesthesia.

Pharynx

Examination of the pharynx should include careful evaluation of the tonsillar crypt for proliferative nodular hyperplasia, a disorder frequently seen in young horses. Nodular hyperplasia is not normally associated with hemorrhage, but can indicate an immune response to conditions such as rhinopneumonitis virus. The glottis should also be examined for lesions affecting the soft palate, arytenoid cartilages, and epiglottis. The epiglottis should be identified and its edges carefully examined for evidence of epiglottic entrapment.

Endoscopic examination of the pharynx can reveal lesions, although these are not commonly the cause of epistaxis. Ulceration of the free margin of the aryepiglottic fold as it envelops the epiglottis might be apparent. In young horses, lymphoid hyperplasia of the dorsal pharynx with nodule formation is considered a normal response to a variety of respiratory tract insults, including the common respiratory viruses. Erosive changes associated with prolapsing of hypertrophied lymphoid tissue from the pharyngeal recess could result in minor nasal blood staining. Other conditions of the pharynx leading to hemorrhage are unusual. Pharyngeal dysfunction, such as dorsal displacement of the soft palate, can, however, lead to aspiration pneumonia, which is sometimes associated with intermittent pulmonary hemorrhage.

Mouth

Examination of the mouth for causes of nasal bleeding is usually unrewarding.

Foreign bodies giving rise to small amounts of blood-flecked mucopurulent nasal discharge are recorded occasionally. Fragments of wood from small branches bitten off and wedged between the upper molars causing erosive lesions on the hard palate are found occasionally. Dental lesions affecting the upper arcade might be detected by visual examination but usually require radiographic confirmation.

Heart and Lung Sounds

Routine auscultation of the heart and lungs can occasionally provide positive confirmation of lesions, although most cases of hemorrhage originating in the lungs are not accompanied by any specific auscultatory signs. Racehorses with EIPH are generally indistinguishable from unaffected racehorses using clinical methods. Some have mildly increased airway sounds over the more caudal and dorsal lung field. In cases of lung abscess, lung sounds and percussion can be more specific, with wheezing, crackles, or dullness over affected areas. More serious conditions that only rarely induce bloody nasal discharge, such as pleuropneumonia and terminal left heart failure, have easily identifiable clinical symptoms. Ventral thoracic dullness, moist rales, and wheezing are indicative of pleuropneumonia, whereas arrhythmias or tachycardia, an enlarged cardiac zone on auscultation, jugular pulses, and sometimes loud murmurs suggest heart failure.

Lung

Endoscopy and radiography are the best initial means of investigating suspected pulmonary hemorrhage. The order in which these techniques are used depends on the horse's signs and the immediate availability of a flexible endoscope of 1.5 m or longer. In a horse that had been bleeding in the last 1 to 2 hours or that is actively bleeding at the time of examination, immediate endoscopic examination is indicated to ascertain that the hemorrhage is in fact of pulmonary origin. Pulmonary hemorrhage is confirmed if blood is detected in the trachea, particularly if it is in a thin stream on the ventral tracheal floor or running up over the epiglottis. Small amounts of blood, either in flecks or mixed with mucus, particularly if the blood is beyond the larynx, also indicates pulmonary hemorrhage.

If the hemorrhagic episode is less recent, endoscopic examination might be negative. Transtracheal aspiration or endoscopic aspiration of the tracheal mucus is indicated to verify the presence or absence of hemosiderophages (macrophages containing hemosiderin). These cells are evidence of past hemorrhage, but do not indicate the time elapsed since the most recent episode. The widely used collection technique has been well described and has minimal side effects. Generally, 50 to 60 ml of a normal saline solution is injected into the trachea. The solution comes to rest in the lowest point of the trachea at the thoracic inlet and is then aspirated immediately either from an endoscopically guided catheter or from a catheter passed through the outer sheath of the needle/cannula assembly inserted between the rings of the trachea in the midsection of the neck. Smears should be made immediately on glass slides and the remaining aspirate retained for bacteriologic and cytologic examination. The smears are stained with Gram's and Wright-Giemsa's stains.

The technique of bronchoalveolar lavage was recently adapted for use in horses. Bronchoalveolar lavage requires a long (at least 1.5 m) endoscope or cuffed narrow-bore tube. The tube or endoscope is wedged in a distal bronchus, and at least 60 ml of buffered saline solution (up to 300 ml have been used in three separate aliquots) is flushed into the bron-

chial segments. The fluid is aspirated and examined cytologically. Bronchoalveolar lavage has been found to be more sensitive than transtracheal aspiration in determining distal airway cytology and can also be used to detect evidence of past pulmonary hemorrhage.

If pulmonary hemorrhage is diagnosed by endoscopic examination, by identification of hemosiderophages on transtracheal aspiration or bronchoalveolar lavage, or in a horse with EIPH, radiographic examination of the lungs is indicated. This examination requires a high-powered machine (250 mA, 90 kv minimum rating), particularly if the more cranial and ventral portions of the lung fields are to be visualized. Four standard views from each side of the thorax are recommended for complete examination Lesions of the lung associated with hemorrhage are shown in Figure 9–3.

In EIPH, definite radiographic lesions are identified in only a small proportion of cases (10 to 20%). These lesions are diffuse bronchointerstitial opacification of the dorsocaudal angle of the lung. An alveolar pattern is also seen in some cases in the days following the hemorrhagic incident. Several weeks later, the interstitial pattern reduces, leaving a more prominent bronchial pattern with occasional linear opacities of uncertain origin.

Some cases also have dorsocaudal opacities typical of pulmonary abscesses, superimposed on the interstitial pattern. These opacities are usually seen either as poorly defined circular regions of dense interstitial opacity, or, in later stages, as well-defined circular structures often containing fluid-air interfaces. They are usually evident in the caudal lung overlying the diaphragm, ventral to the mainstem bronchi and ventral and cranial to the diffuse opacities in the dorsocaudal angles.

In many horses with a history of EIPH, a mild but equivocal increase in interstitial markings is noted in the dorsal and caudal lung fields. Some evidence indicates that this marginally increased opacification is due to increased interstitial infiltration of hemosiderophages from previous hemorrhage. Subgross and histologic evidence suggests that in long-standing lesions of EIPH, cellular infiltration of the perilobular and interstitial spaces is also accompanied by alveolar septal destruction and widespread enlargement of air spaces without bulla formation. Thus, despite increased cellularity, the volume of air retained (much of it probably trapped) maintains overall radiographic lucency in the area. Overall opacity is therefore only slightly increased.

Another lesion leading to hemorrhage less commonly is bronchopneumonia (sometimes associated with pleural effusion). Lesions are often in the ventral lung fields, with a markedly increased alveolar and interstitial pattern masking the normal lung pattern. Bleeding from pneumonic lesions is most likely in the presence of accompanying abscesses. Because pleural effusion is not associated with a fluid-gas interface, ultrasonography might be required to separate the similar radiographic appearances of effusion and ventral lung consolidation from bronchopneumonia. Aspiration pneumonia gives a similar radiographic appearance and should be suspected following any history of choke or recent anesthesia. Patchy pneumonia in other areas of the lung is more readily diagnosed.

Unfortunately, radiographic evaluation of the lungs for hemorrhage, particularly EIPH, is unrewarding in more than half of cases. In addition, radiographs provide information about only the structure of the lung lesions; any conclusions on function have to be deduced by association with previous autopsy information, which remains incomplete.

Lung function can, however, be determined by scintigraphy using a gamma camera and short-lived radioisotopes. Suitable facilities for ventilation-perfusion evaluation are now available in a few referral institutions, mainly those associated with university veterinary teaching hospitals. Although radioactive gases such as xenon and krypton, widely used in human lung imaging, are not practical for the study of ventilation in horses, recent advances in the production of satisfactory radioaerosols of technetium-99m has led to the development of practical methods to determine regional ventilation function in clinical cases. Regional perfusion of the lung is readily demonstrated by imaging after intravenous injection of technetium-99m attached to macroaggregated albumin, which lodges in the pulmonary capillaries. The most recent developments in image analysis allow production of ventilation-perfusion ratio images of the whole lung and generation of numeric data for areas of deficit. Although these techniques have only recently been introduced to clinical diagnosis, results on a variety of pulmonary conditions have demonstrated their sensitivity to mild changes not evident on radiographs. Correlation of scan results with autopsy studies of EIPH cases not only has demonstrated ventilatory deficits in the dorsocaudal lung fields, but has identified even more serious deficits in the pulmonary arterial supply to the caudal lung field. Histologic evidence from similar cases suggests that bronchial proliferation with functional displacement of the pulmonary supply from this area of the lung is probably the cause of the deficits in pulmonary arterial supply. These preliminary findings indicate that for cases of EIPH or other pulmonary hemorrhage with no evidence of radiographic abnormality, pulmonary scintigraphy can provide valuable functional information.

TREATMENT

Treatment of most of the common hemorrhagic lesions of the upper airways, paranasal sinuses, and guttural pouches requires some form of surgical intervention. In conditions causing partial obstruction of the upper airways, a tracheostomy might also be required to provide temporary relief until the primary condition is treated. (Detailed description of these procedures is beyond the scope of this text; the reader is referred to specialized surgical texts and articles in the supplemental reading list.)

NASAL CAVITY

Nasal cavity masses, foreign bodies, or septic erosions usually require removal of the mass or inciting cause under anesthesia, followed by some form of cautery to control hemorrhage in the highly vascular turbinate mucosa. Severe cases might require extensive resection of the turbinates and surrounding tissues. Access is gained through the nares for more rostral and minor lesions or by a nasal bone flap on the dorsal midline.

PARANASAL SINUSES

Paranasal sinus lesions invariably require some form of surgical exposure to remove progressive hematomas, cystic structures, or other masses and to establish drainage. Two main approaches are used. In uncomplicated sinusitis, drainage and irrigation with antibacterial or antifungal preparations is readily achieved by trephination into either the cranial or the caudal compartments of the maxillary sinus and into the rostral extremity of the frontal sinus. The frontal site often serves mainly as an entry point for irrigation fluid and for improved visualization of the sinus contents. Following surgery, the sinuses are flushed with an antimicrobial solution such as 5% povidone-iodine, initially in large volumes, then two or three times a day until the trephine sites close. The key to successful resolution is to re-establish normal drainage of the sinus into the nasal cavity through the nasomaxillary opening.

The second method uses a bone flap procedure for more extensive exposure of the sinus for removal of masses, cysts, or granulomas. Techniques for resecting abnormal tissue vary, but generally involve extensive dissection, curettage, aspiration, flushing, and in some cases cautery of the mucosa. For progressive ethmoid hematomas and cysts, removing all the affected material from the ethmoid labyrinth can prove difficult, even with extensive curettage and flushing. Regrowth can occur in 6 months to 2 years in some cases, but can be controlled by repeated surgery.

Fractures involving the paranasal sinuses and nasal cavity are usually impacted. Most are also compound or open fractures because only a thin layer of mucosa separates the overlying bone from the nasal cavity or paranasal sinus, both of which are contaminated spaces. In most cases, conservative treatment with suitable antimicrobial therapy is satisfactory. When impaction is severe, surgical decompression might be needed to alleviate airway obstruction or reduce facial deformity.

Periapical abscesses and other tooth-root infections usually require repulsion of the tooth into the mouth. The tooth root is exposed through a trephine site or by creating a bone flap in the maxillary sinus. Numerous techniques for performing the surgery and avoiding contamination of the sinus with food material following removal of the tooth have been described elsewhere.

GUTTURAL POUCH

Guttural pouch lesions require vigorous therapy. If in mycotic infection an aneurysm is present, surgical ligation of the offending artery proximal to the lesion is necessary. Some veterinarians have recommended ligation on both sides of the lesion because anastomoses partially maintain pressure, but ligation is usually unnecessary. Successful occlusion of the internal carotid artery has also been achieved by balloon catheter, but this technique is more involved than ligation techniques. As in paranasal sinus lesions, irrigation of the guttural pouch with antimicrobial solutions to remove secretions and reduce the number of microbial agents is important in controlling septic conditions. However, owing to the risk of damaging exposed nerve tissue in the pouch, concentrated irrigation solutions should be avoided. Diluted povidone-iodine solution (1%) has been recommended. A self-retaining catheter should be placed in the auditory tube to drain irrigation fluid into the nasal cavity and to maintain an effective airway between the guttural pouch and nasal pharynx. Air exchange promoted by respiratory movement is the most effective way of controlling mycotic infections. The catheter can be left in place for 1 to 2 weeks to ensure patency of the auditory tube (see also Chapter 8). In cases of strangles abscesses, antibiotic therapy with a suitable penicillin is indicated.

Opinions on the surgical approach to the guttural pouch vary. Although entry through Viborg's triangle facilities removal of foreign material such as chondroids and allows temporary drainage of the space by gravity, complications from nerve damage are reportedly more common than when a lateral approach ventral to the linguofacial vein is used. The prognosis for guttural pouch lesions must always be guarded, especially if the horse has signs of neurologic deficits. Experience has shown that damage to nerves, particularly those controlling glutition, is often permanent, carrying with it the risk of inhalation pneumonia. Follow-up should therefore include careful evaluation of the lung for developing aspiration pneumonia.

PHARYNX

Of the pharyngeal lesions, only epiglottic entrapment is likely to require surgical intervention, and is a rare cause of epistaxis. Two main methods are described: a full surgical approach through a laryngotomy, a pharyngotomy, or the oral cavity; or use of a flexible endoscope with the horse under sedation. Usually all that is required is trimming of the aryepiglottic fold overlying the epiglottis.

LUNG

Lung lesions leading to hemorrhage are generally treated by medical means. Treatment of EIPH is the most problematic. Treatment regimens aimed at prophylactically avoiding the condition have been largely empiric, because the exact cause of EIPH is not known and, until recently, evidence on the pathogenesis was only fragmentary. Furosemide pretreatment is routinely employed in some states of the U.S., despite the absence of a rationale for its use. Opinions on the efficacy of furosemide vary considerably. At present no evidence indicates that furosemide is effective in preventing EIPH. Recent studies suggest that performance can be improved in some horses, but the number of animals evaluated is small. Because the racing and training management of many furosemide-treated horses suffering EIPH is altered, often by improving stable hygiene, pretreatment and post-treatment comparisons are difficult. Until more research into the actual pathogenesis and cause is performed, treatment regimens with furosemide will continue to be empiric, based on little satisfactory evidence for its continued use.

Other treatments suggested in the literature include supplementing feed with hesperidin and citrus bioflavinoids for their supposed strengthening of capillary integrity. No evidence supports their use, however. Similarly, conjugated estrogens and other agents that accelerate blood clotting, such as oxalic and malonic acids, have been used to treat bleeding, despite lack of evidence that clotting disorders contribute to the condition. Bronchodilators have been used based on suggestions that small-airways disease contributes to EIPH. Indeed, recent detailed autopsy evidence indicates that chronic small-airways disease with accompanying multifocal enlargement of air spaces in the dorsocaudal lung fields occurs in EIPH. Other important findings are intense focal, peribronchiolar proliferation of the bronchial arterial circulation and large accumulations of hemosiderophages in both the interstitium and alveolar air spaces. While many of the small-airway changes are probably secondary to the noxious effects of macrophage infiltration in response to previous hemorrhage, evidence indicates that small foci of bronchiolitis are also the primary site of hemorrhage. Based on these findings, treatments such as bronchodilators and mucolytics aimed at improving small-airway function might be more appropriate than the variety of therapeutic agents currently employed. Because inhaled dust, particularly from hay and straw, might be involved in the cause of equine small-airways disease, environmental improvement should be considered in the management of these cases (see Chapter 7).

Lung abscesses are best treated with antimicrobials selected on the basis of culture and sensitivity, determined from transtracheal aspiration samples. Serial radiographs also are useful in following the progress of these cases. Similar treatment regimens are indicated for bronchopneumonia and pleuropneumonia. For pleuropneumonia, drainage of the pleural cavity is recommended if the pleural fluid is purulent, contains visible bacteria on Gram's stain, shows large quantities of floccular or fibrinous material by ultrasonography, or causes severe dyspnea. Thoracic fluid is drained either by placing an indwelling tube aseptically and tunneling subcutaneously, or by repeatedly inserting a drain every 2 to 3 days. Thoracostomy is indicated only for severe septic pleuritis with abscessation.

SUPPLEMENTAL READING

Boulton, C.H.: Equine nasal cavity and paranasal sinus disease: A review of 85 cases. Equine Vet. Sci., 5:268, 1985.

Cook, W.R.: Diseases of the auditive tube diverticulum (guttural pouch). *In* Current Therapy in Equine Medicine. 2nd ed. Edited by N.E. Robinson. Philadelphia, W.B. Saunders, 1987, p. 612.

Farrow, C.S.: Radiography of the equine thorax: Anatomy and technique. Vet. Radiol., 22:62, 1981.

Gibbs, C., and Lane, J.G.: Radiographic examination of the facial, nasal and paranasal sinus regions of the horse. II. Radiological findings. Equine Vet. J., 19:474, 1987.

Haynes, P.F.: Dorsal displacement of the soft palate and epiglottic entrapment: Diagnosis, management and interrelationship. Compend. Contin. Educ., 5:S379, 1983.

Lane, J.G., Gibbs, C., Meynink, S.E., and Steele, F.C.: Radiographic examination of the facial, nasal and paranasal sinus regions of the horse. I. Indications and procedures in 235 cases. Equine Vet. J. 19:466, 1987.

Lattimer, J.C.: Equine nasal passages, sinuses and guttural pouches. *In* Textbook of Veterinary Diagnostic Radiology. Edited by D.E. Thrall. Philadelphia, W.B. Saunders, 1986.

O'Callaghan, M.W., Hornof, W.J., Fisher, P.E., and Pascoe, J.R.: Exercise-induced pulmonary haemorrhage in the horse: A detailed clinical, post mortem and imaging study. VII. Ventilation/perfusion scintigraphy in horses with EIPH. Equine Vet. J., 19:423, 1987.

O'Callaghan, M.W., Pascoe, J.R., Tyler, W.S., and Mason, D.K.: Exercise-induced pulmonary haemorrhage in the horse: A detailed clinical, post mortem and imaging study. III. Subgross findings in lungs subjected to latex perfusions of the bronchial and pulmonary arteries. Equine Vet. J., 19:394, 1987.

Pascoe, J.R., et al: Exercise-induced pulmonary hemorrhage in racing Thoroughbreds: A preliminary study. Am. J. Vet. Res., 42:703, 1981.

Pascoe, J.R., O'Brien, T.R., Wheat, J.D., and Meagher, D.M.: Radiographic aspects of exercise-induced pulmonary hemorrhage in racing horses. Vet. Radiol., 24:85, 1983.

Pascoe, J.R., and Raphel, C.F.: Pulmonary hemorrhage in exercising horses. Compend. Contin. Educ., 4:S411, 1982.

Scott, E.A.: Surgery of the oral cavity. Vet. Clin. North Am. (Large Anim. Pract.), 4:3, 1982.

Sweeney, C.F.: Endoscopic findings in the upper respiratory tract of 479 horses. J. Am. Vet. Med. Assoc., 181:470, 1982.

Sweeney, C.F.: Pleuropneumonia. In Current Therapy in Equine Medicine. 2nd ed. Edited by N.E. Robinson. Philadelphia, W.B. Saunders, 1987, 592.

Sweeney, C.F., and Soma, L.R.: Exercise-induced pulmonary hemorrhage in Thoroughbred horses: Response in furosemide and hesperidin-citrus bioflavinoids. J. Am. Vet. Med. Assoc., 185:195, 1984.

Tobin, T., Roberts, B.L., Swerczek, T.W., and Crisman, M.: The pharmacology of furosemide in the horse. III. Dose and time relationships, effects of repeated dosing and performance effects. J. Equine Med. Surg. 2:216, 1978.

Whitwell, K.E., and Greet, T.R.C.: Collection and evaluation of tracheobronchial washes in the horse. Equine Vet. J., 16:499, 1984.

chapter 10

HEART MURMURS, IRREGULARITIES, AND OTHER CARDIAC ABNORMALITIES

Virginia B. Reef

NORMAL HEART

The horse's heart is different from that of other domestic animals in many ways. Its large size and slow resting heartbeat result in physiologic flow murmurs and normal arrhythmias. From 2 to 4 heart sounds can be auscultated in a normal horse, and split heart sounds are common. At maximum performance the horse's heart rate can be greater than six to ten times its resting rate. A thorough knowledge of the normal horse's heart is necessary to determine the presence of cardiac disease and to accurately diagnose the problem.

LOCATION

The location of the heart within the thorax determines where percussion and auscultation are performed. The heart is located in the cranioventral portion of the thorax from the second to sixth intercostal spaces between the points of the shoulder and elbow. The axis of the equine heart is primarily cranial to caudal, with the right ventricle being cranial and the left ventricle being caudal.

Percussion helps to delineate the heart's size. The normal cardiac silhouette can be percussed as an area of dullness from the left fourth intercostal space, level with the point of the shoulder at the caudal border of the triceps muscle caudally and ventrally, to the sixth intercostal space, level with the point of the elbow. The area of cardiac dullness is smaller on the right side and extends dorsally from the level of the point of the elbow for 5 to 8 cm in an arc in the fourth intercostal space. Placing the horse's foreleg more cranially might facilitate percussion, especially on the right side. These areas for percussion vary somewhat with the size and shape of the thorax.

Auscultation of the cardiac valves on the thoracic wall helps localize heart sounds and murmurs. The mitral valve area is located in the left fifth intercostal space midway between the level of the points of the elbow and shoulder. The aortic valve area is found in the left fourth intercostal space underneath the caudal border of the triceps muscle just below the level of the point of the shoulder. One interspace more cranial (the third intercostal space) and slightly more ventral is the pulmonic valve area. The tricuspid valve area can also be auscultated from the left side in the second or third intercostal space midway between the level of the points of the shoulder and elbow. However, the tricuspid valve area is more easily auscultated from the right third to fourth intercostal space halfway between the level of the points of the shoulder and elbow, deep to the triceps brachii muscle.

the contained blood. From two to four heart sounds are associated with normal hemodynamic processes. The first heart sound (S_1) is a long, loud, low-pitched sound heard best over the mitral and tricuspid valve areas and toward the apex. It occurs at the onset of mechanical systole, simultaneously with the apex beat, and is immediately followed by the arterial pulse. The components of S_1 include the initial movement of the ventricle, followed by atrioventricular (AV) valve closure, the opening of the semilunar valves, and the initial ejection of blood. This sound can be split.

The second heart sound (S_2), usually shorter, softer, and higher-pitched than S_1, is heard best over the aortic and pulmonic valves and the great vessels. It is caused primarily by the closure of the semilunar valves and the rapid reversal of blood flow. The opening of the AV valves also contributes to S_2. S_2 can vary with respiration in normal horses and can be split.

The third heart sound (S_3) is a low-amplitude sound heard best over the cardiac apex. S_3 is associated with the end of the rapid filling phase and with deceleration of the rapidly filling ventricle; it occurs usually 0.14 to 0.17 seconds after S_2 in approximately half of normal horses.

The fourth heart sound (S_4) is associated with atrial contraction and atrioventricular blood flow. The later component is associated with transient AV valve closure and sudden checking of ventricular distension. The fourth heart sound is audible in most resting horses when their PR interval exceeds 0.28 seconds. Isolated S_4 can be heard in normal horses with second-degree AV block at rest.

HEART SOUNDS

Heart sounds are produced by vibrations of the heart and great vessels and by sudden accelerations and decelerations of

HEART MURMURS

Heart murmurs are prolonged audible vibrations occurring during a normally silent period of the cardiac cycle.

Functional or physiologic murmurs can occur in the absence of organic heart disease; abnormal murmurs are associated with obstruction to forward flow, regurgitant flow through an incompetent valve, or flow through an intracardiac or extracardiac shunt. Murmurs are described according to timing, intensity, radiation, and quality (Fig. 10–1).

FUNCTIONAL MURMURS

Low-intensity (grade III/VI or less), soft, decrescendo or crescendo-decrescendo, early systolic to holosystolic murmurs located over the aortic to pulmonic value areas are typical functional murmurs. These murmurs can be heard in up to 66% of normal horses and are thought to

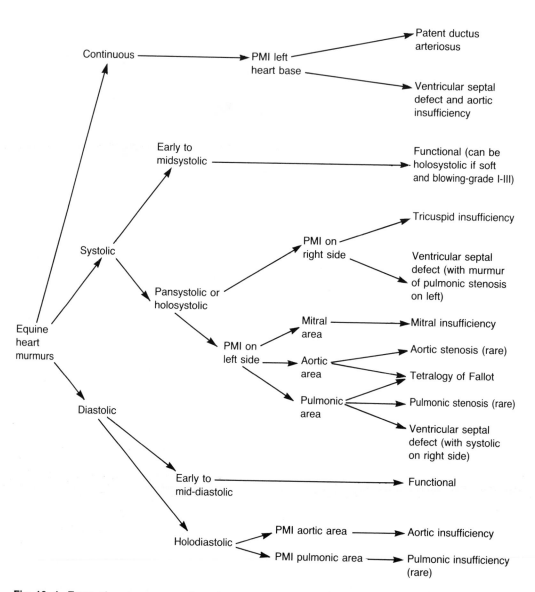

Fig. 10–1. Types of equine murmurs, based on their timing, intensity, radiation, and quality. (PMI = point of maximum intensity.)

be associated with the rapid ejection of blood in early systole. Exercise associated with an increased stroke volume makes these murmurs louder in some horses and makes them disappear in other horses.

Soft, early diastolic, decescendo murmurs (grade III/VI or less) usually occur between S_2 and S_3 in association with rapid ventricular filling. Musical, squeaky, early diastolic murmurs that are best heard in the mitral and aortic valve areas also can be auscultated between S_2 and S_3 and detected intermittently. These sounds are thought to be associated with rapid atrioventricular blood flow. The early diastolic squeaks are most common in 2- and 3-year-olds, although they have been heard in horses up to 5 years of age.

Presystolic murmurs occur between S_4 and S_1, are usually low-pitched, rumbling murmurs, and are associated with atrial vibrations.

Any horse with a murmur that does not meet the above criteria should be evaluated for the existence of organic heart disease. Continuous murmurs (occurring throughout systole and diastole), holodiastolic murmurs, and holosystolic or pansystolic murmurs that are grade III-IV/VI or greater, coarse, and of uniform intensity are probably caused by underlying cardiac disease.

MURMURS CAUSED BY CONGENITAL CARDIAC DISEASE

Although congenital cardiac disease is detected most commonly in foals and young horses, older horses also can present with congenital cardiac abnormalities.

Two-dimensional echocardiography is the technique of choice for determining the malformations that exist in foals with intracardiac defects. Contrast and Doppler echocardiography are useful in deter-

mining the path of abnormal blood flow in these hearts. Electrocardiography and radiology add little in the accurate diagnosis of congenital cardiac disease because they are insensitive and nonspecific.

Ventricular Septal Defect

A grade III-IV/VI, coarse, band-shaped, pansystolic murmur loudest over the right cranioventral thorax in the third to fourth intercostal space is characteristic of a ventricular septal defect (VSD). This murmur usually radiates widely over the right side, and a precordial thrill (grade IV–VI/VI) is usually palpable. A similar murmur (grade III–VI/VI) is usually auscultated over the left heart base, with the point of greatest intensity over the pulmonic valve area. This murmur is associated with increased flow across a normal pulmonic valve (relative pulmonic stenosis). The murmur on the right side is usually louder, associated with shunting of blood from the left to the right ventricle through the VSD. A murmur on the left side that is as loud or louder than that detected on the right can occur with an uncomplicated VSD but might be a feature of a more complex congenital cardiac defect like tetralogy of Fallot. If the relative pulmonic stenosis murmur cannot be auscultated, tricuspid regurgitation is likely.

VSDs are the most common congenital cardiac malformation in the foal. The clinical signs exhibited by the foal and the prognosis are determined by the size an location of the VSD. An animal with small defects might grow normally and perform successfully. With larger defects the foal might grow poorly, have exercise intolerance or weakness, or develop congestive heart failure.

Two-dimensional echocardiography is the most sensitive and specific diagnostic technique available to the practitioner for evaluating foals with VSDs. Pulsed-wave Doppler echocardiography can also be used to delineate the direction and location of the abnormal blood flow. The VSD, usually located in the membranous septum underneath the septal leaflet of the tricuspid valve and the right coronary cusp of the aortic valve, is imaged as a drop-out or lack of echoes from this region of the heart. VSDs that measure 2.5 cm in diameter or smaller are usually associated with normal growth and performance. Larger VSDs are usually associated with a volume-overloaded left ventricle and poor growth and performance.

Right-sided cardiac catheterization with measurements of pressure and oxygen saturation have also been used to diagnose a VSD. An increase in right ventricular pressure and partial oxygen tension is seen with larger defects. Elevated right ventricular pressure is also a feature of other complex congenital cardiac defects.

Tetralogy of Fallot

The loudest murmur detected in horses with tetralogy of Fallot is usually a grade IV–VI/VI, coarse, band-shaped, pansystolic murmur with the point of maximal intensity (PMI) over the left heart base. A prominent precordial thrill is usually present. A similar, almost equally loud murmur is usually heard over the right cardiac silhouette. Cyanosis is present infrequently, although affected foals usually grow poorly and have decreased exercise tolerance. Clinical signs usually develop at an early age (before 1 year). The severity of the clinical signs depends on the size of the VSD and the degree of right ventricular outflow tract obstruction. Prognosis for survival is poor.

Polycythemia is frequently present along with decreased arterial oxygen saturation owing to the right-to-left shunting of blood. Cardiac catheterization reveals elevated right ventricular

pressures similar to left ventricular and aortic pressures. Right atrial and pulmonary atrial pressures are normal.

Two-dimensional echocardiography coupled with contrast echocardiography allows all portions of the defect to be successfully imaged. The VSD is usually large (> 3 cm) and located in the membranous portion of the septum. The aorta is displaced to the right and overrides the interventricular septum. The hypertrophied right ventricle has a thickened free wall and enlarged chamber. The right ventricular outflow tract obstruction is often a hypoplastic pulmonary artery or pulmonic stenosis.

Contrast echocardiography, using aerated saline, results in simultaneous opacification of the right ventricle, left ventricle, and aorta with a right-sided injection, confirming the right to left shunt.

Tricuspid Atresia

A loud (grade IV–VI/VI), coarse, crescendo-decrescendo murmur loudest over the left heart base is characteristic of tricuspid atresia. Affected foals usually exhibit severe exercise intolerance beginning at birth, rarely moving faster than a trot and often collapsing. These foals are severely stunted by several months of age and are usually cyanotic, with weak pulses and rapid labored respiration. Venous distension is common. Prognosis for survival is grave.

Polycythemia and low arterial oxygen tension are associated with the right to left shunt. Elevated right atrial pressures and similar ventricular pressures are detected with cardiac catheterization. The atretic tricuspid valve can be imaged echocardiographically as a band of tissue where the tricuspid valve should be. The other components of the defect include an atrial septal defect (usually a patent foramen ovale), a VSD, a hypoplastic right ventricle, and an enlarged mitral valve and left ventricle, all of which can be imaged with two-dimensional echocardiography. The flow of blood from right atrium to left atrium to left ventricle and simultaneously to the right ventricle and aorta can be demonstrated with contrast echocardiography.

Patent Ductus Arteriosus

Systolic murmurs are commonly auscultated in neonatal foals up to 4 days of age. These murmurs, associated with blood flow through a patent ductus arteriosus (PDA), are considered abnormal when detected after 4 days of age. Continuous murmurs associated with a PDA can be auscultated in normal foals but usually disappear within 24 hours of birth. These systolic and continuous murmurs are usually loudest over the left heart base.

A continuous machinery murmur, grade III–VI/VI, loudest over the left heart base, is typical of a PDA. The diastolic portion is usually localized to the left third or fourth intercostal space at the level of the point of the shoulder. The systolic component often radiates more widely. The arterial pulses are hyperkinetic, rising and declining rapidly. Foals with large PDAs might develop congestive heart failure early in life, whereas horses with small PDAs might not develop clinical signs until later in life.

Cardiac catheterization reveals an increased pressure and elevated partial oxygen saturation in the pulmonary artery. Two-dimensional echocardiographic diagnosis is difficult because the ductus is hard to image. Often, only left atrial and ventricular volume overload are detected. Doppler echocardiography (both pulsed and continuous wave) has been used successfully in foals to document the direction and velocity of blood through a PDA. Surgical correction of a PDA would be possible if the ductus remained patent.

Other Defects

Many other congenital cardiac defects have been reported in horses, most frequently in Arabians. Some of these include truncus arteriosus, pseudotruncus arteriosus, pentalogy of Fallot, malformations and stenosis of the semilunar valves, persistent foramen ovale, abnormalities of the aortic arch, transposition of the great vessels, cor triloculare biatriatum, pulmonary atresia, and double-outlet right ventricle.

MURMURS CAUSED BY ACQUIRED CARDIAC ABNORMALITIES

Acquired abnormalities, like congenital abnormalities, can lead to valvular insufficiency in foals as well as adults. Therefore, careful assessment of the history, clinical signs, physical examination, and auscultatory findings is necessary to arrive at the most likely diagnosis (Fig. 10–1). Echocardiography can then be used to confirm the diagnosis.

Aortic Insufficiency

A grade II–VI/VI, holodiastolic, decrescendo murmur with the PMI at the aortic valve area, radiating to the left cardiac apex, is typical of aortic insufficiency (AI). The murmur can be musical or noisy. Bounding arterial pulses indicate significant aortic regurgitation, and the pulses become more hyperkinetic as the left ventricular volume overload becomes more severe. Although aortic regurgitation can occur in horses of any age, it is most common in older horses and associated with degenerative changes of the aortic valve. The prognosis for life and performance is good. Infrequent performance problems occur with concurrent mitral regurgitation. The cause of death is not usually cardiac disease, unless mitral regurgitation leads to congestive heart failure.

AI can be diagnosed by the detection of the characteristic murmur with hyperkinetic arterial pulses. Echocardiographic evaluation reveals a left ventricular volume overload. High-frequency vibrations of the septal leaflet of the mitral valve are typically detected, resulting from the turbulence caused by the regurgitant jet. High-frequency vibrations are seen less frequently on the aortic valve cusps occurring with a rupture, fenestrations, or prolapse of an aortic valve leaflet. High-frequency vibrations of the interventricular septum might also be identified.

Pulsed-wave Doppler echocardiography can be used to determine the area of the regurgitant jet, as the incompetence of the valve leaflets is neither easy to image nor a sensitive indicator of AI. Thickening of the aortic valve cusps is commonly seen as a nodular or fibrous band parallel to the free edge of the cusp. Nodular lesions, prolapse, and vegetative endocarditis are less frequently detected. However, vegetative endocarditis should be considered in any horse with a history of fever, as the aortic valve is one of the common sites for bacterial endocarditis.

Pathologic studies indicate that degenerative changes of the aortic valve, nodules, fibrous bands, and plaques are the most common valvular lesion in horses. Fenestrations of the aortic valve are common but are often incidental findings. Congenital malformations of the aortic valve occurs infrequently, but AI can be seen in horses with VSDs associated with a prolapse of an aortic leaflet into the VSD.

Mitral Insufficiency

A grade III–VI/VI, coarse, band-shaped, pansystolic murmur with the point of greatest intensity over the mitral valve area radiating to the left heart base is typical of mitral insufficiency (MI). The murmur is often loudest in the aortic valve area in horses with severe MI, as the murmur radiates in the direction of the regurgitant flow. The murmur can be crescendo and holosystolic, as in mitral valve prolapse, or honking, as in ruptured chorda tendineae. Arterial pulses are usually normal unless congestive heart failure is present. Coarse vesicular sounds, end-inspiratory crackles, or wheezes can be auscultated with severe MI and pulmonary edema. Atrial fibrillation is frequently present in horses with severe left atrial enlargement. Tachycardia and tachypnea is common with severe MI. A loud third heart sound might be detected with a large left ventricular volume overload.

Clinical signs vary with the acuteness and degree of regurgitation. When the clinical course is slowly progressive, the initial signs include decreased performance, increased respiratory rate and effort during exercise with prolonged recovery to resting state, and coughing. The next signs, frequently detected as the horse develops congestive heart failure, are venous distension, jugular pulsations, and ventral edema. Frothy fluid is rarely seen in the nares or expectorated unless the mitral regurgitation is acute and severe. In these horses, severe respiratory distress with increased respiratory rate and effort, coughing at rest, weak arterial pulses, prolonged capillary refill times, cool extremities, and cyanosis are characteristic. Death from congestive heart failure or rupture of the pulmonary artery is common. Horses of all ages can be affected, with older horses more frequently having slowly progressive clinical signs. Severe acute MI has been reported in foals, as well as adults, most commonly associated with a ruptured chorda tendineae.

Echocardiographic diagnosis of MI is best when coupled with pulsed-wave Doppler mapping of the regurgitant jet. Left atrial and left ventricular volume overload become more marked as the regurgitation worsens. Because no changes in left atrial or ventricular chamber size are detectable with mild MI, pulsed-wave Doppler echocardiography is needed to confirm the existence of a regurgitant jet. Thickening of the valve leaflets is seen frequently with chronic MI. Mitral valve prolapse (a bulging of the valve leaflet into the left atrium during systole) often is associated with mild MI, whereas ruptured chordae tendineae or vegetative endocarditis frequently cause acute severe regurgitation. Echocardiographic detection of a dilated pulmonary artery is a bad prognostic sign in horses with MI and indicates existing or impending congestive heart failure.

Degenerative changes in the mitral valve are common; MI can also occur secondary to severe left ventricular dysfunction or bacterial endocarditis. Congenital abnormalities of the mitral valve are rare.

Treatment of horses with congestive heart failure usually includes digoxin and furosemide (Table 10–1). Afterload reducers might be helpful in improving cardiac output, but little pharmacokinetic data is available on the use of these drugs in horses. Promazine appears to be a safe and effective vasodilator and can be administered orally in the feed. Life expectancy for severely affected horses is short even with symptomatic therapy.

Tricuspid Insufficiency

Murmurs of tricuspid insufficiency (TI) are usually a grade III–VI/VI, holosystolic or pansystolic, coarse, and band-shaped. These murmurs are heard best over the tricuspid valve area and radiate over the right cardiac silhouette. Honking murmurs indicating a ruptured chorda tendineae are auscultated infrequently. Jugular pulsations, venous distension, and ventral edema occur as the horse develops congestive heart failure. Pleural effusion and hepatic congestion occur with advanced congestive heart failure. Atrial fibrillation can occur.

TABLE 10–1. DRUGS USED FOR THE TREATMENT OF EQUINE CARDIOVASCULAR DISEASE

Drug	Dose (mg/kg)	Clearance Rate (hr)	Side Effects
Digoxin*	20 μg/kg/24 hr PO 6 μg/kg/ 24 hr IV dosage usually divided and given BID	18–23 hrs	Depression, anorexia, weakness, lethargy, diarrhea, colic, cardiac arrhythmias
Furosemide	0.5–2.0 mg/kg IV, IM 1.0– 2.0 mg/kg PO usually given BID or as needed	0.5 hr	Dehydration, hyponatremia, hypokalemia, metabolic alkalosis, prerenal azotemia, tachycardia
Quidinine	20 mg/kg Q 2 hrs to 60 g (quinidine sulfate) PO 0.25–0.5 mg/kg to 5 g IV (quinidine gluconate) usually given q 10–20 minutes or as needed	5–7 hrs	Depression, diarrhea, laminitis urticaria, ataxia, convulsions, nasal mucosal swelling, hypotension, cardiac arrhythmia prolongation of QRS, >25%
Lidocaine	0.25–1.0 mg/kg to effect, up to 2.0 mg/kg total dose	3 hrs	Excitement, convulsions, hypotension
Propranolol	0.25–1.0 mg/kg to effect	1.7 hrs	Hypotension, bradycardia

* When used to treat congestive heart failure, digoxin's toxicity must be carefully monitored.

Horses of any age can be affected. Prognosis varies with the degree of regurgitation. Some horses can compete acceptably with mild TI. However, the presence of venous distension and jugular pulsations indicates advanced regurgitation and a poor prognosis.

In advanced cases, diagnosis can be made from the clinical signs. Echocardiographic confirmation is needed in horses without jugular pulsations. Right atrial and ventricular volume overloads are usually detected unless the regurgitation is mild. In these cases, pulsed-wave Doppler echocardiography confirms the presence of the regurgitant jet. In more advanced TI, paradoxical septal motion is present, associated with the large right ventricular overload. Changes on the tricuspid valve, seen less frequently, include thickening, prolapse, ruptured chordae tendineae, and vegetative endocarditis.

Tricuspid regurgitation occurs less frequently than MI and is often secondary to MI and congestive heart failure. Treatment is similar for horses with MI and congestive heart failure (Table 10–1). Congenital lesions are rare.

Other Defects

Other valvular abnormalities occur infrequently in horses. Pulmonic insufficiency can occur in horses with signs of left-sided congestive heart failure, but rarely can a murmur be auscultated. Congenital stenosis of the AV or semilunar valves is rare but can occur with bacterial endocarditis.

IRREGULARITIES OF CARDIAC RHYTHM

CYCLIC AND REGULAR VARIATIONS

Cardiac arrhythmias are seen at normal or slow heart rates and should disappear with exercise or excitement when the horse develops a sinus tachycardia. At rest, the horse most frequently has a sinus rhythm, with a heart rate of 26 to 50 beats/minute. The overall classification and features of equine arrhythmias are shown in Figure 10–2.

Second-Degree Atrioventricular Block

The most common arrhythmia associated with high vagal tone is second-degree atrioventricular block. This is seen in 15 to 20% of normal horses. Ausculation reveals a relatively regular slow rhythm with occasional isolated fourth heart sounds. The isolated S_4 occurs in a pause approximately equal to two diastolic periods. The S_4 is also typically heard immediately preceding S_1. With the Wenckebach type of second-degree AV block, a gradual prolongation of the time between S_4 and S_1 can be auscultated before a beat is dropped. Although the Wenckebach type of second-degree AV block is more common, Mobitz type II second-degree AV block (fixed interval between S_4 and S_1) is also found in normal horses. Occasionally, two beats can be dropped in succession.

An electrocardiogram (ECG) reveals occasional P waves not followed by QRS and T complexes (Fig. 10–3). Mobitz I type block has a gradual prolongation of the PR interval, while a fixed PR interval is characteristic of Mobitz type II block. Second-degree AV block can also occasionally be seen at higher heart rates immediately after exercise, associated with changing autonomic tone.

Sinus Arrhythmia

Sinus arrhythmia is a less frequent manifestation of high resting vagal tone and is usually associated with bradycardia (heart rate less than 26 beats/minute). Sinus arrhythmia is associated with a waxing and waning of vagal tone and can vary with respiration (rate increases during inspi-

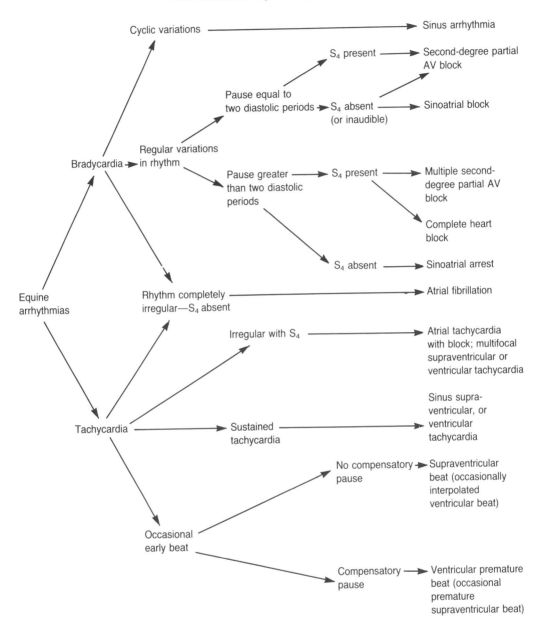

Fig. 10–2. Types of equine arrhythmias, based on heart rate and auscultatory findings.

ration). From 2 to 4 heart sounds can be auscultated; frequently all four heart sounds are heard owing to the slow heart rate. The P, QRS, and T complexes are normal, with the RR intervals varying cyclically. A wandering sinus or atrial pacemaker (variations in the configuration of the P wave) is often seen on the ECG in horses with sinus arrhythmia.

Sinoatrial Block or Arrest

High resting vagal tone infrequently causes sinoatrial block or arrest. Sinoatrial block

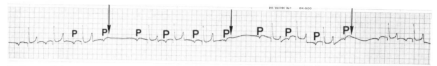

Fig. 10–3. Second-degree partial atrioventricular block. Several P waves are not followed by QRS and T complexes (arrows).

occurs when the PP interval is twice the duration of preceding or subsequent beats (Fig. 10–4). Sinoatrial arrest occurs when the PP interval is greater than twice the duration of preceding or subsequent beats. Affected horses usually have a sinus arrhythmia, and auscultation reveals a diastolic pause equal to two beats (block) or greater than two beats (arrest). No S_4 can be auscultated during the pause, as atrial contraction does not occur. From two to four heart sounds can be associated with each heartbeat. In normal horses, these vagally mediated arrhythmias should be seen only at normal to slow heart rates and should disappear with exercise, excitement, or atropine administration.

IRREGULARITIES AFFECTING PERFORMANCE

Atrial Fibrillation

Atrial fibrillation is the most common arrhythmia affecting performance in horses, with exercise intolerance the most frequent complaint. Other presenting signs include exercise-induced pulmonary hemorrhage, tachypnea, collapse, congestive heart failure, myopathy, and colic. The arrhythmia can also be detected as an incidental finding during a routine physical examination. Atrial fibrillation most commonly occurs in the absence of detectable cardiac disease. However, the presence of other underlying cardiac disease (usually mitral insufficiency) needs to be ruled out.

Completely irregular cardiac rhythm with heart sounds and arterial pulses of variable intensity is characteristic of atrial fibrillation. A fourth heart sound is not detectable. The ECG reveals baseline fibrillation (f) waves with irregularly spaced but normally configured QRS and T complexes. No P waves are seen (Fig. 10–5). The detection of a grade III/VI or louder heart murmur, a resting heart rate in excess of 60 beats/minute, or signs of congestive heart failure all indicate the presence of significant underlying cardiac disease.

Treatment of atrial fibrillation depends on the severity of the underlying cardiac disease, the duration of the arrhythmia, and the intended use of the horse. Horses with atrial fibrillation and congestive heart failure should be treated with digoxin and furosemide (Table 10–1). Spontaneous conversion to sinus rhythm in approximately 24 hours occurs in horses with paroxysmal atrial fibrillation. Conversion with intravenous quinidine gluconate is successful in horses with a recent (<72 hours) onset of atrial fibrillation. In horses with a longer or unknown duration of atrial fibrillation or with evidence of other cardiac disease (but not congestive heart failure), conversion with oral quinidine sulfate is usually successful.

The duration of the arrhythmia is significantly associated with conversion and the likelihood of recurrence. In our study, all horses with a duration of atrial fibrillation of less than 4 months and no other cardiac disease converted to sinus rhythm and the rate of atrial fibrillation recurrence was low. Most horses with a longer-duration arrhythmia converted to sinus rhythm (80%), but the recurrence rate was high (>60%). Almost all animals

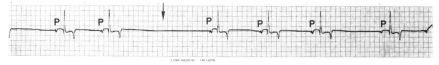

Fig. 10–4. Sinoatrial block. A long diastolic pause (arrow) is twice the normal PP interval, and no P waves occur during this period (compare with Fig. 10–3).

who experience conversion to sinus rhythm return to their previous performance levels.

Quinidine sulfate is usually administered at a dosage of 20 mg/kg every 2 hours until the horse's heartbeat converts, the horse develops toxic side effects, or 60 g has been given in 1 day. Horses that do not tolerate this dosage can be given the drug every 6 hours. The addition of digoxin might be necessary in some horses with high ventricular response rates or myocardial dysfunction. The horse's ECG should be monitored during treatment to detect quinidine toxicity, revealed by a 25% prolongation of the QRS interval. Idiosyncratic and toxic side effects of quinidine include depression, tachycardia, urticaria, nasal mucosal swelling, ataxia, diarrhea, laminitis, hypotension, collapse, and congestive heart failure. Acute quinidine toxicity can be treated with intravenous sodium bicarbonate (1 mEq/kg), which promotes quinidine protein binding and decreases the amount of active drug. If the arrhythmia recurs, treatment should be reinstituted as soon as possible to maximize the likelihood of successful conversion. Treatment of horses with longstanding atrial fibrillation might not be needed if the arrhythmia is an incidental finding.

Atrial Premature Systoles and Tachycardia

Atrial (or supraventricular) premature beats can be associated with atrial myocardial disease, electrolyte imbalances, toxemia, septicemia, hypoxia, ischemia, autonomic imbalance, or chronic valvu-

lar disease. Atrial myocardial disease should be suspected if the extrasystoles are frequent, occur with exercise or appear following a systemic infection, and if other causes have been ruled out. On auscultation, the underlying rhythm is usually regular with a short diastolic period preceding the premature systole, which might or might not be followed by a compensatory pause. The P wave associated with the premature systole is usually different from normal, might be buried in the preceding wave or in the QRS or T complex (junctional), and might not be followed by a QRS and T complex. The QRS configuration is usually normal. Digoxin therapy is indicated if congestive heart failure is present. Quinidine sulfate can be used to suppress the atrial extrasystoles if they are frequent. Corticosteroids are a controversial treatment for horses with suspected myocarditis but might be effective.

Atrial tachycardia is a rapid regular rhythm of 120 to 220 beats/minute that can occur in paroxysms or be sustained (Fig. 10–6). Varying degrees of AV block are common with sustained atrial tachycardia and can mimic atrial fibrillation on auscultation. Supraventricular tachycardia usually has a P-wave configuration different from normal and has normal-appearing QRS and T complexes. This arrhythmia can be seen with ventricular pre-excitation or during quinidine sulfate therapy for atrial fibrillation. Supraventricular tachycardia often indicates underlying atrial myocardial disease and sometimes is successfully treated with quinidine sulfate therapy, though this

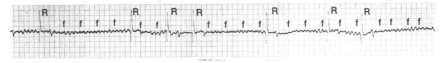

Fig. 10–5. Atrial fibrillation. No P waves are recorded, but baseline fibrillation (f) waves are present. The ventricular complexes (R) are irregularly spaced.

treatment tends to be less effective than it is for atrial fibrillation.

Atrial flutter is uncommon except in horses being treated for atrial fibrillation with quinidine sulfate therapy. The ECG shows 220 to 350 large, saw-toothed flutter (F) waves/minute, uniform in amplitude, shape, and frequency.

Ventricular Premature Systoles and Tachycardia

Ventricular premature contractions (VPC) can be associated with electrolyte or autonomic imbalance, sepsis, toxemia, hypoxia, ischemia, or ventricular myocardial disease. The other causes should be ruled out before ventricular myocardial disease is suspected. Frequent ventricular premature beats, in the absence of any other problem, indicate myocardial disease. The degree of myocardial damage can be greater when the VPCs are induced by exercise, arise from more than one ectopic focus, or are associated with paroxysms of ventricular tachycardia.

On auscultation, the underlying rhythm is regular, with a short diastolic period preceding the premature systole. A compensatory pause usually follows the premature beat. The S_1 associated with the VPC is usually loud and prolonged. The S_2 and peripheral pulse can be absent if the VPC occurs immediately following a normal beat. ECG reveals that the QRS complexes associated with the VPCs are prolonged (Figs. 10–7 and 8). The normal P wave occurs when expected but can be buried in the ectopic

QRS or T complex. The direction of the ectopic QRS is usually opposite to that of the ectopic T wave. Unifocal ventricular arrhythmias are most common; multiple different QRS configurations indicate several ectopic foci.

Treatment should be aimed at correcting the underlying cause. If the arrhythmia is frequent or multifocal or if the R or T phenomenon exists, antiarrhythmics can be used. Quinidine is effective in the treatment of ventricular arrhythmias in horses. Lidocaine must be used carefully in horses with ventricular arrhythmias, as it causes excitability and convulsions at high dosages. Propranolol also has been effective in some horses. Corticosteroids can be helpful in the treatment of horses with myocarditis.

Ventricular tachycardia (paroxysmal or sustained) is uncommon but can persist in some horses for days or weeks. Heart rates of 60 to 240 beats/minute have been seen in horses with ventricular tachycardia. A rapid regular rhythm is usually auscultated, unless multifocal ventricular tachycardia exists. ECG shows a series of bizarre QRS and T complexes with slower, regular P waves that are independent of the ventricular rhythm. Occasional capture of fusion beats can occur (Fig. 10–8). Any underlying causes should be ruled out or treated. This rhythm usually indicates more severe ventricular myocardial disease and should be treated if the rate is rapid, the arrhythmia is multifocal, the R or T phenomenon is seen, or signs of cardiac disease are present; otherwise, ventricular fibrillation could occur. Digoxin can be administered cautiously if congestive

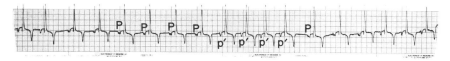

Fig. 10–6. Paroxysm of atrial tachycardia. The normal P wave is bifid. Abnormal P waves (p') occur at a more rapid but regular rate than the normal ones. These complexes could originate either in the sinoatrial node or within the atrial myocardium.

heart failure exists. If the arrhythmia if life threatening, lidocaine or quinidine gluconate should be administered carefully.

Ventricular fibrillation is characterized by the sudden absence of heart sounds and pulses with a rapid drop in blood pressure. Large, bizarre, irregular baseline undulatious with no QRS-T complexes are seen on an ECG. This arrhythmia is usually rapidly fatal in the adult horse, and electrical defibrillation has not been successful.

Complete Heart Block

Third-degree AV block, though an uncommon rhythm disturbance in horses, is a definitive sign of cardiac disease, as is advanced second-degree AV block. With complete heart block no impulses are conducted from the atria to ventricles through the AV node. The horse has a rapid regular sinus rhythm and a slower independent ventricular rhythm. Fainting (Adams-Stokes syndrome) is common, as pauses of 60 seconds or longer can occur between beats. Affected horses are usually exercise intolerant, with a heart rate of 10 to 20 beats/minute. The heart rhythm is usually regular, with a single idioventricular pacemaker. Additional ventricular ectopic activity or occasional conducted sinus or atrial beats can result in an irregular rhythm. The ECG reveals rapid regular P waves with normal configurations. The QRS complexes are usually widened and bizarre, with T waves oriented in the opposite direction. The QRS complexes are usu-

ally complexes are usually infrequent but regular unless other arrhythmias are present (Fig. 10–9). Prognosis is grave, and often electrical pacing is necessary. Atropine sulfate (7.5 mg/450 kg body weight intravenously or 20 to 30 mg/450 kg body weight subcutaneously) can increase ventricular rate if AV block is not complete. Corticosteroids can be helpful in acute cases, as chronic inflammatory changes have been seen in the AV node of some horses with complete heart block.

Other arrhythmias such as accelerated conduction syndromes and bundle branch block have been reported but are rare. Pre-excitation syndromes (PR interval <0.20 seconds) can occur with normal QRS and T complexes or with an abnormal configuration of the QRS and T complexes (a widened and bizarre QRS with a delta wave and a T wave oriented opposite to the delta wave) known as Wolff-Parkinson-White syndrome. Horses with ventricular pre-excitation can perform successfully.

PERICARDITIS

A pericardial friction rub or muffled heart sounds indicate pericardial disease, usually pericarditis. Pericardial friction rubs are usually triphasic, occurring with atrial and ventricular systole and ventricular diastole. These are short, scratchy rubbing sounds that can be very localized or heard over the entire cardiac silhouette. Occasionally, friction rubs are heard only during ventricular systole and diastole or only during systole. During

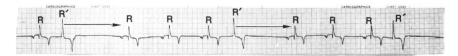

Fig. 10–7. Premature ventricular depolarizations (R') occur earlier than the normal complexes (R) and are not preceded by a P wave. They are followed by a compensatory pause (arrow).

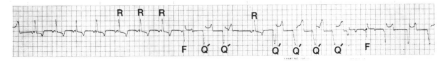

Fig. 10–8. Short runs of bizarre-shaped ventricular complexes (Q') originating within the ventricles. They are different in shape from the normal complexes (R) and are not preceded by a P wave. Fusion beats (F) occur when normal and abnormal complexes occur simultaneously.

systole this rub can often be mistaken for a coarse systolic murmur. As more fluid or fibrin accumulates in the pericardial sac, the heart sounds become more muffled. Venous distension, tachycardia, ventral edema, exercise intolerance, and dyspnea occur as cardiac compression and impaired venous return become more severe. The rate and amount of fluid accumulation affects clinical signs greatly, as the rapid accumulation of fluid can lead to cardiac tamponade and death. Affected horses can have weight loss, anorexia, depression, and fever, especially if pericarditis is associated with pleuropneumonia.

Electrical alternans, low-voltage QRS and T complexes, and abnormalities of ST segments and T waves are commonly seen. Radiographs reveal a pumpkin-shaped cardiac silhouette with large effusions. Echocardiography (M-mode and two-dimensional) is useful in diagnosing pericardial effusion, selecting the site for pericardiocentesis, and monitoring treatment. Pericardiocentesis (cytology and culture, as well as therapeutic drainage) is essential in establishing an etiologic diagnosis. Pericardiocentesis using a 16-gauge over-the-needle intravenous catheter should be performed in the fifth to seventh intercostal spaces on the left side just above the lateral thoracic vein, where the fluid accumulation is the largest. A large-bore (No. 16 to 26 French) chest tube can be inserted for lavage and drainage if a large effusion is present.

Broad-spectrum antimicrobial therapy should be instituted until results of cytology and culture are available. Successful treatment of horses with septic pericarditis has been reported using systemic broad-spectrum antibiotics, lavage, and drainage of the pericardial sac using an indwelling chest tube. A number of horses with idiopathic pericardial effusion have responded to drainage or corticosteroids. Cytologic evaluation of the pericardial fluid revealed an eosinophilic fluid in several horses. Prognosis in horses with pericarditis should be guarded until response to therapy can be assessed. However, aggressive treatment with drainage, lavage, and parenteral antibiotics or corticosteroids has resulted in complete recovery in numerous horses.

ENDOCARDITIS

Bacterial endocarditis occurs infrequently in horses and usually results in the development of valvular insuffi-

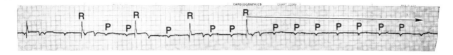

Fig. 10–9. Complete heart block. The P waves occur at a more rapid and independent rate when compared to the ventricular complexes (R). The ventricular pacemaker arrested, leading to a long diastolic pause (arrow).

ciency and congestive heart failure. Affected horses often have chronic weight loss, anorexia, fever, lameness, tachycardia, and heart murmurs. Laboratory abnormalities include anemia, hyperproteinemia, hyperfibrinogenemia, and a neutrophilic leukocytosis. Serial blood cultures are important for determining the identity and sensitivity of the causative organism(s). Echocardiographic detection of masses on the endocardial surface of the heart coupled with the clinical signs is diagnostic of endocarditis.

Aggressive long-term treatment with broad-spectrum bacteriocidal antimicrobials based on culture and sensitivity results should be instituted, but prognosis is poor because significant valvular dysfunction, embolism, and life-threatening arrhythmias often occur. Aortic and mitral valves are affected most commonly, followed by tricuspid and pulmonic valves.

MYOCARDITIS

Various infections and toxins have been associated with myocardial disease in the horse. Signs of myocarditis often occur 1 to 4 weeks after a primary infection, usually respiratory. The horse often has a history of fever, anorexia, depression, and respiratory disease that responded to treatment. Several weeks later, when the horse is returned to work, signs of exercise intolerance, dyspnea, fainting, or congestive heart failure appear. Auscultation of the heart reveals arrhythmias, tachycardia, murmurs, or gallop rhythms. Stall rest and broad-spectrum antibiotics or corticosteroids are indicated until the clinical signs have resolved. Prognosis is poor once cardiac dilation and congestive heart failure have occurred. In these cases, treatment with digoxin, furosemide, and possibly vasodilators is indicated.

SUPPLEMENTAL READING

Bonagura, J.D., Herring, D.S., and Walker, F.: Echocardiography. Vet. Clin. North Am. [Equine Prac.], 1:311–333, 1985.

Brown, C.M.: Acquired cardiovascular disease. Vet. Clin. North Am. [Equine Prac.], 1:371–382, 1985.

McGuirk, S.M., and Muir, W.W.: Diagnosis and treatment of cardiac arrhythmias. Vet. Clin. North Am. [Equine Prac.], 1:353–370, 1985.

Muir, W.W., and McGuirk, S.M.: Pharmacology and pharmacokinetics of drugs used to treat cardiac disease in horses. Vet. Clin. North Am. [Equine Prac.], 1:335–352, 1985.

Reef, V.B.: Cardiovascular disease in the equine neonate. Vet. Clin. North Am. [Equine Prac.], 1:117–129, 1985.

Reef, V.B.: Evaluation of the equine cardiovascular system. Vet. Clin. North Am. [Equine Prac.], 1:275–288, 1985.

chapter 11

LIMB AND
VENTRAL EDEMA

Christopher M. Brown

About 70% of an adult horse's body is water, distributed in three major compartments: intravascular, interstitial, and intracellular. The relative distribution among the three compartments is fairly constant, but not static; water is constantly moving from one to another. When the forces that promote and control water distribution and movement malfunction, the distribution can become abnormal. Accumulation of excessive amounts of water in the interstitial space leads to the clinical sign of edema. In horses, the most frequent sites for edema are the limbs, ventral abdomen, and ventral thorax. This chapter also discusses the mechanisms and causes for swelling and thickening of these areas other than edema.

DISTRIBUTION OF EXTRACELLULAR WATER

The intravascular water and interstitial water, which make up the extracellular water, account for about 30% of total body water. The distribution is fairly constant; about 25% is in the blood vessels, and the remainder in the interstitial spaces.

The constant exchange between the two areas is controlled and promoted by various forces both inside and outside the vessel. Within the vessel, the primary force that promotes efflux of the fluid through the semipermeable basement membranes of the small vessels is the hydrostatic pressure of the fluid. The major force within the vessel that opposes efflux is the oncotic pressure created by protein molecules, many of which are large enough not to readily leave the normal vessel and enter the interstitial space. Albumin is the most significant serum protein fraction generating this intravascular oncotic pressure. The maintenance of the oncotic pressure gradient between vessel and interstitial space depends on a relatively tight barrier to protein movement between the two spaces. Within the interstitial space, the hydrostatic force, called tissue tension, opposes the entrance of water.

At the arteriolar end of capillaries, the difference between the intravascular and interstitial forces—the high hydrostatic and low oncotic pressures within the

vessel, and the low hydrostatic pressure in the interstitial space—promotes the movement of water and crystalloid solutes into the interstitial spaces. Fluid is removed from the interstitial spaces by the lymphatics and is also probably absorbed into the venous ends of capillaries. At the venous end of capillaries, hydrostatic pressure is lower than at the arteriolar end, and the colloidal, protein-derived oncotic pressure is higher owing to water loss at the arteriolar end and the subsequent concentration of plasma proteins. The lowered hydrostatic pressure together with the increased oncotic pressure promotes flow of water from the interstitial space to the intervascular space (Fig. 11–1). Any significant change in any of the forces or structures that control water movement can lead to edema.

PATHOGENESIS

Edema develops when the rate of water entry into the interstitial space exceeds the rate of removal (Fig. 11–2). The imbalance creating edema might last for only a short period, after which a new steady-state is established, with fluid entering

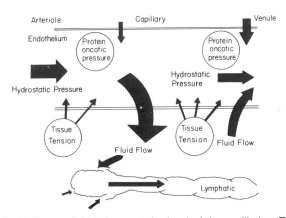

Fig. 11–1. The forces that influence fluid balance at the level of the capillaries. The size of the arrows is proportional to the force or flow. Hydrostatic pressure is greater at the arteriolar end of the capillary than at the venular end. Protein onocotic pressure is lower at the arteriolar end than at the venular end. Tissue tension is a little lower at the arteriolar end. The net flow of the fluid (largest curved arrow) is into the tissue. Fluid leaves the tissues via lymphatics and also goes back into the capillary at the venular end.

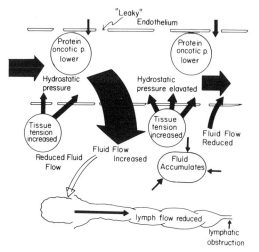

Fig. 11–2. The possible mechanisms leading to increased fluid accumulation in the interstitium (edema). The endothelium can be more permeable to protein and fluid, intravascular protein can be low, venous obstruction can increase pressure at the venular end of the capillary, and the lymphatics can be obstructed. The net result is increased flow of fluid into the tissues, and reduced flow away via the lymphatics and the capillaries.

and leaving the edematous tissue at balanced rates.

Increase in the intravascular pressure at the capillary level can promote increased water movement into, and reduced water removal from, the interstitium, and hence edema. The increased pressure can arise from local venous obstruction or from generalized venous distension secondarily to heart failure. Arterial hypertension is uncommon in horses and does not usually elevate capillary pressure significantly. Increased venous pressure could also develop in horses given intravenous fluids at a rate greater than that at which the kidney can excrete them. Unless renal function is impaired this imbalance is unlikely to occur in adult horses, but it is possible in foals.

Lowered intravenous oncotic pressure occurs in hypoproteinemia, particularly hypoalbuminemia. Hypoalbuminemia can occur in liver disease involving reduced albumin production and in renal and gas-

trointestinal diseases involving increased albumin loss. The severity of the hypoalbuminemia is not always correlated with the development of edema, and in some human patients with congenital absence of serum albumin, edema does not always develop. Generally, in horses, concentrations of albumin below 1.5 g/dl (15 g/L) are associated with the development of edema, although many horses do not show clinical signs until the value falls below 1 g/dl (10 g/L).

Lymphatic flow depends on several factors. The pressure gradient from the interstitial space to the lymph vessels favors lymphatic flow. Also, the contractile lymph vessels pulsate, promoting the forward flow of lymph. In addition, the vessels have valves that inhibit retrograde flow. Finally, lymph flow is promoted by local muscle contraction, and by the increased tissue pressure resulting from body movement.

Lymphatic obstruction or damage, by reducing or eliminating the pressure gradient, reduces the rate of fluid clearance from tissues and leads to edema. Because the external pressure around the vessels causing local obstruction usually compresses local veins as well, increased venous pressure contributes to edema. Distension or infection of local lymph nodes obstructs or reduces lymph flow by reducing the contraction and pulsations of the vessels, and the distension makes the valves incompetent, allowing retrograde flow. Infiltration of lymph nodes with neoplasms also can reduce or obstruct lymph flow. Physical immobility reduces the "pumping" effect of local muscle contraction, and the resulting swelling and edema can further reduce mobility and promote more edema development.

All lymph eventually flows centrally and enters the venous system at the vena cava. Increases in central venous pressure reduce the pressure gradient that promotes this lymph flow and can lead to generalized edema. In congestive heart failure this increased pressure is one of the mechanisms causing edema and ascites.

An intact barrier to the flow of intravascular protein to the interstitial space is an integral part of body fluid homeostasis. Damage to the barrier, allowing protein to escape with water, lowers the oncotic pressure gradient between the intra- and extravascular spaces and promotes edema development. In horses, damage to capillary endothelial and basement membranes results from a variety of causes including chemical agents, viruses, bacterial toxins, and immune-mediated reactions. Mediators of the inflammatory response increase the permeability of the barrier and lead to increased local fluid accumulation.

Whatever the mechanisms whereby fluid is lost from the vascular system, the arterial blood volume decreases. This decrease induces renal conservation of sodium and water hormonally in an attempt to restore arterial volume. Depending on the cause of the edematous state, the conservation measures might stabilize arterial volume, and a new steady-state might be established, with excess fluid trapped extravascularly. In other states, fluid loss into the interstitium continues, and attempts to restore arterial volume are not successful; edema continues to develop.

CLINICAL EVALUATION

Generalized edema becomes obvious initially in the most dependent parts of the body, the lower limbs, ventral abdomen, and ventral thorax. Localized edema occurs wherever local conditions favor its development, such as the head or a single limb. History, physical findings, and laboratory tests all assist the clinician in determining which of the possible causes are involved, and indicate appropriate therapy.

CLASSIFICATION OF SWELLING AND EDEMA (Table 11–1)

Swelling and edema can be divided arbitrarily into two main types, acute and chronic, and two subtypes, localized and generalized. Acute swellings are those that developed rapidly and have been present for only 2 or 3 days. Chronic problems are those that have been present for over a week. Obviously, because an unresolved acute problem will progress to a chronic one, the above division is not rigid or mutually exclusive. In addition, chronic problems can recur after periods of remission or reduction.

ACUTE

Localized

Trauma. Trauma is the most common cause of localized edema and swelling in horses. Trauma affects the limbs most of-

TABLE 11–1. SWELLING AND EDEMA

Duration	Extent	Major Causes
Acute	Localized	Trauma
		Infection
		Chemical irritants
		Burns
		Photosensitization
		Venomous bites
		Parasites
	Generalized	Immobility
		Vasculitis
		Acute heart failure
Chronic	Localized	Infections
		Venous obstruction
		Lymphatic obstruction
		Chemical agents
		Photosensitivity
	Generalized	Hypoalbuminemia
		Elevated central venous pressure
		Generalized skin disease

ten but can occur anywhere. Diagnosis is easy if the skin is broken and hemorrhage is obvious. In severe cases, fractures can be present, and hemorrhage within surrounding soft tissues contributes to the swelling. The local inflammatory response in all of these cases, with release of vasoactive substances, leads to increased vascular permeability. The local edema that develops occludes local venous and lymphatic drainage. Often the entire limb distal to the injury becomes swollen. If the horse is presented for evaluation several hours or days after injury, the initial local site of trauma might not be obvious, and all possibilities for the swelling will have to be considered. Physical examination might help rule out many of the causes considered below, and obvious bruising can support a diagnosis of trauma. If the animal is otherwise well, has good appetite, and is afebrile, laboratory tests are probably not justified at initial evaluation.

Therapy is aimed at reducing the inflammatory response and the swelling. Hosing the area with cold water is often helpful, causing vasoconstriction and keeping the owner involved and observant, but it is tedious and needs to be done two or three times daily for 30 minutes. Alternatively, the area can be packed with ice and the horse held in cross-ties. Nonsteroidal anti-inflammatory drugs (NSAIDs) (e.g., phenylbutazone) can be useful. Leg wraps are valuable for reducing and controlling limb swelling and edema. They should be applied from the coronary band upward to above the level of the problem, if possible. They should be well padded, applied firmly but not tightly, and changed daily. Once the animal can walk, exercise periods of 20 to 30 minutes several times daily promotes lymph flow and reduces edema.

Acute edema and swelling of the distal limbs should be controlled and resolved as quickly as possible. If edema persists for over a week, severe fibrosis can develop in the interstitial space; this fibrosis can lead to permanent swelling, disfigurement, and reduced function.

Infections. Localized infections, which can follow trauma, cause local swelling and edema primarily by means similar to those described for trauma. Physical examination can reveal pain, heat, and occasionally exudation. The infection can be a diffuse cellulitis secondary to a puncture wound. Even severe bacterial dermatitis can lead to significant local swelling. If the lesions are localized, systemic signs are not seen. The appetite is good and the animal is afebrile, but often lame.

Therapy for these animals is fairly straightforward. Fluid at the affected site can be cultured if a suitable sample can be obtained, though culture is not usually justified in most cases, and empiric therapy is probably best. Systemic antibiotic therapy with intramuscular procaine penicillin G 20,000 U/kg twice daily is the least expensive and most logical choice. In addition, the general measures described for the management of problems resulting from trauma should be followed. If the horse shows no response after 2 to 3 days, or if the problem worsens, the antimicrobial spectrum should be expanded, probably by the addition of an aminoglycoside, such as gentamicin, 2 mg/kg three times daily. Again, swelling must be reduced as soon as possible to reduce the risk of permanent fibrosis.

This management protocol should not be followed if clostridial organisms are involved. These organisms are introduced into the site following an intramuscular injection of a nonantibiotic substance. Infection with clostridial organisms often involves one of the rear limbs, but can also develop in the neck. The organisms multiply rapidly, producing tissue necrosis, often gas, and many toxins. Horses become severely ill, with profound systemic signs, and are often in shock by the time the problem is discovered. Usually a nonantibiotic intramuscular injection was given 2 or 3 days previously. In contrast to the horses with other localized infections, these animals require aggressive, emergency therapy. High dosages of crystalline sodium penicillin (50,000 U/kg) should be given intravenously every 4 hours. Intravenous fluid therapy is usually needed, and radical surgical exposure of the infected tissue should be considered to remove necrotic material, relieve pressure, and irrigate the site. Treatment of clostridial myositis is expensive and has a poor prognosis. Treatment can take several weeks, and extensive muscle loss can occur.

Chemical Irritants. Chemical irritants applied directly to the skin cause swelling and edema owing to the inflammatory response induced. Edema is often the desired effect when "blisters" and other "counter irritants" are applied to the skin to treat underlying soft-tissue or even skeletal lesions. Overzealous use of this questionable therapy can cause much more harm than good, and severe painful inflammation can ensue. Therapy for chemical irritation involves removing as much of the excess chemical as possible, together with the general protocol for the management of swelling as outlined above.

Burns. Massive swelling and edema can develop in any area of the body exposed to fire. Such burns are rare in horses, and diagnosis is easy based on the history. Management is empiric. Severe burns often lead to such severe tissue loss and pain that euthanasia may be the most humane choice.

Photosensitization. Photosensitization is associated with localized swelling of white or nonpigmented skin that has been exposed to the sun. Occasionally, it can occur from ingestion of primary photosensitizing agents such as St. John's wort or buckwheat, but more commonly photosensitization in horses occurs secondary to liver disease. In liver disease the breakdown product of chlorophyll, phylloerythrin, is not metabolized. Phylloerythrin is a photodynamic agent, and a severe reaction occurs when the skin is exposed to ultraviolet light. Most typical sites are the white areas of the muzzle, forehead, and limbs. Management of both primary and secondary photosensitivity involves removing the animal from the sunlight and identifying and removing the inciting agent, either the primary photodynamic agent or the hepatotoxin. In severe cases extensive sloughing of the skin can require extensive and expensive skin grafting.

Other Causes. Snake and insect bites can also cause localized swelling and edema. Single bites are difficult to ascertain. Management is empiric and similar to that suggested for trauma. In severe cases, antihistamines, corticosteroids, or both might be helpful.

Helminth parasites are not usually associated with acute localized swelling and edema, although occasionally the microfilaria of Onchocerca cervicalis are. Some horses with onchocerciasis, when treated with the anthelmintic invermectin, develop plaques of ventral edema. Presumably this edema is secondary to the death of Onchocerca microfilaria and an inflammatory reaction to them. No specific therapy is required, and the problem usually resolves in a few days. However, owners should be warned of the problem following the use of ivermectin.

Generalized

Immobility. Immobility and rest are by far the most common causes of swelling and edema of the limbs in horses. This well-recognized "stocking-up" is of uncertain origin and develops in many stalled, immobile horses in 10 to 12 hours. Although some have suggested that changes in blood flow, hematocrit, and serum proteins in rested horses promote edema development, the evidence for this theory is not strong; more likely a reduction in movement-assisted lymph flow predisposes to edema. The resolution of this edema after 15 to 20 minutes of light exercise supports this idea. Edema resulting from immobility is benign and does not usually need specific therapy. Some horses that recurrently develop severe edema when stalled might need leg wraps.

Vasculitis. Generalized vasculitis involving small vessels and capillaries can lead to edema secondary to protein leakage. The most likely causes in horses are endotoxemia, purpura hemorrhagica, and equine viral arteritis.

Endotoxemia can occur in a variety of conditions, mostly gastrointestinal. Peracute and acute enterocolitis from a variety of causes, such as salmonellosis, Clostridium perfringens Type A, Ehrlichia risticii, and grain overload, often lead to endotoxemia, together with severe diarrhea and fluid and electrolyte abnormalities (Chapter 3). Vascular endothelial damage can become clinically obvious 1 or 2 days into the disease. Edema in these patients can be secondary to the vasculitis and leakage of protein and water into the interstitium, and also to hypoalbuminemia secondary to an acute protein-losing enteropathy. Typically these patients are severely ill, depressed, febrile, anorexic, and dehydrated, with profuse fluid diarrhea. Clinical pathologic data are consistent with endotoxemia (Chapter 3). Ventral and limb edema often persists 10 to 14 days, even if the enteric problems resolve. Usually specific therapy for the edema is neither indicated, nor helpful.

The profound pathophysiologic problems of endotoxemia require aggressive fluid therapy, flunixin meglumine, and in selected cases, systemic antibiotic therapy. Because the edema is due in part to leaky vessels, and these patients are often dehydrated, diuretic therapy is not helpful and is often contraindicated. Leg wraps to reduce the formation of permanent lower-limb fibrosis might be helpful.

Purpura hemorrhagica is an immune-mediated vasculitis usually associated with streptococcal infections, usually developing after a second infection. Hence, the disease tends to occur in older horses. The second infection might not be obvious, although other horses in the group can have typical signs of strangles. Uncommonly, the problem can occur in horses previously sensitized that are given S. equi vaccines.

The clinical signs of purpura hemorrhagica include swelling and edema that is often extensive and severe. The skin of the legs can split and ooze serosanguineous fluid. It can become infected. Multiple petechiae and occasional ecchymotic hemorrhages are present on the mucous membranes. Animals can be febrile, anorectic, and reluctant or unable to move. Clinical laboratory data are often consistent with an active inflammation or infection, revealing leukocytosis, hyperfibrinogenemia, hyperglobulinemia, and anemia. Thrombocytopenia is not a feature.

Management is directed at reducing the swelling and suppressing the inflammatory response. Leg wraps are usually needed, particularly when the skin has split. Wraps should be changed daily and a suitable dressing applied to the skin. Procaine penicillin G (20,000 U/kg) twice daily intramuscularly is used empirically, because streptococci are most frequently suspected. Immunosuppressive dosages of prednisolone (2 mg/kg orally once daily) are used initially. Prednisolone might have to be given for several weeks at decreasing dosage. Diuretic therapy probably will not help, because endothelial damage is extensive. As the horse improves, daily exercise can be introduced. Severe cases of purpura hemorrhagica do not usually respond well to treatment, and permanent fibrosis often develops.

Though skin biopsy stained for specific antibodies might be helpful in confirming a diagnosis, the result usually is not available in time to have any impact on decision-making and management.

Equine viral arteritis is a panvasculitis whose most important clinical signs result from damage to small vessels, lymphatics, and capillaries. The horse is initially febrile (temperature 104°F, 40°C), with conjunctival congestion, limb edema, and possibly a serous to purulent nasal discharge. Pregnant mares with viral arteritis might abort. The edema can spread to the ventrum, including the prepuce, and in some cases palpebral edema can develop. A lymphopenia can be present at the onset of signs.

The disease is probably spread by aerosol transmission, and outbreaks can occur in susceptible groups of horses. Serologic surveys indicate that many horses do not develop clinical signs although they seroconvert. Therefore, not all animals in a group will become clinically affected even if they are susceptible.

Diagnosis is based on clinical signs and laboratory data. Attempts at isolating the virus are only moderately useful in natural outbreaks but might be successful using nasal swabs or the buffy coat. Serologic testing detects seroconversion following exposure. However, in many areas large numbers of normal animals are seropositive, and a fourfold increase in titer over 10 days is needed to confirm recent exposure.

Therapy is empiric and similar to that used in trauma-induced edema. Corticosteroids should be avoided and diuretics usually are not helpful. Antibiotics are indicated only if secondary bacterial infections are suspected. NSAIDs such as flunixin meglumine or phenylbutazone might be helpful in restoring appetite in the acute febrile phase.

Breeding stallions should be vaccinated to prevent transmission of the virus in semen. Horses on large breeding farms could be vaccinated if there is a high risk of infection, but vaccination would not probably be of much value against an outbreak.

Acute Heart Failure. Acute heart failure, uncommon in horses, is an uncommon cause of acute leg and ventral edema and swelling. Acute monensin toxicity can cause acute myocardial failure, but death usually occurs before edema develops. Occasionally one of the mitral chordae tendineae ruptures, causing acute left heart failure, pulmonary edema, pulmonary hypertension, and subsequently acute right heart failure. This rupture can cause acute peripheral edema. However, these animals are more likely to be presented for acute respiratory signs secondary to the pulmonary edema. The peripheral edema is of secondary importance and not always present (Chapter 10).

Other Causes. Equine infectious anemia is a viral disease of horses producing a wide range of clinical signs. In some acute severe cases, edema of limbs, ventral abdomen, and, in males, the prepuce can occur. The horse is usually febrile and jaundiced, and can have widespread petechiae. Some animals that recover relapse days to weeks later, with similar signs. Diagnosis is based on clinical signs and a positive result with the gel diffusion test (Coggins test) (Chapter 13).

The use of black-walnut shavings as bedding in some areas has been associated with the development of laminitis. Edema of the lower limbs has also been reported in experimental and field exposure to black-walnut shavings. In occasional cases this edema involves the ventral abdomen, thorax, and neck. The mechanism whereby black-walnut shavings cause laminitis and edema has not been determined. The laminitis appears to be clinically different from that induced by grain overload, that is, endotoxemia. If the laminitis is not too debilitating and resolves, the associated edema resolves in 1 to 2 days.

Hemostatic abnormalities can lead to many areas of subcutaneous hemorrhage, particularly over areas likely to be traumatized, such as the lower limbs. These coagulopathies can be induced by overdosage with anticoagulants such as warfarin or can be secondary to idiopathic thrombocytopenias. Extensive swelling can develop at the site of hemorrhage, and petechiation or frank hemorrhage can be noted on the mucous membranes. A coagulation profile and platelet count are indicated if hemostatic disorders are considered a possible cause of the swelling. Specific therapy depends on the cause.

CHRONIC

Chronic localized or generalized edema and swelling, whatever the cause, often presents more of a diagnostic and therapeutic challenge than acute. Often, severe fibrosis leads to permanent thickening and often dysfunction, usually refractory to all therapy.

Management of chronic problems is often unrewarding. Specific problems such as infections can be resolved, but the scarring and thickening can persist no matter how well treated. Pressure bandages, cold hosing, and exercise can have little or no effect.

Localized

Infections. Chronic infection with a range of agents can produce a combination of inflammatory exudate, lymphatic obstruction, and venous hypertension that leads to localized swelling. Localized chronic infections of the limbs often involve the lymphatics and can be bacterial or fungal. These infections include Corynebacterium pseudotuberculosis, which causes ulcerative lymphangitis; staphylococci; streptococci; and Pseudomonas aeruginosa. In infected animals, chronic recurrent nodular lesions develop at the pastern, grow, and rupture, discharging greenish pus. The infection slowly ascends the limb, with lymphatic distension, repeated nodal development, and rupture. Culture of the discharge or nodular aspirate will identify the organism involved. The limb can scar and thicken extensively.

Therapy is both local and systemic. The affected area should be drained and cleansed, and procaine penicillin G (20,000 U/kg) intramuscularly twice daily should be given initially pending culture results. Usually therapy is needed for at least 10 days and often for up to 30 days. The scarring and thickening might not resolve.

Fungal infections of the lower limbs, often involving lymphatics, are uncommon causes of persistent thickening and swelling. Pustules and nodules are present, ascending the lymphatics, and Sporothrix schenckii (Sporotrichum schenckii) and, rarely, other fungi such as Hyphomyces destruens can be isolated. (Histoplasma farciminosus, the cause of epizootic lymphangitis, does not occur in the U.S.) Diagnosis is based on clinical signs and isolation of the yeastlike cells or other fungal elements on smear. Culture will confirm the diagnosis, but culture results might take a long time to be reported. Often long-term therapy (30 to 60 days) is needed, and the infection does not always resolve. Especially severe lesions, particularly those caused by Hyphomyces destruens, should be surgically excised prior to medical therapy. Oral iodide therapy, such as 15 g sodium iodide for a 400-kg horse once daily, might resolve the problem, although systemic signs of iodism such as lacrimation and depression can develop. Griseofulvin orally at 10 g/day for 2 weeks, then 5 g/day for 20 days can be effective in some cases, but might be too expensive. Many cases are refractory.

Glanders, caused by Actinobacillus mallei, is no longer present in North America, but in some areas of Europe, Africa, and Asia it must still be considered as a possible cause of chronic lymphadenitis and lymphangitis.

Venous and Lymphatic Obstruction. Chronic local venous and lymphatic obstruction often occur together and lead to chronic edema of the drainage area. No specific diseases are recognized, and many different causes are possible. Chronic infection causing lymphatic obstruction is discussed above. Local invasion by neoplasms or metastasis to local nodes can obstruct lymph flow and venous return. Physical examination might indicate the cause, and aspiration or biopsy confirms the diagnosis. Therapy is based on the suspected cause.

Other Causes. Many of the causes of acute localized swelling or edema result in chronic localized problems if left untreated. These causes include chronic or repeated exposure to chemical irritants and recurrent photosensitization.

Generalized

Generalized chronic edema and swelling usually involves all four limbs and often the ventral abdomen.

Hypoalbuminemia. Hypoalbuminemia leads to lower intravascular oncotic pressure and retention of water in the interstitium. In horses, chronic hypoalbuminemia occurs in three main syndromes: chronic liver disease, chronic renal disease, and chronic protein-losing enteropathy. In all of these conditions, chronic weight loss is another feature (Chapter 2). Laboratory data might indicate the possible cause of the hypoalbuminemia.

Chronic liver disease is suggested by low serum urea nitrogen (below 10 mg/dl; 3.5 mmol/L), elevated serum gamma glutamyltranspeptidase (above 40 iu/L), and varying changes in other hepatic-associated enzymes. Serum bilirubin can be elevated and the horse jaundiced, and the clearance rate of sulfobromophthalein sodium might be prolonged (over 5 minutes). Hypoalbuminemia can mask the prolonged clearance rate (Chapter 14).

Chronic renal disease is suggested by polyuria and polydipsia (Chapter 12); along with the hypoalbuminemia can be elevated serum urea and creatinine, and often elevation of serum calcium (over 13 mg/dl; 3.25 mmol/L). Other serum electrolytes are not consistently altered, although hyponatremia and hypochloremia are common. Urine is dilute and highly proteinaceous.

Chronic protein-losing enteropathy is suggested in animals that, though thin and hypoalbuminemic, are bright and alert, eat well, and have few or no other serum biochemical abnormalities. Malabsorption, which is present frequently, possibly exacerbates the hypoproteinemia. Many possible causes exist, and any horse with chronic generalized edema and hypoalbuminemia with no clinical or biochemical signs of renal or hepatic disease should be suspected of having protein-losing enteropathy (Chapter 2).

Management of cases of hypoalbuminemia depends on the cause. Defining the cause may require a biopsy of the suspected problematic organ. Many forms of liver disease cannot be treated, although some horses with histologic features of chronic active hepatitis respond to corticosteroid therapy. Severe renal disease is usually too advanced at the time of presentation to warrant therapy, although if the biopsy suggests an immune-mediated glomerular disorder, immuno-suppressive therapy could be considered. The bowel diseases leading to protein-losing enteropathy are for the most part unresponsive to therapy, although plasmacytic/lymphocytic enteropathies and granulomatous enteritis might respond to parenteral corticosteroids.

Response to therapy in all cases of hypoalbuminemia is based on weight gain, serum biochemistry, and in renal cases of disease, urinalysis.

Elevated Central Venous Pressure. Chronic elevation of central venous pressure can cause chronic peripheral edema. The two major causes of elevated central venous pressure in horses are intrathoracic disorders such as large cranial mediastinal masses, chronic pleural effusion, and pleural abscesses, and cardiac disease of varying types affecting the pericardium, myocardium, and valves.

Horses with cranial mediastinal masses, often lymphosarcomas, might have edema of only the forelimbs, head, and neck, because only the cranial vena cava is obstructed, causing venous congestion of just the front end. In these animals the jugular veins are very distended but do not pulsate. Other possible findings of cranial mediastinal masses include normal white blood cell count, mild anemia, and normal serum biochemistry. In some the serum calcium is elevated, and in some the serum IgM concentration is low. More generalized intrathoracic disease such as pleuritis, pleural abscesses, and diffuse thoracic neoplasia are often associated with generalized edema, although weight loss and severe respiratory signs can predominate. Laboratory data vary with the cause of the intrathoracic disease. Thoracic auscultation and

percussion may indicate the cause of the disease, and thoracic radiography and ultrasonography confirm the diagnosis. Thoracocentesis with fluid analysis refines the diagnosis and indicates appropriate therapy, which could include bilateral pleural drainage, antibiotics, diuretics (furosemide 1.0 mg/kg three times daily), or euthanasia.

Cardiac causes of generalized edema are not common in horses. Chronic valvular disease leading to heart failure is much less common in horses than in dogs. Many horses with severe valvular incompetence, particularly of the mitral valve, develop atrial fibrillation. These animals can have heart failure, with tachycardia, jugular distension and pulsation, and obvious murmur(s), arrhythmia, or both. Heart failure owing to myocardial disease is rare in horses, although a few cases of dilated cardiomyopathy have been described, and one of the possible chronic sequels to monensin toxicity in horses is chronic myocardial disease. Clinical signs are nonspecific and are similar to those seen in other forms of heart failure, and murmurs can develop if the atrioventricular valve orifices become dilated. Pericarditis is also rare, and a chronic fibrinous form is recognized. These animals have muffled heart sounds, distended but not pulsatile veins, tachycardia, and generalized edema. Echocardiographic assessment is particularly useful in all cases of heart failure. Electrocardiography is of limited value if no arrhythmias occur.

Therapy is not indicated for all cases of heart failure. Animals intended to have an athletic career probably cannot be restored to a safe competitive state. However, therapy might be warranted in breeding animals (Chapter 10). Pericardiocentesis, often repeated, is indicated for cases of pericarditis combined with appropriate or empiric antibiotic therapy. In addition, diuretics (furosemide 1 mg/kg intramuscularly three times daily) promote fluid loss. Animals with heart failure secondary to valvular disease benefit from diuresis and digoxin (3 μg/kg twice daily intravenously). The use of other agents in the treatment of heart failure in horses has not been evaluated.

Skin Diseases. A rare cause of generalized edema and swelling in horses is generalized skin diseases, such as pemphigus foliaceus and equine granulomatous disease. Skin biopsy in these horses, based on the severity of the skin condition, can indicate appropriate therapy.

SUPPLEMENTAL READING

Dalton, R.G.: Oedema in the rested-immobilised horse: A physiological pathology or a pathological physiology? Equine Vet. J., 5:81–84, 1973.

Munford, J.A.: Preparing for equine arteritis. Equine Vet. J., 17:6–11, 1985.

Reef, V.B.: Vasculitis. *In* Current Therapy in Equine Medicine. 2nd Ed. Edited by N.E. Robinson. Philadelphia, W.B. Saunders, 1987, pp. 312–314.

Staub, N.C., and Taylor, A.E. (Ed.): Edema. New York, Raven Press, 1984.

chapter 12

POLYURIA AND POLYDIPSIA

Allen J. Roussel, Jr.
G. Kent Carter

WATER BALANCE

Water balance in the horse is determined by water consumption, metabolism, excretion, and insensible loss. Drinking and urination are not always the most important parts of the total water dynamics in the horse, because other sources of water gain and loss can be significant. Under certain conditions, metabolic water and water ingested in feed contribute significantly to total body water. For example, under normal circumstances, 10% of the horse's body water requirement is supplied by metabolism of fats, carbohydrates, and protein. Also, the water content of lush pasture grasses can be as high as 90%. Although urination is often assumed to be the major route of water excretion, fecal water loss in the normal horse is far greater than urinary water loss. Other routes of water loss include sweat, insensible loss through the skin, and loss of vapor in expired air.

Although drinking and urination are not the most important routes of water consumption and excretion quantitatively, they are the most important means of *controlling* water balance in the horse. Water intake is controlled by the thirst center in the hypothalamus. Osmoreceptors in this region of the brain detect changes in osmolality and sodium concentration in the extracellular fluid (ECF). Increased osmolality of the ECF stimulates thirst, and the horse seeks water. Secondary stimuli of thirst centers can also trigger drinking. Decreased stimulation of stretch receptors in the large veins and atria causes decreased vagal tone and increased sympathetic tone, which stimulates the thirst centers. Angiotensin II, which has major effects in the kidneys, also stimulates thirst centers.

When water is consumed and absorbed, ECF osmolality returns to normal and the thirst center is no longer stimulated. Because this process is not immediate, however, other mechanisms must temporarily suppress these thirst centers. Wetting of the oral mucous membranes, swallowing water, and filling the stomach cause transient satiety with such accuracy that animals usually drink only the exact amount they require.

Renal water excretion is influenced by the same factors that regulate water intake. Osmoreceptors in the hypothalamus respond to increased ECF osmolality by transmitting impulses to the posterior pituitary, which releases stored antidiuretic hormone (ADH). ADH allows water but not solute to move from the lumen of the collecting duct into the hyperosmolar interstitium of the renal medulla. This selectivity concentrates urine and conserves water. For this system to function properly, several criteria must be met. First, the animal must be able to produce and release biologically active ADH. Second, receptors must be present on the renal tubular cells to bind the hormone and begin the intracellular process. Third, the medullary interstitium must be hyperosmotic.

Water balance is also affected by the renin-angiotensin system. When dehydration and volume depletion occur, renin is released by the juxtaglomerular cells of the kidney. Renin converts renin substrate to angiotensin I, which is immediately converted to angiotensin II. The direct effect of angiotensin II on renal blood flow results in water conservation. Angiotensin II also stimulates the adrenal cortex to secrete aldosterone, which causes conservation of sodium and water and excretion of potassium.

Inappropriate function of the kidneys or any of these mechanisms can disrupt water balance.

CLINICAL EVALUATION

The first step in evaluating a horse with polyuria (excessive urination), polydipsia (excessive thirst), or both is to document that a problem exists. The owner's opinion that the horse drinks or urinates too much is usually subjective. Excessive stall wetness might lead the owner to suspect polyuria, when the true cause might be water leaks or horses' playing in their water.

Owners can mistake pollakiuria (unduly frequent passage of urine) for polyuria. Urethritis, cystitis, vaginitis, metritis, and estrus can cause a horse to void small amounts of urine frequently. Pollakiuria requires evaluation of the reproductive and lower urinary tracts.

Water consumption is much easier to measure than its equivalent, urine output. Although daily water consumption is highly variable, under normal management, dietary, and environmental conditions, horses consume 22 to 90 L of water/day. Exercise, fever, and high environmental temperatures cause increases in consumption, whereas high-moisture feed causes decreases. Accurate measurement of actual water consumption is extremely important and can be determined by the owner or the veterinarian.

Normal healthy adult horses produce about 16 L of urine/day. If necessary, urine production can be quantitated with minimal equipment but with a moderate expenditure of time.

Urine collection in male patients is easily accomplished by fitting the animal with a urine collection device constructed by removing the base of an empty plastic gallon jug and attaching a valve to its mouth (Fig. 12–1). The cut edges of the container should be covered with a nonabsorbent padding that protects the

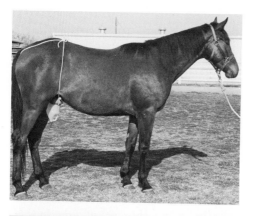

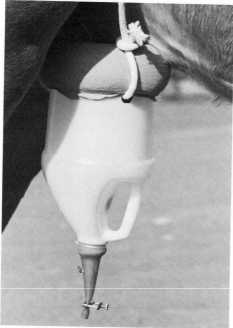

Fig. 12–1. Urine collection device in place on a gelding. The device is made from a gallon plastic jug. *B,* Close-up of the urine collection device.

animal but does not absorb urine. A valve constructed from rubber tubing and a stopcock makes sample collection easy. Depending on the rate of urine production, samples are collected and the volume recorded at 1- to 4-hour intervals.

For collection in mares, a self-retaining urinary catheter can be placed in the bladder. The retention catheter should be connected to a collection vessel, such as an empty 5-L fluid bag supported beneath the mare, with flexible tubing such as a disposable intravenous infusion set run between the animal's rear legs. Animals should remain tied throughout the collection period to prevent them from lying down.

When collection documents polyuria or polydipsia, the veterinarian should initiate a systematic diagnostic workup. This chapter emphasizes the most important and common causes of polyuria and polydipsia.

The minimum laboratory data base includes a complete blood count, serum protein and albumin, blood urea nitrogen and creatinine, serum glucose, and complete urinalysis (Fig. 12–2). In most cases, serum chemistry profiles include the suggested chemistries and cost less than individual tests.

CAUSES

CHRONIC RENAL FAILURE

Although renal failure is not encountered frequently in horses, it is diagnosed more often than previously, probably owing to improved diagnostic techniques and awareness, rather than to a true increased incidence of the disease.

Causes. Causes of chronic renal failure in horses include proliferative glomerulonephritis, chronic interstitial nephritis, pyelonephritis, amyloidosis, and oxalate nephropathy. Glomerulonephri-

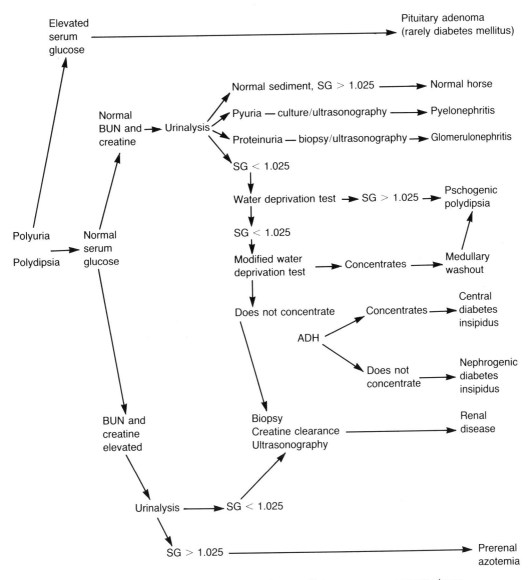

Fig. 12–2. Investigation of polyuria and polydipsia in horses. Only common causes are shown.

tis, although commonly found in horses post mortem, causes clinical disease infrequently. Glomerulonephritis caused by deposition of circulating immune complexes in the glomerulus has been recorded in horses. The immune complexes activate complement, which attracts leukocytes. Lysozymes and other mediators of inflammation cause damage to the basement membrane and endothelial cells in the glomerulus. Chronic in-

terstitial nephritis causing chronic renal failure usually is a sequel of acute renal failure. Aminoglycoside antibiotics, pigments (myoglobin and hemoglobin), vitamin K_3 toxicosis, and septic, toxic, or hypovolemic shock can cause acute renal failure and subsequent chronic interstitial nephritis. Pyelonephritis is rare in horses but is usually associated with nephrolithiasis, urolithiasis, neurologic deficits, or other causes of urine retention. Bacterial virulence factors such as fimbria that attach to uroepithelial cells and toxins that decrease ureteral motility can play a role in the pathogenesis of pyelonephritis. Coliforms are the most frequent cause of pyelonephritis in horses, but Corynebacterium renale (a cause of bovine pyelonephritis) and Staphylococcus aureus have also been reported.

Amyloidosis is rare in horses, almost always occurring in horses used to produce antiserum. Oxalate nephropathy has been attributed to consumption of oxalate-accumulating plants in several animal species, including the horse. However, oxalate crystals in the renal tubules of equine kidneys are usually considered secondary to renal disease.

Clinical Evaluation. Clinical signs of chronic renal failure include poor body condition, lethargy, anorexia, and, less consistently, emaciation, oral ulcers, dental tartar, and ventral edema. Polyuria and polydipsia probably occur in most horses at some stage of the disease, but they are not found consistently.

Rectal examination might be helpful in the diagnosis of some cases of renal disease, although only the left kidney is usually palpable. In pyelonephritis, the affected kidneys and ureters can be enlarged. In most cases of chronic renal failure, the diseased kidneys are smaller than normal. An irregular surface of the palpable left kidney also suggests renal disease.

Ultrasonography can be helpful in diagnosing renal disease. Both kidneys can be imaged by scanning from the body surface, whereas only the left kidney can be imaged routinely from the rectum. The kidneys can be accurately measured and the structure noted. Cortical atrophy, hydronephrosis, renal cysts, nephrolithiasis, and pyelonephritis are often identified using ultrasonography.

Endoscopy can be useful in evaluating suspected cases of pyelonephritis or renal hematuria. The endoscope is passed through the urethra into the trigone area and the ureters visualized. Urine from one kidney containing exudate or blood can be identified as it exits the ureter.

Laboratory evaluation of patients with chronic renal failure should include a complete blood count, serum chemistry profile, serum electrolytes, and complete urinalysis. A presumptive diagnosis of renal failure can be made on the basis of azotemia (elevated serum urea and creatinine) and inappropriate urine concentration. Azotemia is almost always present by the time clinical signs of renal failure appear. Loss of three fourths of the functional capacity of the kidneys produces primary renal azotemia, whereas loss of two thirds of functional capacity produces prerenal azotemia, or loss of ability to concentrate urine above a specific gravity of 1.025. In equine practice, such as in patients with acute diarrhea or colic (Chapter 3), prerenal azotemia is encountered more frequently than primary renal azotemia. Differentiating between the two is crucial. Primary renal azotemia occurs when the blood urea nitrogen and creatinine concentrations are above normal, and if urine specific gravity is <1.025, urine osmolality is <1000 mOsm/ml, or fractional excretion of sodium is >1.0.

Hypercalcemia and hypophosphatemia are observed in about 50% of horses with chronic renal failure. This abnormality in calcium and phosphorus concentration is seldom seen in other species. In the equine intestine calcium absorption remains constant, unresponsive to changes in plasma concentration, metabolic needs, or dietary intake. Whereas normally excess calcium is excreted by the kidneys, horses with renal failure lose the ability. In experimentally nephrectomized horses, plasma calcium concentrations varied according to the amount of calcium in their rations. Probably, dietary calcium also affects the plasma calcium concentration of horses in naturally occurring renal failure. Other unidentified factors must also be involved, because some anorectic horses with renal failure are hypercalcemic.

One of the functions of the normal kidney is to conserve sodium and to excrete excess potassium. In chronic renal failure, plasma sodium and chloride concentrations tend to be low, while plasma potassium concentration tends to be high. Hypoproteinemia, particularly hypoalbuminemia, often accompanies glomerulonephritis, because albumin, a small protein molecule, leaks through the diseased glomerulus. Hyperglobulinemia can accompany pyelonephritis. Other abnormalities in the chemistry profile of horses with chronic renal failure can include hyperlipemia, hypercholesterolemia, and hypermagnesemia.

A complete blood count usually reveals nonspecific changes such as anemia of chronic disease and leukocytosis. Another possible mechanism of anemia is decreased erythropoietin production by the kidneys.

Urinalysis in chronic renal failure reveals inappropriate urine concentration, progressing to fixed specific gravity. Although a complete urinalysis should always be performed, in chronic interstitial nephritis causing chronic renal failure, inappropriate concentration might be the only abnormality. Proteinuria is a consistent feature of glomerular disease, while hematuria and pyuria are often seen in pyelonephritis. Bacteriuria is usually present in pyelonephritis. Urine bacterial counts of greater than 10^5/ml from a catheterized sample are consistent with urinary tract infection and warrant urine culture and sensitivity testing.

Urine indices can be used to confirm or refine a diagnosis of chronic renal failure. Fractional excretion of sodium and ratios of urine to plasma urea, plasma creatinine, and plasma osmolality can be used to differentiate prerenal azotemia from primary renal azotemia. Fractional excretions of potassium, chloride, and phosphate also can be increased in renal disease. Although fractional excretion of electrolytes is frequently measured in horses with renal disease, they offer little additional information regarding cause, severity, therapy, or prognosis.

Perhaps the most accurate quantitative estimation of renal function can be obtained by determining creatinine clearance values. Creatinine clearance should not be confused with fractional excretions of electrolytes, which is also referred to as creatinine clearance ratios. Because creatinine is neither secreted nor absorbed by equine renal tubules, creatinine clearance correlates well with glomerular filtration rate (GFR). Creatinine clearance is determined by collecting and quantitating urine over a period of time, measuring creatinine in the urine and in the serum, and applying the formula

$$C_{Cr} = (U_{Cr}/P_{Cr}) \times V_u/T/BW$$

where C_{Cr} = creatinine clearance; U_{Cr} = concentration of creatinine in the urine; P_{Cr} = concentration of creatinine in the plasma; V_u = total urine volume in milliliters; T = time of collection in minutes; and BW = body weight of the horse in killograms. Creatinine clearance is not consistent over a 24-hour period, and micturition does not occur at consistent intervals over 24 hours. Hence, urine should be collected over the entire period, especially if spontaneously voided urine is being collected. However, the protocol in Table 12-1 eliminates the necessity of a 24-hour collection period. If fractional excretions are to be determined, blood and urine collected at the beginning of the collection period can be used. The bladder lavage before and after collection adds accuracy to the study and allows the use of shorter collection periods. The two serum creatinine values are averaged, and the average is used in the calculations to compensate for variation in serum creatinine concentrations during the study.

The value for creatinine clearance can be compared to normal values, and a percentage of the patient's normal renal capacity can be estimated. The greatest flaw in the test is the difficulty of interpretation brought about by the variety of "normal" values published, which range from 1.39 to 3.68 ml/min/kg. A recent study reported a value of 1.88 ± 0.46 ml/min/kg.

A sodium sulfanilate clearance test is also used for determining the GFR in horses. Because it involves injecting sodium sulfanilate and obtaining blood samples two to three times within 90 minutes of injection, it is much easier to perform than a creatinine clearance. However, little information exists about its application in clinical cases. The GFR in horses has also been determined using the radioactive compound technetium-99m diethyltriamine-pentacetic acid. Regulations regarding use of radioactive compounds limit its use.

Renal biopsy is essential in determining the nature of the renal lesions and in formulating a prognosis. Biopsy of the left kidney can be performed percutaneously with guidance given per rectum or with ultrasound guidance, but ultrasound guidance is recommended for biopsy of the right kidney in most horses. All patients should be evaluated for hemostatic deficiencies prior to biopsy. Hematuria occurs following almost all renal biopsies, but usually resolves in 24 to 48 hours. Proper restraint is essential because excessive movement increases the chance of laceration and hemorrhage. Although valuable information can be obtained from renal biopsies, the veterinarian must weigh the risk against the reward, and should inform the owner of the

TABLE 12–1. DETERMINATION OF CREATININE CLEARANCE VALUES

0 hour —Collect blood for creatinine concentration
—Catheterize, empty, and lavage bladder with 1 L of saline—discard lavage fluid
—Attach urine collection device
—Periodically observe animal, remove and save urine produced

12 hours—Collect blood for creatinine concentration
—Catheterize, empty, and lavage bladder with 1 L of saline—save lavage fluid
—Mix all urine produced with lavage fluid and submit aliquot for creatinine determination
—Submit 0- and 12-hour blood samples for creatinine determination

possible complications. Biopsy samples should be fixed in 10% formalin for routine histopathology. If immunofluorescent staining and examination for antibody is to be performed, other fixatives such as Michel's solution may be preferred. The veterinarian should consult the laboratory to which the sample will be submitted prior to performing the biopsy so that the samples can be fixed properly.

Treatment. Seldom is treatment of horses in chronic renal failure successful. At best, life is prolonged. The greatest chance for successful therapy exists with an acute exacerbation of a chronic problem. If the horse can be supported through the acute crisis, it can return to a state of compensated chronic renal failure and survive for several months if no other disease or stress causes decompensation. Treatment consists of correcting dehydration and electrolyte imbalances, and then producing diuresis by overhydration. If oliguria is not present, up to three times maintenance fluid requirements can be given intravenously and orally. Monitoring acid-base and electrolyte balance daily is essential when massive amounts of fluids are administered. Usually a combination of isotonic solutions such as 0.9% NaCl, 1.3% $NaHCO_3$, and 5% dextrose is given to maintain fluid and electrolyte balance. If edema is present, overhydration must be avoided and dietary sodium should be restricted. Severe hypoalbuminemia can be treated with plasma, but it is likely to recur. Diuresis results in loss of B vitamins, so these should be supplemented.

The ration should provide the minimum requirement of high-quality protein and minimal calcium. Grass hay is preferable to calcium-rich alfalfa. Weight loss in chronic renal failure can be decreased by feeding concentrates. Salt is usually provided ad libitum but should be restricted in animals demonstrating edema. In most cases of renal failure, nephrotoxic drugs should be avoided. Administration of anabolic steroids can decrease muscle wasting and stimulate hematopoiesis.

Pyelonephritis is usually not diagnosed early enough to respond to antimicrobial therapy. Culture and sensitivity testing should precede any attempts at antimicrobial therapy. The chronic nature of the disease makes long-term therapy necessary. Unilateral nephrectomy is sometimes successful in horses if only one kidney is involved. In general, the prognosis for survival in pyelonephritis is poor.

PITUITARY ADENOMA AND DIABETES MELLITUS

Pituitary tumors are usually seen in old horses and are almost always pituitary adenomas of the pars distalis (Fig. 12–3). The incidence is higher in mares. The pars distalis produces and processes pro-opiolipomelanocortin to form several peptides, including ACTH. Tumors of the pars distalis secrete excessive amounts of these peptides. The pars distalis is indirectly inhibited by dopamine and stimulated by serotonin but is resistant to glucocorticoid feedback. Some of the clinical and laboratory changes associated with pituitary adenoma in horses are due to in-

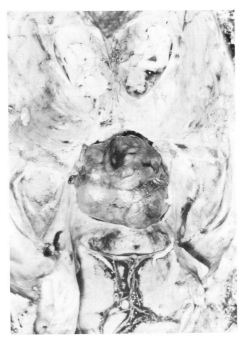

Fig. 12–3. Pituitary adenoma of the pars distalis in situ.

creased ACTH secretion (cushingoid syndrome), some are the result of physical impingement of the tumor on the brain, particularly the hypothalamus, and some are probably due to both mechanisms.

Horses with pituitary adenomas can present with a history of weight loss or muscle wasting, lethargy, abnormal estrus cycles, failure to shed their coats, polyuria and polydipsia, or behavioral changes. Frequent clinical findings include hirsutism (Fig. 12–4), sweating, laminitis, and chronic infections. Other clinical signs include tachypnea, exophthalmos, blindness, ataxia, bradycardia, and seizures. The weight loss, abnormal estrus, laminitis, and chronic infections are probably caused by increased production of ACTH and, subsequently, glucocorticoids. Hyperhydrosis, hirsutism, tachypnea, bradycardia, blindness, and central nervous system abnormalities most likely result from the impingement of the tumor on the optic chiasma and hypothalamic structures such as the thermoregulatory center. Polydipsia or

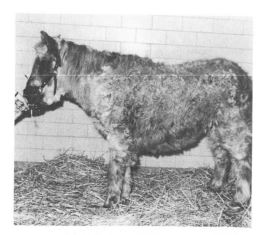

Fig. 12–4. Aged pony with pituitary adenoma. Notice the abnormal long, curly-hair coat.

polyuria seen in pituitary adenoma can have several possible causes. Increased glucocorticoids can inhibit ADH at the level of the collecting duct. In hyperglycemic horses, glucosuria resulting in osmotic diuresis can contribute to the polyuria. Finally, the tumor can damage or obliterate the supraoptic nuclei that secrete ADH, or the infundibulum that delivers it to the posterior pituitary.

The most consistent clinicopathologic findings in pituitary adenoma include neutrophilic leukocytosis with lymphopenia and eosinopenia (stress leukogram) and hyperglycemia. Other findings include hypercholesterolemia and hyperlipemia. Several diagnostic tests and protocols have been proposed to confirm pituitary adenoma in the horse. The ACTH stimulation test, dexamethasone suppression test, or both are traditionally used to evaluate adrenal and pituitary function in horses. The suppression and stimulation tests can be conducted on different days or performed sequentially. Table 12–2 shows a recommended protocol for performing these tests. In the 2-day dexamethasone suppression test, cortisol concentration should be suppressed to 30% of baseline in 4 hours and should still be at or below 30% of baseline in 24 hours. The ACTH stimulation test performed the following day should show a

two- to threefold rise in cortisol concentration by 8 hours postinjection. If the tests are run on consecutive days, the 24-hour dexamethasone suppression samples serve as the 0-hour ACTH stimulation sample. In the time-saving combined dexamethasone suppression–ACTH stimulation test, cortisol concentration should be suppressed to less than 35% of baseline at 3 hours, and it should rise to about 2.5 times baseline at 5 hours. The obvious advantage of this combined method is that the entire procedure takes only 5 hours. However, cosyntropin used in the 1-day procedure is more expensive than corticotropin gel, used in the 2-day procedure, and corticotropin gel works well in the 2-day protocol.

A recent study suggests that a definitive diagnosis of pituitary adenoma can be based on dexamethasone suppression, thyrotropin-releasing hormone (TRH) response, and insulin concentration measurement. In horses with pituitary adenoma given TRH (1 mg intravenously), plasma cortisol concentrations rose significantly to peak at 30 minutes postinjection. Resting insulin concentrations in horses with pituitary adenoma are elevated above 100 μ U/ml and do not respond normally to intravenous glucose challenge.

Treatment of pituitary adenoma has been attempted with serotonin antagonist cyproheptadine (Periactin). The dose rate is 0.6 mg/kg increased to 1.2 mg/kg over a period of weeks. Clinical response to treatment should occur in 6 to 8 weeks. Treatment reduces the secretion of peptides but does not affect tumor size; therefore, only those signs caused by excess ACTH and related peptides will be ameliorated. Less frequently used drugs include the dopamine agonists pergolide and bromocriptine.

Diabetes mellitus is rare in the horse. Early case reports of diabetes mellitus in the literature were actually cases of pituitary adenoma. A few cases of diabetes mellitus have been associated with chronic pancreatitis.

Hirsutism and hyperhydrosis are not seen with diabetes mellitus, while ketonuria is. Horses with diabetes mellitus should be responsive to insulin and have low resting insulin concentrations, in contrast to horses with pituitary adenoma. Two cases of insulin-resistant diabetes mellitus without pituitary adenoma have been reported.

PSYCHOGENIC POLYDIPSIA-POLYURIA

Psychogenic or primary polydipsia is commonly encountered in equine medicine, particularly in the southern states with high ambient temperatures and humidity. In our experience, psychogenic water drinking is the most common cause of polyuria and polydipsia. It is more commonly diagnosed in horses kept stalled and is almost always diagnosed during hot and humid seasons. Apparently, polydipsia commonly develops out of boredom and becomes habit or a stall vice. Psychogenic polydipsia is usually diagnosed by ruling out other causes of polyuria and polydipsia. If psychogenic polydipsia is not long-standing, the water deprivation test (Table 12–3) should result in appropriately concentrated urine. Initiating the test in the evening ensures better and more convenient observation at more critical periods of deprivation (i.e., at 12 to 20 hours). If urine specific gravity approaches but does not exceed 1.020 at 20 hours, further deprivation to 24 hours can be considered. Concentrating ability might not be normal in long-standing cases of psychogenic water drinking because of medullary washout. Restricting water intake to approximately 40 ml/kg body weight/day for several days and reassessing urine specific gravity should confirm medullary washout. Alternatively, hypertonic saline can be given to help establish renal medullary hypertonicity.

TABLE 12–2. DEXAMETHASONE SUPPRESSION AND ACTH RESPONSE TEST

2-Day Procedure

0 hour —Collect blood for baseline cortisol
 —Inject 40 μg/kg dexamethasone intramuscularly

4 hours—Collect blood for cortisol

24 hours—Collect blood for cortisol
 —Inject 1 U/kg corticotropin gel intramuscularly

32 hours—Collect blood for cortisol

1-Day Procedure

0 hour —Collect blood for baseline cortisol
 —Inject 10 mg dexamethasone intramuscularly

3 hours—Collect blood for cortisol
 —Inject 1 mg cosyntropin intravenously

5 hours—Collect blood for cortisol

Psychogenic polydipsia can usually be corrected by judiciously limiting water intake and employing management changes to eliminate it. Water restriction should be initiated only if other causes of polyuria and polydipsia have been ruled out.

Relieving the animal's boredom by increasing exercise or providing a toy or stallmate can be helpful in correcting psychogenic water drinking. Increasing the roughage content of the feed to increase eating time and thus decrease boredom as well as increasing satiety can also be helpful. Pasturing the horse is often the easiest management change.

Polyuria and polydipsia secondary to psychogenic salt consumption is rarely encountered. Psychogenic salt consumption developing out of boredom can become a habit. The increased sodium chloride intake should result in high fractional excretions of sodium and chloride as well as a sodium diuresis and dilute urine. Salt deprivation and water limitation should allow correction of the polyuria and polydipsia. As with psychogenic polydipsia, management practices to reduce bore-

TABLE 12–3. WATER DEPRIVATION EST

Never perform a water deprivation test on a
  horse with azotemia or dehydration
If possible, determine the animal's weight
Remove feed and water
Catheterize to empty the bladder and
  determine urine specific gravity
Determine urine specific gravity, weight loss,
  and blood urea nitrogen or creatinine
  concentrations every 4 hours for a maximum
  of 20 hours' deprivation
Water deprivation should be terminated before
  20 hours if **any** of the following occur:
    urine concentration above 1.020
    blood urea nitrogen or creatinine elevation
      above normal
    evidence of clinical dehydration or loss of
      5% body weight

dom such as turning the horse out to pasture or providing a stallmate often correct such vices. Removal of ad libitum salt and feeding it in the ration might be necessary to alleviate the problem.

DIABETES INSIPIDUS AND MEDULLARY WASHOUT

Diabetes insipidus is characterized by the inability of the kidney to concentrate urine owing to a lack of ADH or an insensitivity of the kidney to ADH. Central diabetes insipidus is due to interference with production or release of ADH by the supraoptic nuclei of the hypothalamus, transport of ADH down the infundibulum of the pituitary, or release of the hormone by the neurohypophysis. In the horse, central diabetes insipidus is often associated with pituitary adenoma. Inability of the tubules to respond to ADH is termed nephrogenic diabetes insipidus. This condition can occur secondary to renal infection such as pyelonephritis. Bacterial toxins might render the renal tubules insensitive to ADH. Medullary washout is the loss of hypertonicity of the medullary interstitium. It can occur secondarily in any animal with polyuria and polydipsia. It is particularly important when it results from psychogenic polydipsia, because it can be confused with nephrogenic diabetes, insipidus.

A horse with central diabetes insipidus is unable to concentrate urine when water intake is restricted, but it concentrates urine in response to exogenous ADH. Horses with nephrogenic diabetes insipidus cannot concentrate urine even when ADH is injected. In order to differentiate nephrogenic diabetes insipidus from the more common medullary washout, a modified water deprivation test as described in psychogenic polydipsia is performed.

One ADH response test involves three injections of the administration of 60 IU ADH/450 kg body weight every 6 hours.

SUPPLEMENTAL READING

Beech, J., and Garcia, M.: Hormonal response to thyrotropin-releasing hormone in healthy horses and in horses with pituitary adenoma. Am. J. Vet. Res., 46:1941–1943, 1985.

Divers, T.J.: Chronic renal failure in horses. Compend. Contin. Educ., 5:S310–S317, 1983.

Grossman, B.S., et al.: Urinary indices for differentiation of pre-renal azotemia and renal azotemia in horses. J. Am. Vet. Med. Assoc., 180:286–288, 1982.

Koterba, A.M., and Coffman, J.R.: Acute and chronic renal disease in the horse. Compend. Contin. Educ., 3:S461–S470, 1981.

Morris, D.D., Divers, T.J., and Whitlock, R.H.: Renal clearance and fractional excretion of electrolytes over a 24 hour period in horses. Am. J. Vet. Res., 45:2431–2435, 1984.

chapter 13

ANEMIA—PALE MUCOUS MEMBRANES

Christopher M. Brown

Benjamin J. Darien

Anemia is not a disease, but a clinical sign or problem. Frequently, equine veterinarians diagnose anemia and treat the horse without determining the cause of the problem. Many horses so handled do not respond to the therapy, and the problem persists and can even worsen. The problem should be defined at the outset to allow a logical approach to therapy and management.

DEFINING THE PROBLEM AND ITS SIGNIFICANCE

Anemia is a reduction below reference levels in the number of red cells, the amount of hemoglobin, or both in a given volume of blood. In routine equine practice this reduction is usually defined in terms of packed cell volume (PCV, %, or L/L) and total hemoglobin (g/dl of plasma). Other indices, such as red cell size and hemoglobin content, are less useful in the horse than in other species, and hence total red cell counts are not as useful.

Although this definition of anemia appears straightforward, the circulating red cell mass in the horse is extremely labile. The spleen has a large reserve of red cells (up to 30% of the red cell mass) that can be discharged into the circulation when the spleen contracts. Thus, the PCV depends on the state of splenic contraction. In excited or recently exercised horses, the contracted spleen elevates the PCV above "resting" levels. On the other hand, splenic relaxation, induced, for example, by promazine tranquilizers, causes red cell sequestration and the lowering of the PCV below resting levels. For example, a Thoroughbred in training, tranquilized with acepromazine, could have a PCV of 34% (0.34 L/L); the same horse untranquilized and after strenuous exercise could have a PCV of 54% (0.54 L/L).

In addition, the PCV and hemoglobin levels vary greatly among breeds of horses. The more athletic horses, such as Thoroughbred and Standardbreds (the "hot-blooded" horses), have markedly higher PCVs than "cold-blooded" animals, such as draught horses and ponies. Values are usually in the range of 38 to 48% (0.38 to 0.48 L/L) for resting PCV in the first group and 28 to 35% (0.28 to 0.35 L/L) in the latter group.

A deviation from the usual values can be detected if several previous evaluations, taken under similar conditions, are available for the same horse. A single sample taken from a horse can be difficult to interpret without any previous data for comparison. If the animal is very pale with tachypnea and tachycardia and has a PCV of 15% (0.15 L/L), no matter what its original normal value, the horse is profoundly anemic. On the other hand, a value that is only 4 to 5% (0.04 to 0.05 L/L) below reference normals might or might not indicate a reduced red cell mass.

Once a reduction below normal values has been ascertained, its significance must be determined. The impact of the reduced oxygen-carrying capacity of the blood in anemia depends on its magnitude and the use of the horse. A small drop in red cell mass could have a significant impact on the maximum performance of a competitive racehorse but could go completely undetected in a broodmare. However, as already mentioned, these small deviations are difficult to detect using routine techniques. In experimental situations in racehorses, a correlation between total blood volume and performance has been shown. Horses with a reduced red cell mass and those with an excessively large mass ("overtrained" horses) perform poorly compared to those in the optimum range. However, these determinations are not routinely available. Subtle anemias are difficult to detect and have vague, ill-defined effects.

More severe anemias cause a variety of signs, depending on the degree of anemia, its cause, and its rate of development. Acute, severe blood loss leads to hypovolemic shock, with pale mucous membranes, weak, rapid pulse, cold limbs, and tachypnea. Less severe or less acute anemias have less-severe signs, and often are a secondary disease, with other clinical signs predominating.

CLINICAL EVALUATION (FIG. 13–1)

PHYSICAL EXAMINATION

Physical examination can reveal obvious pallor of the mucous membranes; petechiation suggesting coagulopathy or vasculitis; localized swellings suggesting subcutaneous hemorrhage; or an obvious site of hemorrhage, such as the nose, anus, or urinary tract.

LABORATORY TESTS

Initial laboratory data might be helpful. Usually the anemia will have been discovered based on hematologic data, a lowered PCV and hemoglobin. Indices of red cell size (mean corpuscular volume, or MCV) and hemoglobin content (mean

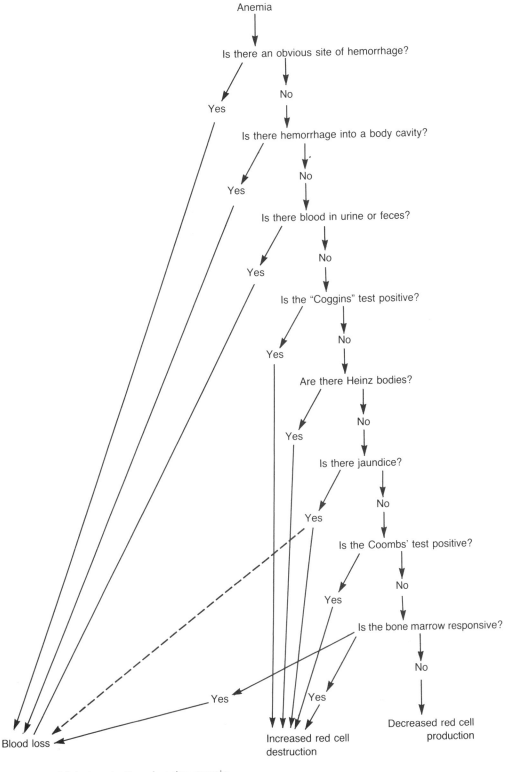

Fig. 13–1. Clinical evaluation of equine anemia.

corpuscular hemoglobin content, or MCHC) are much less useful in horses than in other species. The erythrogram generally does not clearly indicate the type or cause of the anemia, nor does it strongly suggest if a regenerative response occurs. In many species, in response to blood loss or increased red cell destruction, the bone marrow increases the rate of production of red cells, and immature and nucleated red cells are often released into the peripheral blood. Because this release does not occur in the horse, however, a complete blood count and differential cell count cannot be used to determine if an anemia is responsive or unresponsive. In the horse, the MCV might increase somewhat in responsive anemias, usually before the PCV increases. This small-magnitude change is most clearly demonstrated when blood samples are processed through automatic analyzers, which produce an erythrogram showing the size distribution of the red cell population. Though analyzers are not yet widely available for processing equine blood samples, they probably will be in the future.

Heinz bodies that might be seen on the peripheral blood smear suggest possible causes of anemia. Heinz bodies are produced from hemoglobin following the action of various oxidative chemicals. In horses, phenothiazine and compounds found in onions and wilted red maple leaves have been responsible for the production of Heinz-body anemias. In addition, aggregation of red cells suggests autoagglutination and an immune-mediated problem. If active severe intravascular hemolysis is present, free hemoglobin in the plasma can give a pink to red supernatant in the microhematocrit tube. Similarly, the plasma can be deep yellow in cases of significant hemolysis and increased production of bilirubin (Chapter 14).

In patients with chronic inflammatory disorders, mild anemia marked by an increased white blood cell count, predominantly a mature neutrophilia, is expected.

Serum globulin and fibrinogen are also elevated in many of these patients.

An impression of the platelet count can be obtained by examining the blood smears, and a total count is needed if thrombocytopenia is suspected as a cause of a coagulopathy and anemia. Thrombocytopenia is indicated by widespread petechiation of the mucous membranes and coagulopathy, with normal partial thromboplastin time and prothrombin times.

If the initial laboratory data (complete blood count) does not clearly indicate the cause of the anemia, a series of tests can be done. Lacking an obvious site of blood loss, the possibility of hemorrhage into a body cavity or loss in feces or urine should be considered. Fecal or urine blood evaluations are simple and inexpensive. Many horses have a positive test result for fecal blood at 60 seconds or longer, probably owing to pseudoperoxidase present in plant material. The result should not be considered significant unless the test becomes positive within 20 seconds. Equally, a trace of blood in a urine sample probably is not significant. Samples not voided spontaneously, but obtained by catheterization or rectal examination, might be contaminated with blood produced by trauma from collection, giving a false-positive result.

Abdominocentesis to determine the presence of intra-abdominal hemorrhage is safe and simple. However, because the spleen is easily tapped, if a bloody sample is obtained the tap should be repeated at another site, preferably well to the right of midline. In addition, the PCV of the abdominal fluid should be checked. Splenic blood usually has a higher PCV than peripheral blood, whereas fluid that accumulates in the abdomen following hemorrhage has either a lower PCV or the same PCV as peripheral blood.

Although thoracocentesis is simple and can determine the presence of interpleural hemorrhage, some risks are involved. Thoracic auscultation, percussion, radiography, and ultrasonography are noninvasive and if possible should be performed to determine if thoracocentesis is justified.

Lacking obvious hemorrhage or evidence of blood loss into the feces, urine, or body cavities, additional tests can be undertaken. Whenever an anemia cannot be explained based on physical and initial laboratory findings, blood should be submitted for the gel diffusion test (the Coggins test) to detect antibodies against the equine infectious anemia virus. However, the significance of a positive test is unclear. Many horses that test positive have no clinical signs. If the clinical findings are consistent with equine infectious anemia, however, the test confirms the etiology.

The Coombs' test is now more widely available for the horse than before and can be used to determine the possible role of immune-mediated phenomena in the cause of the anemia.

Finally, because the peripheral erythrogram is relatively unhelpful in horses, bone marrow aspiration, biopsy, or both can be used to determine the response of the erythropoietic tissue to the anemia. Of the three sites that can be used for aspiration (the sternum, the ribs, or the tuber coxae), we find the ribs or the sternum the most accessible and reliable. Techniques vary, but the simplest method is to use a 16-gauge disposable bone marrow needle. The stylet is introduced through a small incision in a prepared anesthetized site. The needle must be driven firmly into the bone using a rotating action. When the needle is well-seated, the stylet is removed and suction applied with a 3-ml syringe. Frequently, only a small amount of material enters the hub of the syringe. If blood flows freely, the sample obtained will usually be diluted with peripheral blood and hence inadequate for assessment. The sample should be transferred to a tube with a small amount of ethylenediaminetetra-acetic acid (EDTA), or applied directly to prepared microscope slides that should be processed immediately. The best results and interpretations can be obtained only with fresh, well-prepared material and slides. Because most practitioners are not experienced with bone marrow cytology, the advice of a clinical pathologist should be obtained before the samples are collected.

An alternative and useful method of obtaining bone marrow aspirate is to bore a hole into the bone marrow using a Steinmann's pin inserted in a Jacob's chuck. A small hypodermic needle is passed down the bore hole to aspirate a sample.

A more complete assessment of the bone marrow can be obtained if a core biopsy is performed and the material examined histologically. Biopsy requires a suitable trephine, 2 to 3 mm in diameter. The core of bone and marrow obtained should be quickly fixed in Zenker's fixative, although impression smears can be made first for immediate processing and interpretation. The disadvantage of the biopsy is that several days are needed to process the sample for histologic evaluation. This delay is not usually a drawback to patient management, however, as many of the horses that require a bone marrow assessment have slowly progressive disorders.

Following this protocol should allow a definitive diagnosis, or at least classification of the anemia based on one of three causes—blood loss, increased red cell destruction, and decreased red cell production. Additional tests might be required to further refine the diagnosis and to develop a management plan.

CAUSES (Fig. 13–2)

BLOOD LOSS

Overt Hemorrhage. Overt hemorrhage is the easiest and most obvious problem to diagnose. The amount and rate of blood

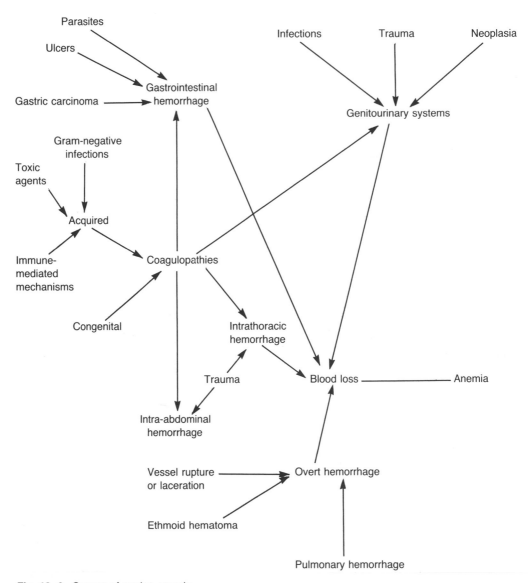

Fig. 13–2. Causes of equine anemia.

loss depends on the vessel lacerated and the duration of hemorrhaging. Severe systemic hemorrhage can result from disorders of hemostasis as well as direct vessel rupture.

Respiratory Hemorrhage. The respiratory system can be a source of hemorrhage. Spontaneous rupture of aneurysms of the internal carotid artery within the guttural pouch, as a consequence of mycotic infection, can cause repeated severe hemorrhage that can be fatal (Chapter 9). Pulmonary hemorrhage is common in athletic horses (Chapter 9), but the amount of blood lost is usually not sufficient to cause demonstrable anemia. Occasionally, severe pulmonary hemorrhage can be induced by exercise. Horses with pulmonary abscesses, particularly abscesses caused by mixed bacterial infections, including anaerobes, can suffer from severe repeated pulmonary hemorrhage if large vessels become necrotic. The source of the hemorrhage can be localized by endoscopy and radiography.

Ethmoid hematomas (Chapter 9) frequently cause intermittent unilateral nasal bleeding. The amount of blood lost is usually fairly small, but if the hemorrhage is continuous, mild anemia might ensue. Endoscopy and skull radiography confirm the diagnosis.

Gastrointestinal Hemorrhage. Gastrointestinal hemorrhage, though rarely spectacular, can be chronic and insidious and result in chronic anemias. The incidence of gastrointestinal ulceration in adult horses is unknown. Some data indicate that many horses have varying degrees of gastric erosions and ulceration, but exactly how much blood is lost through these lesions is unknown. Some animals, particularly foals, can develop more discrete deep ulcers that can involve larger vessels and result in significant hemorrhage. These ulcers can develop as a result of either stress or overusage of nonsteroidal anti-inflammatory drugs. Occasionally, the bleeding will be extensive and rapid enough to cause acute hypovolemic shock requiring emergency therapy. Usually, however, blood loss is slower and less severe, resulting in mild to moderate anemia (PCV 20 to 25%, 0.20 to 0.25 L/L). Additional signs of gastric ulceration are vague and include mild intermittent colic, occasional diarrhea, inappetence, weight loss, and grinding of the teeth in some cases (Chapters 3 and 5).

Gastric squamous cell carcinomas are well-recognized, but uncommon in horses. Some of these tumors bleed and cause chronic anemia. Occasionally a horse will suffer an acute severe hemorrhage if the tumor erodes through a major vessel. Diagnosis is based on analysis of abdominal fluid, fecal blood evaluation, and, if available, gastroscopy.

Parasitism is probably the most common cause of chronic blood loss through the gastrointestinal system in horses. Mature strongyles, particularly the large ones, attach to the mucosa, eroding it and causing ulceration and blood loss. A heavy infestation can lead to chronic anemia. Though the small stronglyes are less pathogenic, heavy infestations can result in mild anemia.

Diagnosis of parasitism is based on clinical signs, including weight loss (Chapter 2), detection of worm eggs in the feces, and an elevation of serum β globulin or IgG(T). A response to appropriate anthelmintic therapy often supports a diagnosis of parasitism.

Genitourinary Hemorrhage. Genitourinary hemorrhage is a relatively uncommon source of blood loss in horses. Parturient injuries in mares such as laceration of major vaginal or cervical vessels can lead to significant blood loss but usually present no major diagnostic problems. Rupture of the middle uterine artery is an uncommon but well-recognized problem occurring at parturition in older multiparous mares. Hemorrhage from the vagina or into the abdomen is not immediately obvious. The blood collects within the broad ligament, causing a large swelling, pain, and varying degrees of hypovolemia. Rectal examination is useful in diagnosis. There is no specific therapy, and if the hematoma in the broad ligament ruptures, the hemorrhage is usually fatal. If hemorrhage stops the mare might survive but will be markedly anemic for some time.

Hematuria can develop from lesions within the bladder and kidneys. (Hemoglobinuria, which develops following severe intravascular hemolysis, can be distinguished from myoglobinuria by electrophoretic urinalysis.) In adult horses, cystic calculi are often associated with chronic cystitis, erosion of the bladder mucosa, and hemorrhage. Other clinical signs, such as tenesmus and pollakiuria, are often present. Rectal examination confirms the presence of the calculus. Cystitis without calculi is less commonly associated with recurrent chronic hemorrhage, although occasional bleeding ulcers are found in chronic cystitis. Neoplasia of the bladder is uncommon in horses and hence is a rare cause of blood loss from this system. The bladder can be evaluated by rectal examination, transrectal ultrasonography, and fiberoptic endoscopy. The location and severity of lesions can be assessed. Urinalysis is indicated in all cases of hematuria. Renal lesions that uncommonly cause significant blood loss include infarcts, abscesses, and neoplasms. Diagnosis is based on rectal, ultrasonographic (transrectal and transabdominal), and laboratory findings.

Trauma. Trauma can lead to either intrathoracic or intra-abdominal hemorrhage, without any overt signs of bleeding. A history of a traumatic accident is important. Splenic rupture is rarely recognized in horses. Diagnosis is based on clinical findings, radiography, ultrasonography, thoracocentesis, and abdominocentesis.

Coagulopathies. Coagulopathies can result in hemorrhage or thrombosis of varying severity at almost any site. A problem with hemostasis should be suspected when spontaneous hemorrhage or thrombosis at one or more sites cannot be explained by an obvious underlying cause, such as a lacerated vessel or an erosive or necrotic lesion. Further suspicion is aroused when sites of venipuncture bleed profusely for prolonged periods or spontaneously form a thrombus. Clinical signs vary. Hemorrhage in hypocoagulopathies can be massive and even fatal. More typically, repeated bouts of hemorrhage or chronic continuous bleeding occur. Hemorrhage into a body cavity might

go unnoticed. The severity of the anemia and the signs depend on the rate and degree of blood loss.

Though hemostatic disorders have many potential causes, relatively few need consideration. Overdosage with warfarin, which some veterinarians use in the management of navicular disease, can lead to an abnormality in several clotting factors (factors II, VI, IX, and X, protein C, and protein S) because it is a vitamin K antagonist. Its impact on factor VII is first detected as an increase in the prothombin time. Prolongation of the activated partial thromboplastin time occurs somewhat later. Thus, both the intrinsic and extrinsic systems are involved. Diagnosis is based on evidence of hemorrhage, from a body orifice, into a body cavity, or under the skin; a history of warfarin exposure (either therapeutically or accidentally); and prolongation of prothrombin time and possibly activated partial prothrombin time.

Therapy is based on eliminating exposure to the drug and administering vitamin K_1 (400 to 500 mg) subcutaneously every 6 hours until the prothrombin time is within the normal range. Fresh plasma might be necessary if the bleeding tendency is life-threatening, and a transfusion of whole blood should be considered if severe blood loss has occurred. Approximately 5 to 10 ml/kg body weight of fresh plasma is administered, usually three times, until bleeding is controlled.

Because clotting factors are produced in the liver, hemostasis can be impaired in the terminal phases of severe liver diseases; however, the anemia of blood loss following a coagulopathy is not usually recognized in equine liver disease. Other clinical signs predominate (Chapter 14).

Thrombocytopenia in horses is not common, but bleeding becomes a tendency when the platelet count falls below 20,000/μl. The cause of the thrombocytopenia is not usually apparent. Thrombocytopenia developing while a horse is receiving medication suggests a drug-induced phenomenon. Some animals can have active or recent infectious diseases, but most have no apparent inducer. In most cases the mechanism is probably immune mediated, the affected platelets being removed by the reticuloendothelial system. Rarely, thrombocytopenia develops from reduced production in the bone marrow following toxic damage or neoplastic infiltration. These situations are usually marked by a pancytopenia.

Diagnosis is based on clinical signs of spontaneous hemorrhages and mucosal petechiation, pronounced thrombocytopenia, and normal prothrombin time and activated partial prothrombin time. Management includes discontinuing medication that might be responsible. Transfusion of fresh whole blood might be necessary if potential life-threatening hemorrhage or severe hypovolemia has occurred. The majority of horses respond well to a course of corticosteroids. Initially, prednisolone at 2 mg/kg once daily intramuscularly should be given until the platelet count has risen to at least 50,000/μl. The dosage should be gradually reduced to 0.2 mg/kg and then be discontinued after 14 to 24 days of treatment. Occasional animals relapse and require repeated courses of therapy to maintain adequate platelet status.

Occasionally horses are presented with adequate platelet numbers, a normal prothrombin time and activated partial thromboplastin time, and clinical features similar to those described for thrombocytopenia. These horses can have defects in platelet function, which can be detected only with special testing and ultrastructural evaluation usually beyond the scope of most laboratories offering a routine diagnostic service.

Congenital abnormalities of the clotting mechanisms are rarely recognized in horses. Hemophilia A, a deficiency of factor VIII, has been described in Arabians, quarter horses, Standardbreds, and Thoroughbreds. Apparently it is a sex-linked recessive trait, carried by females and clinically manifested in males. Signs can occur anytime after birth, and most horses show signs in the first few weeks of life. Intra-articular hemorrhage is common, but hemorrhages can occur anywhere, particularly at sites of trauma. Activated partial thromboplastin time is prolonged. Diagnosis of hemophilia A can be confirmed by assay for factor VIII, and the client should be referred to an appropriate laboratory. Therapy is not indicated, but genetic counseling is important.

In uncomplicated cases of anemia caused by blood loss, bone marrow is responsive, with an increase in the erythroid series. If blood has been lost chronically, serum iron concentrations might be low, and serum iron-binding capacity will be increased. However, these indices are not routinely required in the assessment of these patients.

Blood loss anemias usually do not require treatment if the cause of the bleeding is identified and treated. Blood transfusions might be needed if the anemia is critical (PCV below 10%, 0.10 L/L). Some horses with chronic blood loss, particularly foals, require iron supplementation. However, the use of iron supplementation is much more widespread than is necessary. In adult horses, most of the breakdown products of hemoglobin are retained and recycled, and these animals rarely become iron deficient. The bilirubin released by this breakdown is excreted via the bile. If extensive hemolysis occurs, bilirubin production can exceed hepatic processing and excretion and icterus can ensue (Chapter 14).

INCREASED RED CELL DESTRUCTION (FIG. 13–3)

Infectious Diseases. The infectious diseases that directly affect the equine red cell and lead to increased destruction and anemia are equine infectious anemia, equine

Fig. 13–3. Causes of increased red cell destruction leading to equine anemia.

babesiosis (piroplasmosis), and equine ehrlichiosis.

Equine infectious anemia is a retroviral disease spread by biting insects, particularly horseflies. It is most common in the southern states, but is recorded throughout North America. Clinically, it varies from being inapparent, to being mildly to acutely severe and even fatal. In addition, chronic and recurrent cases occur.

Initially, signs can include fever with mucosal petechiation. Recurrent bouts of

fever occur with anemia, anorexia, icterus, and edema. Weight loss occurs in chronic cases. During periods of remission the anemia can resolve, although it can recur with subsequent episodes. The anemia results from increased red cell destruction, which is probably immune mediated, and also from reduced red cell production. Also associated with the anemia is multiorgan involvement, with evidence of liver disease based on serum enzymes (Chapter 14). Confirmation of a suspected diagnosis is based on the demonstration of antiviral antibodies using the gel diffusion test (Coggins test). However, this test can give a false-negative result in the peracute phase of the disease, and some chronic cases are also seronegative. No effective therapy for equine infectious anemia exists, and local regulations might require destruction or quarantine of horses with confirmed cases.

Equine babesiosis occurs in tropical and subtropical areas. In the U.S., Babesia caballi, the most common cause of equine babesiosis, is transmitted by the tick Dermacentor nitens. This tick is found in Texas and Florida and around the Caribbean. B. equi, the other agent of equine babesiosis, is uncommon in the U.S.

The disease mostly affects horses newly introduced into endemic areas; horses raised in these areas acquire the infection as foals and achieve a status of tolerance (premunition), in which they are permanently infected but not clinically affected. Susceptible horses have anemia, fever, depression, edema, and ecchymoses on the mucosae. Diagnosis is based on clinical signs and history. In some cases the parasite can be seen on blood smears, and detection of antibodies by a complement fixation test can confirm the diagnosis. Details for the submission of samples should be obtained from local state diagnostic laboratories before collection of samples.

Therapy depends on the location of the horse. In endemic areas the objective is not to clear the infection but to suppress it so the premunition will ensue. A single intramuscular dose of imidocarb diproprionate at 2.2 mg/kg body weight is suggested as a means of achieving suppression. Horses moving to nonendemic areas should receive the same drug at 2 mg/kg on 2 successive days. Although this dosage usually clears infection of B. caballi, it will resolve B. equi only in about 60% of the cases, even at dosages of

4 mg/kg every 3 days for four or five treatments. In endemic areas tick control can play a role in disease management.

Ehrlichia equi is a rickettsial agent found mostly in California, but occasionally recorded elsewhere. It is probably transmitted by ticks. Affected horses have fever, anorexia, depression, edema, petechiation of mucosae, and occasional ataxia. The anemia is moderate, and leukopenia and thrombocytopenia occur. Diagnostic inclusion bodies might be seen in neutrophils and eosinophils. The disease is not serious, and horses usually recover in about 2 weeks. Oxytetracycline, 2.5 mg/kg intravenously twice daily, might reduce the recovery period.

Toxic Agents. Toxic agents that cause equine anemias by increasing red cell destruction are not commonly encountered. Three main agents have been described—wilted red maple leaves, onions (wild and domesticated), and phenothiazine. All can produce Heinz bodies by oxidation of hemoglobin, and red maple leaves can produce methemoglobin by oxidation of iron. The clinical signs resulting from the three agents are similar. If sufficient amounts of the agent is eaten, an acute hemolytic crisis occurs with tachypnea, tachycardia, and weakness. Mucous membranes can be jaundiced or can be bronze-colored if large amounts of methemoglobin are present. Urine is often red-brown or black. Laboratory data reflect the hemolysis and its mechanism. The PCV can be below 10% (0.1 L/L), and the red cells can have Heinz bodies. Serum can be icteric or red owing to free hemoglobin, and many serum enzymes, particularly liver-associated enzymes, can be elevated, probably reflecting tissue anoxia. Some animals with red maple toxicosis have evidence of disseminated intravascular coagulation, based on an abnormal activated partial thromboplastin time and elevation of fibrinolytic degeneration products. Many of these animals have a rapidly progressive fatal disease, such as pulmonary thrombosis and renal failure.

Treatment with intravenous fluids and fresh whole blood can reverse the anemia and the coagulopathy and promote volume diuresis to clear the metabolites. Methylene blue has not been useful for the treatment of methemoglobinemia associated with red maple leaf toxicity.

Intravascular hemolysis can occur as a terminal event in severe liver disease (Chapter 14). The cause is unknown, and other clinical signs predominate. Similar hemolysis can occur if large volumes of hypotonic fluids are given intravenously. Such hemolytic accidents are unlikely if commercially prepared solutions are used, but the risk is increased if homemade fluids are used.

Immune-Mediated Mechanisms. Immune-mediated mechanisms can lead to increased red cell destruction. Foals can develop an isoimmune problem in which alloantibodies against the foals' red cells are present in the colostrum. On absorption of colostral antibodies, a hemolytic crisis occurs with hemoglobinemia, hemoglobinuria, jaundice, severe anemia (PCV 15% or below; 0.15 L/L), weakness, tachycardia, tachypnea, and sometimes convulsions. The severity of the clinical signs depends on the specific blood-group incompatibility and the amount of antibody absorbed. Data indicate that antigenic factors Aa and Qa are the two factors most often responsible for neonatal isoerythrolysis.

The antibodies are produced by the dam in response to the foal's red cells, to which she is exposed by placental bleeding. Sensitization occurs if the foal has inherited from the sire a blood group different from the dam's. The foal is treated with appropriate crossmatched red cells or washed cells from the dam. (This problem is discussed in Chapter 19, and as a cause of jaundice in Chapter 14.)

In adults, autoimmune anemias can occur secondary to many diseases, including infections and neoplasia, and during various drug therapies. Many unexplained anemias are primarily idiopathic. These horses generate antibodies that coat the red cells and lead to their removal by the reticuloendothelial system. The rate of red cell destruction depends on the intensity of the immune response, and the resulting anemia can be acute, chronic, or recurrent.

Diagnosis is based on failure to identify other causes of anemia and a positive Coombs' test. Autoagglutination can be noticed in the blood sample, and erythrophagocytosis can be seen in the blood smear.

Therapy depends on the cause. Autoimmune anemia secondary to other diseases can be managed by treating the primary diseases. Drugs should be stopped, or at least changed to medications chemically different from the current ones. Transfusions can be necessary in severe acute cases. Corticosteroids—dexamethasone (0.2 mg/kg) or prednisolone (2 mg/kg) divided into two dosages/day, intramuscularly—are recommended. The PCV should be taken daily; when a steady rate of increase (0.5% or more/day; 0.005 L/L) has been achieved, the dosage can be gradually tapered to alternate-day therapy and then held at maintenance or stopped. Dosages and duration of therapy vary from case to case, and laboratory data and clinical signs should be used to guide the protocol.

In all of these horses with increased red cell destruction, the bone marrow will respond.

DECREASED RED CELL PRODUCTION

Chronic low-grade anemias resulting from reduced red cell production are common in horses; most are secondary to other diseases (Fig. 13–4). The anemia is not usually clinically important, and it resolves when the primary problem resolves.

Chronic inflammation, due to infection, necrosis, or neoplasia, is commonly associated with mild anemia. The mechanism is probably mediated by products released from the cells of the inflammatory process. Anemia of chronic disease is associated with altered iron metabolism resulting in lowered serum iron and reduced erythrocyte survival, without a compensatory increase in red cell production. Similar anemias often accompany chronic liver or renal disease and can result in part from decreased erythropoietin levels and chronic inflammation.

Deficiencies are apparently rare as causes of anemia resulting from decreased red cell production. In chronic blood loss, iron deficiency could develop, and folate deficiency is possible with prolonged use of trimethoprim-sulfa combinations. Diagnosis is based

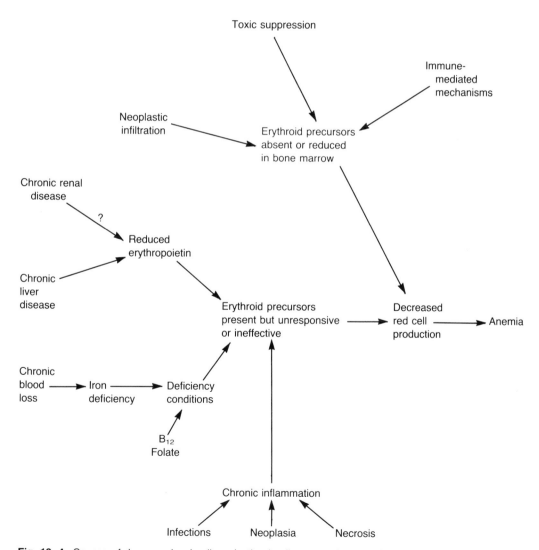

Fig. 13–4. Causes of decreased red cell production leading to equine anemia.

on the patient's history and response to dietary supplementation with the substance thought to be deficient.

Toxic agents, such as heavy metals, organic solvents, and possibly phenylbutazone, can occasionally cause direct bone marrow suppression and affect all cell lines. Similar problems can ensue from radiation exposure. Infiltration of the bone marrow by neoplastic cells also affects production of all cells. Under these circumstances, an aplastic anemia develops, with low PCV, leukopenia, and thrombocytopenia, that is, pancytopenia.

In all of these anemias, bone marrow evaluation is essential to define the problem. If a specific cause can be identified, such as deficiency or drug toxicity, appropriate action can be taken. The many idiopathic aplastic anemias in which no clear inciting agent is found can be assumed to be immune mediated. Affected animals should be treated with corticosteroids using the same protocol as that suggested for hemolytic anemias.

TREATMENT WITH BLOOD TRANSFUSIONS

GENERAL CONSIDERATIONS

Based on red cell surface antigens (alloantigens), at least eight equine blood groups are recognized. In addition, many other red cell proteins and serum proteins are genetically determined. As a result, a huge number of phenotypes for red cell and serum proteins is possible, and probably no two horses will have an identical profile and therefore be perfectly matched as blood donor and recipient. Compatibility is assessed using standard crossmatching procedures, which primarily detect agglutinins. Equine alloantibodies act more as hemolysins than as agglutinins. Testing for hemolysins, however, is not straightforward and not practical in most situations. Coombs'

test, though useful to test for agglutinins not detected by standard crossmatching, is not usually available to the general practitioner. Hence, crossmatching is used to screen donors and recipients, although apparent compatibility does not guarantee that a transfusion reaction will not occur.

Generally, a horse that has not had a previous transfusion or been sensitized to equine blood products can have a transfusion fairly safely, although some apparently naïve horses will react. If no reaction occurs, the transfusion can be repeated if necessary within days of the first, but after this time alloantibodies will have been produced and a transfusion reaction is likely.

Though normal equine red cells have a life span of about 150 days, transfused cells survive for only 2 to 4 days. Hence, transfusions are useful only for short-term support. The horse must be able to mount an efffective bone marrow response and begin to replace red cells as the effects of the transfusions decline. Because about 4 days are required for a red cell to mature from a stem cell, the transfusion provides just enough support for the horse to initiate increased red cell production and release the first "batch" of replacement cells. Giving a transfusion to an animal with bone marrow depression is useless unless specific therapy against the underlying problem is possible and has been initiated.

INDICATIONS

Only horses with life-threatening anemias or hypovolemia should be considered for transfusion. Fatal reactions can occur even with crossmatching, and the transfusion sensitizes the animal so that therapy in subsequent weeks or years would be impossible. In addition, transfused mares can become sensitized and increase the risk of inducing neonatal isoerythrolysis in their foals.

Three problems occur in acute severe hemorrhage: reduced intravascular volume, reduced red cell mass, and loss of plasma proteins. If the rate of blood loss is rapid, the fall in circulating blood volume results in circulatory failure, and erythrocyte loss causes anemic anoxia. Combined, these two factors can be fatal. The restoration of volume can be more vital than the restoration of red cell mass. Whole blood is the best fluid to give at this time, although crystaloid solutions can be lifesaving if blood is not available. The re-expanded intravascular fluid might be low in red cells, and the osmotic pressure of the plasma might be reduced by dilution of plasma proteins, but tissue perfusion will be restored. The resulting anemia and edema will be corrected in time, providing the blood loss is halted.

Estimating the volume of blood lost is difficult. Owners frequently overestimate the volume of frank hemorrhage; "gallons" are usually pints. Usually, 6 to 10 L of blood loss will not cause a life-threatening problem in a 450-kg horse; after volume expansion, such an animal would be anemic, but not critically so.

In a severe hemolytic crisis the rate of hemolysis as well as its severity determines whether transfusions should be given. If the PCV is falling rapidly toward the critical level of 10% (0.1 L/L), transfusions should be started and specific therapy against the inciting cause begun. If the PCV is 10 to 12% (0.1 to 0.12 L/L) but has stabilized and the hemolytic process has stopped, careful nursing care and support might be all that is needed.

COLLECTION

If possible a crossmatch should be done between the recipient and several potential donors. Large clinics might maintain a "universal" donor, a horse that is both Aa and Qa negative for alloantigens and has no serum alloantibodies. The erythrocyte antigen profile of several potential donors can be analyzed to determine if alloantibodies are present.* A serum sample from a clotted specimen, and a whole blood sample in acid citrate dextrose (ACD) anticoagulant (1.5 ml ACD to 8.5 ml blood) should be sent. Suitable donors have no alloantibodies in their serum, and their red cells lack Aa or Qa antigens. While blood from either of the options is not guaranteed not to cause reactions, the chances are reduced. If neither a universal donor nor crossmatching is available, blood can be taken for any healthy horse, particularly male ponies, as they are often A and Q negative. Mares who have had foals should be avoided. Neonatal isoerythrolysis requires specific treatment (Chapter 19).

Blood should be taken from the jugular vein using large-bore needles (10-gauge) and tubing. We use sodium citrate as a 3.85% solution (10 ml to each 100 ml of blood collected). This process causes little risk to a healthy donor; 10 to 15 ml of blood/kg body weight can be safely drawn from an adult horse at any one time. If possible, blood should be collected into plastic containers, because plastic is less likely than glass to cause mediators to be released from the white cells. Also, plastics do not activate platelets or factor XII or cause red cell destruction, as glass can. Collected blood should be used within 24 hours and refrigerated if not used immediately.

ADMINISTRATION AND COMPLICATIONS

The volume of blood needed in different situations varies. Because 6 to 8 L is the most that can normally be taken from a single horse at one time, this is often the

* Two laboratories currently provide this service: Serology Laboratory, Department of Veterinary Reproduction, School of Veterinary Medicine, University of California, Davis, CA 95695. Stormont Laboratories, Inc., 1237 E. Beamer St, Suite D Woodland, CA 95695.

amount administered to another horse. The objective is to maintain red cell mass just above the critical level until the animal can respond and replace the loss itself. Some severely anemic horses with critical PCVs (8 to 10%; 0.08 to 0.1 L/L) and with ongoing hemolysis (e.g., in red maple toxicity) might need 10, 12, or even 20 L of whole blood to keep pace with problems and prevent tissue anoxia.

Immune-mediated reactions or other reactions resulting from products released within the collected blood vary from mild to severe. Clinical signs include restlessness, tachycardia, tachypnea, sweating, and, in foals, diarrhea. Sudden death also is possible.

As these reactions are unpredictable, the initial rate of administration should be slow, about 5 to 10 ml/minute. The patient should be carefully monitored. If no adverse signs develop in the first 120 minutes of administration, the rate can be increased to up to 20 ml/hour/kg body weight (9 L/hour in 450-kg horse); in a young foal, 40 ml/hour/kg might be necessary (e.g., 3 L in 2 hours). Problems developing at high flow rates might be less severe if the transfusion rate is slowed. If an adverse reaction occurs with the blood from one donor, it tends to happen with blood from another; therefore, collecting from another horse might not be worthwhile.

SUPPLEMENTAL READING

Byars, T.D., Greene, C.E., and Kemp, D.T.: Antidotal effect of vitamin K, against warfarin-induced anticoagulation in the horse. Am. J. Vet. Res., 47:2309–2312, 1986.

George, L.W., Divers, T.J., Mahaffey, E.A., and Suarez, M.J.H.: Heinz body anemia and methemaglobinemia in ponies given red maple (Acer rubrum) leaves. Vet. Pathol., 19:521–533, 1982.

Kallfelz, F.A., Whitlock, R.H., and Schultz, R.D.: Survival of ^{59}Fe-labeled erythrocytes in cross-transfused equine blood. Am. J. Vet. Res., 39:617–620, 1978.

Moore, J.N., Mahaffey, E.A., and Zboran, M.: Heparin-induced agglutination of erythrocytes in horses. Am. J. Vet. Res., 48:68–71, 1987.

Radin, M.J., Eubank, M.C., and Weiser, M.G.: Electronic measurement of erythrocyte volume and volume heterogeneity in horses during erythrocyte regeneration associated with experimental anemias. Vet. Pathol., 23:656–660, 1986.

Tschudi, P., Archer, R.K., and Gerber, H.: The cells of equine blood and their development. Equine Vet. J. 7:141–147, 1975.

Wong, P.L., Nickel, L.S., Bowling, A.T., and Steffey, E.P.: Clinical survey of antibodies against red blood cells in horses after homologous blood transfusion. Am. J. Vet. Res., 47:2566–2571, 1986.

chapter 14

ICTERUS

Erwin G. Pearson

DEFINITION

Icterus (jaundice) is a syndrome characterized by hyperbilirubinemia and deposition of bile pigment in the skin and mucous membranes with a resulting yellow appearance. Icterus is impossible to detect in pigmented skin and unless severe is difficult to see in unpigmented skin covered with hair. Probably the area that best shows icterus is the sclera, although other mucous membranes, such as the mouth and vulva, can also show it.

Icterus indicates that the bilirubin metabolism has been altered by increased production of bilirubin, decreased removal of bilirubin from the blood, or both.

In the normal horse, serum total bilirubin levels are reported to range from about 0.5 to 2 mg/dl (8.5 to 34 μmol/L), depending on the method and the investigator, and most is unconjugated or indirect reacting. Bilirubin levels in normal horses vary greatly. Some particularly "hot-blooded" and exercised horses have higher levels; other horses, such as Shetland ponies, mules, and donkeys, have lower levels.

A poor correlation exists between the degree of icterus and the concentration of plasma bilirubin in horses when bilirubin is below 2 mg/dl (34 μmol/L), but with marked icterus, the serum bilirubin is invariably elevated.

NORMAL BILIRUBIN METABOLISM

The pathway of bilirubin metabolism is illustrated by Fig. 14–1. The initial step is the destruction of the erythrocyte. If the erythrocyte destruction is intravascular, hemoglobin is bound to haptoglobin for transport. If the erythrocytes are re-moved by the reticuloendothelial system, hemoglobin is broken down and not released into the plasma. Within the reticuloendothelial system, the heme is converted first to biliverdin and then to bilirubin.

Next, the unconjugated (indirect) bilirubin, bound to albumin, is transferred to the liver. This insoluble protein-bound free bilirubin will not be removed by the kidney.

The third step is the uptake of unconjugated bilirubin by the hepatocytes. In the hepatocyte, some bilirubin is conjugated to the diglucuronide; in the horse, over half of bilirubin in bile forms this conjugate. Conjugated bilirubin is water soluble, and some is regurgitated into the sinusoids and thus enters the

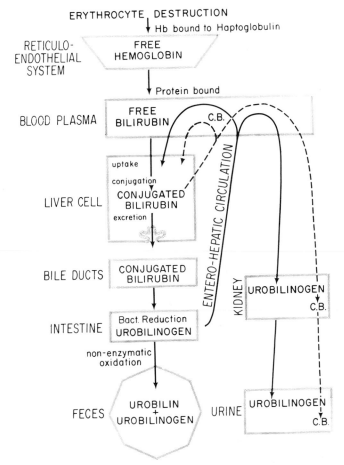

Fig. 14–1. Pathway of bilirubin metabolism. (From Pearson, E.G.: Clinical management of the icteric horse. Compend. Contin. Educ., 4:S114–S122, 1982.)

plasma; if the concentration is high enough, some will be excreted by the kidney.

The final step of bilirubin metabolism in the hepatocyte is the secretion of conjugated bilirubin into the bile canaliculi. Whereas in most species this energy-dependent process is the rate-limiting step, this might not be true in the horse, as conjugated bilirubin levels in the plasma are not excessive unless bile flow is obstructed. Disruption of hepatocyte energy metabolism slows this excretory process. Conjugated bilirubin enters the intestine through the bile ducts. If these are blocked, plasma concentrations of both conjugated and unconjugated bilirubin increase. In the intestinal tract, anaerobic bacteria convert bilirubin to urobilinogen. Some urobilinogen is absorbed and re-excreted by the liver. Normally, a small fraction of absorbed urobilinogen passes through the liver and is excreted in the urine.

In the horse, about 75% of the bile pigment originates from the metabolism of hemoglobin released from erythrocytes. Hepatic and erythropoietic heme account for some of the remainder. A direct correlation exists between the percentage of erythrocytes replaced each day, and the endogenous bile pigment excretion. Total bile pigment excretion in ponies is about 1.4 μg/minute/kg.

Problems in bilirubin metabolism can result from increased red blood cell destruction; impairment of the ability of the hepatocyte to pick up, conjugate, and excrete bilirubin; and obstruction to the flow of bile. In addition, fasting in horses can cause hyperbilirubinemia.

CLINICAL EVALUATION OF ICTERUS (Fig. 14–2)

Many diseases of horses cause icterus. Increasing the data base and considering the patient history, signs, and geographic location helps eliminate many unlikely causes. Icterus can be divided into several major categories—hemolytic

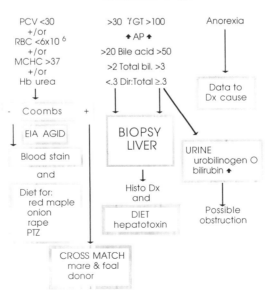

CONCEPT OF ICTERUS DIAGNOSIS
Mucous membranes yellow
Total bilirubin >2mg/dl

Fig. 14–2. Diagnosis of icterus.

anemias, hepatocellular disease, bile obstruction, fasting, and diseases restricted to neonates. However, some of the diseases fit into more than one category; for example, many horses with hemolysis or hepatic damage are anorectic, and hemolysis has been reported in terminal liver disease. Within each category, specific tests might be needed to confirm or rule out the suspected diseases.

PATIENT HISTORY

The season of the year might be important, especially in eliminating some of the arthropod-transmitted diseases, such as equine infectious anemia. Knowledge of the food intake allows fasting to be considered. Pastured animals might have access to hemolytic plants or hepatotoxins, although these could also be present in the hay. A vaccination history will reveal whether the horse has received equine serum, for example, tetanus antitoxin or pregnant mare's serum.

The chronicity of the disease can be important. Many of the toxic hepatic diseases and neoplastic diseases are chronic. In most instances, complete bile obstruction and the hemolytic diseases are acute. Geographic location is important, as certain toxic plants occur only in certain areas. Also, some blood infections such as babesiosis are seen more commonly in the southern states.

Conditions causing icterus in foals under 2 weeks of age include normal increased bilirubin, neonatal isoerythrolysis, neonatal hepatic failure, Tyzzer's disease, in utero herpes infection, anorexia, and foal septicemia.

PHYSICAL EXAMINATION

Table 14–1 shows some of the common signs in icterus and their possible causes. Icteric horses with hepatocellular disease can have signs resulting from failure of other liver functions. None of these signs is pathognomonic for liver disease, as all can be caused by other mechanisms. None is consistently present in all cases. Neurologic signs resulting from hepatic encephalopathy are common in hepatic disease in horses. The most common finding is a change in behavior; the animal might be more docile or depressed, or a well-mannered horse might become vicious. In the terminal stages, aimless walking and head-pressing are observed, and some horses seem ataxic. Most of the signs point to cerebral dysfunction. Though the signs are often subtle, the

TABLE 14–1. CLINICAL SIGNS ASSOCIATED WITH ICTERUS IN THE HORSE

Sign	Category	Pathophysiology	Other Cause
Hemoglobinuria	Hemolytic	Excess intravascular RBC destruction; hemoglobin exceeds haptoglobin	Urinary hemorrhage with hemolysis
Anemia	Hemolytic	RBC destruction	Blood loss or deficiency, bone-marrow suppression
Enlarged liver	Obstruction, hepatocellular	Bile obstruction	Tumor, abscess
CNS signs	Hepatocellular	Hepatic encephalopathy	CNS disease
Ascites	Hepatocellular	Sinusoidal or portal hypertension	Cardiac, hypoproteinemia
Dermatitis	Hepatocellular	Failure to excrete phylloerythrin	Skin disease
Pruritus	Hepatocellular	Bile salt retention	Skin disease, CNS disease

(From Pearson, E.G.: Clinical management of the icteric horse. Compend. Contin. Educ., *4*:S114-S122, 1982.)

owner, who is more familiar with the animal's behavior, might detect them.

Photosensitization might produce dermatitis in white areas. Such dermatitis is seen in obstructive and hepatic diseases because the phylloerythrin from chlorophyll metabolism, not excreted, acts as a photodynamic agent. Pruritus has been seen in a few cases and is possibly related to accumulation of bile acids in the skin. Diarrhea occurs in some cases, probably as a result of the increased hydrostatic pressures occurring with portal hypertension. Weakness or exercise intolerance can be noted in cases of hemolytic anemia. The pulse and respiratory rates can be elevated owing to the reduced oxygen-carrying capacity of the blood.

Some icteric horses can have colic because of complete bile obstruction owing to biliary calculi. Horses with more traditional forms of gastrointestinal colic also can be icteric. The animals are more likely to be jaundiced with small-intestinal obstruction and proximal enteritis than with large-intestinal obstructions.

LABORATORY TESTS

Table 14–2 lists some of the more useful laboratory tests and the expected abnormalities with each category of icterus.

TABLE 14–2. LABORATORY VALUES IN ICTERIC HORSES

	Hemolytic Anemia	Hepatocellular Diseases	Obstruction or Cholestasis
PCV (L/L)	<30 (<.30)	N	N
RBCs	↓	N to ↓	N
Hb (g/dl)	<11	N to ↓	N
MCHC (%)	>37*	31–37	31–37
Total bilirubin mg/dl (μmol/L)	2.6–8.0 (44–137)	2.6–26 (44–445)	2.6–10 (44–171)
Direct (conjugated) bilirubin mg/dl (μmol/L)	0–0.4 (0–7.0)	0–0.4 (0–7.0)	>0.4 (>7.0)
Indirect (free) bilirubin mg/dl (μmol/L)	>2 (>34)	>1 (>17)	N
Direct:total	<0.1	<0.2	0.3–0.5
Urine bilirubin	0–slight	0–slight	↑ ↑
Urine urobilinogen	↑	N–1	0
Hemoglobinuria	+ or 0	0	0
Serum bile salt	<15 μmol	>20 μmol	>>20 μmol
BSP clearance	↑	↑ >4 min	↑ >4 min
AP	N	↑	↑ ↑
AST (SGOT)	N	↑	N
GGT (IU/L)	4–22	>40	>40
SDH	N	↑ or N	N
Blood ammonia	N	↑	N
Liver biopsy	No visible lesions, central lobular fat if anoxic	Necrosis, biliary hyperplasia, cirrhosis, fatty change	Plugs in bile canaliculi, bile lakes, biliary cirrhosis

PCV = packed cell volume; N = normal; RBCs = red blood cells; ↓ = decreased; Hb = hemoglobin; ↑ = increased; ↑ ↑ = large increase; MCHC = mean corpuscular hemoglobin concentration; BSP = sulfobromophthalein; AP = alkaline phosphatase; AST = aspartate aminotransferase; GGT = gamma glutamyltransferase; SDH = sorbitol dehydrogenase.

Note: values in parentheses are in S1 units.

(From Pearson, E.G.: Clinical management of the icteric horse. Compend. Contin. Educ., *4*:S114-S122, 1982.)

* If intravascular hemolysis is recent.

The most important question is whether the horse has hemolytic anemia or failure of liver function. A number of laboratory tests might be indicated.

Hematology

The hemoglobin concentration, packed cell volume, and total erythrocytes are all decreased in hemolytic anemias. The mean corpuscular hemoglobin concentration might be elevated in the early stages of intravascular hemolysis, before the released hemoglobin has been removed by the reticuloendothelial system. Gross hemolysis can sometimes be detected by observing the plasma. Anemia can also be seen in chronic diseases such as neoplasia and chronic abscesses that block the bile duct. Many animals with chronic disease are anorectic and hence icteric.

Animals with chronic bacterial infections and some abscesses can have leukocytosis, leukopenia with salmonella-caused cholangitis, and equine viral arteritis. Fibrinogen can be elevated in chronic infections. Although fibrinogen is produced by the liver, usually it is not decreased until the terminal stages of liver disease.

Liver Function Tests

Impairment of some of the liver's metabolic functions can change the concentration of some blood constituents, but no test is specific for liver disease. Glucose can be decreased because of diminished gluconeogenesis. Blood urea nitrogen can be decreased and ammonia concentrations elevated, as the liver is the body's only source of urease, needed to convert ammonia to urea.

Total plasma protein is rarely diminished in liver disease in horses. In horses with fatal liver disease, the albumin can be decreased to below 2 g/dl (20 g/L), but the total protein is still within the normal range because of increased globulins.

Clotting factors can be decreased in terminal liver disease.

Excretion tests can be used to evaluate the liver's excretory functions. Sulfobromophthalein clearance is almost always increased in an icteric animal and rarely adds new diagnostic information. It might be removed by some of the same mechanisms that remove bilirubin. To check sulfobromopthalein's clearance, a baseline sample is taken, after which 500 to 1000 mg of sulfobromophthalein is injected intravenously. Three consecutive samples are then taken—for example, at 3, 7, and 11 minutes or 4, 8, and 12 minutes. The blood is analyzed for sulfobromophthalein concentration and the clearance calculated. Normal sulfobromophthalein clearance in the horse is less than 3.5 minutes; in icteric animals a clearance of over 5 minutes is expected. Sulfobromophthalein clearance rates can also be reduced in fasting horses. Other cholephilic dyes are being used now in humans and small animals to test liver excretion. Indocyanine green has been used experimentally in horses but is extremely expensive.

Bilirubin, being a pigment that must be excreted by the liver, can be used as a measurement of liver excretory function. Determining the amount of conjugated and unconjugated bilirubin, as well as calculating the ratio of direct bilirubin to total bilirubin, can be helpful. Hemolytic icterus results from indirect or free bilirubin that has not yet been conjugated by the hepatocyte (although 10% or more of the conjugated bilirubin will react to the test for direct bilirubin). In cholestatic diseases, more of the total bilirubin is direct because excretion, being impaired, is slower than uptake and conjugation. Some of the conjugated bilirubin passes back into the sinusoids and into the general circulation when canalicular excretion is impaired. In chronic cirrhosis, the biliary tree can be obstructed, thus forcing conjugated bilirubin back into the sinusoids and increasing the ratio of direct to total bilirubin. Urine bilirubin is not usually elevated in hemolytic disease, because unconjugated bilirubin is bound to serum protein and will not be filtered through the glomeruli. Conjugated bilirubin is water soluble and will "spill" over into the urine when its amount in plasma is increased secondary to hepatocellular or obstructive cholestasis.

Urobilinogen, present in small amounts in normal horse urine, can be increased in hemolytic icterus. Because it is oxidized rapidly, it must be measured soon after collection. No urobilinogen is present in the urine in a horse with complete biliary obstruction, because no bilirubin reaches the intestine to be converted into urobilinogen.

Bile acid measurements can assess liver function. Bile acids are synthesized by the liver from cholesterol, conjugated with either glycine or taurine, and excreted into the bile. In most species, 95 to 98% of the bile acids are reabsorbed by the ileum and carried by the portal circulation back to the liver for re-excretion. In ponies, the bile acids are circulated about 38 times/day. Because the horse has no gallbladder, bile flows somewhat continuously into the intestine. The small amount of bile acid entering the general circulation can be measured in the serum. Bile acids in the serum increase with failure of liver function and specifically indicate blockage of bile flow or vascular shunting between the portal and systemic circulations. The mean serum bile acid concentration in 51 normal horses was 5.3 μmol/L with a standard deviation of 6.5. Tests of serum bile acid concentrations are also fairly sensitive for detecting chronic liver disease in the horse.

Enzymes normally present in the liver can be found at higher concentrations in the serum or plasma during hepatocellular disease (Table 14–3). Some enzymes present in bile duct epithelium are greatly elevated with cholestasis. In acute hepatocyte destruction, the dehydrogenases such as sorbitol dehydrogenase (SDH), lactate dehydrogenase (LDH), and glutamate dehydrogenase (GLDH) are increased. However, the serum concentrations of these enzymes might not be ele-

TABLE 14–3. LIVER ENZYMES

Enzyme	Specificity	Problems
Gamma glutamyltransferase (GGT)	Liver, kidney*, pancreas	
Alkaline phosphatase (AP)	Liver, bone, intestine, macrophages, placenta	Not specific
Sorbitol dehydrogenase (SDH)	Liver	Not elevated in chronic disease, short life, not stable
Glutamate dehydrogenase (GLDH)	Liver	Not elevated in chronic disease
Aspartate aminotransferase (AST)	Liver, muscle, heart	Not specific
Alanine aminotransferase (AIT) or (SGPT)	see →	Low concentration in horse; not good indicator
Lactate dehydrogenase (LDH)	None, unless isoenzymes	Short life; not elevated in chronic disease
Arginase (Ar)	Liver	Analysis not routinely available
Ornithine carbomyltransferase (OCT)	Liver	Analysis not routinely available
Isocitic dehydrogenase (IDH)	All, higher in liver	Analysis not routinely available
5' Nucleotidase (5'N)	Liver	Analysis not routinely available

(From Pearson, E.G.: Clinical management of the icteric horse. Compend. Contin. Educ., *4*:S114-S122, 1982.)

* Elevated in urine, not blood.

vated when clinical signs are present in chronic liver disease. Some of the transaminases such as aspartate aminotransferase (AST) (formerly called serum glutamic-oxaloacetic transaminase [SGOT]) are also increased. Alkaline phosphatase (AP) and gamma glutamyltransferase (GGT) are often elevated in the more chronic liver diseases, and their levels can be extremely high with bile duct obstruction. A panel of two or three liver enzymes should be sensitive enough to pick up virtually all cases of hepatocellular disease or cholestasis.

Liver Biopsy

Liver biopsy is relatively safe and easy. The site of puncture in the horse is the right fourteenth intercostal space at the intersection, with a line drawn from the tuber coxae to the point of the shoulder. The skin over the site of biopsy should be clipped and prepared for aseptic insertion of the needle. A local infiltration of 2% lidocaine will help reduce the animal's reaction, although the animal might flinch when the pleura and peritoneum are penetrated. A small stab wound is made in the skin at the site of insertion with a No. 11 or 15 scalpel blade. A needle directed slightly anteriorly and slightly ventrally is more likely to remain in the parenchyma of the liver and less likely to penetrate the large vessels on the visceral surface or pass on through the liver into the right kidney, pancreas, or other viscera. A simple instrument for taking the liver biopsy is the "Tru-cut" disposable biopsy needle (Travenol Laboratories, Deerfield, IL 60015). If a liver sample is not obtained at this site, the needle can be inserted further cranially and ventrally, although at this location more lung is penetrated. With ascites, the liver tends to move more dorsally. A cirrhotic liver is smaller and moves forward behind the diaphragm. Ultrasonog-

raphy can be used to guide the biopsy needle. A clotting profile is often performed before the biopsy, but is not necessary.

CAUSES AND CLINICAL ASPECTS OF DISEASES RESULTING IN ICTERUS

FASTING

The causes of anorexia in the horse are too numerous to be considered here; many are discussed in other places in this text. Some of the more common causes are foal septicemia, proximal enteritis, viral arteritis, neoplasia, and intestinal obstruction.

Fasting increases serum bilirubin concentrations in most horses. In some cases, the bilirubin levels will increase to 5 to 7 mg/dl (85 to 120 µmol/L) in 2 to 4 days. This increase is due to a failure of uptake and conjugation of bilirubin, rather than to increased production. The bilirubin levels improve if the appetite returns and the animal begins to eat. The amount of bilirubinemia depends on the baseline level for each particular animal. An animal with a high baseline level is more likely to develop icterus after fasting. Perhaps 15% of the horses show icterus if fasted. Numerous diseases of horses cause anorexia, and all could produce icterus in a given animal. Some of the more common diseases that frequently produce icterus are described here.

Many colicky horses also have icterus, especially those horses with intestinal obstructions. One study showed that the mean bilirubin concentration in horses with intestinal obstruction was 4.2 mg/dl (71 µmol/L). The icterus can be due to hemolysis of extravascular blood or to anorexia, and not necessarily to obstruction. Vascular compromise of the liver could also cause biliary dysfunction.

HEMOLYTIC ANEMIAS

Causes of hemolytic anemias and diagnostic tests are listed in Table 14–4. Some of the diseases causing hemolytic anemia are also discussed in Chapter 13. Hemolysis can be caused by immune-mediated, infectious, or toxic agents. Blood lost into body spaces will eventually be broken down, releasing hemoglobin and elevating bilirubin levels. Increased hemolysis can also be seen with erythrocytosis, neoplasia, and gastrointestinal ulceration.

Immune-Mediated

In immune-mediated hemolysis, antibody reacts to the antigen on the erythrocyte, causing agglutination, lysis, or both. Except in neonatal isoerythrolysis and transfusion reaction, the immune abnormality is unknown. Binding of antibody or complement to erythrocyte membranes results in either extravascular destruction in the reticuloendothelial system, or, with the activation complement, intravascular hemolysis.

Transfusion reaction, not common in horses, occurs if the horse has been previously sensitized to incompatible red blood cell antigens. This sensitization can occur in mares pregnant with a fetus with a different blood type and in horses that have had previous blood transfusions. The clinical signs are those described for hemolytic anemia. Diagnosis is based on a history of blood transfusion and on developing signs of hemolytic anemia.

The most important treatment of hemolytic anemia is to maintain hydration of the animal to ensure proper renal perfusion. If the anemia develops slowly, a fairly marked anemia is tolerated, even to packed cell volumes of 10% (10 L/L). Rapid hemolysis requires transfusion of red blood cells of a type that will not be agglutinated or lysed by antibody previously transfused or naturally produced by the recipient. To prevent transfusion reaction, blood should be crossmatched between the recipient and donor if possible. An alternative is to use blood from donors that are negative for the A or Q antigens.

Autoimmune hemolytic anemia is a manifestation of an immunologic disor-

TABLE 14–4. CAUSES OF HEMOLYTIC DISEASE

Disease	Test	Sample
Isoimmune hemolytic anemia	Crossmatch foal's washed RBCs with mare's serum	Foal's cells, mare's serum
Equine infectious anemia	Gel diffusion	Serum
Autoimmune hemolytic anemia	Coombs'	Whole blood
Cold isoagglutinins	Coombs' at 4°C	Whole blood
Transfusion reaction	Crossmatch blood	Whole blood
Babesiosis	Find insect vector parasite on RBC	Blood smear
Snakebite	History	
Other hemolytic toxins	Heinz bodies	Blood
Phenothiazine poisoning	History	
Red maple poisoning	History, methemoglobin	
Onion poisoning	History, odor	
Trypanosoma	(Exotic)	

(From Pearson, E.G.: Clinical management of the icteric horse. Compend. Contin. Educ., 4:S114–S122, 1982.)

der in which antibody against the body's own erythrocytes or erythrocyte precursors is produced. Excessive destruction or premature removal of erythrocytes from the circulation occurs. Autoantibody can be produced because erythrocyte antigen changes, or because immune cells no longer recognize homologous tissue. In the horse, autoantibody is usually associated with some other disease, such as some cases of purpura hemorrhagica. Some toxins such as dioxin, other chlorinated or bromated hydrocarbons, and Clostridium perfringens infections can cause an immune-mediated hemolysis. Cold-reacting antibodies are sometimes present, so that hemolysis occurs at the cold extremities. Many cases of equine autoimmune hemolytic anemia remain idiopathic. The most common disease causing autoimmune hemolytic anemia is equine infectious anemia, discussed later.

The signs of autoimmune hemolytic anemia include those of hemolytic anemia and those of the primary disease. Diagnosis is based on the finding of auto-agglutinins on the erythrocytes, usually by use of the direct Coombs' test. Rabbit antisera to equine IgG, IgM, and complement is mixed with the erythrocytes at both 37°C and 40°C to detect both warm- and cold-reacting agglutinins. Red blood cell fragility can also be increased. A positive Coombs' reaction occurs with neonatal isoerythrolysis, transfusion reactions, autoimmune hemolytic anemia, equine infectious anemia, and cold autoagglutinins.

Treatment involves the use of corticosteroids to reduce the immune reaction. Prednisolone at 0.1 to 0.5 mg/kg or dexamethasone at 0.11 mg/kg can be used. Higher doses are sometimes needed in the early stages of the disease. With severe hemolysis, blood transfusions of up to 4 ml/kg/hour might be needed. These immune-mediated hemolytic anemias are discussed in more detail in Chapter 13.

Infections

Equine infectious anemia, also known as swamp fever, is an infectious disease caused by a retrovirus and spread by hematophagous arthropods. The disease occurs in most of the U.S., in Europe, and in Canada, but is more prevalent in the Gulf Coast and Eastern Seaboard states. The overall incidence in the U.S. is low.

The virus damages the intima of small blood vessels and causes destruction of macrophages and erythrocytes. Fragility of erythrocytes is increased, probably owing to deposition of viral antigen on the erythrocyte membrane. Most of the fragile erythrocytes are removed by the reticuloendothelial system and destroyed.

Clinical signs vary with the form of the disease. The acute disease following first exposure results in a febrile condition with anorexia but not usually anemia, icterus, or edema. The subacute or intermediate form of the disease can produce anemia, edema, icterus, and weight loss. Petechial hemorrhages are often found on the mucosae. Tachycardia and enlarged spleen can be present. Laboratory tests reveal a decreased platelet count, a packed cell volume between 14 and 20% (14 to 20 L/L), and a reduced ratio of albumin to globulin. Specific diagnosis is made by a positive gel diffusion test. No treatment to eliminate the infection is known, and many state governments require destruction or quarantine of infected animals.

Babesiosis is a tick-borne protozoan infection. In addition to icterus, clinical signs include fever, anemia, depression, thirst, and anorexia. Hemoglobinuria is rare, but sometimes edema is present. The disease is carried by ticks present more in the southeastern U.S. Ecchymosis of the third eyelid has been considered pathognomonic for the disease.

Diagnosis can be confirmed by identifying the parasite in the blood, by inoculating susceptible animals, or by detecting antibody to the Babesia in the serum. Recommended treatments include amicarbalide diiesthionate at 8 mg/kg either intramuscularly or intravenously, or imidocarb dihydrochloride at 2 mg/kg for 2 consecutive days. Babesiosis can be prevented by controlling the vectors or eliminating the carriers.

Equine ehrlichiosis, although more likely to cause edema, can also occur with icterus. The pathogenesis of the icterus is not completely explained, although affected animals are anorectic and can have hemolysis of red blood cells. Other signs of the disease include fever, petechiation, ataxia, depression, anorexia, and reluctance to move. Anemia and leukopenia are fairly frequent. The disease occurs in late fall, in winter, and in spring. Although most cases occur in California, equine ehrlichiosis has also been diagnosed in Colorado, Illinois, Florida, Washington, and New Jersey. The most severe cases occur in horses over 3 years old.

Equine ehrlichiosis is diagnosed by finding the causative agent, Ehrlichia equi, in the cytoplasm of neutrophils using the Giemsa or methylene blue stain. Treatment with oxytetracycline at 7 mg/kg once a day intravenously for 3 to 7 days results in improvement usually within 24 hours. Uncomplicated untreated horses recover in 3 to 16 days.

Leptospirosis is a cause of icterus in the horse, but most cases are asymptomatic.

Trypanosoma infections exotic to North America can cause hemolysis and icterus in horses. These include surra (Trypanosoma evansi), mal de caderas (Trypanosoma equinum), and murrina (Trypanosoma hippicum).

In diagnosing infectious causes of hemolytic anemias, the erythrocytes should be examined closely for blood parasites, especially Babesia, and the neutrophils should be examined closely for Ehrlichia equi. The presence of insect vectors in the area substantiates the diagnosis.

Serology can be useful in detecting some of the infectious causes of hemoly-sis; the gel diffusion tests evaluate for equine infectious anemia; and paired serum samples with a rise in titer tests for leptospirosis or for equine viral arteritis.

Toxic

Red maple leaf ingestion was described in 1981 as causing a Heinz-body hemolytic anemia and methemoglobinemia in horses. In addition to icterus, clinical signs include hemoglobinuria, weakness, lethargy, tachycardia, increased respiratory rate, respiratory distress, and occasionally fever. Affected animals are anemic, and the methemoglobin level of the blood is from 20 to 50%, giving the blood a brown color. Heinz bodies are present in some patients, but not all. Most have remarkable anisocytosis and bilirubinemia. The condition is seen mainly in northeastern North America where red maples grow. Both the leaves and bark are considered toxic. Most cases are seen between June and October. At autopsy, enlargement of the spleen and kidneys, and brownish discoloration of the tissues are found.

Diagnosis is based on finding a Heinz-body hemolytic anemia with methemoglobinemia in horses with access to red maple trees. No treatment has been effective, although a few horses have survived if removed from the source and given massive blood transfusions.

Phenothiazine poisoning can cause a Heinz-body hemolytic anemia in horses. Individual sensitivity varies. Because the drug is being used as an anthelmintic less frequently, a decrease in the number of cases is expected. Clinical signs include icterus, some hemoglobinuria, anemia, and weakness. Diagnosis is based on a Heinz-body hemolytic anemia in a horse that has been administered phenothiazine.

Cultivated and wild onions can cause Heinz-body hemolytic anemia in horses. The clinical picture is similar to that of other hemolytic anemias. Diagnosis is based on a history of access to onions in a horse with hemolytic anemia. Treatment includes removing the source of onions and, in severe cases, administering blood.

Venom from certain poisonous snakes and from bees can contain hemolytic toxins. Some hemolytic anemias and icterus can occur following snakebites and bee stings.

HEPATIC DISEASE

Because hepatic reserve is large, most of the liver must be damaged or not functioning before bilirubin excretion is sufficiently impaired to produce icterus. In horses, the reserve for excretion of bilirubin might not be as great as in other species.

Both infectious and toxic agents can destroy hepatocytes. The mammalian liver has a remarkable regenerative capability. New hepatoctyes are produced near the portal areas and migrate toward the central vein. If the portal areas are destroyed, however, regeneration is impaired. Some antimitotic agents such as pyrrolizidine alkaloids might prevent hepatocyte division and therefore regeneration. Many of the destroyed hepatocytes are replaced with connective tissue, and resulting cirrhosis prevents further regeneration.

Failure of other liver functions can produce other signs. Decreased blood flow through the liver can cause portal hypertension and, therefore, ascites and diarrhea. Just before death, clotting factors or albumin production can fail. Some horses with terminal liver disease have acute intravascular hemolysis with hemoglobinemia. The mechanism is unknown. Hepatic encephalopathy occurs commonly in the horse, and theories about the mechanism abound. The most current is that, following liver failure, an imbalance in amino acids occurs in the blood, with a decrease in the short-branched chain amino acids (e.g., valine, leucine, and isoleucine), and with an increase in the aromatic amino acids (e.g., tyrosine and phenylalanine). These amino acids are competitively transported into the brain, where they act as precursors of certain neurotransmitters. Abnormal amounts of excitatory or inhibitory neurotransmitters, or an increased synthesis of some false neurotransmitters, can produce the neurologic signs.

Table 14–5 lists some of the common hepatocellular diseases in the horse and tests useful in confirming or ruling out each disease. Patient history and examination of the environment are useful. The

TABLE 14–5. CAUSES OF HEPATOCELLULAR DISEASE

Disease	Test	Sample
Pyrrolizidine alkaloid poisoning	History, histopathology	Liver biopsy
Other hepatotoxic plants	History, environment	
Mycotoxicosis	Identify toxin	Feed
Phenol poisoning	FeCl→purple	Urine
Drug intoxication	History	
Serum hepatitis (Theiler's disease)	History of inoculation, histopathology	Liver biopsy
Nonserum acute hepatitis	Histopathology	Liver biopsy
Tyzzer's disease	Histopathology	Necropsy, liver biopsy
Chronic active hepatitis (cause unknown)	Histopathology	Liver biopsy

(From Pearson, E.G.: Clinical management of the icteric horse. Compend. Contin. Educ., *4*:S114-S122, 1982.)

vaccination history will reveal whether tetanus antitoxin or pregnant mare's serum has been used, which would make serum hepatitis a plausible diagnosis. The medication and worming history can reveal possible exposure to hepatotoxic anthelmintics or other drugs. Other environmental factors to look for include sources of iron, elemental phosphorus, moldy grain, and other chemicals.

Clinical signs can indicate possible liver involvement but rarely the specific disease involved. Some of the diseases, such as pyrrolizidine alkaloid poisoning and other types of chronic active hepatitis, have a more chronic course and insidious onset. Other diseases, such as serum hepatitis, drug and chemical intoxication, and Tyzzer's disease, have a more acute onset. Liver function tests indicate failure of liver function in all liver diseases but rarely are diagnostic of a specific cause.

Liver biopsy is rarely valuable in focal liver diseases such as abscesses or tumors, but these diseases do not produce icterus unless the bile duct is blocked. The remaining liver cells can still excrete bilirubin. Liver biopsy can be diagnostic in serum hepatitis, pyrrolizidine alkaloid poisoning, Tyzzer's disease, other forms of chronic active hepatitis, and sometimes mycotoxicosis.

Histologic findings aid in the diagnosis. Biliary hyperplasia, a nonspecific indicator of liver insult, occurs within a few weeks of the insult. It is reversible and seen in cases of pyrrolizidine alkaloid poisoning, aflatoxicosis, other types of toxic hepatitis, and chronic active hepatitis. Megalocytosis, the presence of large hepatocytes and large nuclei, occurs in pyrrolizidine alkaloid toxicity and mycotoxicosis. Nuclear inclusion bodies might be seen in foals who contracted intrauterine herpes infection. Cirrhosis often follows hepatic necrosis, especially if no regeneration occurs. The amount of cirrhosis might be a better prognostic indicator than the specific disease; massive cirrhosis indicates a very poor prognosis. Lipidosis or fatty infiltration of the liver is a reversible change often seen with negative energy balance and is not necessarily related to liver damage.

The location of the liver damage within the lobule is an important diagnostic determinant. The portal areas receive the toxic agents first, along with the oxygen and nutrients, and are affected more by certain toxins and less by hypoxia. Portal cirrhosis occurs with pyrrolizidine alkaloid toxicity, aflatoxicosis, and other forms of chronic active hepatitis. The centrolobular areas are the oldest cells, the last to receive oxygen and nutrients, and are more affected by hypoxia and chemical and infectious agents. Centrolobular necrosis or cirrhosis is seen with Theiler's disease (serum hepatitis), some drug intoxications, and massive pyrrolizidine alkaloid toxicity.

Food analysis might be necessary to determine specific hepatotoxic agents, such as iron fumarate, elemental iron, elemental phosphorus, aflatoxin, carbon tetrachloride, trichloroethylene, pyrrolizidine alkaloids, and certain herbicides.

Pyrrolizidine alkaloid toxicity is not reversible once clinical signs such as icterus develop. Advanced cirrhosis and the antimitotic activity of the toxin prevent regeneration.

Some of the other liver diseases, if they are not too severe, can be treated. The liver's large capacity for regeneration allows some animals to recover. Some general principles of liver therapy are to remove the insult to the liver, such as the toxin or the infectious agent, and to support the metabolic functions of the liver. This support can include administering glucose for energy and providing choline for the production of phospholipids for the mobilization of fat. Oral administration of choline 1 to 2 ounces/day for an adult horse has been recommended.

If hepatic encephalopathy develops, administration of short-branched chain amino acids might be beneficial. Preparations are available but are expensive. A diet that is high in short-branched chain amino acids and low in aromatic amino acids will also be useful. This diet should include alfalfa and beet pulp as a source of protein.

Corticosteroids have been advocated in some cases of liver disease to reduce the cirrhosis and perhaps modify the immune reaction. Athough they have not been adequately evaluated in controlled studies in the horse, there is no evidence of harm from their use. The anabolic steroids, which are analogues of the androgens, are also sometimes useful in liver disease.

Pyrrolizidine Alkaloid Toxicity

The pasture and hay should be examined for pyrrolizidine alkaloid–containing plants or other hepatotoxic plants, although these toxic plants might not be found in pyrrolizidine alkaloid–poisoned horses because clinical signs can occur up to a year after the animal has stopped consuming the toxin.

Pyrrolizidine alkaloid toxicity is caused by the ingestion of pyrrolizidine alkaloid–containing plants. These plants include Senecio jacobae (Tansy ragwort), Senecio vulgaris, Senecio longilobus (groundsel), Amsinckia intermedia (fiddle neck), Crotalaria sp. (rattle box), Echiu plantaqineum (viber's buglos), and Heliotropiuim europaeum (common heliotrope). The alkaloid is absorbed and carried by the portal system to the liver, where it is metabolized to pyrroles. These potent alkylating agents cross-link double-stranded DNA and prevent mitosis as well as inactivate certain liver enzymes.

The disease is delayed and chronic. Sometimes no signs are seen until a year after the plant has been removed from the diet. Once clinical signs of liver failure

develop, the disease is progressive and fatal. Clinical signs include icterus, behavioral changes, weight loss, occasional photosensitization, diarrhea, or ascites. Liver enzymes, especially gamma glutamyltransferase and alkaline phosphatase, are elevated along with bile acids.

A specific diagnosis is made by liver biopsy. The patient has a history of having consumed pyrrolizidine alkaloid–containing plants. Histopathologic changes include megalocytosis, portal necrosis, and portal cirrhosis. Necrotic hepatocytes and islands of connective tissue are also sometimes found within other parts of the liver lobule. There is no effective therapy.

Mycotoxins

Aflatoxin B_1 and perhaps other mycotoxins can cause liver damage. Aflatoxin is a metabolite produced by fungi usually growing on feeds such as sorghum, cereal grains, peanut meal, and cottonseed meal under warm, moist conditions. Few cases of aflatoxicosis have been described. Experimentally, a rise in liver enzymes has been produced in ponies by giving them 2 mg aflatoxin/kg of body weight. Horses might be less susceptible if they are on high-quality rations.

Clinical signs are those of hepatic failure. Histologic lesions seen in the liver are similar to those of pyrrolizidine alkaloid poisoning and include biliary hyperplasia, hepatocyte necrosis, portal cirrhosis, and even megalocytosis. However, livers affected by aflatoxin might be capable of regeneration.

Hepatotoxins

Other hepatotoxic plants can cause toxicity to the liver but do not contain pyrrolizidine alkaloids. These include cocklebur, which may be more toxic to pigs and young animals, Tribulus terrestris (caltrops), Lantana camora (lantana),

Tetradymia sp. (horse brush), and Cycus sp. Gossypol, the pigment in cottonseed that can be present in cottonseed meal, can damage the liver. Continuous feeding of alsike clover has been reported to cause liver damage.

Other chemical hapatotoxins reported to cause hepatic toxicity include carbon tetrachloride, which has been used experimentally and as an anthelmintic; phenol; tetrachloroethylene and other halogenated hydrocarbons; chloroform; dioxin; phosphorus; and certain other herbicides.

Drugs have been reported to be hepatotoxic, at least in other species, if given in high enough doses and for a long enough period. Some of these drugs are tetracycline, erythromycin, ethyl alcohol, phenothiazine tranquilizers, iproniazid, some anesthetic agents, and some anticonvulsants.

Chronic Active Hepatitis

Chronic active hepatitis includes a group of chronic liver diseases with active and progressive liver damage. The exact cause in most cases is unknown, but might be toxins other than the pyrrolizidine alkaloids. History of viral exposure or drug administration, as occurs in humans, is not usual.

Clinical findings are similar to those of other cases of chronic liver failure. In most cases, the liver enzymes are elevated and serum bile acid concentration is increased.

A definitive diagnosis is made by examining liver biopsy specimens. The usual histologic diagnosis is cholangiohepatitis, which includes biliary hyperplasia, evidence of bile stasis, necrosis of hepatocytes that are replaced with connective tissue, and the presence of inflammatory cells, usually in the periportal areas.

Serum Hepatitis

Theiler's disease, or serum hepatitis, occurs usually in horses over 2 years old after serum has been administered. The equine serum might include pregnant mare's serum, tetanus antitoxin, or antitoxin to other diseases such as African horse sickness. Inoculation with equine rhinopneumonitis vaccine and use of dirty needles has perhaps produced the disease. In most cases, the disease develops 4 to 12 weeks after an injection. Some of the liver damage might be immune mediated.

Signs of the disease are similar to other cases of hepatic failure. Diagnosis is based on history of serum administration and the histopathologic lesion. Histologically, a diffuse and sometimes massive necrosis is present. The greater severity of this necrosis in the centrolobular areas might differentiate it from pyrrolizidine alkaloid poisoning or chronic active hepatitis. The mortality rate is above 50%.

Occasionally, hepatitis occurs in horses with no history of serum administration. The clinical signs and histologic appearance can be similar to that of Theiler's disease. This condition can result from transmission of serum hepatitis or Theiler's disease in ways other than by serum injections, such as by arthropod vectors. Also, other liver insults such as chemicals or other infectious agents can occur. These horses are treated for liver failure. Animals with less severe cases recover.

Other Causes

Liver neoplasia is uncommon in horses, although metastatic tumors have been reported. Signs of liver failure, including icterus, can occur if enough of the liver parenchyma is replaced by the tumor, or if the bile duct is obstructed. Diagnosis is made by histopathologic examination of the liver. Because these lesions are focal, the proper tissues might not be obtained by blind percutaneous liver biopsy. Ultrasonography might be helpful.

OBSTRUCTIVE ICTERUS

Obstruction to the flow of bile, cholestasis, can be intrahepatic or extrahepatic. Intrahepatic cholestasis is usually due to canalicular dysfunction. In many cases, the canaliculi are blocked or destroyed by cirrhosis. Some of the bilirubin can be picked up and conjugated by the liver, but because flow through the canaliculi is reduced, some is regurgitated back into the plasma. Direct-reacting, conjugated bilirubin can contribute up to 40% of the total bilirubin in these cases. In other cases, extrahepatic obstruction of the bile duct occurs. Cholangitis, choleliths, parasites, neoplasms, and abscesses have been incriminated as causes of bile duct blockage. The blockage reduces the excretion of other metabolites. Bile acids increase in the plasma. Phylloerythrins, produced from chlorophyll metabolism by intestinal bacteria and normally absorbed and re-excreted through the bile, are retained. These, when deposited in the skin, act as photodynamic agents and can cause photosensitization (see Chapter 11).

Table 14–6 shows some of the more common causes of obstructive icterus. Determining if the obstruction is intrahepatic or extrahepatic is useful.

Intrahepatic Cirrhosis

Intrahepatic cirrhosis is one of the more common causes of cholestasis. A liver biopsy is necessary for diagnosis. Either portal or diffuse cirrhosis and inflammatory cells are present around the bile ducts. Culturing the liver biopsy might also produce significant bacteria.

Liver disease causing intrahepatic cirrhosis is the same as that for hepatocellular diseases. Once the cirrhosis is extensive, no treatment will be effective. Bridging of connective tissue between the liver lobules is a poor prognostic finding.

Cholangitis

Cholangitis, perhaps the most common cause of extrahepatic obstruction, often accompanies hepatitis or cholangiohepatitis. Salmonella infection can extend into the bile ducts and produce cholangiohepatitis. Acinetobacter has been isolated from livers in cases of bile duct inflammation. Extension of infections from the small intestines can also cause inflammation of the bile ducts. This extension can occur with proximal enteritis and perhaps other conditions.

Clinical signs of cholangitis can be those of bile obstruction. In addition, affected animals can have signs of the primary disease causing the inflammation, such as salmonellosis or proximal enteritis. Diagnosis can be difficult. A liver biopsy is useful because the inflammation can extend into the liver with periportal fibrosis, biliary hyperplasia, and bile pigment accumulation. Liver culture can also reveal a significant pathogen. The cause of enteritis is probably

TABLE 14–6. CAUSES OF OBSTRUCTIVE ICTERUS

Disease	Test	Results
Hepatic cirrhosis	Biopsy	Fibrosis, portal or massive
Cholangitis	Biopsy culture	Portal and bile duct inflammation
		Pathogen in liver
Choledocholithiasis	Ultrasonography	Enlarged bile ducts, stones
Parasites	Trial anthelmintics	Improvement
Extraduct mass	Exploratory surgery	Tumor, abscess

also the cause of the cholangitis. Treatment is aimed at curing the primary disease. Once the infection and inflammation are eliminated, many cases will reverse and no longer be obstructive.

Choledocholithiasis

Choledocholithiasis (bile stones in the common bile duct) can produce complete obstruction of bile flow. Clinical signs can include abdominal pain or colic, intermittent in some cases. The animals are also usually depressed and icteric. Most affected animals are over 5 years old. In some instances, they remain asymptomatic if the flow of bile is not obstructed. Laboratory tests reveal an increase in liver enzyme concentrations, especially alkaline phosphatase and gamma glutamyltransferase. Direct bilirubin can account for 20 to 40% of the total bilirubin in some of these cases. Diagnosis is difficult, but ultrasonography has been used successfully in some cases to identify dilated bile ducts or the actual stones. Exploratory surgery can be indicated in other cases if complete obstruction is suspected.

Parasites

Verminous biliary obstruction is occasionally seen on postmortem examination. Few clinical signs suggest this condition, but colic, jaundice, and increased bilirubin levels are commonly seen. Some horses treated with anthelmintics improve. Gasterophilus, ascardis, and strongyles can enter the bile duct and cause obstruction.

Masses

Abscesses and neoplasms can obstruct the flow of bile to the common duct. Obstruction has not been reported as commonly in horses as in cattle. Icterus has been described in many cases of intestinal obstruction. Whether bile outflow is obstructed or the icterus is a result of fasting is not known.

Neonatal Icterus

Table 14–7 lists some of the more common causes of icterus in the foal and some of the useful diagnostic tests. The procedures for older horses can be used also in foals. A complete blood count with indices helps identify a hemolytic anemia. The most likely cause of hemolytic anemia in the newborn is neonatal isoerythrolysis. Crossmatching of the mare's plasma to the foal's erythrocytes and a positive Coombs' test diagnose the condition.

Although many diseases are linked with anorexia, septicemia is the most common cause of anorexia and icterus. Some of the signs of foal septicemia are fever, lethargy, dehydration, elevated fibrinogen, swollen joints, and hypopion. A positive blood culture might be diagnostic. Elevated liver enzymes can be useful in detecting neonatal hepatic failure, Tyzzer's disease, and neonatal herpes infection. Some of these enzymes are higher in the normal foal than they are in the adult. Total and indirect bilirubin is up to four times higher in day-old foals than in animals at 1 year of age. If serum constituents are elevated, liver biopsy might be indicated (see Chapter 19).

Normal Elevated Bilirubin

If physiologic jaundice is suspected in a foal, the animal should be examined for signs of other diseases, and the bilirubin levels should be determined again in several days to make sure that they are going down.

Neonatal Isoerythrolysis

Neonatal isoerythrolysis is an uncommon but important disease of foals, often

TABLE 14–7. CAUSES OF NEONATAL ICTERUS

Disease	Test
Normal elevated bilirubin	Bilirubin going down, no other signs
Anorexia	History of not eating
Neonatal isoerythrolysis	Hemolytic anemia, positive direct Coombs', match mare serum and foal cells
Foal septicemia	Fever, positive blood culture, often low IgG
Neonatal toxic hepatitis	Elevated liver enzymes, biopsy, history of administering iron fumarate
Tyzzer's disease	Histopathology, culture of Bacillus piliformis
In utero herpes infection	Histopathology, inclusion bodies

causing fatal hemolytic crisis. The foal's red blood cells are destroyed by isoantibodies produced by the mare and passed to the foal in colostrum. The mare produces antibodies because of foreign erythrocyte antigen factors of the foal inherited from the stallion and not possessed by the mare, to which the mare is probably exposed during fetomaternal hemorrhage at the placenta. Although the horse has over 30 antigenic factors in eight blood groups, most cases of neonatal isoerythrolysis are due to the antibodies against the A or Q factors.

Neonatal isoerythrolysis usually occurs in foals of multiparous mares. Though the foal is healthy at birth, signs strongly suggesting the condition occur 24 to 48 hours after nursing. The foal is weak and lethargic. Pulse and respiratory rates are elevated at the time icterus occurs. Hemoglobinuria sometimes occurs later. Laboratory signs include signs of anemia, such as low packed cell volume and reduced numbers of red blood cells. Unconjugated hyperbilirubinemia can reach levels

of 20 to 40 mg/dl (340 to 680 μmol/L) in severe cases.

For a specific diagnosis, maternal antibodies must be demonstrated on the foal's red blood cells. The Coombs' test can give false-negative results because the isoantibodies are hemolysins rather than agglutinins. The most reliable test is a hemolytic test using washed foal red blood cells against the mare's serum. This test requires the addition of complement and is usually done in a veterinary laboratory. Using unwashed foal red blood cells against the serum or colostrum provides inaccurate results.

Treatment should first involve eliminating further exposure to the mare's antibodies by preventing nursing by muzzling the foal for the first 48 hours. Alterative nutrition of at least 120 kcal/kg/day must be provided. Blood transfusions are needed if the red blood cell numbers decline rapidly or if the packed cell volume goes down to less than 10% (10 L/L). Donors that are Aa, Qa negative can be used, or a crossmatch can be made between the donor and the foal. Some veterinarians recommend using washed erythrocytes of the mare. The volume given should at least temporarily replace the missing or destroyed erythrocytes.

Prevention is possible by detecting isoantibodies in the dam's serum prior to parturition, and then preventing the foal from nursing this mare for at least 48 hours and providing colostrum from another mare.

Neonatal Toxic Hepatitis

Neonatal toxic hepatic failure is a toxic disease of foals usually less than 1 week of age, caused by the oral administration of a microorganism inoculum that contains ferrous fumarate. This iron compound causes hepatic necrosis and the clinical disease. Now that the cause is known, this condition will probably not be prevalent in the future.

Tyzzer's Disease

Tyzzer's disease is an uncommon acute, focal necrotizing hepatitis of foals caused by Bacillus piliformis, an anaerobic bacillus. The disease is sporadic, and predisposing factors might be involved. Most foals with the disease are between 5 and 42 days old.

Many with Tyzzer's disease are found dead, having died before icterus has developed. Others demonstrate severe depression, convulsions, coma, and icterus. The illness usually lasts less than 2 days. Laboratory findings include increased bilirubin, including direct bilirubin. Enzymes, aspartate aminotransferase, and sorbitol dehydrogenase are elevated. The foal might be hypoglycemic.

Specific diagnosis is based on histopathologic examination of the liver and the finding of bacillus in necrotic foci. Successful treatment has not been recorded in confirmed cases.

In Utero Herpes Infection

Herpes infection of the fetus can lead to abortion or birth of a weak foal. Focal hepatic necrosis occurs, and some foals are born icteric. Most of these foals do not survive. A definitive diagnosis is made by finding intranuclear inclusion bodies in the hepatocytes.

Septicemia

Septicemia often causes an elevated bilirubin, causing icterus (see Chapter 19).

SUPPLEMENTAL READING

Aller, W.W., Edds, G.T., Asquith, R.L.: Effects of aflatoxins in young ponies. Am. J. Vet. Res., 42:2162, 1981.

Bauer, J.E., Harvey, J.W., Asquith, R.L., McNulty, P.K., Kivipecto, J.: Clinical chemistry reference values of foals during the first year of life. Equine Vet. J., 16:361–363, 1984.

Becht, J.L.: Neonatal isoerythrolysis in the foal. Part I. Background, blood group antigens and pathogenesis. Compend. Contin. Educ. Pract. Vet., 5: S591, 1983.

Divers, T.J.: Liver disease and liver failure in horses. Proceedings, Am. Assoc. Eq. Pract., p. 213, 1985.

Divers, T.J., Warner, A., Voala, W.E., Whitlock, R.H., et al.: Toxic hepatic failure in newborn foals. J. Am. Vet. Med. Assoc., 183:1407–1413, 1983.

Gronwall, R., Engelking, L.R., Noonan, N.: Direct measurement of biliary bilirubin excretion of ponies during fasting. Am. J. Vet. Res., 41:125, 1980.

Gulick, B.A., Liu, I.K.M., Quals, C.V., Gribbel, D.H., Rogers, Q.R.: Effect of pyrrolizidine alkaloid-induced hepatic disease on plasma amino acid patterns in the horse. Am. J. Vet. Res., 41:1894–1898, 1980.

Issel, C.J., Coggins, L.: Equine infectious anemia: current knowledge. J. Am. Vet. Med. Assoc., 174:727–733, 1979.

Madigan, J.E., Gribble, D.: Equine ehrlichiosis: diagnosis, treatment, and preliminary epidemiological findings. Proceedings, Am. College Vet. Internal Med. Forum, p. 10–3, 1986.

Pearson, E.G.: Clinical management of the icteric horse. Comp. on Cont. Educ. for Pract. Vet., 4:S114–S122, 1982.

Pearson, E.G., Craig, A.M.: Serum bile acids for diagnosing chronic liver disease in horses. Proceedings ACVIM Forum, Washington, DC, 1986.

Tennant, B., Dill, S.G.: Acute hemolytic anemia methemoglobinemia and Heinz body formation associated with ingestion of red maple leaves by horses. J. Am. Vet. Med. Assoc., 179:143–150, 1981.

Tennant, B.C., Evans, C.D., Kaneko, J.J., Schalm, O.W.: Intravascular hemolysis associated with hepatic failure in the horse. Calif. Vet., 27:15–18, 1972.

Turk, A.M., Gallina, A.M., Perryman, L.E.: Bacillus piliformis infection (Tyzzer's disease) in foals in northwestern United States: a retrospective study of 21 cases. J. Am. Vet. Med. Assoc., 178:279–281, 1981.

Traub, J.L., Rantanen, N., Reed, S., Schecter, L.: Cholelithiasis in four horses. J. Am. Vet. Med. Assoc., 181:59–62, 1982.

chapter 15

FEVER

Christopher M. Brown

DEFINITION

Fever is a state in which body temperature has been reset and is maintained at a level above normal. It is not the same as an elevated body temperature created by a failure to dissipate produced or acquired heat, as occurs in heatstroke. In fever, regulatory mechanisms are working, but the "thermostat" is set at a higher level.

REGULATION OF BODY TEMPERATURE

Heat is produced by all metabolic processes; the most active tissues produce the most heat. At rest the liver is a major source of heat, but during exercise the majority is produced in the muscles. Heat is lost by three main mechanisms. Radiation from the body surface by infrared waves accounts for a large amount of heat loss in temperate environments. Convection, heat loss to the air passing over the body, though not great when the horse is standing or when the air is still, is significant when there is a wind or when the horse is running. Evaporation of water from the respiratory tract and the body cools the surface from which it evaporates; heat loss by sweating is important in the exercising horse, and failure of this mechanism such as anhidrosis can have a serious impact (Table 15–1).

The maintenance of a constant body temperature requires a balance between heat loss and heat production. Within the hypothalamus are cells that increase their discharge frequency in response to local heating, and others that increase in response to cooling. Ablation of these areas destroys the ability of a mammal to control its body temperature. In addition to these central areas monitoring core temperature are widely distributed peripheral thermoreceptors that provide input for the central coordination of thermoregulation. Changes in core temperature activate the central receptors, which then initiate appropriate responses to return the temperature to normal. If the core temperature goes down, cutaneous vasoconstriction will reduce radiant and convectional loss, and shivering will increase heat production by muscle. If core temperature rises, peripheral vasodilation is induced, together with sweating and panting, to promote heat loss by evaporation, radiation, and convection. These responses can be initiated in anticipation of temperature changes. For example, physical exercise initiates vasodilation and sweating to dissipate the heat produced before it causes a rise in core temperature; a cold wind can cause vasoconstriction and shivering to prevent a fall in core temperature.

These control mechanisms are well developed, and in adult horses body temperature is fairly stable under a variety of environmental conditions. Only after hard, prolonged physical exertion will an elevated rectal temperature be found in normal horses. Foals, like many immature mammals, have a less efficient control system and will show more variation in body temperature, depending on environmental temperature and level of activity and excitement. Active, healthy foals who have been difficult to catch on warm days often have an elevated rectal temperature. The temperature is very labile in neonates, particularly in those premature or dysmature (Chapter 19).

THE CONCEPT OF A NORMAL TEMPERATURE

Healthy adult horses maintain a body temperature between 100° and 101° F (37.8° to 38.3° C). However, many normal horses are consistently beyond this range. Most mammals have a diurnal temperature rhythm. Those most active in daylight have the highest temperature late in the afternoon and the lowest in the morning. Thus, a horse's rectal temperature could vary by up to 2° F (about 1° C) between morning and evening. A single temperature reading for a horse is difficult to interpret. If the animal normally has a rectal temperature of 99.5° F (37° C) and at examination has a temperature of 101° F (37.8° C), the elevation might indicate either a mild fever or diurnal variation. Without prior knowledge of baseline values for a particular horse, making an objective assessment of an isolated reading is difficult. The normal morning and afternoon temperature for a horse can be established by taking a series of readings over several days, and using these values as part of the health record.

PATHOPHYSIOLOGY

In fever the thermoregulatory center becomes reset at a higher level, and control mechanisms maintain the body temperature at this new setting. Many different diseases lead to fever, but all fever-causing

TABLE 15–1. DISEASES CAUSING FEVER IN HORSES

Major Clinical Signs	Causes	Additional Signs and Diagnostic Clues
Respiratory	Influenza virus	Fever 102°–106°F (39°–41°C). Cough, serous nasal discharge. Occasionally anemia. May develop pneumonia. Often occurs in outbreaks. Paired serology or virus isolation for diagnosis.
	Herpes virus I (rhinopneumonitis)	Signs similar to influenza. Abortions and neurologic disease in some horses, depending on strain. Pneumonia in foals. Paired serology or virus isolation for diagnosis.
	Viral arteritis	Fever 102°–106°F (39°–41°C). Cough. Seropurulent nasal discharge. Limb and ventral edema. Petechiation of nasal and conjunctival mucosae. Occasional diarrhea and abortions. Paired serology for diagnosis.
	Rhinovirus	Mild disease. Fever 102°–103°F (39°–39.5°C). Cough and nasal discharge.
	Streptococcus equi (occasionally S. zooepidemicus)	Mostly younger horses. Fever 102°–105°F (39°–40.5°C). Serous, becoming purulent, nasal discharge. Marked lymphadenopathy with abscessation and rupture. Often herd outbreaks. Culture confirms etiology.
	Single or mixed bacterial infections (gram-positive and -negative; aerobes and anaerobes). Occasionally Mycoplasma felis	Pneumonias, pulmonary abscesses, pleuritis. Variable signs; fever 102°–105°F (39°–40.5°C), depression, cough, nasal discharge, fetid breath, dyspnea, weight loss. Radiography, ultrasonography, thoracocentesis, transtracheal aspiration; culture of aspirates confirms etiology.
	Tuberculosis	Rare. Chronic granulomatous pneumonia. Recurrent fever 102°–104°F (39°–49°C). Weight loss, dyspnea. Radiographs, culture, and lung biopsy confirm diagnosis.
	Mycoses	Rare, chronic, deep-seated infections, either abscesses or occasional pneumonia or pleuritis. Chronic low-grade fever, cough, weight loss. Radiography, aspiration with culture and cytology for diagnosis.
	Neoplasia	Rare, either pulmonary, primary, or secondary metastases mediastinal or mesothelial. Dyspnea, cough, weight loss. Occasional intermittent fever. Radiography, ultrasonography, aspiration, and cytology confirm the diagnosis.

TABLE 15–1. *Continued.*

Major Clinical Signs	Causes	Additional Signs and Diagnostic Clues
Alimentary	Vesicular stomatitis	Mild fever (102°–104°F, 39°–40°C). Vesicles on tongue and lips, occasionally on udder and prepuce. Salivation and anorexia. Serology and virus isolation confirm the diagnosis.
	Salmonellae and other acute endotoxemic diseases	Fever, 102°–106°F (39°–41°C). Profuse watery diarrhea, neutropenia, dehydration, acid-base/electrolyte disturbances. Signs may be less severe, without diarrhea. Fecal culture may identify the pathogen.
	Ehrlichia risticii (Potomac horse fever)	Depression, fever (102°–104°F, 39°–40°C) followed by diarrhea. Monocytosis may be present. Diagnosis based on paired serology.
	Single or mixed bacterial infections (gram-positive and -negative; aerobes and anaerobes)	Abdominal, often mesenteric, abscessation. Low-grade fever (102°–103°F, 39°–40°C). Weight loss, intermittent colic. Peritonitis, colic, diarrhea, fever, weight loss. Can be fulminating. Diagnosis based on rectal examination, abdominocentesis, and culture and cytology.
	Neoplasia	Almost any type, particularly if necrotic. Rectal examination, abdominocentesis, cytology, and ultrasonography assist diagnosis.
Central nervous	Viral encephalitis (Eastern and Western equine encephalomyelitis; occasionally rabies)	Mild fever (102°–104°F, 39°–40°C). Variable nervous signs, including ataxia, circling, depression, recumbency (some rabid horses are hyperesthetic). Diagnosis based on serology and necropsy.
	Bacterial	Meningitis and abscesses. Most common in foals. Occasionally found in adults by extension from guttural pouch infections. Signs vary, similar to viral encephalitis. Fever variable—often very high with meningitis (106°F, 41°C). Abscesses may cause signs consistent with focal lesions. Diagnosis assisted by CSF analysis and confirmed by necropsy.
	Trauma—CNS	Tissue damage with release of mediators or hypothalamic damage can lead to fever by altering activity of thermoregulatory center. Diagnosis assisted by radiography and CSF analysis.

TABLE 15–1. *Continued.*

Major Clinical Signs	Causes	Additional Signs and Diagnostic Clues
Hematopoietic	Equine infectious anemia	Variable fever 102°–106°F (39°–41°C). Signs—acute to chronic and recurrent. Anemia, edema. Diagnosis assisted by gel diffusion test.
	Ehrlichia equi	High fever (104°–107°F, 40°–42°C), mild anemia, depression, edema. Diagnosis assisted by serology.
	Babesia caballi, equi	Short, mild fever (104°F, 39°C). Ventral edema and jaundice. Diagnosis by hematology and serology.
	Immune mechanisms, or toxic agents (e.g., red maples, onions, phenothiazine)	Acute, severe intravascular hemolysis may cause fever for a short period. Laboratory data and history of exposure support diagnosis.
	Neoplasia	If bone marrow is destroyed, pancytopenia may ensue. Opportunist infections may become established and cause fever. Hematology and bone marrow aspirates support diagnosis.
Cardiovascular	Venous thrombosis and embolism	Particularly after long-term venous catheterization. Even if not septic, embolism may lead to fever.
	Bacterial endocarditis	Recurrent fever, weight loss. Variable murmurs. Cardiac failure late in disease. Diagnosis confirmed by echocardiography, assisted by blood culture.
Dermatologic	Immune-mediated	Pemphigus foliaceus; rare erosive, ulcerative, crusting skin disease, starting on the neck and extending ventrally. May have febrile episodes. Biopsy confirms diagnosis.
Multisystemic or nonspecific diseases	Brucellosis	Very variable. Recurrent fever (103°–104°F, 39°–40°C), joint swellings and stiffness, fistulous withers, general malaise. Becoming rarer as bovine brucellosis is eradicated. Diagnosis based on serology, particularly complement fixation test.
	Leptospirosis	Poorly defined, associated with recurrent uveitis. May have mild fever, hepatic disease, and abortion. Diagnosis suspected based on serology.
	Borrelia burgdorferi (Lyme disease)	Increasingly diagnosed in endemic areas. Fever, inappetence, and arthritis possible. Diagnosis based on serology.
	Anthrax	Acute high fever (106°F, 42°C), ventral edema, colic, rapidly fatal. Diagnosis by necropsy.

TABLE 15–1. *Continued.*

Major Clinical Signs	Causes	Additional Signs and Diagnostic Clues
	Tetanus	Stiffness, hyperesthesia, collapse. Hyperthermia (not a true fever) may develop due to muscle heat production.
	Pyrogens—exogenous	Present in poorly prepared intravenous fluids or serum products. Fever on administration. Trembling, restlessness, and occasionally death possible.
	Massive tissue damage	Induced by trauma, ischemia, or metabolic dysfunction, e.g., exertional rhabdomyolysis. Endogenous pyrogen is released, causing fever. Diagnosis based on clinical signs and history.
	Anhidrosis	Southern hot, humid area. Hyperthermia (not a true fever). Caused by exertion and a failure to sweat.
	Lactation tetany (transit tetany, hypocalcemia)	See Tetanus. Responds to intravenous calcium solution. Also seen in endurance horses.

agents appear to operate by the release of endogenous pyrogen (probably interleukin-1) from macrophages and monocytes. Endogenous pyrogen acts to alter the discharge of thermoregulatory cells of the hypothalamus and initiate the conservation of body heat to raise body temperature, and then to maintain body temperature at the newly achieved level. Nonsteroidal anti-inflammatory drugs (NSAIDs) block the action of endogenous pyrogen, and prostaglandins strongly induce fever when injected into the hypothalamus. These data suggest that the induction of fever by the hypothalamus involves prostaglandins as mediators, although other substances have also been proposed.

When endogenous pyrogen is released, heat is conserved and heat production increases. Peripheral vasoconstriction occurs, as might shivering. The limbs feel cold. Once the body temperature is stabilized at the new level, heat production and loss are adjusted to maintain this level. The animal can appear fairly normal, although a little restless or depressed. If the pyrogen production stops, the process is reversed, and heat is lost. Peripheral vasodilation, sweating, and panting occur until a normal temperature is reached.

Fever worries clients and veterinarians, who often urgently try to reduce the fever before the cause has been determined. Even when the cause has been determined, the reduction of fever using NSAIDs might not be the best therapy; fever and its natural resolution are useful indicators of the effect of therapy, particularly in infectious diseases. In addition, the febrile response can be beneficial, particularly in infectious diseases. Experimental data have indicated that the development of a moderate fever is associated with decreased mortality in infections. Hence, it is unwise to treat merely the fever and not the cause. However, extremely high fevers (e.g., over 106° F,

41° C) should perhaps be reduced empirically, even if the exact cause has not been determined. Treatment is indicated if the animal had stopped eating and drinking or is endotoxemic. Because serious cell damage is not likely even at these temperatures, however, the use of NSAIDs solely to reduce fever should be considered carefully.

POSSIBLE CAUSES (Table 15–1)

The majority of febrile episodes in horses are associated with infectious diseases. Although many infectious diseases are well recognized in horses, in many cases determining the cause of fever is not possible. Often signs are vague and do not indicate a clear cause. A specific cause might not be determined even if additional testing, such as virus isolation, bacteriology, or serology, is undertaken. A recent survey of 4000 febrile episodes in horses over a 7-year period in Japan showed that over 75% of febrile episodes were not related to infections with identifiable equine viral pathogens, based on acute and convalescent serology.

Most of the possible causes of fever in horses have fairly obvious clinical signs and are not too difficult to diagnose. Problems occur when the cause of the fever is not immediately apparent. These cases and their investigation will be considered in more detail.

CLINICAL EVALUATION

The first step is to decide if a problem really exists. Owners and trainers who routinely record rectal temperatures of their horses can provide a reliable record. Low-grade fevers can be more accurately documented in these horses than in others for whom no previous "normal" values are known. Owners are often worried by increases in temperature of 0.5° F (0.2° C) and expect this "problem" to be investigated.

Some owners are concerned that their animals always have a fever after racing or working hard. Normally core temperature can reach 106° F (41° C) during maximal exercise. Depending on environmental conditions, 1 to 2 hours might be needed for a horse's rectal temperature to return to normal following severe exercise. Before an extensive investigation of these animals is undertaken, a record of the course of the postexercise temperature should be made on several occasions. A repeated pattern might demonstrate to the owner or trainer that this phenomenon is normal.

Record keeping is valuable in other animals with suspected or proven fevers. Two readings, one in early morning and one in late afternoon, should be taken. As noted earlier, horses' temperature probably follows a diurnal rhythm, being higher in the afternoon. Because this rhythm will probably be maintained in febrile animals, a fever slightly higher in the evening than the morning should not necessarily be taken as evidence of a worsening situation.

Accounting for a fever is easy if clinical signs suggest a possible cause and if additional investigations support a diagnosis, such as in acute viral infections. Vague, nonspecific illnesses accompanied by fever are more of a problem. Extensive investigation might be necessary to understand these horses and to design a management plan.

The majority of short-duration (2 or 3 days) febrile episodes, without major clinical signs other than depression and anorexia, are probably caused by viral infections. Because probably many more viral respiratory pathogens affect horses than the three or four agents routinely tested for by most laboratories, the cause of many febrile episodes can go unexplained. For the most part, a nonspecific fever associated with mild signs of partial anorexia, depression, and reduced performance need

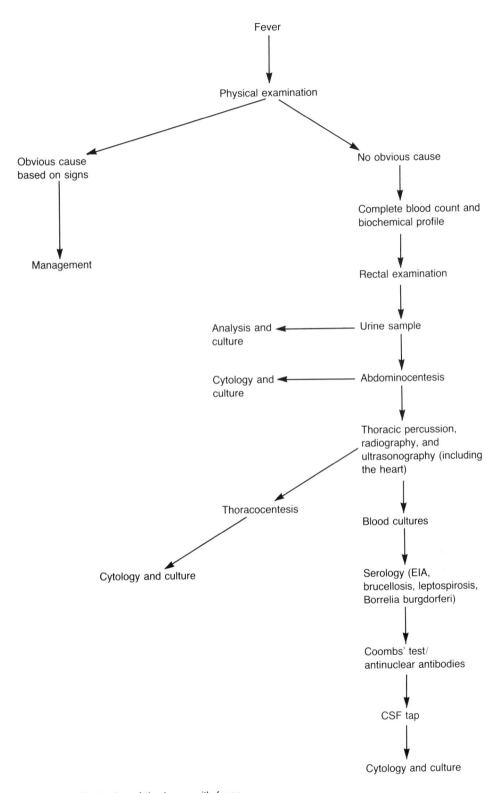

Fig. 15–1. Evaluation of the horse with fever.

only be monitored for a few days, and not investigated extensively. Most will resolve over 3 to 7 days without residual problems.

If a fever persists beyond 3 to 5 days, or if the animal is severely ill, with total anorexia and depression, additional investigations should be undertaken (Fig. 15–1). All the steps in this protocol are not necessary in all cases, and the sequence of the steps is not rigid. The less invasive and less expensive evaluations should be done first, and the investigation ended as test results become available. The increasing cost of the investigation, particularly one with negative results, might cause a halt before an answer is found. If a specific diag-nosis is made, appropriate therapy, if any, can be initiated. If no diagnosis is made, either because of economic considerations or because the diagnostic possibilities have been exhausted, empiric therapy could be undertaken. The value of the horse will to some extent determine the drugs selected. The broadest spectrum of antibiotic therapy should be selected, if affordable. Antibiotics probably will have to be given for at least 10 days. If the horse shows no response, another drug should be considered. Though this approach is not satisfactory, it might be the best that can be offered. The client should be fully informed about the empiric nature of this approach.

SUPPLEMENTAL READING

Dawson, F.M.L., and Durrant, D.S.: Some serological reactions to *Brucella* antigen in the horse. Equine Vet. J., 7:137–140, 1975.

Dinarello, C.A.: Pathophysiology of fever. *In* Cecil's Textbook of Medicine. 18th Ed. Edited by J.B. Wyngaaden and L.H. Smith. Philadelphia, W.B. Saunders, 1988, pp. 1525–1527.

Rumbaugh, G.E., Smith, B.P., and Carlson, G.P.: Internal abdominal abscesses in the horses: A study of 25 cases. J. Am. Vet. Med. Assoc., 172:304–309, 1978.

Smith, B.P.: Pleuritis and pleural effusion in the horse: A study of 37 cases. J. Am. Vet. Med. Assoc., 170:208–211, 1977.

Sugiura, T., Matsumura, T., Imagawa, H., and Fukanaga, Y.: Serological studies on virus agents causing respiratory infection with pyrexia among racehorses at training centers for 7 years. Proc. Vth International Conf. Equine Inf. Dis., Lexington, KY, 1987.

chapter 16

ATAXIA, BIZARRE GAITS, AND RECUMBENCY

Frank M. Andrews

Stephen M. Reed

For horses to stand and move normally, information must be gathered from muscles, tendons, and nerves, processed in the brain and spinal cord, and relayed back to the musculoskeletal system. Damage anywhere along these pathways can lead to ataxia, bizarre gaits, or recumbency. Understanding the nervous system as separate but integrated parts (Fig. 16–1) is important to solving problems like ataxia, weakness, spasticity, hypermetria, and recumbency.

DEFINING THE PROBLEM

A wide range of normal gaits is seen in horses. Differences exist within and among breeds and among individual horses. Owing to unusual conformation or shoeing, some horses can show excessive flexion, pronounced external rotation (winging out), circumduction, or decreased action at normal gaits. Asking the owner or caretaker about the horse's gait can help distinguish between normality and abnormality for that individual.

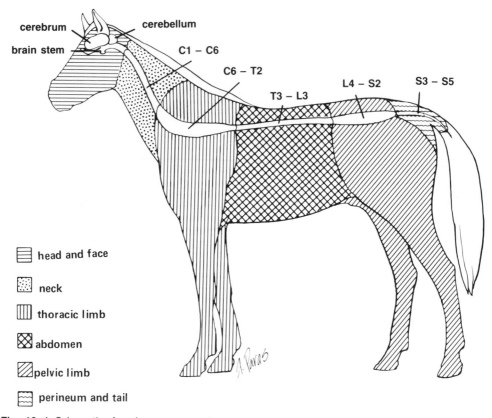

Fig. 16–1. Schematic of equine nervous system.

Once a gait deficit is recognized, regardless of its severity, it must be defined in its simplest form and a problem list generated. Ataxia, weakness, spasticity, and hypermetria describe gait problems suggestive of neurologic disease. These names are used to describe the outward manifestation or the result of more basic problems. In other words, each one of these complex problems is associated with a group of simpler problems. For instance, increased swaying of the trunk, prolonged pelvic limb stride, waving the limb in the air before placement, abduction of the limb during forward movement, crossing the limb under the body, and stepping on the opposite limb defines the proprioceptive problem *ataxia*. Knuckling, stumbling, or dragging of the limb and dipping of the trunk during weight bearing defines the motor problem *weakness* or *paresis*. A stiff-stilted, short-strided (tin soldier) gait, with a lack of joint flexion, defines *spasticity*. Increased or exaggerated joint flexion defines *hypermetria*. These problems can occur together, which might make distinguishing them difficult. Also, some horses with musculoskeletal disease can show signs of weakness when painful limbs are passively lifted off the ground or spasticity when they use painful joints (reluctance to flex). However, *when more than two gait deficits are seen together they are probably the result of a neurologic, rather than a musculoskeletal problem.* Therefore, when defining gait problems it is important to describe the distribution of the problem, so that the lesion can be localized anatomically. The severity of the problem can be graded according to the method of deLahunta (Table 16–1).

Basic understanding of nervous system organization and integration facilitates neuroanatomic localization, which allows the clinician to develop a list of differential diagnoses (Table 16–2). Many lesions affecting the nervous system can be neuroanatomically localized to a single focus. When such localization is not possible, a diffuse or multifocal disease of the nervous system should be considered. Some examples are equine herpesvirus type 1 (EHV 1) encephalomyelitis, polyneuritis equi, and equine protozoal encephalomyelitis (EPM).

ATAXIA AND BIZARRE GAITS

CAUSES

The causes of neurologic gait abnormalities such as ataxia, weakness, spasticity, and hypermetria can be classified into general categories. Horses can have ataxia and bizarre gaits owing to altered motor and conscious proprioceptive impulses from the integrative centers in the brain and brain stem; altered motor and unconscious proprioceptive impulses in the cerebellum; altered motor and proprioceptive impulses along the spinal cord; altered motor impulses along the ventral roots and peripheral nerves; and altered sensory impulses from peripheral end organs in muscles, tendons, ligaments, and joints.

CLINICAL EVALUATION

Patient History and Data Base (Fig. 16–2)

The patient history is important in developing a data base to define problems associated with ataxia and bizarre gaits. In many cases a thorough history will decrease the list of differential diagnoses. The history should define the animal's

TABLE 16–1. GRADING SYSTEM OF EACH LIMB DURING GAIT ANALYSIS

Grade	Description
0	No gait deficits detected (normal horse).
1	Gait deficits barely detectable at walk and trot but present with special manipulatory tests, backing, circling, swaying, head elevation, and neck extension.
2	Gait deficit easily detected at walk and trot or posture; exaggerated by backing, turning, swaying, and head elevation.
3	Gait deficits very prominent at walk and trot or posture; horse buckles and falls with backing, turning, swaying, and head elevation.
4	Stumbling, tripping, and falling occurs spontaneously at walk and trot.
5	Recumbency, inability to rise.

(Adapted from Mayhew, I.G., et al.: Spinal cord disease in the horse. Cornell Vet., *68*[Suppl. 6]:24–29, 1978.)

age, sex, and breed, the duration of the condition, and the use of the animal.

Characteristics of Horse. Breed-, age-, and sex-related neurologic diseases include cervical stenotic myelopathy (CSM) (wobbler syndrome), commonly reported in young, rapidly growing male Thoroughbreds 1 to 2 years of age. An increasing incidence of CSM has also been seen in weanling Thoroughbreds, Standardbreds, and other breeds.

Cerebellar abiotrophy is commonly reported in young male Arabian horses and Gotland ponies (onset < 6 months of age), and atlanto-occipital malformation is reported in Arabian or Arabian crosses. Narcolepsy has been reported in Shetland ponies, with clinical signs beginning at 4 to 6 months of age. Night blindness has been seen in Appaloosas, which can have intermittent ataxia and bizarre gaits, especially during dusk and early morning, when lighting is poor, or when going from a lighted area to a dark

TABLE 16–2. MOST COMMON CAUSES OF ATAXIA AND BIZARRE MOVEMENTS IN THE HORSE

Major Group of Causes	Minor Group of Causes	Specific Diseases
Altered cerebral function	Metabolic	Hypoglycemia Hyperglycemia Renal encephalopathy Hepatic encephalopathy Hyperlipidemia
	Electrolyte imbalance	Hyperkalemia Hypokalemia Hypocalcemia Hypomagnesemia
	Traumatic	Skull fractures
	Infectious	EPM EHV 1 EEE, WEE, VEE Rabies Abscesses (S. equi, Corynebacterium)

	Noninfectious	Toxicosis
		  Organophosphate
		  Lead
		  Arsenic
		  Strychnine
		Neoplasia
		  Pituitary adenoma
		  Lymphosarcoma
		  Cholesteatoma
		Malformations
		  Hydrocephalus

Altered brain stem function	Traumatic	Fracture of basisphenoid-basioccipital bone
	Infectious	EPM EHV 1 EEE, WEE, VEE Rabies Parasitic migration Abscesses (S. equi, Corynebacterium)

	Noninfectious	Toxicosis
		  Yellow star thistle
		  Russian knapweed
		Neoplasia
		  Pituitary adenoma

Altered cerebellar function	Traumatic	Basisphenoid-basioccipital fractures

	Noninfectious	Malformations
		  Cerebellar abiotrophy
		  Cerebellar hypoplasia

Altered spinal cord function	Traumatic	Cervical stenotic myelopathy Atlanto-occipital malformation Thoracolumbar malformation Synovial cysts Fractures of vertebrae
	Infectious	EPM EHV 1 Tetanus Nonsuppurative myelitis

TABLE 16–2. *Continued.*

Major Group of Causes	Minor Group of Causes	Specific Diseases
	Noninfectious	Aberrant parasite migration
		Degenerative myelopathy
		Fibrocartinolaginous infarct
		Polyneuritis equi
		Shivers
		Neuraxonal dystrophy
Altered peripheral nerve function	Traumatic	Suprascapular nerve paralysis (sweeny)
		Radial nerve paralysis
		Femoral nerve paralysis
		Brachial plexus injury
		Sciatic nerve paralysis
		Cranial gluteal nerve paralysis
	Infectious	Botulism
	Noninfectious	Polyneuritis equi (cauda equina neuritis)
		Parasitic migration
		Myotonia
		String-halt
		Tic

area. Dorsal lateral strabismus may also be observed.

Neuroaxonal dystrophy, a progressive degenerative spinal cord disease, has been observed in young Morgan and Standardbred horses. EPM, a diffuse granulomatous spinal cord disease, occurs with high incidence in mature Standardbreds and at a lower incidence in Thoroughbreds. Lumbar fractures and sacroiliac luxations are seen most often in horses at least 5 years of age, whereas cervical vertebral fractures occur most often in horses less than 5 years old. Neoplasia is seen mostly in aged horses.

Color-related neurologic diseases include melanomas, which have a high incidence in gray horses and horses with large areas of depigmentation.

Use of Horse. The use of the horse can be important in determining the cause of the ataxia and gait deficits. Horses with subtle gait deficits can have musculoskeletal lameness or chronic myopathies that confuse the differential diagnosis. Painful hock lesions and chronic lumbar muscle pain can occur with horses being trained or raced excessively. These horses can use bizarre gaits as they attempt to guard against pain.

Duration of Condition. The duration of the condition can be important in defining problems associated with ataxia and bizarre gaits. Frequently, horses demonstrate ataxia following a traumatic episode, such as falling while lunging or being loaded in a trailer. However, careful questioning of the owner or trainer might reveal that subtle gait deficits were present prior to the trauma, instead of being a result of the traumas. Horses with acute rapidly progressing neurologic problems may have EHV 1 encephalomyelitis or traumatic lesions, whereas EPM and CSM often have a slower onset and progression. The owner or trainer can be helpful in answering questions related to duration and onset, although the possibility of providing misleading information exists.

Racing History. Questions about the prior racing history can be important in deter-

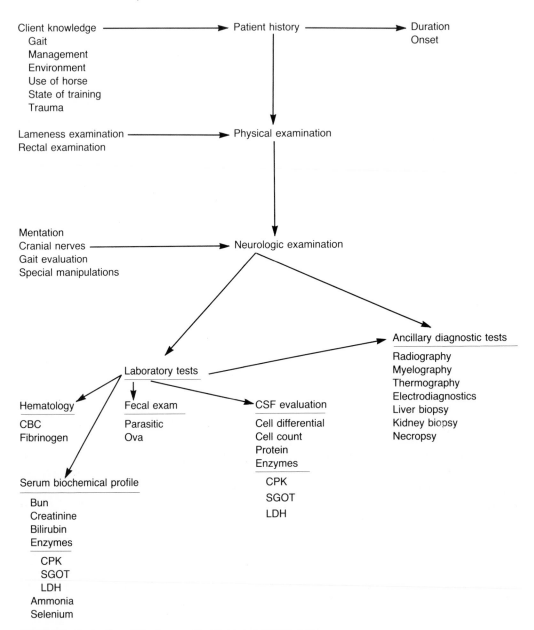

Fig. 16–2. Evaluation of the horse with ataxia and bizarre gait.

mining the cause of ataxia or bizarre gaits. It is unlikely that horses with a prior racing record have congenital or acquired malformations. In our experience, Standardbreds with CSM usually do not attain mile times of less than 2 minutes 30 seconds during training and hence might be presented for evaluation of poor athletic performance. However, some horses with later onset of CSM can attain race speeds. Horses with

the more subtle gait deficits, secondary to EPM, can have a history of lateral digital extensor tenectomy or medial patellar tendon desmotomy for correction of what was thought to be a hock or stifle lameness.

Physical Examination

Once a thorough history is taken, a general physical examination of the patient should be done. Physical examination might reveal other problems that suggest a metabolic cause for the abnormal gaits. Diarrhea and colic can accompany neurologic disease secondary to ingestion of toxins. Icterus can be present in horses with hepatoencephalopathy (see Chapter 14). Wounds may be found on horses in whom tetanus is suspected. Decreased blood flow in the terminal aorta, asymmetries of the pelvic canal, and crepitus in the pelvis can be detected by rectal palpation. If these conditions are suspected, further laboratory tests can be done (Fig. 16–2). Laboratory tests necessary to generate a good data base should include complete blood count, serum chemistry profile, fecal flotation, and fibrinogen.

Neurologic Examination

A neurologic examination should be performed if the physical examination localizes the causes of the gait deficits to the neurologic system. The examination should be done systematically to neuroanatomically localize the lesion (Fig. 16–3), and the details should be recorded for future reference and comparison. Most lesions in the nervous system can be localized to a focal area, while a few can be diffuse or multifocal. In a systematic approach to the neurologic examination, several questions allow the examination to flow logically (Fig. 16–3) and generate rational differential diagnoses.

Are ataxia, bizarre gait deficits, cranial nerve signs, or abnormal behavior present?

Cerebral, brain stem, and cerebellar lesions can produce abnormal gaits in all four limbs, cranial nerve deficits, and mentation changes. Cerebral lesions can produce mild paresis, wide circling, and

mentation changes. The horse's mental status might be difficult to assess, although the caretaker can help with this evaluation.

Altered Cerebral Function. Cerebral disease can be secondary to metabolic abnormalities, electrolyte imbalances, trauma, infectious agents, and noninfectious agents (Table 16–1).

Metabolic abnormalities that should be considered include hypoglycemia, hyperglycemia, renal disease, liver disease, and hyperlipidemia. Some metabolic abnormalities can be differentiated using serum biochemical analysis. The most common metabolic cause of cerebral disease is hepatoencephalopathy. Horses present with dementia, head pressing, aimless wandering, stargazing, and in some cases, icteric mucous membranes (see Chapter 14). Frequently the problems are most pronounced following feeding, especially after a high-protein meal. Increased serum ammonia and aromatic amino acids are thought to diffuse across the blood-brain barrier and act as false neurotransmitters, leading to typical clinical problems. The diagnosis of hepatoencephalopathy is made on the basis of a characteristic history, clinical signs, increased serum ammonia concentrations, which can exceed $30\,\mu g/dl$ (8.0 to $16.2\,\mu g/dl$), and histopathologic changes seen on liver biopsy. Hepatic encephalopathy in the young horse can be secondary to portacaval shunts; though rare, portacaval shunts should be considered in stunted foals with signs of hepatoencephalopathy. Other metabolic abnormalities occur sporadically in the horse and can be diagnosed with careful evaluation and appropriate serum biochemical tests.

Electrolyte imbalances causing neurologic signs also occur sporadically in the horse. One electrolyte abnormality that has gained attention recently is hyperkalemic periodic paralysis. Tetraplegia,

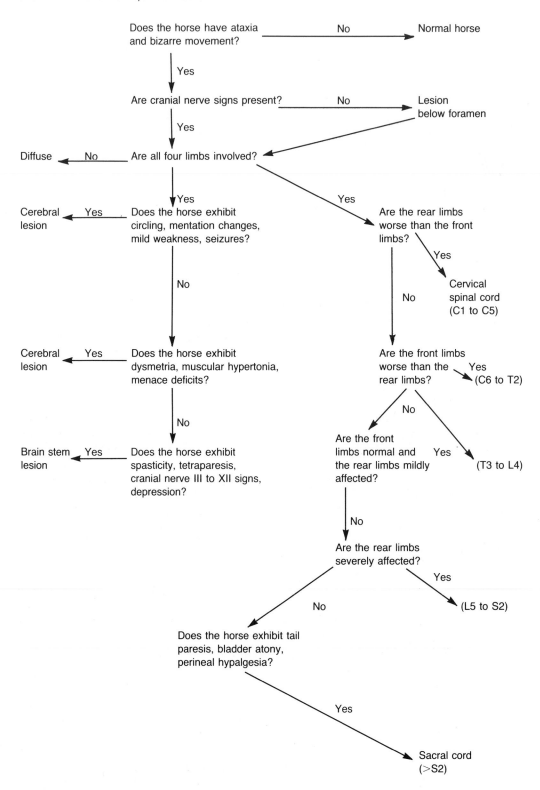

Fig. 16–3. Neuroanatomic localization of lesions.

ataxia, weakness, muscle tremors, and seizures are problems seen in some genetic lines of quarter horses. This syndrome can be differentiated from others by repeated increases in serum potassium concentrations and the onset of typical clinical signs postprandially, during exercise, or during extreme stress or excitement.

Hypomagnesemia and hypocalcemia can lead to signs of cerebral disease. These conditions can occur following stress or severe exercise or secondary to diseases that cause intestinal stasis, decreased feed intake, or decreased absorption, such as anterior enteritis, colic, and granulomatous enteritis.

Infectious cerebral disease can result from viral infections such as eastern equine encephalomyelitis (EEE), western equine encephalomyelitis (WEE), Venezuelan equine encephalomyelitis (VEE), rabies, and EHV 1, from protozoal organisms such as Sarcocystis and Toxoplasma, and from bacteria such as Streptococcus equi and Corynebacterium. Streptococcal cerebral abscesses are rare and can follow outbreaks of strangles. Rabies is of greatest importance because of its sporadic occurrence and potential zoonosis. Rabies should be considered in any horse with acutely developing local hyperesthesia, lameness, ataxia, and mentation changes of less than 10 days' duration. Death usually occurs in these horses within 7 days after the onset of clinical signs. A diagnosis of rabies can be made from the history, the acutely developing clinical signs, and the necropsy findings. Negri bodies in the hippocampus pyramidal cells, fluorescent antibody testing of brain tissue, and mouse inoculation are currently used in most laboratories to test for rabies. Samples of the brain should be submitted to a regional pathology laboratory, half in formalin and half cold or frozen; full necropsy should be delayed until the results are received.

Eastern and western equine encephalomyelites occur sporadically throughout the U.S. These togaviruses, which are transmitted by biting insects, cause extensive inflammation of the cerebrum. Horses demonstrate lethargy, unresponsiveness, aimless wandering, circling, and in some cases, blindness. The clinical signs can worsen acutely and progress to recumbency and death. Viral titers can be helpful in making a differential diagnosis in horses that survive long enough to produce an antibody response. EHV 1 encephalomyelitis and EPM can also cause diffuse cerebral disease (see the section on diffuse multifocal neurologic diseases).

Noninfectious agents causing cerebral disease include toxicosis, neoplasia, and malformations. Organophosphate, lead, arsenic, and strychnine toxicosis can cause cerebral disease. Careful historical information and farm visits can be helpful in determining toxic cerebral disease. Although serum concentrations of these toxins can be measured, if the exact toxin is not suspected, multiple analysis can be very costly and frustrating.

Neoplasia of the brain is rare and usually occurs in the aged horse. Most common tumors include pituitary adenoma, lymphosarcoma, and cholesteatoma, although melanomas of the central nervous system have been observed. Seizures, blindness, mentation changes, and abnormal gaits can be present, depending on the exact location of the tumor. Pituitary adenoma is the most commonly encountered tumor. Additional presenting problems with pituitary adenoma include polydipsia or polyuria (see Chapter 12), hirsutism, a pot-bellied appearance, and hyperglycemia. Electroencephalography can be helpful in determining the presence of space-occupying masses in the cerebrum. Low-frequency, high-amplitude slow waves suggest areas of destroyed neurons; high-frequency, low-amplitude waves suggest an irritation or an inflammatory process.

Congenital malformation such as hydrocephalus rarely occurs in young horses. A foal with an open fontanelle that shows progressive depression, ataxia, and weakness can have congenital hydrocephalus. Radiographs of the skull might show a ground-glass appearance to the brain, due to thinning of the cortex. Opening atlanto-occipital cerebrospinal fluid (CSF) pressure can be increased. A presumptive diagnosis can be made based on history and clinical signs, but a definitive diagnosis can be difficult without computed tomography (CT) or necropsy. If the fontanelle is open, ultrasonography through the foramen could be attempted, and the size of the ventricles assessed.

Cranial trauma can occur from horse's falling over backwards and striking the poll, colliding with obstacles, and kicking by other horses. Skull fractures involving the mandible, the maxilla, and the incisive, frontal, parietal, basioccipital, and basisphenoid bones can lead to brain or brain stem trauma and the presence of bizarre gait, head tilt, ptosis, and anisocoria. Trauma usually results in cerebral edema, which causes a redistribution of brain tissue within the rigid calvaria. This redistribution leads to compression and the characteristic signs of cerebral and brain stem disease. Death can occur from depression of the respiratory or cardiac centers in the brain stem. Cerebral trauma can result in mild weakness but does not lead to ataxia or bizarre gait deficits unless severe. Skull radiographs can be helpful in diagnosing fractures.

Altered Brain Stem Function. Brain stem disease frequently causes spasticity and ataxia of all four limbs, tetraparesis, ptosis, ear droop, deviated muzzle, head tilt, circling and leaning toward the affected side, spontaneous horizontal or rotary nystagmus, or depression. Common causes of brain stem lesions are trauma, toxicity, and infectious disease such as EHV 1

and EPM. (EPM and EHV 1 will be discussed below under diffuse diseases).

Russian knapweed or yellow star thistle ingestion causes nigropallidal encephalomalacia. Usually the disease occurs in late summer and fall in horses in the western U.S. on native overgrazed pastures. Characteristic presenting clinical problems include acute onset of impaired prehension and mastication, hypertonicity of the facial and masticatory muscles, and dysphagia. Other possible problems are seizures, head pressing, incoordination, and falling down. These animals can swallow but cannot prehend or chew feed. A diagnosis can be made based on a history of ingestion of the plants and typical clinical signs. Affected horses do not recover, and treatment consists of supportive therapy. Characteristic necropsy findings include irreversible malacia of the substantia nigra and globus pallidus in the brain stem.

Brain stem trauma occurs frequently in the horse. Trauma without evidence of fractures is not uncommon. Basisphenoid-basioccipital bone fractures often occur when horses fall over backward and strike the poll, causing damage to the medulla and pons. Additional presenting problems include hemorrhage into the external ear canal, leakage of CSF from nose and ear, and intention tremors, if the cerebellum is affected. A diagnosis can be made based on history of trauma, clinical signs, and skull radiographs showing displacement of the basisphenoid-basioccipital bones. Prognosis is guarded; horses progress to recumbency and death, probably from respiratory failure. Horses that recover might have residual head tilt and mild circling but can be salvaged for breeding.

Altered Cerebellar Function. Cerebellar disease causes ataxia and symmetric spasticity without loss of strength, muscular hypertonia, intention tremors, and loss of or delayed menace response. Inflammatory or traumatic lesions affecting the cerebellum are usually associated with cranial nerve signs. The most common cerebellar disease is congenital cerebellar abiotrophy, which occurs in highest incidence in young Arabian foals. A base-wide stance is present at rest and increased extensor tone is noted in the front limbs, producing a characteristic "goose step" at a walk and trot. Foals with cerebellar abiotrophy usually present without head tilt, visual deficits, or nystagmus, but have tremors during intentional movements (intention tremors) such as eating and drinking. Radiographic examination can help rule out atlanto-occipital malformation and cranial trauma. CSF values are usually within normal limits, except for a mild increased creatine kinase concentration in some cases, which can be a result of demyelination.

Are ataxia and bizarre gait deficits present in all four limbs without cranial nerve deficits or abnormal mentation?

Ataxia, weakness, spasticity, limb hyperreflexia, and normal deep pain without cranial nerve signs are observed in lesions below the foramen magnum.

Altered Spinal Cord Function. Cervical spinal cord lesions are the most common cause of ataxia and bizarre gait. Clinical signs include ataxia, paresis, and spasticity in all four limbs, with the rear limbs appearing to be most affected. Causes of cervical spinal cord disease include malformations, trauma, and infectious diseases. Other conditions such as injection site abscesses occur, but less frequently. A history of previous cervical injection can be helpful in making the differential diagnosis of spinal cord abscess.

Cervical vertebral malformations include atlanto-occipital malformation and cervical stenotic myelopathy. Compression of the spinal cord results in the clinical signs. Atlanto-occipital malformation is a rare congenital malformation that occurs in Arabians. It usually involves the occipital bone, atlas, and axis. Various subtypes of this condition are classified on the basis of different anatomic features. Problems characteristic of cranial cervical spinal cord compression occur within the first few months of life; in some cases the onset of problems can be delayed until 2 to 3 years of age. Differentiation from other cervical spinal lesions can be made from the history, from palpation, which reveals a characteristic click on flexion and extension of the head and neck, from the rigid extension of the neck, and from cervical radiographs. Prognosis is poor and breeding is not recommended.

Cervical stenotic myelopathy (spinal ataxia, cervical vertebral malformation or instability, wobbler syndrome) is the term given to a variety of conditions that lead to cervical spinal cord compression. Problems usually develop within the first 6 to 30 months of life, can progress very rapidly, or can remain static. The horse might have a history of trauma. Problems characteristic of cervical spinal cord compression are seen. In some cases, mild asymmetric ataxia and spasticity can be present. A presumptive diagnosis can be made based on history, clinical signs, and cervical radiographs with normal CSF parameters. However, a definitive diagnosis of spinal cord compression can be made only with a cervical myelogram. Cervical myelography is also indicated to localize the site of spinal cord compression for possible surgical intervention. Ventral stabilization or dorsal decompression can be done in select cases, and improvement has been noted. Prognosis for future performance is partially related to the severity and duration of clinical problems. Horses with grade III/V gait deficits or worse or a long duration of clinical signs have a poorer prognosis for return to performance because of the limited regenerative capacity of the central nervous system. Because cervical stenotic myelopathy has been linked to developmental orthopedic disease (metabolic bone disease), cartilage defects can occur at other sites.

Cervical spinal cord trauma most commonly occurs when horses fall or collide with a relatively immovable object. Foals appear to be more susceptible to vertebral trauma than adult horses and frequently suffer fractures of the cranial cervical and caudal thoracic vertebrae. Fractures and luxation of the dens, secondary to hyperflexion, and epiphyseal fractures, resulting from hyperextension injuries, are most common, as epiphyseal growth plates do not close until 4 to 5 years of age. Adult horses are more susceptible to injury of the caudal cervical vertebrae (C5 to C7) and caudal thoracic vertebrae. Cervical radiographs can be helpful in elucidating these fractures if displacement is present. The absence of radiographic evidence of a fracture does not rule it out. Without displacement, fractures are difficult to identify. Increased number of red blood cells and xanthochromia can be present in CSF of horses with spinal and vertebral injuries. Serial CSF collections over several days might be helpful in determining if continued hemorrhage into the subarachnoid space is occurring.

Are the front limbs worse than the rear limbs?

Profound weakness and hyporeflexia in the front limbs with hyperreflexia to normoreflexia in the rear limbs is consistent with a cranial intumescence lesion. Lesions in this area are usually traumatic, although malformations of the thoracic vertebrae, fibrocartilaginous infarcts, and inflammatory diseases also occur. Diagnosis can be made based on history, clinical signs, CSF changes, and sometimes radiographic evidence of fracture. Radiographs of this region can be helpful, although the depth of this region often makes study inconclusive. Necropsy can provide the definitive diagnosis if improvement does not occur within several days.

Are the front limbs normal and the rear limbs mildly affected?

Progressive symmetric ataxia, paresis, and spasticity of the pelvic limbs at 6 months to 2 years of age can suggest equine degenerative myelopathy (EDM). A presumptive diagnosis can be made based on history, typical clinical signs, normal cervical radiographs, and normal CSF parameters. A definitive diagnosis of EDM can be made only based on histopathologic examination of the spinal cord. Although this condition has been reported in all equine species and in several breeds, some reports indicate that Morgans, Standardbreds and some quarter horses might be more often affected. Prognosis is poor.

Trembling and pectoral and pelvic limb muscle fasciculations, especially during backing-up in young draft horses (especially Clydesdales), suggests shivers or shivering. Diagnosis can be made based on the history and typical clinical signs. Electromyography can reveal the presence of occasional denervation potentials, fibrillation potentials, and positive sharp waves. CSF parameters are normal. Histochemical staining of skeletal muscle biopsies in one case showed a decrease in glycogen concentration, which suggests rapid fatigue as a possible cause.

Altered Peripheral Nerve Function. *Are all four limbs weak?* Profound weakness, limb hyporeflexia, limb hypotonia, and decreased deep pain reception is consistent with a lesion in the peripheral nervous system or muscle (lower motor neuron) (LMN). Diseases of the motor unit can be divided into several categories, depending on their anatomic location along the motor unit. Peripheral neuropathies cause profound weakness, rapid muscle atrophy, hyporeflexia, and hypotonicity. Diseases that sometimes affect the ventral column of the spinal cord and internuncial neurons include EPM, aberrant parasite migration, and tetanus. Diseases that affect the ventral roots of the LMN include polyneuritis equi and neoplasia. (Polyneuritis equi and EPM are discussed below under diffuse diseases, owing to their multifocal distribution.) Diseases of the peripheral nerve such as suprascapular nerve paralysis (sweeny), radial nerve paralysis, cranial gluteal paralysis, femoral nerve paralysis, and sciatic nerve paralysis can occur in horses after trauma or general anesthesia. Neuromuscular junction lesions like equine botulism (forage poisoning) and myasthenia-like syndrome are uncommon but occur in some horses. Equine botulism leads to profound weakness. The heat-labile exotoxin produced by the Clostridium botulinum type C and B organisms binds to the presynaptic membrane of the neuromuscular junction, preventing release of acetylcholine and causing the characteristic clinical signs of weakness. Initially horses have dysphagia, decreased eyelid and facial muscle tone, delayed palpebral and pupillary light reflex, and weakness in all four limbs. Normally these horses respond to the examiner but appear depressed, weak, and listless. Horses usually progress to recumbency and can die of respiratory arrest. Colic resulting from ileus, constipation, and urinary retention can occur. Prognosis is guarded to poor, especially after the horse has progressed to recumbency.

Other unclassified disorders of the peripheral nerve include shivers, tics, and string-halt. The exact cause of these conditions is unknown, but abnormal sensory impulses might be a possible cause of tics and string-halt.

Diffuse Central Nervous Diseases. *Are the ataxia and bizarre gait deficits present in only one or two limbs and accompanied by cranial nerve deficits?*

Cranial nerve deficits and ataxia, paraplegia and muscle atrophy only in the rear limbs or distributed asymmetrically suggest a multifocal or diffuse lesion. Polyneuritis equi (neuritis of the caudal equina), EHV 1 encephalomyelitis, EPM, and nonsuppurative myelitis are multifocal or diffuse. Subtle clinical differences between these multifocal diseases make separating them possible.

Progressive symmetric paresis and analgesia of the tail, anus, bladder, and perineum, sometimes with cranial nerve signs in mature horses, suggest polyneuritis equi (cauda equina neuritis). Other problems in these horses include fecal incontinence, paraphimosis, urine scalding of the perineum, and bacterial cystitis. The owner can mistake bilateral gluteal and coccygeal muscle atrophy, as well as facial muscle atrophy, for weight loss. The cause of polyneuritis equi is unknown, but bacterial, viral, and immune-mediated mechanisms have been proposed, and antimyelin antibodies have been detected in some cases. Diagnosis can be made based on history and clinical signs, including weight loss and progressive neurologic signs. Prognosis is poor as the disease progresses despite treatment.

Symmetric ataxia, bladder atony, urinary incontinence, and hypotonia of the anus and tail, with or without cranial nerve signs, that begins acutely and sometimes stabilizes rapidly is consistent with a diagnosis of EHV 1 encephalomyelitis. The disease can occur 7 to 10 days after an outbreak of respiratory disease or abortion on the farm. EHV 1 causes a severe vasculitis and thrombosis, which leads to infarcts in tissues supplied by the vessels, resulting in neurologic signs. The vasculitis is thought to be an immune-complex disease. Serologic testing of the serum and CSF can be helpful in making a diagnosis. A fourfold increase in antibody titer between the acute sample and one taken 10 to 14 days later is considered diagnostic of acute neurologic or respiratory infection. However, the absence of a rising titer does not exclude the diagnosis. Many of the horses with EHV 1 encephalomyelitis that remain standing recover spontaneously in 1 to 4 weeks. In some cases, residual neurologic gait deficits persist. The prognosis is guarded to poor if the horse becomes recumbent.

Progressive asymmetric ataxia, weakness, muscle atrophy, and cranial nerve signs suggest EPM. This disease usually occurs in the mature horse, especially Standardbreds. Obscure lameness, lateral digital extensor tenectomy, and medial patellar desmotomy are often part of the history. Sarcocystis and Toxoplasma species are thought to be etiologic agents in EPM, although the exact cause is not determined. The protozoal organisms randomly invade the gray and white matter of the spinal cord, resulting in multifocal upper and lower motor neuron disease. Rising serum Sarcocystis and Toxoplasma titers, history, and clinical signs can help in arriving at a presumptive diagnosis of EPM. Necropsy and identification of characteristic lesions or isolation of the organisms in the nervous tissue provide the only definitive diagnosis. Prognosis for horses with EPM is guarded, although long-term treatment has proven effective in some cases (see below).

Once the neurologic examination is completed, ancillary diagnostic tests can be used to further limit the differential diagnosis so that appropriate therapy can be started. Ancillary diagnostic tests most helpful in determining the cause of ataxia and bizarre gaits are radiographs, which sometimes include myelography, CSF analysis, electrodiagnostic testing (electromyography, electroencephalography, auditory brain stem response testing), thermography, and, in some cases, necropsy. Not all these diagnostic tests are necessary or indicated on every animal with ataxia and bizarre gait; with a thorough history, physical examination, and neurologic examination, essential tests will become apparent.

Radiography

Radiographs of the skull can be of value as an ancillary diagnostic test if cranial nerve and gait deficits appear simultaneously. Radiographs of the head can reveal fractures of the basisphenoid bones and basioccipital bones of the skull. Skull fractures can cause dense areas of air accumulation, which can highlight the fracture line. Also, head tilts caused by middle ear infections, guttural pouch mycosis, or temporomandibular osteitis might be seen radiographically. Radiographs of the cervical vertebrae, taken with the horse standing or under general anesthesia, can be useful in evaluating causes of ataxia, weakness, or spasticity of all four limbs without cranial nerve signs. Cervical vertebral radiographs can reveal malformations or fractures or suggest compressive lesions. Radiographs of the thoracic and lumbosacral vertebrae are difficult to obtain in the adult horse owing to the horse's large size. However, such radiographs are valuable in foals and small horses and can be done with the horse standing or in lateral recumbency under mild tranquilization. Fractures of vertebrae might be difficult to see in the absence of displacement. If compression of the spinal cord is suspected, a myelogram can be done using iodine compounds injected into the atlanto-occipital space under general anesthesia.

Cerebrospinal Fluid Analysis

When is it necessary to do a CSF tap?

A CSF tap or any other ancillary diagnostic test is indicated when making or confirming a diagnosis. If the diagnosis has already been made, further diagnostic tests might not be indicated. CSF analysis can be of great value in determining the cause of neurologic disease. Normal CSF values are listed in Table 16–3. CSF can be collected from the lumbosacral space in standing horses and the atlanto-occipital space in anesthetized horses. In foals and older horses it can be collected with the horses in lateral recumbency under heavy xylazine and butorphanol sedation and restraint. Generally, CSF from the atlanto-occipital space is more diagnostically used for diseases above the foramen magnum (or at least cranial to C2), and CSF from the lumbosacral space is better diagnostically for diseases below the foramen magnum (caudal to C2). Atlanto-occipital CSF must be obtained with great care, as negative pressure applied too rapidly can cause brain swelling leading to herniation of the cerebellum through the foramen magnum. Sometimes, CSF parameters from the atlanto-occipital space and the lumbosacral space can be compared and the space closest to the lesion confirmed.

The CSF parameters that are most helpful in differentiating problems of ataxia and bizarre gaits are appearance of the CSF, total leukocyte count with differential, total protein, and erythrocyte count. Before the results of more in-depth analysis are received, an initial examination of the CSF appearance can be helpful. Normal CSF is clear and colorless and does not clot; the presence of a clot indicates an increased concentration of fibrinogen secondary to inflammation or peripheral blood contamination, and a red tinge to the CSF indicates peripheral blood contamination. Hemorrhage into

TABLE 16–3. NORMAL VALUES FOR EQUINE CEREBROSPINAL FLUID ANALYSIS

Cisternal pressure	150–500 mm H_2O
Refractors index	1.334–1.335
Red blood cell	none
White blood cell	0–10/μl
Total protein	20–80 mg/dl
Pándy's test	negative
Glucose	35–75% blood glucose
Creatine kinase	0–8 IU/ml
Aspartate aminotransferase	15–50 Sigma Frankel units
Lactic dehydrogenase	0–5 IU/ml

the CSF secondary to trauma will not result in a clot. Turbid CSF (assessed by difficulty reading newsprint through the sample) can indicate increased white blood cells or red blood cells, bacteria, fungal organisms, or epidural fat. An increased number of red blood cells in the CSF can indicate peripheral blood contamination, the origin of which is sometimes difficult to determine. Repeated hemorrhagic taps over several days suggest continued trauma, because most red blood cells are cleared from the CSF within 24 hours after acute trauma. A slight orange to yellow tinge to the CSF (xanthochromia) can indicate previous hemorrhage from trauma, protein leakage from a vasculitis, or bilirubin from leakage across the blood-brain barrier. EHV 1 encephalomyelitis commonly leads to xanthochromic CSF.

The most sensitive CSF parameters used in arriving at a diagnosis are, in order of importance, total protein, differential cell count, and total cell count. Increased CSF total protein concentration is a sensitive indicator of changes in the CNS. Damage to the blood-brain barrier, which allows leakage of protein from the plasma or an increased production of gamma globulins, can lead to increased CSF protein. This damage can occur from inflammation of the meninges, vasculitis (EHV 1), infection, and degenerative disease. EHV 1 encephalomyelitis, EPM, polyneuritis equi, bacterial meningitis, and viral encephalitis can result in an increased CSF protein. EHV 1 encephalomyelitis can cause a marked increase in CSF protein, whereas equine protozoal encephalomyelitis, polyneuritis equi, bacterial meningitis, and viral encephalitis can result in a more modest increase.

An increased total white blood cell count or changes in the normal distribution of white blood cells in the CSF can indicate inflammation or peripheral blood contamination. Normal CSF should contain less than 20 cells/μl, with a population of approximately 70% small mononuclear cells and 4 to 40% large mononuclear cells with an occasional neutrophil (1 to 2%). Eosinophils and basophils are not part of the normal CSF cell population. Several formulas have been developed to determine if the cells present are contaminants from the peripheral blood. In the formula we use, 1 white blood cell in the CSF/1000 red blood cells in the CSF is assumed to be from peripheral blood contamination.

Many times in neurologic disease although the total cell counts can be normal, the differential cell counts shift; this shift in cell types can be missed if a differential count is not done.

Increased CSF neutrophils are consistent with an infectious or bacterial cause, necrosis, repeated collection of CSF, and reactions to hemorrhage or contrast media injection. We have observed increased neutrophil counts (up to 50%) in polyneuritis equi, bacterial meningitis, and abscesses. Also, increased CSF neutrophil counts have been reported early in eastern and Venezuelan equine encephalomyelitis.

Increased CSF lymphocytes are consistent with spinal cord compression, axonal degeneration, and granulomatous infectious processes such as EPM and fungal and higher bacterial etiologic agents. Also, mild increases in lymphocytes can be seen in WEE, trauma, and rabies.

Increased CSF eosinophils can occur in severe inflammatory diseases such as parasitic myelitis, EPM, and immune-mediated myelitis.

Increased macrophages can be seen in spinal cord compression, axonal degeneration, and equine protozoal encephalomyelitis. Often these cells are present in response to the need to remove debris secondary to inflammation or axonal degeneration, but occasionally macrophages are found in otherwise normal CSF.

Other CSF parameters that can be of value in defining problems associated with the neurologic system include CSF pressure, refractive index, glucose, Pándy's test, creatine kinase (CPK), lactic dehydrogenase (LDH), aspartate aminotransferase (AST), bacteriologic culture, virus isolation, and virus titers. These parameters can sometimes help differentiate problems associated with the neurologic system. Increased CSF pressure indicates an obstruction to normal CSF flow, which could be caused by brain edema, hemorrhage, inflammation, and neoplasia. CSF pressure that decreases 25 to 50% after a few milliliters of fluid is removed might suggest a space-occupying intracranial mass or spinal cord compression cranial to the site of CSF collection.

Chronic infections and immune-mediated diseases can lead to increased globulins in the CSF that can be evaluated using Pándy's test. Extensive myelin degeneration can cause increased CPK and AST in CSF. CPK values are independent of peripheral serum values; severely increased values indicate a poor prognosis. Increased LDH values in the CSF have been reported in lymphosarcoma of the brain and spinal cord.

Normal CSF parameters do not always rule out the presence of disease related to the neurologic system. Normal CSF values can be seen with an extradural lesion, in CSF taken away from the lesion, with ventral root changes and peripheral neuropathies, and early or late in the neurologic disease condition.

Electrodiagnostic Testing

Electromyography, auditory brain stem response testing, and electroencephalography are electrodiagnostic aids helpful in the localization, diagnosis, and prognosis of neurologic disease. Electromyography, which consists of needle EMG and nerve conduction velocity, is helpful in diagnosing disease of the lower motor neuron or motor unit. Auditory brain stem response testing is helpful in diagnosing and identifying the presence of diseases affecting cranial nerve VIII and its projections along the brain stem. Electroencephalography is helpful in diagnosing focal and diffuse intracranial lesions. These ancillary diagnostic tests done on the conscious animal further localize diseases of the neurologic system.

Thermography

Local changes in skin temperature can indicate underlying inflammation, vascular disruption, or neoplasia. Thermographic units are helpful in identifying areas of skin temperature change. Decreased skin and muscle temperature can be present with denervation atrophy of muscles; increased skin temperature in the cervical and facial region can suggest Horner's syndrome or abscessation.

CT Scan

The use of CT is becoming more common in the evaluation of equine neurologic diseases. Congenital anomalies such as hydrocephalus, brain abscesses, vertebral abscesses, fractures, spinal cord compressive lesions, and hematomas can be diagnosed using this procedure. Contrast media can be injected into the jugu-

lar vein to highlight areas in the brain (hot spots) that have unusual vascularity, such as tumors. Even though this technique is relatively new in veterinary medicine, its use is increasing and will provide an excellent ancillary diagnostic tool in select cases.

Necropsy

Necropsy and histopathologic examination might be the only way to definitively diagnose some cases of neurologic disease. Horses that do not respond to therapy, horses that rapidly deteriorate, or horses presented as part of a herd health problem might be candidates for necropsy evaluation. Neurologic postmortem examination can be difficult in the field because of the rapid autolysis of nervous tissue. The brain can be removed and half of it frozen and the other half placed in formalin. The spinal cord can be removed in sections by debulking the muscles around the vertebrae and removing the dorsal laminae with a hacksaw. The sections of the cord should be placed in formalin immediately. Multiple histologic sections can be cut to allow microscopic examination for small focal lesions. A complete history, physical examination data, and neurologic examination data as well as the pertinent laboratory data should be included along with samples submitted to the diagnostic laboratory. This information aids the pathologist in making a definitive diagnosis.

TREATMENT

Once the horse has been accurately assessed, aggressive medical, surgical, and physical management are essential to restore function. The goal of medical and surgical management is stabilization and prevention of further damage to the nervous system. The goal of physical management is to help restore function to the injured nervous system or promote compensation. In some cases a better recovery can be expected. Most of the horses with ataxia and bizarre gaits are not in critical conditions and can be tested as described above. However, some horses with ataxia and bizarre movements have rapidly progressing clinical problems or recumbency and need immediate treatment. The assessment and management of the critically ill and recumbent patient is discussed later.

Medical

General medical treatments are employed to reduce inflammation and edema in the central and peripheral nervous systems. A variety of pharmacologic agents can be used.

General Pharmacologic Agents. Dimethyl sulfoxide (DMSO) is an industrial solvent with anti-inflammatory properties. Its principal action is to scavenge hydroxyl radical released from damaged tissue. DMSO also maintains blood flow in hypoxic tissues by reducing the generation of prostaglandins and thromboxane, thus preventing platelet aggregation and vasoconstriction. DMSO can also have a central-mediated analgesic effect. Horses that benefit most from DMSO treatment are those with acute cranial or spinal cord trauma and those with rapidly progressing neurologic signs. Improvement can also be noted in horses in which the neurologic signs have stabilized. Experience suggests that 1g/kg as a 10% solution in normal saline (0.9%) or 5% dextrose in water, given intravenously twice daily, will achieve adequate blood levels. Using a 10% DMSO solution is important, as higher concentrations can result in intravascular hemolysis. This therapy can be used for up to 3 days.

Corticosteroids are commonly used in spinal cord traumas and inflammation. The use of corticosteroids such as dexamethazone and prednisone has resulted in a dramatic improvement in some horses with neurologic disease. Corticosteroids decrease edema by stabilizing capillary endothelium and lysosomal membranes, which decreases or prevents the release of proteolytic enzymes. Corticosteroids and DMSO are synergistic. The side effects of corticosteroid therapy include laminitis, adrenal insufficiency, increased susceptibility to bacterial infections, loose stool, and serum electrolyte abnormalities. A single dose of 0.1 mg/kg or 0.2 mg/kg of dexamethasone initially, followed by re-evaluation the next day, has been helpful in cases of brain and spinal cord trauma, EHV 1 encephalomyelitis, and polyneuritis equi. Corticosteroids should be avoided in EMP, having been noted to exacerbate clinical signs.

Mannitol is the alcohol of the sugar mannose. Its greatest value is in reducing brain and spinal cord edema secondary to trauma, principally by acting as an osmotic diuretic removing accumulated fluid from the nervous system. Mannitol can cause hypertension and exacerbation of already dehydrated states. At least two doses of 0.25 to 2.0 mg/kg intravenously as a 20% solution, each dose injected over 30 to 60 minutes, has proven effective in reducing spinal cord and brain edema. Mannitol is prohibitively expensive for use in the adult horse, but can be used in foals.

Specific Pharmacologic Agents. Folate antagonists pyrimethamine and trimethoprim-sulfadiazine are currently being used to treat EPM. These drugs inhibit bacterial and protozoal production of folinic acid, a coenzyme essential for the formation of many amino acids. These synergistic drugs have been successful in treating toxoplasmosis in humans. Doses of 15 mg/kg of trimethoprim-sulfadiazine and 0.275 mg/kg pyrimethamine once or twice daily for 30 days has proven helpful in improving or arresting the clinical signs in some horses. These doses are empiric, as the pharmacokinetics of pyrimethamine have not been established for the horse.

Vitamin E has been used to prevent some forms of equine degenerative myelopathy. Vitamin E functions as a scavenger of oxygen-free radicals, produced during normal biochemical reactions and inflammatory responses. Oral administration of 600 to 1800 mg of vitamin E daily (DL-alpha-tocopherol acetate) has been suggested as a dietary supplement.

Surgical

The principal goal of surgical treatment is to stabilize and decompress the injured nervous system. Exploratory craniotomy can be done to treat progressive subdural hematomas, which are rare in the horse. Ventral stabilization and decompressive dorsal laminectomy of the cervical vertebrae have been developed to treat horses with cervical stenotic myelopathy. These techniques are usually available only in a well-equipped equine surgical facility. The prognosis for surgical treatment is guarded and depends on the duration and severity of clinical problems and the age of the horse. Younger horses seem to improve more rapidly, though this improvement might reflect the shorter duration of clinical signs.

Successfully treated horses, especially mares, might become functional breeding animals. Some horses can return to strenuous exercise, although many perform at a lower level than previously.

Physical

Physical therapy is effective in developing compensatory mechanisms and strength in horses with or recover-

ing from residual neurologic problems. Horses with resolving inflammatory spinal cord disease improve 1 to 2 grades with regular exercise on a lunge line, treadmill, or pasture. Exercise allows the unaffected parts of the nervous system to compensate for the affected nervous system by increasing strength and conscious proprioception. Physical therapy can be one of the most valuable tools in helping horses with ataxia and bizarre movement return to useful functions.

RECUMBENCY

DEFINING THE PROBLEM

The recumbent horse presents not only a diagnostic challenge but a difficult patient management problem to the equine clinician and owner. Using a systematic evaluation, a list of problems can be generated and differential diagnosis made. Neuroanatomic localization of the lesion helps define the problem of recumbency. If the lesion cannot be localized to the nervous system, abnormalities of other body systems that cause recumbency must be considered.

The initial evaluation and treatment of an acutely recumbent horse involves stabilization. If the patient is in distress, the airway must be checked and cleared if it is not patent; if needed, artificial breathing should be started immediately using nasotracheal intubation or tracheostomy tube inserted into the trachea. The respiratory rate should be approximately 12 breaths/minute. Circulation should be sustained using external cardiac massage at approximately 60 strokes/minute, and drugs and fluids should be used as necessary. Once the patient has been stabilized, a thorough history, physical examination, and systematic neurologic evaluation can be done to localize the impaired site.

A data base is necessary to determine the immediate needs for fluids, electrolytes, or both. A complete blood count, specifically a packed cell volume and total protein count, can be helpful in evaluating the state of hydration. A serum chemistry profile and blood gas analysis can be helpful in determining electrolyte imbalances and metabolic causes of recumbency. A CSF tap can help in differentiating traumatic and infectious causes of neurologic disease (Table 16–3). Once the lesion has been neuroanatomically localized, radiographs can be taken to identify fractures, luxations, or subluxations. Negative radiographic findings do not rule out fractures.

Recumbent horses present a great challenge to the equine clinician. Because of the horse's size and weight, management is labor intensive and hence often limited in duration. Therefore, the initial therapeutic goals are to get the horse to its feet as soon as possible. A definitive diagnosis might not always be possible and might be made in response to treatment.

CLINICAL EVALUATION (Fig. 16–4)

Patient History

The history should include duration and onset of signs. Horses with acute spinal cord trauma can be normal one minute and recumbent the next, whereas horses with infectious spinal cord disease or botulism can show a progressive onset of signs over several days. The breed, sex, age, and use of the horse helps the clinician make a differential diagnosis.

Physical Examination

A physical examination including mucous membrane color, heart rate, peripheral pulse characteristic, respiratory pattern, and abdominal distension helps rule out abdominal crisis (endotoxemia). Skin turgor should be checked to determine the degree of dehydration, as recumbent horses are frequently dehy-

drated. Tacky mucous membranes with normal skin turgor suggests 3% dehydration, tacky mucous membranes and delayed skin turgor suggests 5% dehydration, and tacky mucous membranes, delayed skin turgor, and sunken eyes suggests 10% dehydration. A rectal examination in lateral recumbency can help in diagnosing distended abdominal viscus, which can cause colic. Palpation of the muscle tone can help identify exertional rhabdomyolysis or other muscle diseases. Palpation of the limbs can help elucidate crepitus secondary to limb fractures or joint instability. The character and consistency of the stool can also help in evaluating horses with possible toxicosis or diarrheal syndromes.

Laboratory Tests

Once the patient history and physical examination have been completed, appropriate laboratory tests can be ordered to further refine the diagnosis (Fig. 16-2). Whole blood selenium can be helpful in ruling out selenium deficiency myopathy (white muscle disease). This diagnosis should be considered in selenium-deficient areas.

Neurologic Examination

When the problem of recumbency has been localized to the neurologic system, several questions can assist the neurologic examination and neuroanatomic localization of the lesion (Fig. 16–4).

Is the horse recumbent and unable to rise?

Recumbent horses often thrash around, causing trauma. When the horse is first presented, the clinician should determine whether the horse can get up. An attempt to get the patient up should be deferred until the horse is stabilized and

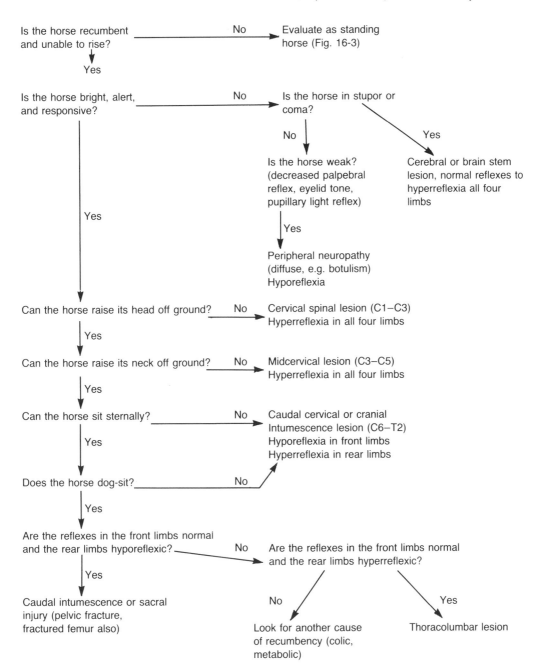

Fig. 16–4. Evaluation of the recumbent horse.

a careful examination has been done to rule out fractures. If a fracture or crepitus is palpated, stabilization of the affected area should be attempted and radiographs taken to determine the extent of the damage. Attempts to get the horse up without prior examination can result in severe damage to the brain, brain stem, or spinal cord. Horses with fractures have severe pain when manipulated. However, some recumbent horses get to their feet with the slightest help and can be evaluated standing (Fig. 16–3).

Is the horse bright, alert, and responsive?

Recumbent horses that are bright, alert, and responsive most likely have lesions below the foramen magnum. Stupor, coma, dementia, or seizures suggest brain or brain stem disease. Profoundly weak horses can be somnolent, be depressed, or have delayed cranial nerve reflexes, but they will respond to the examiner. In equine botulism, a neuromuscular junction disease producing these signs, seizures, coma, and dementia are not features. Also, delayed limb reflexes can occur with equine botulism; increased to normal limb reflexes can be present with brain or brain stem disease.

Is the horse able to lift its head off the ground?

A horse's inability to lift its head off the ground can suggest a cranial cervical lesion. Cranial cervical vertebral fractures and luxations occur most often in horses less than 5 years of age. Therefore, trauma must be strongly considered in young recumbent horses. These horses are usually alert and responsive but cannot raise their heads or can have severe pain when raising the head.

Is the horse able to lift its neck off the ground?

Horses that can lift their heads but not their necks off the ground probably have a mid to caudal cervical lesion. The most common causes of mid to caudal cervical lesions leading to recumbency are cervical fractures and luxations secondary to trauma. Cervical fractures frequently occur in younger horses.

Is the horse able to sit sternally?

Horses that are not able to sit sternally and that have delayed reflexes in the front limbs might have lesions in the cranial intumescence or brachial plexus. The rear limbs have normal to increased reflexes. Careful palpation of the cervical vertebrae can reveal crepitus or subcutaneous emphysema and suggest fractures or trauma. Sometimes rib fractures can be palpated, especially if the trauma was secondary to a kick. Radiographs might or might not be helpful, depending on the degree of displacement. Negative radiographic findings do not rule out fractures or trauma.

Is the horse able to dog-sit?

Horses that are able to dog-sit might have a lesion caudal to the second thoracic vertebra. Also, horses with severe cervical spinal cord trauma secondary to cervical vertebral stenosis or subluxation that are too weak to stand might dog-sit. Cases of degenerative myelopathy, polyneuritis equi, and EHV 1 myelitis occasionally present in a dog-sitting posture. These signs can be progressive, and a previous history of either ataxia or cranial nerve signs is sometimes noted. Pelvic fractures, sacroiliac fractures, and femur fractures can also cause a horse to dog-sit. Careful palpation of the limbs and pelvis might help differentiate these causes. Rectal examination can help in elucidating pelvic asymmetries and crepitus. Rear limb reflexes can be helpful in localizing the lesion in the pelvic limbs. Normal to increased rear limb reflexes suggest a thoracolumbar lesion (T3–L3), and flaccid paralysis with decreased reflexes suggests a caudal intumescence (L4–S2) or lumbosacral injury.

If the horse is recumbent and cannot get up but has normal reflexes and mentation, it should be evaluated for other causes of recumbency. Capillary refill time, heart rate, mucous membrane color, peripheral pulse character, and appropriate laboratory tests should be done to elucidate these causes.

Treatment

In most cases of recumbency, treatment can precede the establishment of a definitive diagnosis or the results of laboratory tests. In the recumbent horse, treatment must be aggressive and broad to cover all possible etiologies pending establishment of an accurate diagnosis. Some horses develop compartmental syndrome, muscle necrosis, and severe trauma owing to recumbency, and in general, the shorter the period of recumbency, the more favorable the prognosis. Broad-spectrum treatment should include anti-inflammatory therapy, fluids, and prophylactic broad-spectrum antibiotics, as well as diligent nursing care.

If neurologic disease is suspected, anti-inflammatory agents can be used to reduce inflammation. DMSO has been shown to be an effective nervous system anti-inflammatory agent. A dose of 1 g/kg body weight as a 10% solution in normal saline or 5% dextrose solution can be given intravenously twice daily for 3 days, then every other day for 6 days. The solution can be administered after that as needed to prevent deterioration of neurologic signs. DMSO must be used with caution, however, as it is hyperosmotic (1600 mosm/L) and can compromise an already dehydrated animal.

Corticosteroids are indicated in acute cranial and spinal cord trauma and EHV 1 encephalomyelitis. Early and short-term administration seems to be most beneficial. Dexamethasone or dexamethasone sodium phosphate at a dosage of 0.1 to 0.2 mg/kg body weight intravenously can be used initially and administered every 8 hours for 24 hours to decrease central nervous system inflammation. Generally, improvement should

be seen in 4 to 6 hours after administration. The dose can be tapered over a 5-day period to avoid secondary complications. Failure to achieve a favorable response within 4 hours or deterioration of neurologic signs indicates the need for more aggressive therapy, such as osmotic diuretic agents. At higher doses or longer-term administration, corticosteroids can cause laminitis, adrenal suppression, and immune suppression.

Osmotic diuretic agents such as mannitol at a dosage of 0.25 to 2 g/kg as a 20% solution can be helpful but is very expensive. Intravenous mannitol can be repeated. Mannitol must be used with caution in the dehydrated horse. Monitoring skin elasticity, packed cell volume, total solids, urinary output, and central venous pressure can be helpful in evaluating the horse's state of hydration.

Nonsteroidal anti-inflammatory drugs (NSAIDs) can be used at recommended dosages to reduce inflammation in the central nervous system and also to decrease muscle inflammation from recumbency. Phenylbutazone at a dosage of 4.4 to 8.8 mg/kg body weight, flunixin meglumine at a dosage of 0.55 to 1.1 mg/kg body weight, and naproxen at a dosage of 4.4 to 8.8 mg/kg body weight can be used. NSAIDs must be used with caution in horses with severe dehydration and reduced renal function because these drugs can cause renal toxicity.

Antibiotics can be used prophylactically in recumbent animals. Pyrimethamine and trimethoprim-sulfadiazine are currently being used in the treatment of equine protozoal encephalomyelitis. Trimethoprim-sulfadiazine is a broad-spectrum antibiotic that concentrates in the nervous system as well as other tissues such as the lungs. This antibiotic can be helpful in preventing secondary pneumonia. Broad-spectrum antibiotics such as aminoglycosides should be avoided in the dehydrated horse to avoid renal toxicity.

Diligent nursing care is important in treating the recumbent horse. Owing to horse's large muscle mass, pressure necrosis of the muscles and nerve trauma can occur within a few hours of recumbency. The horse must be turned frequently (every 4 to 6 hours if possible) to maintain adequate blood supply to the muscles. The horse should be placed on thick pads or bedded in deep straw to minimize pressure-related complications. The legs should be wrapped, past the carpus on the front legs and above the hocks on the rear legs, to prevent self-trauma and decubital ulcers. Metal shoes should be removed or at least wrapped with tape to minimize self-induced trauma and maximize safety for the handler. If the horse tries frequently to get up, a head bonnet should be used to prevent cranial trauma and abrasions. These bonnets also help protect eyes from corneal ulceration, which are common secondary complications of the recumbent horse. Prophylactic treatment with antibiotic ophthalmic ointment can help prevent corneal ulcers.

Horses that are marginally weak might be able to function in a sling, although without the cooperation of the horse slings can become dangerous to the animal and handler. The horse must be able to use the sling as a "fifth wheel" and push off while in it. If the horse hangs motionless in the sling, its use should be discontinued.

Recumbent horses present a great challenge to the equine clinician. Because of the horse's great size and weight, management is very labor intensive and often limits the length of time treatment can be continued. Therefore, initial therapeutic goals have to be directed at getting the horse to its feet as soon as possible. A definitive diagnosis might not always be possible and might be made on response to treatment.

SUPPLEMENTAL READING

DeLahunta, A.: Veterinary neuroanatomy and clinical neurology. 2nd Ed. Philadelphia, W.B. Saunders, 1983.

Mayhew, I.G., and MacKay, R.J.: The nervous system. *In* Equine medicine and surgery. 3rd Ed. Edited by R.A. Mannsman and E.S. McAllister, Santa Barbara, Santa Barbara American Veterinary Publications, 1982, pp. 1159–1252.

Reed, S.M.: Neurologic diseases. Vet. Clin. N. Am. Equine Pract., 3(2):255–440, 1987.

Reed, S.M., et al.: Ataxia and paresis in horses. Part I. Differential diagnosis. Compend. Contin. Educ., 3(3):888–899, 1981.

Smith, J.M., Cox, J.H., and DeBowes, R.M.: Central nervous system disease in adult horses. Part I. A data base. Compend. Contin. Educ., 9(5):561–570, 1987.

Smith, J.M., De Bowes, R.M., and Cox, J.H.: Central nervous system disease in adult horses. Part II. Differential diagnosis. Compend. Contin. Educ., 9(7):772–780, 1987.

Smith, J.M., DeBowes, R.M., and Cox, J.H.: Central nervous system disease in adult horses. Part III. Differential diagnosis and comparison of common disorders. Compend. Contin. Educ., 9(10): 1042–1053, 1987.

chapter 17

POOR OR REDUCED ATHLETIC PERFORMANCE

Christopher M. Brown

Most horses are bred and raised to spend at least part of their lives in some form of work. The intensity and demands of this work vary tremendously, perhaps being greatest on the racetrack or in the competitive endurance trail ride. Not only does the intensity of the work vary, but also the style; compare, for example, a Quarterhorse in a 10-second dash to a Belgian in a pulling competition, or a steeplechaser racing over a 3-mile course to an Arabian gelding competing in a 50-mile mountainous trail ride.

Given the variations in the type of horse and the workload, a universal approach to animals showing reduced or poor athletic performance is useless. The problem must be defined before the investigation is undertaken.

DEFINING THE PROBLEM

The clinician should obtain a full understanding of the type of work expected of the animal. If unfamiliar with the specific form of equestrian activity, he or she should not be reluctant to seek clarification. Although some owners might regard this questioning as an admission of ignorance and themselves question the veterinarian's ability to solve the horse's problem, no solution will be found if the problem is not defined and understood. If the veterinarian feels uncomfortable about investigating a problem with which he or she is unfamiliar, or if the owner indicates a lack of trust, referral to someone more familiar with the particular activity should be considered.

No matter what type of athletic activity is involved, two situations prompt owners to seek veterinary advice concerning performance. One is failure of a young or recently acquired animal to achieve its potential expected by its breeding. The second is failure of a horse to perform at its own clearly established performance level. Although similar problems can lead to the poor performance seen in both situations, specific approaches are used for each group of horses (Fig. 17–1).

Although problems and subgroups of problems are considered separately here, more than one problem might be causing reduced performance. Each problem, if small and isolated, might have no or minimal impact on performance, but in conjunction with others can have a significant effect.

The investigation of many of these horses is extremely frustrating for the veterinarian, particularly when assessing a high-performance horse that has suffered a reduction in performance that is only marginal, but enough to remove it

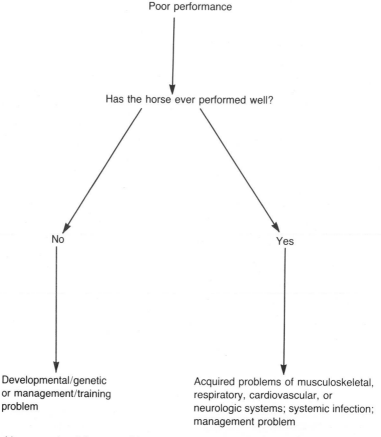

Fig. 17–1. Problems causing failure to achieve potential and reduced performance.

from the top three in a race. For example, for a Standardbred pacer who consistently went a mile in 1 minute 56 seconds and won and now paces in 1 minute 59 seconds and places third, these 3 vital seconds represent an increase in time of 2.6%. Obviously, the dysfunctions that can cause this small but very important performance change are not the severe respiratory, cardiac, or musculoskeletal abnormalities considered elsewhere in this book. Subtle subclinical alterations in a variety of systems are enough to cause this degree of reduced performance. Current knowledge and technology are often inadequate to detect minor deviations from normality. Equine sports medicine, still in a developmental phase, is now defining normality. The pathophysiologic abnormalities that account for the differences between winners and losers have not been defined.

FACTORS DETERMINING FITNESS AND PERFORMANCE

FACTORS

Virtually every aspect of equine structure and function can have an impact on athletic performance, and many are interdependent.

Most horses bred for athletic performance are the product of controlled matings, with the objective of using the best genetic material to produce the most competitive animal possible. Analyses of pedigree and racing performance indicate that, at least to some extent, athletic ability can be inherited and selected. However, the genetic factors predetermining the potential of a horse are by no means the most important factors, as the many examples of well-bred horses that never do well, and poorly bred horses that are outstanding, attest. Nevertheless, the genetic background of an animal should be determined.

Among inherited factors, conformation strongly influences the performance of an animal. Other aspects of conformation are influenced by growth and development, which are partly features of postnatal management and nutrition. The influence of conformational variations on performance has not been determined scientifically, and what is good conformation is determined mostly by opinion based on experience. Many perfectly conformed horses race poorly, and many poorly conformed horses race well. How much better the latter ones might perform with better conformation is open to speculation. Some conformations predispose to joint or tendinous injury and therefore indirectly influence performance.

No information exists about the inheritance of various physiologic functions, such as cardiac output and pulmonary function, although these are important determinants of athletic performance.

As indicated, the final shape and structure of an adult horse is a product of genetic and environmental influences, including the horse's nutrition during growth. Dietary imbalances and deficiencies can have a significant impact on the final ability to perform. Gross imbalances can lead to significant abnormalities, such as in bone growth and development. The impact of less severe imbalances and minor deficiencies on the development of maximum athletic performance is not known. Often, determining the previous dietary history of a horse, particularly its nutrition during growth, is difficult.

The current nutritional program also has an impact on maximum performance. Experts do not agree on the best way to feed different horses for different types of work and performance. Similar horses whose feeding programs vary widely can have similar successes at the racetrack or arena. Although a well-informed veterinarian can detect gross deviations from acceptable programs, minor, potentially influential ones are hard to detect.

In addition to genetic, developmental, and nutritional influences, management probably has a great impact on performance, although again the exact mechanisms are yet to be determined. So far, confirming or refuting claims that one protocol is superior to another has not been possible. For example, scientific data are not yet available to prove that "interval training" of Standardbred horses is superior to conventional programs. Indeed, it is likely that one type of horse will do well in one program, and another in a different program. Nonetheless, variations in training schedules and trainers are often the most frequent changes made to bring about improvements in athletic performance. The training and management of horses is still largely based on empirically obtained information and experience.

The other determinant of performance lies within the horse's brain. Undoubtedly, some horses appear keen to compete, and others on similar programs and without detectable problems have no will to win. This poorly understood and difficult-to-evaluate element often is blamed for a poor performance.

ASSESSMENT

Much effort has been devoted to measuring fitness parameters to judge how well a training program is progressing or why a particular horse is no longer performing well. Though such indices would be useful, none is routinely available. The many evaluations performed on treadmills indicate that under controlled experimental conditions it is possible to assess the level of fitness of a particular horse. However, because most assessments require that the samples be drawn or measurements be made during a set level of work, or because they require

techniques that are not routinely available, apparently no simple "stable-side" or "track-side" tests that are good, consistent indicators of the level of fitness can be routinely applied to horses preparing for, or involved in, athletic activities. As more equine sports medicine units are developed, probably such tests will be devised, and owners and trainers will be able to assess the animals' degree of fitness and the progress of training programs.

CLINICAL EVALUATION (Fig. 17–2)

The evaluation of the poorly performing horse is in principle no different from that of any other equine patient. However, because most of these animals are not ill in the conventional sense, routine physical and other diagnostic techniques will probably not define the problem.

The patient history, which helps define the problem, might not be complete, particularly in recently acquired animals, such as those obtained in "claiming" or "selling" races. Horses' performances often worsen when they are suddenly changed from one training and management program to another, and the new owners or trainers are often suspicious that the animal had been receiving some sort of medication that alleviated or masked some performance-limiting problem.

At the outset the veterinarian should determine if the animal has never performed well or if a reduction from previous levels of performance has occurred, and if the latter whether the decline was sudden or gradual. Racing records or other documentation can help establish the type of problem. Management or training changes might not be obvious. Changes in grooms or food suppliers might not be considered important enough to be mentioned. In addition, changes can occur unknown to owners or trainers. Grooms can decide to feed a par-

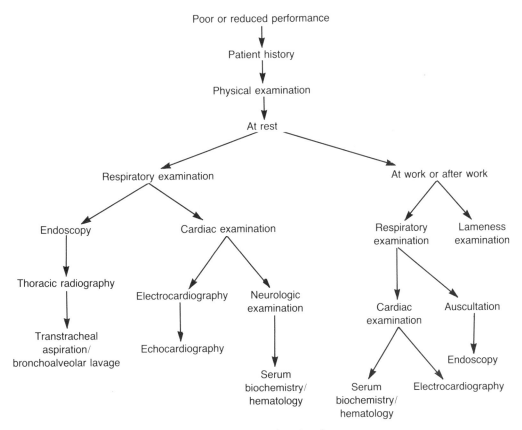

Fig. 17–2. Clinical evaluation of horses with poor or reduced performance.

ticular horse more or less, or modify the work schedule, without consulting the trainer.

A routine physical examination might indicate a cause of reduced performance, such as a loud heart murmur that suggests congenital heart disease, but many horses have minor abnormalities requiring more detailed examination. This examination can include several special procedures, including endoscopy of the upper airways, trachea, and bronchi; transtracheal aspiration or bronchoalveolar lavage; echo- and electrocardiography; neurologic examination; and hematology and serum biochemistries.

If the examination at rest has not revealed the cause of the problem, horses should be examined at varying grades of work. The final level of work should be that at which the problem occurs.

Because musculoskeletal disease is the greatest cause of abnormalities in performance horses, particularly racehorses, *the veterinarian should try to prove that the horse has a significant lameness to account for reduced performance.* Only after exhaustive effort has failed to prove that musculoskeletal disease is present is pursuit of possible diseases of other systems justified. A detailed consideration of musculoskeletal diseases is beyond the scope of this book (see supplemental reading list).

No well-developed methods for measuring physiologic functions in exercising horses are routinely available. Animals are usually worked to their maximum and then examined immediately afterward. Although this method can be useful, particularly for assessing upper-airway function, it is inadequate because, as soon as a horse is stopped and begins to recover, the respiratory and cardiovascular systems function differently. At centers able to study heart rate and record the electrocardiogram (ECG) in exercising horses, maximum heart rate can be assessed and some arrhythmias detected. Hematology and biochemistry can be done before and immediately after exercise and perhaps at 24 and 48 hours after exercise.

Because no two horses are the same and no two training programs are identical, it is difficult to apply a standard exercise testing protocol to all horses and obtain comparable results. Each animal, and each program, should be considered separately and evaluated accordingly.

HORSES THAT HAVE NEVER PERFORMED WELL

There is a saying in horse breeding, "breed the best with the best, and hope for the best." When hopes and expectations are not realized, owners and trainers might seek explanations. While the patient history, physical examination, and evaluation of the management and training might uncover a problem, often horses are evaluated exhaustively and no problem is identified. Owners should be warned about this possible outcome before an evaluation is undertaken.

At the outset of these investigations the veterinarian must establish if the expectations for the horse are realistic. This determination usually requires knowledge of the breed, the sport or work to be done, and the genetic background and management of the horse. If the veterinarian is not familiar with the breed or task, he or she should not rely on the opinion of the owner, who has a certain expectation or otherwise would not have presented the animal. The majority of these clients will not accept, based

on history alone, that their animals are merely of lower quality than they believe. They expect a full assessment (Fig. 17–3).

These animals are usually fairly young, 2 or 3 years old, at the beginning of their athletic careers. The stage of their training or work program at which the problem becomes apparent varies. Horses that have never performed well fit into one of two groups: animals born with a congenital anomaly, such as a heart defect, that limits performance; and animals that have acquired a problem during early growth and development, such as metabolic bone disease, or severe permanent lung damage following pneumonia.

Many of these animals will be assessed from one end to the other anatomically, physiologically, and metabolically and no abnormalities will be found. If, after several months of different management and training schedules, performance does not improve, one can conclude that the horse does not have a detectable problem; the horse might have a problem that cannot be found, or the horse might just not be capable of achieving its owner's expectations.

Congenital Lesions

Congenital lesions causing poor performance are uncommon. Gross lesions of the musculoskeletal system or other systems are unlikely to be overlooked even by owners. Other abnormalities might not become obvious until the animal is stressed by severe work. Many horses grow and reach maturity without ever having been examined carefully by a veterinarian; examples can be cited of horses with fairly large interventricular septal defects progressing into training programs. This most common congenital cardiac lesion in horses is easily detected by auscultation in most cases. Auscultation can also detect most of the other significant cardiac anomalies, although echocardi-

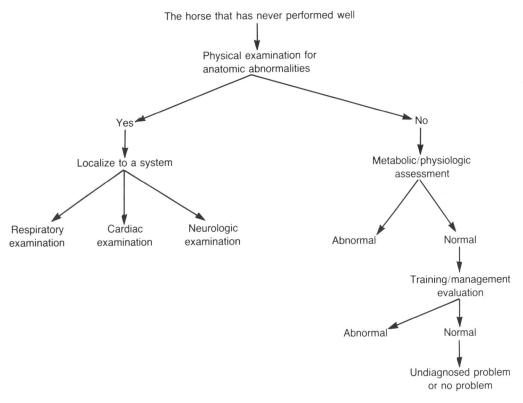

The horse that has never performed well

Physical examination for
anatomic abnormalities

Yes — No

Localize to a system

Metabolic/physiologic
assessment

Respiratory examination   Cardiac examination   Neurologic examination

Abnormal   Normal

Training/management
evaluation

Abnormal   Normal

Undiagnosed problem
or no problem

Fig. 17–3. Evaluation of horses that never performed well.

ography is most useful to evaluate and confirm a diagnosis.

Respiratory congenital anomalies are rare. Occasional horses have abnormalities of the external nares involving their failure to flare on exercise, and in rare cases, pharyngeal, palatial, and laryngeal abnormalities interfere with airflow. These abnormalities are detectable by physical and endoscopic examination, particularly after exercise, and some can be corrected or relieved by surgical procedures.

Whereas subtle physiologic and metabolic abnormalities are difficult to detect, gross physiologic and metabolic abnormalities have a marked effect on growth, development, and performance. However, few data indicate how frequently congenital metabolism abnormalities play a role in poor performance. Exhaustive hormonal and metabolic investigations, particularly thyroid hormonal assays, are often pursued in poorly performing horses. Usually the results are negative or equivocal. Nonetheless, many animals are given thyroid supplementation or anabolic steroids to boost their metabolisms. Data indicate that these therapies do not improve growth or athletic performance, and anabolic steroids often have an adverse effect on behavior.

Acquired Lesions

Previous severe diseases can result in permanent damage to an organ and lead to reduced performance, particularly in the lung. Severe pneumonia, bacterial, viral, or mixed, can cause permanent fibrosis and reduced pulmonary function. Because all evidence of active infection and disease will probably be gone when the animal is presented for evaluation of failure to perform well, historical information is extremely useful if prior lung disease is suspected. The lungs might be unremarkable on auscultation, and endoscopically no abnormality is found. The animal can be dyspneic with exercise and afterwards take longer to return to a normal respiratory rate, and thoracic radiography can demonstrate an overall increase in density, suggesting prior lung disease. Not all severe lung disease in young horses leads to permanent performance-limiting damage, however. Prior to the use of rifampin and erythromycin for the treatment of pneumonia caused by Rhodococcus equi, foals with this problem had a poor prognosis for both life and function. Even severely affected horses can now be treated, however, and many will perform successfully.

Nutritional imbalances can be responsible for the development of various bone abnormalities such as osteochondritis dissecans and cervical spinal stenosis. These abnormalities can lead to various forms of lameness and ataxia. In addition, vitamin E deficiency can be involved in the cause of equine degenerative myeloencephalopathy, although this disease might also involve a genetic predisposition. The role of selenium deficiency in the development of myopathy in horses is not clear but might be important. An accurate dietary history and analysis, though important, often is unreliable, as the current diet might be totally different from previous ones, and often the owner remembers poorly what and how much was fed.

Most horses that fail to reach expected levels of performance lack detectable hematologic or clinicopathologic abnormalities. The animals have usually been aggressively dewormed and frequently supplemented with a wide range of proprietary tonics.

If no apparent anatomic, physiologic, or metabolic abnormalities account for the alleged problem, the management and training program should be evaluated. This evaluation should be done on the farm or track rather than in the clinic so that the environment, the food and food stores, and the work area can be examined directly. Critical assessment of training and management protocols is difficult. As pointed out, horses vary tremendously and so do successful programs. No "perfect" program exists for all horses, even those of the same age and type. However, if a trainer or owner is having problems with many horses rather than a single individual, a management problem should be suspected. Even if a veterinarian knows a great deal about a particular area of equestrian activity, he or she might be able to comment critically on only the most obvious deviations from common practices. Horse training and management is still mostly an art with an empiric base, and few data objectively compare various methods, horses, and performances.

Nevertheless, management and training is the area that will be most frequently addressed by trainers dealing with these underachievers. Dietary and training adjustments are often made, in the hope that no harm will be done, and perhaps some good will result.

HORSES THAT PREVIOUSLY PERFORMED WELL

Horses that previously performed well are perhaps a little easier to assess than those that never performed well, if only because the proper level of achievement has been established. The degree of reduced performance usually correlates with the likelihood that a diagnosis will be made. Current diagnostic tests are not sensitive enough to detect reductions in performance of 2 to 3%. Surveys indicate that the most common reason young racehorses are withheld from training and racing is some form of lameness, and the second most common reason is respiratory disease. Although these data do not directly assess reduced performance, they indicate where the major problems occur and where diagnostic efforts should be directed (Fig. 17–4).

Thus, when a history is taken, lameness should be the first possibility considered, and considered in depth. In many horses whose chronic lameness is controlled and whose performance is adequate, performance is reduced by the development of a new problem or the exacerbation of an old one. Owners and trainers are often aware of the existing problems in their horses and their limiting effects on performance. If they believe that a new problem has arisen, their concern should be given careful consideration.

The severity and speed of onset of the reduced performance should be estab-

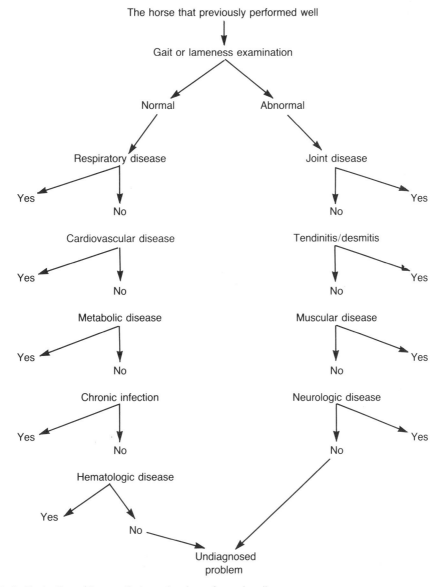

Fig. 17–4. Evaluation of horses that previously performed well.

lished. Problems that develop from one athletic event to the next suggest acute conditions such as tendinitis or articular problems. More gradual changes suggest progressive problems such as chronic lung disease or anemia. Viral respiratory diseases are important causes of reduced performance, and the vaccination status and recent medical history of the horse and of associated horses should be determined.

Musculoskeletal Disorders

Musculoskeletal diseases are important causes of reduced performance, and a lameness/gait analysis is vital in all cases, unless the history clearly suggests another problem, such as acute onset of a respiratory noise. The details of the lameness examination and the possible problems it would uncover are beyond the scope of this chapter.

If a specific arthritis, tendinitis, or desmitis is not uncovered and the gait is still considered abnormal, neurologic, neuromuscular, or muscular disease should be considered. Neurologic problems are discussed in Chapter 16. Muscular disease, particularly subclinical muscular disease, is difficult to document and evaluate. In horses with subclinical muscular disease, vague signs of muscle soreness and stiffness and elevation of the enzymes creatine kinase (CPK) and aspartate aminotransferase (AAT) in the serum can be the only evidence of myopathy. These enzymes will not be elevated several hundredfold, as in the "tied-up" horse with severe exertional rhabdomyolysis; rather, CPK is elevated three to four times above baseline, and AAT two or three times. These values can be obtained 6 to 24 hours after a workout or race. Although elevation of these serum enzymes might suggest a myopathy, it is not absolute evidence. Many apparently normal working horses have moderate elevations of these enzymes, from either muscle

bruising or exercise. However, if the clinical signs suggest a myopathy and enzymes are elevated, exercise-associated myopathy is a realistic consideration, particularly if the elevations are consistent over a period of time and exercise periods. In addition, the observation that when the enzymes return to normal, the horse is often performing well suggests an association between the leakage of these enzymes and the poor performance. The cause of this syndrome of subclinical myopathy is poorly understood. Serum selenium estimation in some affected horses suggests a deficiency of selenium, supplementation of which can be associated with improvement in performance.

These muscle problems are treated empirically for the most part. Oral multimineral supplementation appears to help some horses, and in others adjustment of the training schedule can help. Usually this adjustment involves reducing the intensity and frequency of the severe workouts or races.

Respiratory Disorders

Respiratory disorders reducing performance in mature horses affect the upper airways, lungs, or both. Those affecting the upper airways are usually associated with abnormal respiratory noises at exercise and include any lesion from the nostril to the trachea (Table 17–1). Some conditions are more common than others. All the upper-airway problems are best assessed by endoscopic examination at rest, immediately after exercise, or both. Some clinicians have suggested that light tranquilization with xylazine is useful, and that a diagnosis of laryngeal dysfunction is more likely when using this agent. I suggest that endoscopy be done without tranquilization, if possible.

Pharyngeal lymphoid hyperplasia is common in young horses (Fig. 17–5) and might be normal. By the time the horse is

TABLE 17–1. CONDITIONS OF THE UPPER AIRWAY CAUSING EXERCISE INTOLERANCE

Condition	Clinical Signs
Excessive alar folds	Inspiratory and expiratory noise Exercise intolerance only rarely
Thickened nasal septum	Inspiratory obstruction
Nasal polyps	If large, exercise intolerance, nasal discharge, fetid odor to the breath, occasional epistaxis
Ethmoid hematomas	If large and expansive, exercise intolerance, hemorrhagic nasal discharge, inspiratory noise
Epiglottic entrapment	Inspiratory and expiratory noises, coughing, exercise intolerance
Dorsal displacement of the soft palate	Depends on frequency and severity of displacement; cough, expiratory noise, exercise intolerance
Pharyngeal cysts	Respiratory noises, dysphagia, exercise intolerance
Laryngeal hemiplegia	Inspiratory noise, exercise intolerance

5 years old, hyperplasia is usually less obvious. Some young horses with poor performance have marked hyperplasia and can have exercise-associated respiratory noises. What constitutes a significant degree of hyperplasia is not determined. Experimental induction of pharyngeal inflammatory disease in horses does not cause any consistent measurable changes in respiratory function as reflected by arterial blood gas measurements. Many horses with normal performance have marked hyperplasia. Reduced performance should not be ascribed to lymphoid hyperplasia unless extensive investigations have ruled out all other possibilities. Even then, lymphoid hyperplasia is often a diagnosis of convenience. Surgical or chemical cautery of the pharyngeal lesions used to be popular but is rarely advocated today. Various throat sprays, usually containing an antiseptic and corticosteroid, are also popular treatments that probably do no harm but little good. They are swallowed immediately, and probably remain in contact with the membranes for only a few minutes. Monthly vaccination against influenza and rhinopneumonitis has also been claimed as effective in controlling pharyngeal lymphoid hyperplasia. The effectiveness of

these approaches is increased if the horse is rested for 2 to 3 weeks. In most cases, these pharyngeal nodules are not a significant problem and do not require any therapy.

Entrapment of the epiglottis by the aryepiglottic folds (Fig. 17–6) might or might not cause respiratory obstruction, as the patient history will help determine. Entrapment is probably a congenital disorder that becomes a problem only when the tissue becomes thickened and inflamed. The obstruction to airflow can occur during both inspiration and expiration, with resultant noises. Therapy is surgical. The development of the transendoscopic electrosurgical technique for the standing horse has made treatment less difficult. Because this technique is suitable only when the entrapping membranes are fairly thin, electrosurgery is recommended in an asymptomatic horse with entrapment before the membrane becomes thickened and ulcerated, causing obstruction. Obstructed cases require surgical treatment under general anesthesia and an approach through a laryngotomy.

The performance of a horse that works at maximum speed for more than 10 seconds will be compromised if the horse

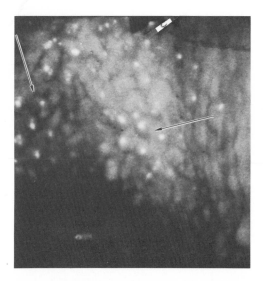

Fig. 17–5. Endoscopic appearance of the pharynx of a 3-year-old Standardbred with moderate lymphoid hyperplasia (arrows).

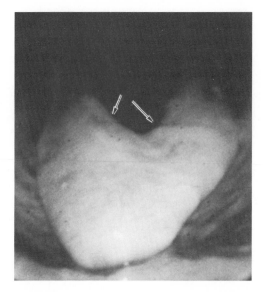

Fig. 17–6. Endoscopic appearance of the larynx of a horse with the epiglottis entrapped by the aryepiglottic fold (arrows).

has laryngeal hemiplegia. The disease is a common idiopathic one, usually affecting the left side of the larynx. Diagnosis is based on history and endoscopic findings (Fig. 17–7). Severe total hemiparalysis is relatively easy to diagnose. The horses make a whistle or roar on inspiration with exercise. Animals affected less severely might be more difficult to diagnose. They are best evaluated endoscopically, immediately after exercising almost to the point of fatigue. The only useful management of these horses is surgical stabilization of the arytenoid in the abducted position to restore normal upper-airway resistance.

Usually, horses with intermittent dorsal displacement of the soft palate perform well until suddenly the palatolaryngeal seal is broken, the free edge of the palate lies within the rima glottidis, and inspiratory and expiratory noises begin. The animals soon begin to slow and finish poorly. Diagnosis is not always easy, and the history might give the most useful clues. Some horses have permanent displacement, which is seen endoscopically (Fig. 17–8). In others displacement can

be induced by occluding both nostrils while observing the larynx and soft palate endoscopically. If the condition is suspected, the veterinarian should perform a tongue-tie; the tongue is pulled forward and tied down firmly with a cloth band to draw the larynx rostrally, which makes a tighter seal with the soft palate and reduces the ease of displacement. If the soft palate continues to displace, a myotomy of the sternothyrohyoid muscles, or neurectomy of the nerves supplying these muscles, can be performed to prevent the larynx from being drawn caudally. Both a tongue-tie and surgery might be necessary. The less common upper-airway conditions listed in Table 17–1 can be diagnosed by endoscopic examination and digital palpation of the external nares. Some can be resolved surgically.

Chronic low-grade lung disease is probably common in performance horses. Most of these horses spend much of each day confined in poorly ventilated dusty stalls or working in dusty environments. They also are repeatedly exposed to a

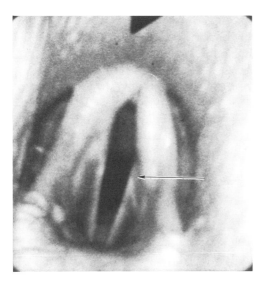

Fig. 17–7. Endoscopic appearance of the larynx of a horse with left laryngeal hemiplegia. On the affected side the vocal fold and arytenoid cartilage are not abducted (arrow).

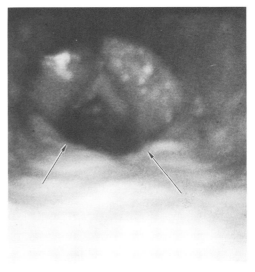

Fig. 17–8. Endoscopic view of the larynx and pharynx of a horse with dorsal displacement of the soft palate. The epiglottis is not visible, and the free edge of the soft palate lies across the opening to the larynx (arrows).

large number of viral respiratory pathogens. Again, the lung disease is not severe enough to cause clinical signs of heaves (Chapter 7), but could be enough to reduce performance. Arriving at a diagnosis and grading the severity of the problem is not easy based on physical examination alone. Auscultation, particularly after severe exercise, might reveal harsh lung sounds. Endoscopy might visualize mucopurulent material in the trachea, and thoracic radiographs might show varying degrees of increased interstitial density. Additional information could be obtained by transtracheal aspiration, although bronchoalveolar lavage might give more information about changes in distal airways. Neutrophils are normally less than 10% of the cell population in bronchoalveolar lavage fluid, and lymphocytes and macrophages account for 70 to 85% of the cells. In horses with chronic airway disease, the neutrophil count is increased, often exceeding 25% of the cell population. These animals are not usually infected with bacteria, so culture of these fluids is not indicated. Cy-

tology usually indicates an inflammatory condition.

Exercise-induced pulmonary hemorrhage is common in athletic horses (Chapter 9). Severe hemorrhage itself could cause reduced performance, but for the most part the hemorrhage reflects underlying chronic lung disease. Radiographically, a shadow might be seen in the caudodorsal lung field in horses who have recently bled, and airway fluids can have cytologic evidence of recent hemorrhage.

The cause of these respiratory problems is not known, although many can have an allergic component. No consistently effective therapy for these horses exists. Because environmental contamination might play a role, a "fresh-air" regimen is often advocated. The horses should be kept outside at all times and be fed grass, wet hay, pelletized feed, and grain. The role of viruses in these problems is unknown, but monthly vaccination against influenza and rhinopneumonitis have been suggested to reduce the severity of the respiratory disease. Horses suffering from pulmonary hemorrhage are frequently treated with furosemide before they race or train. Though of questionable value, this treatment is practiced widely and is legal in many states.

Cardiac Disorders

Cardiac disease is fairly common in adult horses based on necropsy surveys and auscultatory findings, but otherwise it is apparent only when significant. Clearly defined problems such as atrial fibrillation or severe aortic insufficiency undoubtedly have an impact on performance and are easy to detect (Chapter 10). It is unknown, however, whether irregularities such as occasional ectopic beats or soft, grade II ejection murmurs reflect problems that can affect performance. Cardiac function during exercise, recorded by radiotelemetry or by on-board tape recorders, can be different from that in the immediate postexercise period. At rates of 200 beats/minute or more, however, ECGs are often difficult to read accurately. Frequent ectopic beats, or pauses owing to various blocks at high heart rates, probably reduce cardiac output and influence performance. Some clinicians have suggested that the ECG, taken by various limb leads and augmented chest leads, can be used to assess "heart strain" in horses; this diagnosis is based mostly on apparent T-wave abnormalities. The equine T wave is an extremely labile waveform, however, and depends on lead position and heart rate. Recordings should not be overinterpreted, and T-wave changes cannot be relied on as indicators of heart abnormalities that cause reduced performance.

Echocardiography is extremely valuable for assessing equine cardiac anatomy and motion and is useful in determining the significance of murmurs. Because it is an assessment with the horse at rest, however, it will not determine what is happening at high heart rates.

Other Disorders

Metabolic and endocrine dysfunctions as causes of reduced performance in horses are poorly documented. Much has been made of hypothyroidism, but little data support its existence. Anhidrosis (failure to sweat) is well documented as a cause of reduced performance in horses in hot, humid climates. In these animals, either native or introduced, the sweat glands' sensitivity to circulating epinephrine is reduced. The problem can begin suddenly, with failure to sweat, hypothermia, and tachypnea. More chronic cases involve a dry, flaky skin, some alopecia, anorexia, and poor performance. Clinicopathologic data are inconsistent, although some horses can be hypochloremic; diagnosis is based mostly on clinical signs. The animal should be restored to a temperate atmosphere, either in another geographic region or in an air-conditioned stall.

Chronic abnormalities in electrolyte balance could be responsible for reduced performance. Abnormalities are difficult to document, as serum electrolyte determinations do not always reflect total body electrolyte status. Measurement of urinary fractional excretion of electrolytes, particularly sodium, potassium, and chloride, might be more reliable. In particular, reduced fractional excretion of potassium might reflect a relative potassium deficiency. Development of this problem is unlikely, as most equine diets are rich in potassium.

Chronic infections, such as equine infectious anemia or deep-seated abscess, could also affect performance. These infections might be detected by routine laboratory testing or by additional tests such as thoracic radiography, ultrasonography, and abdominocentesis.

Anemia can be present in chronic infections owing to bacteria or as part of equine infectious anemia. In addition, chronic low-grade anemias can develop owing to chronic blood loss, such as from gastric ulcers. Gastric ulcers are probably more common in competing adult horses than is realized. They are difficult to diagnose and can be confirmed only by gastroscopy or necropsy, and gastroscopy is available only in a few centers. Clinical signs of gastric ulcers are vague. Mild intermittent pain, reduced or selective appetite, and intermittent low-grade fever have been recorded. Feces can contain occult blood. The condition might be more common in horses receiving nonsteroidal anti-inflammatory medication.

Immune-mediated anemias tend to be fairly severe and acute and therefore are less likely to be a cause of chronic low-grade anemia resulting in reduced performance. Reduced red cell production in the bone marrow, secondary to neoplastic infiltration or toxic suppression of the stem cells, also causes anemia and reduced performance. Routine hematology and possibly bone marrow aspiration help diagnose the problem (see Chapter 13).

Evidence in Standardbreds indicates that performance can be correlated with total red cell mass. Horses with low red cell mass perform poorly; however, "overtraining" causes a high red cell mass, which also leads to poor performance. Measuring the red cell mass is difficult. Horses have a huge splenic reserve that is mobilized with exercise, which a resting packed cell volume (PCV) might not reflect. Equally, a PCV after exercise can suggest polycythemia. The techniques for measuring total red cell mass in horses are not routinely available. A racehorse at rest in the stall can have a packed cell volume (PCV) of 36% (0.36 L/L), which some practitioners would say is anemic, and after severe exercise a PCV of 58% (0.58 L/L), which some would consider to be high.

CONCLUSION

Having considered all possible abnormalities, the veterinarian is often left with little or no understanding of why a horse is performing poorly. Advice is hard to give. Frequently, any apparent abnormality detected by either the physical or laboratory examination is used to account for the problem. Specific therapy for the perceived problem is tried, such as hematinics for anemia. Often a period of rest (30 to 60 days) is suggested. Rest can in fact be the most beneficial therapy, and the use of various medications might be the best way to ensure that a rest period is given. Many low-grade problems, regardless of the cause, will resolve with this management. A 30- to 90-day layoff is expensive for the owner, and for horses with a lower value such a recommendation is neither popular nor realistic. These animals will be continued in work and might or might not improve, in spite of or because of various recommendations and therapies. These horses are often taken from one veterinarian to another in the hope that something will be revealed. The system considered to be at fault might depend on the particular emphasis of the practitioner; one might diagnose chronic lung disease, another "sore back" and another anemia. These cases are often frustrating and unsatisfactory for the veterinarian and owner.

SUPPLEMENTAL READING

Clark, A.F., Madelin, T.M., and Allpress, R.G.: The relationship of air hygiene in stables to lower airway disease and pharyngeal lymphoid hyperplasia in two groups of Thoroughbred horses. Equine Vet. J., 19:524–530, 1987.

Gillespie, J.R., and Robinson, N.E. (eds.): Equine exercise physiology 2. International Conference on Equine Exercise Physiology Publications. Philadelphia, Davis, 1987.

Jones, W.E.: Equine Sports Medicine. Philadelphia, Lea & Febiger, 1988.

Mayhew, I.G., and Ferguson, H.O.: Clinical clinico-pathologic and epidemiologic features of anhidrosis in central Florida Thoroughbred horses. J. Vet. Int. Med., 1:136–141, 1987.

Persson, S.G.B., and Ullbery, L.E.: Blood volume in relation to exercise tolerance in trotters. J.S. Afr. Vet. Assoc., 45:293–299, 1974.

Rossdale, P.D., Hopes, R., Wingfield-Digby, N.J., and Offord, K.: Epidemiological study of wastage among race horses 1982 and 1983. Vet. Rec., 116:66–69, 1985.

Snow, D.H., Persson, S.G.B., and Rose, R.J. (eds.): Equine exercise physiology. Cambridge, UK, Granta Editions, 1983.

Stashak, T.S.: Adam's Lameness in Horses. 4th Ed. Philadelphia, Lea & Febiger, 1987.

chapter 18

SUDDEN AND UNEXPECTED DEATH

Christopher M. Brown
Thomas P. Mullaney

INVESTIGATION OF SUDDEN AND UNEXPECTED DEATH

All horses eventually die. In most cases the death is expected or euthanasia is performed because the horse has an incurable condition or because of old age. When an apparently healthy horse dies suddenly when being worked or observed, or was apparently normal when last seen alive, owners are often distressed and alarmed. They often seek veterinary assistance to determine the cause of death.

These cases should be approached with caution and investigated thoroughly and systematically. They cannot usually be investigated in the time allotted to a routine farm call. Surveys of cases of sudden and unexpected deaths in horses indicate that over one third are unexplained despite extensive and thorough environmental, pathologic, and toxicologic investigations. At the outset, owners should be made aware of this likelihood, particularly if preliminary in-

investigations do not suggest an obvious cause. They might otherwise become involved in a protracted and expensive investigation that ultimately can leave many questions unanswered.

Many factors will determine how thoroughly these cases will be investigated. The death of insured horses and animals that die at the racetrack usually requires full investigation. Owners of animals with high monetary or sentimental value might seek an answer, and if other horses are at risk, a full investigation might be justified. Generally, the higher the value of the animal and the greater the likelihood of litigation, the more probable it is that a full investigation of the cause of death will be required.

The overall plan used to investigate one of these cases is illustrated in Fig.18–1. All aspects of each phase may not be applicable in every case, and financial and other constraints can limit the scope of the investigation.

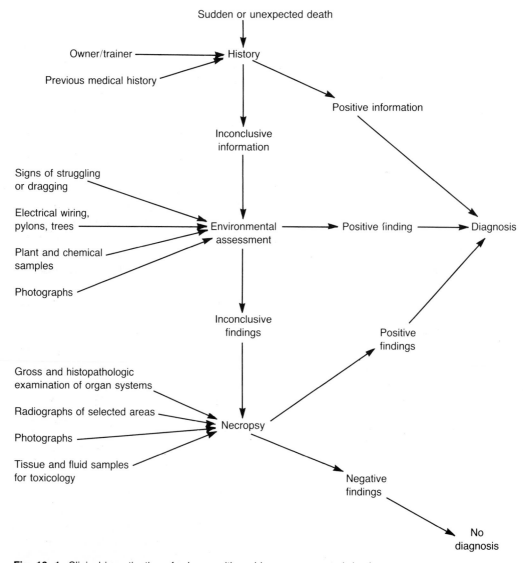

Fig. 18–1. Clinical investigation of a horse with sudden or unexpected death.

PATIENT HISTORY

An accurate and thorough patient history can provide invaluable clues. The history can be difficult to obtain, however, and assessing its reliability can be difficult. Owners and trainers might not be available, or they might be too upset to communicate effectively. In addition they might conceal information, hoping that possible neglect or management errors will not be revealed.

Recent management changes, including changes in work and feeding schedules, could be important. Past and recent medical history could indicate possible causes for the death. This information might not always be available, as horses, particularly racehorses, change hands frequently, and previous treatments and diseases are not always known. When a recently acquired horse dies unexpectedly, the new owners often suspect that they have been sold an animal with a pre-existing problem. They seek veterinary assistance to confirm their suspicions.

If the animal's death was observed, an accurate description of what happened might indicate possible causes. Was the animal being worked? Was medication being administered? Did blood appear at the nostrils? The possibility that deliberate harm occurred is most likely when a recent domestic or professional dispute involving an owner or trainer has occurred, or in competitive situations such as the racetrack or show-ring.

Owners vary tremendously in the closeness and detail with which they observe their horses. Some notice the slightest deviation from normal, and others overlook the most obvious signs. Thus, what one owner might see as an unexpected death in an apparently healthy horse, another owner might be prepared for. In a survey of 151 unexpected deaths in horses and ponies, 10 animals were considered to be emaciated, and yet had not apparently aroused concern in the owners. Other horses in the group or on the farm should be examined; any that are apparently ill should be examined in detail prior to an evaluation of the dead horse.

EXAMINATION OF THE ENVIRONMENT

The environment can give valuable clues or confirm the cause of death. Not all animals die in their usual surroundings or at the site where they encountered what killed them; for instance, a horse could ingest a toxic substance in its grain, and collapse and die on the trail or in the show-ring. However, a detailed examination of the surrounding area is always indicated.

Owners might move dead horses to create circumstantial evidence to support a damages or insurance claim; animals might be moved under a tree after a storm to suggest lightning strike, or under pylons to suggest electrocution. The ground and animal should be carefully examined to determine if the horse has been dragged or transported to its current site, and any evidence should be photographed.

The entire area to which the horse had access should be examined. Poisonous plants, empty chemical containers, open feed bins, new or worn electrical wiring, or any other suggestive features should be noted. Samples of food, chemicals, and plants should be collected into separate, labeled containers, indicating the time and place of collection. Photographic records may be invaluable later, and a camera with flash and close-up lens is useful. Signs of struggling on both the body and the ground might indicate how a horse died; for instance, horses struck by lightning drop dead where they stood, but those with gastrointestinal distension and rupture probably struggle and thrash about before death.

NECROPSY EXAMINATION

If the environmental examination has not clearly determined the cause of death, necropsy might be indicated.

A thorough necropsy examination of an adult horse is difficult and time-consuming. It should not be undertaken without adequate facilities, equipment, and assistance. In most cases the general practitioner should refer the client to a fully equipped diagnostic laboratory if a thorough examination is needed. Necropsy might be particularly desirable if legal action is anticipated, although in some areas distance or time precludes necropsy. In addition, a full necropsy examination including gross pathologic, histologic, and toxicologic investigations can be expensive. For these reasons the owner might request a more cursory examination in the field, although it can reduce the chances of confirming the cause of death.

Wherever the necropsy is performed, the investigation should be started as soon as possible. This is particularly true in midsummer in areas where large carcasses rapidly develop postmortem changes that can prevent accurate diagnosis. An accurate record of the necropsy findings, either written or tape-recorded, should be made, and selected areas photographed. A particularly careful record should be made of the animal's distinguishing features, including color markings, brands, and tattoos, for insured horses.

The investigation should not be hurried and will proceed more efficiently if a knowledgeable assistant, preferably another veterinarian, is available. If all organs including the brain and spinal cord are to be removed, sharp knives, scissors, shears, and saws should be available. Containers, some with fixative for obtaining histologic samples, and others that can be frozen for toxicologic samples, are required. Sterile needles and syringes are useful for the collection of body fluids,

and sterile containers are needed to hold samples for bacteriology and virology. Samples should be taken from all major systems, although not all will need to be processed further. They can easily be discarded when the case is closed.

Despite the circumstances under which a postmortem examination may have to be conducted, it must be done systematically. Postmortem examination of the horse can be approached several ways. We prefer to place the carcass in lateral recumbency with the right side down. The external carcass should be thoroughly examined. The first incision should be midventral, extending from the symphysis of the mandibles to the prepubic tendon. The skin on the upper side is reflected dorsally over the withers and back as far as possible. The left foreleg and left hind leg are reflected back by incising the underlying muscles and attachments. For the hind leg, the coxofemoral joint is exposed and the round ligament is severed.

The wall of the abdominal cavity is removed by cutting the muscles along the last rib and continuing the incision along the flank and ventral midline. Care should be taken not to incise the underlying viscera. The ribs are cut both dorsally and along the costochondral junctions, preferably with a costotome, the diaphragm is severed, and the thoracic cavity exposed. All exposed organs should then be examined in situ and evidence of displacement, torsion, strangulation, hemorrhage, or discoloration noted.

The abdominal viscera should be examined. First, the pelvic flexure of the large colon is exteriorized and pulled ventrally. The spleen, left kidney, left adrenal, small colon, small intestine, and stomach are removed in that order. Prior to removal of the large colon and cecum, the anterior mesenteric artery should be examined. The large colon and cecum, liver, right kidney, and adrenal are then removed, followed by the thoracic organs. We prefer to remove the tongue, pharynx, larynx, thyroids, trachea, esophagus, lungs, and heart together.

Each organ is carefully examined. When appropriate, the pelvic organs are also removed and examined. The head is disarticulated at the alantooccipital joint and the brain removed after sawing and elevation of the overlying calvaria. When indicated, the spinal cord, long bones, joints, marrow cavities, and nares are exposed and examined. Each body system is then examined individually and appropriate specimens selected for histopathologic, microbiologic, and toxicologic examination. When no obvious lesions are identified on gross postmortem examination, careful attention should be paid to selection of cardiac specimens for histopathologic examination and to selection of specimens for toxicologic examination. From the heart, blocks of tissue should be removed to allow examination of components of the conduction system, including the sinus node, atrioventricular node and bundles, branching bundle, and right bundle branch. For toxicologic examination, approximately 30-g samples of liver, kidney, urine, stomach content, heart blood (clot from left ventricle), and fat should be frozen in plastic bags.

At the end of the gross examination, the findings should be summarized. Collected samples should be clearly labeled, and selected samples submitted for further evaluation.

CAUSES

Sudden death, an observed event that occurs within a few minutes of the onset of signs and without previous warning, is different from unexpected death. In unexpected death, a horse previously considered healthy is found dead; such an animal may have died overnight. Because the two problems are somewhat different they will be considered separately. However, conditions that cause sudden death can also be responsible for some unexpected deaths, the difference being that no one was around to see the animal collapse and die. In other cases of unexpected death, several hours might have passed before death ensued, but again no one was present to observe the signs.

SUDDEN DEATH

Animals that experienced sudden death collapsed and died within minutes or instantaneously. Based on our experience and that of others, a thorough investigation of these cases yields no diagnosis in about 30% of cases, as should be emphasized to all interested parties at the outset. More than one significant lesion can be present in an animal, and the investigation should not be stopped after one lesion is found.

Cardiovascular Lesions. Cardiovascular lesions are often incorrectly thought to be responsible for sudden death in horses, primarily because they are a major cause of the problem in humans. Although many cases of unexplained sudden equine death might have been due to fatal arrhythmias, no specific lesions at necropsy account for death. Small foci of inflammation and degeneration are found in equine ventricular myocardium commonly, and the majority of such animals have no symptoms of cardiac disease. Such lesions found at necropsy should not be automatically assumed to be the cause of death. On the other hand, the ingestion of monensin-contaminated feed can cause massive myocardial necrosis and death. Usually, however, other signs including depression and diarrhea might be present for several hours to a few days before death. Some horses show signs of heart failure.

Ruptures of major components of the cardiovascular system also can lead to sudden death. These lesions include rupture of the atrium, pulmonary trunk, and probably mitral chordae tendineae. In breeding stallions a specific syndrome of coital or postcoital death is a rare but well-documented problem. The cause is rupture of the aortic root; typically an older stallion early in the breeding season collapses and dies while breeding a mare or immediately afterward.

In racehorses in particular, many sudden deaths are associated with massive hemorrhage into either the thorax or the abdomen. Often the specific site of bleeding cannot be identified, even with the most careful dissection.

Respiratory Lesions. Lesions of the respiratory system leading to sudden death include pulmonary hemorrhage and pneumothorax. Nonfatal pulmonary hemorrhage is common in racing and other exerted horses. The cause is unknown but probably is related to underlying chronic lung disease (Chapter 9). Occasionally a racehorse collapses and dies of massive pulmonary hemorrhage, perhaps a variation of the common nonfatal form. Necropsy reveals massive hemorrhage spread throughout both lungs, and blood often pours out of the nostrils at death.

Pneumothorax, rarely diagnosed in horses, presumably follows trauma, either to the chest wall or lung. It could be easily overlooked during necropsy because the lung normally collapses when the chest is opened.

Acute respiratory distress is often a feature of acute adverse drug reactions in horses. These reactions are usually associated with deliberate or accidental intravascular injections, particularly with procaine penicillin G. Owners might conceal the fact of injection. Venipuncture sites, particularly the jugular veins, are examined carefully. The accidental injection of medications into the common carotid artery is likely to cause sudden severe signs or death. Again, patient his-

tory might be helpful, although both arteries should be examined carefully for signs of injection. A hematoma might be present at the puncture site. In addition, a toxicology screen might be indicated if adverse reactions to medications are suspected. Many animals dying from adverse drug reactions have few necropsy findings. There may be foam in the trachea and histologic evidence of acute pulmonary edema.

Gastrointestinal Lesions. Acute gastrointestinal lesions rarely cause horses to die suddenly; they more typically are associated with death preceded by signs of pain and shock. Occasionally a horse with peracute colitis dies suddenly when stressed. The cause of the acute colitis might not be determined, but colitis caused by Salmonella species and Clostridium perfringens type A could be implicated. Many affected horses are diagnosed simply with the idiopathic colitis X. Necropsy findings are nonspecific, with edema and petechiation of the large bowel wall, together with fluid gut contents in the lumen.

Neurologic Lesions. Neurologic causes of sudden death are often associated with trauma producing skull and spinal fractures that directly traumatize the brain and spinal cord or that rupture vessels and produce fatal hemorrhage within the neural axis. Not all trauma causes fractures; some animals die from severe hemorrhage of the central nervous system without evidence of fractures. The most common site of skull fracture is between the basisphenoid and basioccipital bones. Animals usually incur this fracture by having reared up and fallen over backward, striking the poll of the head on the ground. The horse can die instantaneously, live for several hours, or recover, though with severe deficits (Chapter 16). Except for trauma-induced bleeding, cerebrovascular accidents of the type commonly seen in humans are apparently rare causes of sudden death in horses. However, occasional cases of severe nontrauma-induced diffuse hemorrhage have been found in some horses that died suddenly.

Other Causes. Electrocution and lightning strike are both difficult to diagnose, as necropsy findings can be unhelpful. All the evidence might be circumstantial; for instance, the horse is found dead under trees after a storm, or the horse's stall has broken or bare wires. It is a convenient diagnosis but difficult to substantiate in court.

Gunshot wounds and other forms of major trauma are not difficult to document if an accurate history is available. Similarly, the death of horses observed to have been administered toxic material should be fairly easy to investigate and resolve. When toxic substances are administered maliciously, the animal is more likely to be *found* dead (see Unexpected Death).

Racehorses

Although racehorses can die suddenly from any of the conditions discussed above, they present problems different from a general equine population. If their deaths occur during or immediately after a race, they will be observed by thousands of people and might receive widespread publicity. Often great pressure is placed on veterinarians and racing authorities to come up with an explanation within a short period. The press invariably raises the suggestion that deliberate drugging is involved in these cases. Surveys of sudden death in racehorses, particularly deaths occurring during races, suggest that many go unexplained. Up to 60% of such deaths might not be accounted for, although in some series the percentages have been much less. Of the documented causes, massive hemorrhage into the lung, thorax, abdomen, or brain

is the most frequent finding. Predisposing causes for this hemorrhage have not been determined, and locating a specific ruptured vessel is often impossible.

As many of these horses do not have significant postmortem lesions, these animals should be taken to a diagnostic laboratory as soon as possible for a full necropsy and possible toxicology screen. This investigation should not be performed on the backstretch of a racetrack, or at the local rendering plant.

UNEXPECTED DEATH

Animals that experienced unexpected death are found dead after having been apparently healthy when last seen. "Apparent health" is determined by the owner, who might not be the most astute observer; these animals can have several diseases that might have been present for several days or even weeks but were unobserved.

Causes of unexpected death are the same as those of sudden death, in addition to several others. Many horses die suddenly, for example, from lightning strike, but are not found dead until the next day. Many diseases leading to the death of horses have a clinical course of several hours. Depending on the cause of the disease, the antemortem course of the disease can cause clinical signs that can be found postmortem. For instance, horses with colic can have self-inflicted abrasions on the body and evidence of struggling and pawing within the general surroundings. Up to 30% of these cases of unexpected death will not be explained after a full investigation.

Cardiovascular Lesions. Cardiovascular lesions, in addition to those discussed as causing sudden death, include laceration or rupture of moderately sized vessels. Middle uterine artery rupture is a well-recognized, usually fatal problem in older postparturient multiparous mares.

Death occurs several hours after the onset of signs of pain and hypovolemic shock. Necropsy lesions are diagnostic.

Rupture of aneurysms of the internal carotid artery within the guttural pouch can cause fatal hemorrhage. These aneurysms are usually associated with mycotic infections over the vessel. Profuse epistaxis occurs when the aneurysm ruptures, and blood is sprayed around the stall (Chapter 9). Necropsy confirms the problem.

Laceration of major vessels following fractures also can lead to fatal hemorrhage. These fractures often involve the bones of the pelvis and occasionally the ribs. The hemorrhage might remain within fascial planes and not be obvious from external examination. Splenic rupture is apparently rare in horses, as the organ is well protected by the ribs.

Gastrointestinal Lesions. Gastrointestinal lesions account for a large number of unexplained deaths in horses, in our survey, over 33%. Rupture of a viscus, particularly the stomach or cecum, occurs frequently. Determining if the organ ruptured before or after death can be difficult, particularly if the animal has been dead for some time. When the rupture occurs before death, the ingesta is often spread widely throughout the abdomen. The edges of the rupture can be hemorrhagic, and acute inflammation can be evident histologically along the edges and on the peritoneal surface.

Gastric rupture occurs from ingestion of large amounts of highly fermentable food or from ingestion of very dry food followed by large amounts of water, causing the food to swell. In addition, small intestinal obstructive disorders, such as anterior enteritis, prevent gastric emptying, allowing fluid from the intestine to reflux back into the stomach, distending it. Rupture can occur because horses do not vomit. Gastric ulceration can predispose to rupture, particularly in foals.

Rupture of the cecum, perhaps exacerbated by the recent use of nonsteroidal anti-inflammatory drugs, occurs in two groups of horses—broodmares just after parturition, and horses with apparent failure of cecal emptying. Acute anatomic displacements of bowel, with or without rupture, can lead to severe pathophysiologic changes and death within hours. Necropsy usually confirms the diagnosis.

Acute grain overload can lead to severe gastrointestinal changes, endotoxic shock, and death within hours. An "outbreak" of unexpected deaths can occur when a group of horses gains access to open feed bins. Historical and environmental information can be as valuable as necropsy findings.

Respiratory Lesions. Respiratory lesions such as peracute pneumonias or pleuritis might be found only at necropsy. Occasional cases of acute fatal laryngeal edema have been reported, as well as cases of severe pulmonary hemorrhage and hemothorax.

Central Nervous Lesions. Central nervous lesions other than those causing sudden death are uncommon causes of unexpected death. However, an occasional case of equine encephalomyelitis or acute menigitis can go unnoticed and the affected horse found dead.

Musculoskeletal Disorders. Musculoskeletal disorders, other than fractures causing vessel laceration, are rare as causes of unexpected death. Fatal pathophysiologic changes might ensue following severe exertional rhabdomyolysis, such as when an unfit horse is taken out and worked excessively hard, turned into a stall or paddock, and not observed for several hours. Death is even more likely if the horse is deprived of water. Unexpected death can also occur in horses with clostridial myositis. These cases

TABLE 18–1. POTENTIALLY TOXIC SUBSTANCES CAUSING SUDDEN AND UNEXPECTED DEATH, NECROPSY FINDINGS, AND SAMPLES USEFUL FOR DIAGNOSIS

Toxic Substance or Chemicals	Necropsy Findings	Samples
Chemical Toxins		
Arsenic and arsenicals	Intense hyperemia of gastrointestinal tract, fluid hemorrhagic feces	Liver, kidney
Chlorinated hydrocarbons	Nonspecific; random petechiae	Blood, liver, fat, brain
Fluoroacetate	None	Stomach contents, liver, kidney
Monensin	Acute myocardial necrosis	Gut contents, foodstuffs
Nicotine	Nonspecific	Blood, liver, kidney, gut contents
Organophosphates and carbamates	Nonspecific; excess fluid in lungs and gastrointestinal tract	Blood for cholinesterase, urine, brain, gut contents
Warfarin and other anticoagulants	Massive hemorrhage into a space or viscus	Liver, kidney, whole blood
Strychnine	Rapid onset of rigor mortis	Stomach contents, liver, kidney
Animal Toxins		
Cantharidin (blister beetle)	Severe gastroenteritis with sloughing of mucosa; fluid gut contents; pale kidney; inflamed renal pelvis; bladder inflammation; myocardial degeneration	Foodstuffs (hay), gut contents, urine
Snakebite and insect bite	Nonspecific; possible local swelling or evidence of acute anaphylaxis	None
Plant Toxins		
Black nightshade (Solanum nigrum)	Nonspecific	Plants, gut contents to examine for poisonous plant
Blue-green algae	Nonspecific	Water sample
Caster bean (Ricinus communis)	Nonspecific; fluid gastrointestinal contents	Plants, gut contents to examine for poisonous plant
Chokecherry and other cyanogenic plants (Prunus spp.)	Bright red mucous membranes	Plants, gut contents to examine for poisonous plant
Oleander (Nerium oleander)	Nonspecific	Plants, gut contents to examine for poisonous plant
Red maple leaves (Acer rubrum)	Icterus, splenomegaly, swollen black kidneys, brown urine, tubular nephrosis with hemoglobin casts	Plants
Poison hemlock (Conium maculatum)	Nonspecific	Plants, gut contents to examine for poisonous plant
Yew	None; contaminated food often in mouth	Plants, gut contents to examine for poisonous plant
Pigweed (Amaranthus retroflexus) and other plants containing nitrate	Dark brownish blood and mucous membranes	Plants, gut contents to examine for poisonous plant

(Modified from Brown, C.M., Taylor, R.F., and Slanker, M.R.: Compend. Contin. Educ., *9*:78–86, 1987.)

usually develop 2 to 3 days after an intramuscular injection with a nonantibiotic medication. A fulminating myositis or cellulitis develops, with severe and often fatal systemic effects. Death can occur within 24 hours from the onset of signs (Chapter 11). Necropsy findings are strongly suggestive, and histopathology, culture, and fluorescent antibody staining of material can confirm the diagnosis.

Heatstroke. Heatstroke, like lightning strike, is diagnosed more on circumstantial evidence than on necropsy findings. Animals so diagnosed have been confined in poorly ventilated areas on very hot days, often without water.

Toxicologic Causes. Toxicologic causes of sudden and unexpected deaths in horses are probably overemphasized. Few confirmed cases of sudden and unexpected equine death are due to poisonings in most surveys. In our series of 200 cases of sudden and unexpected death, we found only 2 cases of poisoning. This low representation might reflect the expense and unavailability of toxicologic screening in some areas; many horses are not evaluated for toxic principles.

When gross and histopathologic investigations fail to account for a horse's death, screening tissues and fluids for toxic substances might be necessary. Screening for "everything" is expensive and slow, and the investigating veterinarian might be able to suggest what particular agents should be screened for based on historical, environmental, and pathologic findings. Generally, liver, kidney, urine, blood, fat, and gut contents should be saved for toxicologic processing.

Although thousands of substances can kill a horse, only a few common ones need to be considered (Table 18–1).

A major diagnostic problem occurs when substances normally present in the body, such as insulin, calcium, or potassium, are used to kill horses. If nonequine insulin is used (no commercial source of equine insulin exists) to kill the horse, immunologic evaluation of serum insulins might identify the abnormal insulin. Whole-blood potassium concentrations can be elevated in horses that have been killed by an intravenous overdose of potassium.

Ponies

In our survey of sudden and unexpected deaths in horses and ponies, no ponies died suddenly while being observed; all were found dead. Several explanations are possible. First, ponies are not usually subjected to the severe stresses associated with sudden death, such as racing. Second, ponies are not as closely observed as other types of horses. Often they are turned out in paddocks and might be seen only once daily. Third, they are often not very valuable, and therefore when they die, their deaths are less likely to be investigated.

SUPPLEMENTAL READING

Brown, C.M., Kaneene, J.B., and Taylor, R.F.: Sudden and unexpected death in horses and ponies: an analysis of 200 cases. Equine Vet. J., 20:99–103, 1988.

Brown, C.M., Taylor, R.F., and Slanker, M.R.: Sudden and unexpected deaths in adult horses. Compend. Contin. Educ., 9:78–86, 1987.

Cranley, J.J., and McCullagh, K.C.: Ischaemic myocardial fibrosis and aortic strongylosis in the horse. Equine Vet. J., 13:35–42, 1981.

Gelberg, H.B., et al.: Sudden death in training and racing Thoroughbred horses. J. Am. Vet. Med. Assoc., 187:1354–1356, 1985.

Lucke, V.M.: Sudden death. Equine Vet. J., 19:85–86, 1987.

Platt, H.: Sudden and unexpected death in horses: A review of 69 cases. Br. Vet. J., *138*:417–429, 1982.

Smith, H.: Necropsy procedures for the horse. *In* Veterinary Necropsy Procedures. Edited by T.C. Jones and C.A. Gleiser. Philadelphia, J.B. Lippincott Co., Philadelphia, 1954.

Vaughan, L.C., and Mason, B.J.E.: A clinicopathological study of racing accidents in horses. London, Horserace Betting Levy Board, 1974.

chapter 19

THE SICK NEONATAL FOAL

Ioana Sonea

This chapter deals with medical problems encountered in foals up to about 2 weeks of age. Newborn foals present a tremendous challenge to the practitioner. Unlike adult horses, in whom disease processes are often slow, foals can appear normal in the morning and be dead by evening. Furthermore, symptoms are usually vague, and some clinical signs, for example lung sounds, can misleadingly seem normal. Because foal diseases can be fulminating, early detection is critical. The veterinarian should be familiar with the behavior and clinical parameters of the normal foal and should be alert to any deviation from normality. Treatment must be swift and appropriate.

THE NORMAL FULL-TERM FOAL

The normal 335- to 365-day gestation should produce a strong foal with a full, thick coat, firm ears, and normal angulation of the limbs. Behavior of full-term foals follows a fairly set pattern, and any deviation should be regarded with suspicion.

The amnion is ruptured by the foal as the foal is born or immediately thereafter. The first breath is taken within 30 seconds, and the mucous membranes, initially purple, become pink or grayish pink and show a rapid capillary refill time (≤ 1.5 seconds) in less than 2 minutes. The foal sits sternally 5 to 10 minutes after birth and then tries to stand. The umbilical cord usually breaks by this activity, if the mare has not risen and broken it earlier. The pulse is regular and can easily be felt over the heart or over the facial, brachial, or dorsal metatarsal arteries (Table 19–1). Breathing immediately after birth is fast but effortless, and it slows after 1 hour. Some coughing or snorting is not unusual (Table 19–1). By 20 minutes after birth, foals show a strong suckling reflex, often sucking their upper lip until they find the mare's teats. On average, foals first stand about 1 hour after birth and usually have found the udder and suckled by 2 hours of age. Thereafter they suckle often, about four times an hour, so the mare's udder is never turgid.

Young foals spend a great deal of time taking short naps. They quickly learn to arise and lie down, and their initial wide-legged and unsteady stance and gait improve rapidly. They tolerate fairly wide ranges of environmental temperatures as long as they are well fed and protected from wet, wind, or extreme heat. Body temperature is maintained between 99 and 102° F (37° to 38.3° C) once foals are more than 2 hours old, but it can rise in hot weather. Chilled foals will shiver to get warm, but they lack sufficient energy stores to maintain body temperature in that way for long.

Pasty to firm, brownish black meconium is passed, with some straining, 1 to 1½ hours after birth, followed later by pasty yellow "milk" feces. Green, formed fecal material containing some foodstuff may be passed as early as 2 days of age. Foal heat diarrhea starts between 6 and 14 days of age and usually lasts 3 to 4 days. Most foals urinate within 8 to 12 hours of birth and quite frequently thereafter, because of their liquid diet.

PHYSIOLOGIC CONSIDERATIONS

Newborn foals are not miniature versions of adult horses; they differ in several important ways. Normal laboratory values for neonatal foals are given in Tables 19–2 and 19–3.

Immune Status

Although foals can manufacture antibodies in utero if challenged, compared to adults they respond more slowly and inefficiently to an antigenic stimulus. Immediately after birth, serum concentrations of IgG, IgM, and IgA are almost undetectable. After absorption of colostrum, neonatal serum antibody levels approach those of adults, providing passive protection against many equine pathogens.

Failure of Passive Transfer of Maternal Antibodies (FPT). Foals that do not suckle colostrum in the short period (8 to 12 hours)

TABLE 19–1. NORMAL CLINICAL VALUES FOR NEONATAL FOALS

	At Birth	At 1 to 2 Hours	At >2 Hours
Temperature	37°C/98.6°F	38°C/100.4°F	37.2 to 38.3°C/99 to 101.5°F
Pulse	40 to 80/min	80 to 130/min	70 to 120/min
Breaths		60 to 80/min	30 to 44/min
Mucous membranes	Purplish	Pale pink to grayish	Pink

TABLE 19–2. NORMAL NEONATAL HEMOGRAM

	1 Day	3 Days	2 Weeks
PCV (%)	40†	38	34
(×0.01 L/L)*	(34–46)‡	(33–43)	(25–43)
RBC (10/μL)	9.9	9.6	8.9
(×10⁶; cells/L)*	(8.8–11)	(8.3–10.7)	(9.6–16.4)
WBC (/μL)	8440	7550	8530
(×10⁶; cells/L)*	(4500–11500)	(5100–10700)	(6500–14400)
Neutrophils (μL)	6800	5700	6000
(×10⁶; cells/L)*	(3040–9570)	(3210–8720)	(3990–11520)
Band neutrophils (/μL)	<50	<50	<5
(×10⁶; cells/L)*			
Lymphocytes (/μL)	1430	1450	2220
(×10⁶; cells/L)*	(630–2060)	(740–2080)	(1550–3350)
Monocytes (/μL)	190	320	240
(×10⁶; cells/L)*	(50–380)	(80–710)	(70–580)
Eosinophils (/μL)	11	45	63
(×10⁶; cells/L)*	(0–108)	(0–214)	(0–212)
Basophils (/μL)	3	32	12
(×10⁶; cells/L)*	(0–35)	(0–130)	(0–72)
Fibrinogen (mg/dl)	246	310	338
(×10; g/L)*	(108–448)	(160–449)	(155–617)

Normal neutrophil:lymphocyte ratio is >2:1.

Data from Harvey, J.W., et al.: Haematology of foals up to one year old. Equine Vet. J., *16*:347, 1984.
* Factor used to convert the values to units of the International System.
† Values given are the mean obtained from 22 normal neonatal foals.
‡ Values in parenthesis represent the actual range of values obtained.

during which they can absorb proteins intact from the gut suffer from a failure of passive transfer of maternal antibodies (FPT) and are prone to overwhelming infections. *FPT is the major predisposing factor for neonatal septicemia, pneumonia, septic arthritis, and other infectious conditions.* FPT or partial failure can result from failure to ingest colostrum at an early age, leakage of some of the mare's colostrum before parturition (half of foals born to such mares have FPT), or inadequate concentrations of antibodies in colostrum (occurring most frequently in maiden mares and certain breeds such as Thoroughbreds and Standardbreds). FPT also can occur without apparent cause.

Because FPT or partial FPT is common (occurring in up to 25% of foals), serum antibody concentrations should be evaluated routinely at 18 to 24 hours of age. Serum or plasma antibodies can be measured by several methods. Radial immunodiffusion (RID) tests, the most accurate method of determining IgG, IgM, and IgA concentrations, require serum or plasma and need a 12- to 24-hour incubation period, leading to a delay in treatment if treatment is needed. They are also relatively expensive to perform. An enzyme-linked immunosorbent assay (ELISA) test is rapid (lasting 5 minutes), can be done with whole blood or serum, and can be performed on the farm, allowing for immediate diagnosis and treatment. However, values in the intermediate zone (400 to 800 mg/dl, or 4 to 8 g/L) of IgG are often equivocal. Latex agglutination tests are rapid (lasting 5 minutes) and can be done with either whole blood or serum.

TABLE 19-3. SERUM BIOCHEMISTRY OF NORMAL NEONATAL FOALS

	1 Day	2 Days	2 Weeks
Total protein (g/dl) ($\times 10$; g/L)†	5.7 ± 0.8	5.8 ± 0.7	5.4 ± 0.7
Aspartate aminotransferase (SGOT; IU/L)	175.4 ± 45.5	244.8 ± 97	389.5 ± 131.5
Lactate dehydrogenase (IU/L)	496.9 ± 106.2	407 ± 135.5	526 ± 73.5
Alkaline phosphatase (IU/L)	1073	1073	1000
Gamma glutamyl transpeptidase* (IU/L)	40 ± 27	40 ± 27	62 ± 42
Total bilirubin (mg/dl) ($\times 17.1$; μmol/L)†	3.9 ± 3.6	2.1 ± 0.6	1.3 ± 0.4
Blood urea nitrogen (mg/dl) ($\times 0.36$; mmol/L urea)†	16.4 ± 3.6	6 ± 1.2	5.7 ± 2.2
Creatinine‡ (mg/dl) ($\times 88.4$; μmol/L)†	2 ± 0.8	1.4 ± 0.3‡	1.4 ± 0.2
Glucose (mg/dl) ($\times 0.055$; mmol/L)†	160.2 ± 45.7	158.4 ± 5.3	158.3 ± 8
Calcium (mg/dl) ($\times 0.25$; mmol/L)†	11.5 ± 1.1	11 ± 0.8	11.1 ± 0.9
Sodium (mEq/L)** ($\times 1.0$; mmol/L)†	136	136	137
Potassium (mEq/L)** ($\times 1.0$; mmol/L)†	4.0	4.0	4.3
Chloride (mEq/L)** ($\times 1.0$; mmol/L)†	99	99	98

Mean ± SD reported where available.
Data from Rumbaugh, G.E., and Adamson, P.J.W.: J. Am. Vet. Med. Assoc., *183*:769–772, 1983.
* Gossett, K.A., and French, D.D.: Am. J. Vet. Res., *45*:354–356, 1984.
† Factor used to convert the values to the International System (for BUN the converted value is for mmol of *urea,* not urea nitrogen).
‡ Bauer, J.E., et al.: Equine Vet. J., *16*:361–363, 1984. Data obtained from 3-day-old foals.
** Gossett, K.A., and French, D.D.: Am. J. Vet. Res., *44*:1744–1745, 1983.

However, they are sensitive to temperature and fail to detect up to 20% of cases of FPT. The zinc sulfate turbidity test was the first method used to specifically detect serum globulin concentrations. It is slow (lasting 1 hour), requires serum or plasma and a laboratory, and is about as accurate as the latex agglutination tests. Although refractometer measurement of serum or plasma total solids has been used, it is highly inaccurate for detecting FPT and cannot be recommended except as a screening method; foals with total solids of less than 3.5 g/dl (35 g/L) are likely to have FPT, but so are many foals with "normal" total solids.

Normal serum IgG concentrations of 1-day-old foals are over 1000 mg/dl (10 g/L); FPT is usually defined by a serum IgG concentration less than or equal to 400 mg/dl (4 g/L), and partial failure between 400 and 800 mg/dl (4.8 to 8 g/L). Very young foals (<8 hours) with FPT can be given 1 to 2 L of colostrum over 2 to 3 hours to attempt to treat FPT if the problem is recognized early, such as in a foal whose dam died or a foal that fails to suckle. Most foals are older when FPT is diagnosed, however, and can no longer absorb antibodies intact from the gut. Their only treatment is intravenous administration of compatible equine plasma.

Because plasma has lower concentrations of immunoglobulins than colostrum has, larger amounts must be given. Usually 3 L or more, given over 2 to 3 hours, are needed to raise a 100-lb (40-kg) foal's serum antibodies to acceptable levels. Serum IgG concentrations should be determined 18 to 24 hours after treatment with plasma or colostrum. Serum IgG concentrations over 400 mg/dl (g/L) are generally considered adequate, although serum concentrations over 800 mg/dl (8 g/L) are preferable, particularly if infection is suspected.

Neonatal foals also have poorly developed cellular responses to inflammation and infection. Neutrophil functions such as phagocytosis and migration are not as well developed as in the adult. Therefore, bactericidal antibiotics should be used if possible.

HYDRATION STATUS

Because newborn foals are unable to concentrate urine effectively, careful attention should be paid to hydration and renal function in sick neonates. Oliguria can be a sign of decreased renal perfusion rather than increased tubular reabsorption of water in hypovolemic foals. Extracellular fluid volume is greater in foals than in adults (44% vs. 25%), and little correlation exists between total solids, packed-cell volume, and degree of dehydration.

RESPIRATORY FUNCTION

Foals have a very compliant chest wall, predisposing them to pulmonary atelectasis, especially of the down lung in a recumbent animal. In weak, premature, or neurologically impaired foals, abnormal respiratory reflexes can compound the problem.

THERMOREGULATION

Thermoregulation in neonates is somewhat inefficient, and hypothermia is a common consequence of illness, prolonged recumbency, exposure, or failure to drink. Although normal foals can tolerate wide variations in temperature, sick or weak foals must be kept warm and dry.

DRUG METABOLISM

Hepatic metabolism has not been studied extensively, but apparently some drugs are metabolized as efficiently by foals as by adults. Because body fat content is lower than that of adults, lipid-soluble drugs such as barbiturates have longer effects.

CLINICAL EVALUATION

Although newborn foals can have many problems, the symptoms are rarely distinctive and can result from more than one disease. To avoid overlooking problems, a standard neonatal diagnostic plan should be applied in each case (Table 19–4). Many of these tests can be accomplished in the field.

The initial assessment should include assessment of temperature, pulse, and respiration. If the foal is not breathing or has no pulse, CPR should be performed. If the foal is cyanotic or dyspneic, O_2 (5 to 10 L/minute) should be administered via nasal insufflation. After the initial assessment, a complete physical examination should be performed.

Blood should be drawn aseptically for reagent strip blood glucose analysis. If blood glucose is less than 40 mg/dl (2.2 mmol/L), the veterinarian should immediately administer 20 ml of dextrose 50% slowly, or 100 ml of 10% or 200 ml of 5% dextrose rapidly. Aerobic and anaerobic blood cultures should be done, as should determination of serum or plasma IgG

TABLE 19–4. NORMAL VALUES FOR BLOOD GAS ANALYSIS

	At Birth	2 Hours	4–12 Hours	1–14 Days
Arterial				
P_{O_2} (mm Hg)	50–60	6 ± 10	75 ± 5	75 ± 96
P_{CO_2} (mm Hg)	52–60	49 ± 2	47 ± 24	47–50
HCO_3 (mEq/L)	24–36	26 ± 2	28 ± 2	28 ± 2
pH	7.2–7.3	7.37 ± 0.01	7.39 ± 0.01	7.4 ± 0.01
Venous				
P_{O_2} (mm Hg)	—	42 ± 2	42 ± 2	36–45
P_{CO_2} (mm Hg)	—	56 ± 2	52 ± 2	50–55
HCO_3 (mEq/L)	—	28 ± 2	30 ± 2	27–33
pH	—	7.33 ± 0.01	7.38 ± 0.01	7.38 ± 0.01

Response to insufflation of 10 L/minute 100% O_2:
Normal foals aged ½–4 hours: Pa_{O_2} 200–300 mm Hg
Normal foals over 12 hours old: Pa_{O_2} 250–400 mm Hg

Note: To convert mm Hg to kPa, multiply by 0.133

(Adapted from Rossdale, P.D., and Ricketts, S.W.: Equine Stud Farm Medicine. 2nd Ed. Philadelphia, Lea & Febiger, 1980, 299–302.)

concentrations and routine hematology and biochemistry.

The veterinarian should aseptically place an intravenous catheter and start treatment of hypoglycemia, dehydration, or hypovolemia, if indicated.

An arterial sample should be obtained for blood gas analysis. For evaluation of acid-base status, a venous sample can be used if an arterial sample is unobtainable.

If the body temperature is less than 99° F (37.2° C), the foal should be warmed with heating pads, lamps, or blankets.

In selenium-deficient areas, an injectable preparation of vitamin E and selenium should be administered.

If wet, the umbilicus should be cauterized or disinfected. Iodine solutions greater than 3% should not be used.

The foal should be weighed, and the placenta, if available, submitted for gross and possibly histologic examination.

The thorax should be radiographed if blood gas analysis is abnormal or if the foal is dyspneic or cyanotic.

The veterinarian should evaluate laboratory results and response to treatment, then begin other treatments and routine nursing care.

PATIENT HISTORY

Obtaining a patient history for both the dam and foal is essential. Dystocia can have serious deleterious effects on both, and a retained placenta suggests that an in utero problem such as a bacterial or fungal infection might have affected the foal. The presence, absence, or prepartum loss of colostrum can have a major impact on the foal's immune status. The dam's vaccination record and any mineral or vitamin supplementation during pregnancy should be noted. Some mares have recurrent problems best discovered early.

BLOOD GLUCOSE

If a foal is very depressed or unable to rise, the most useful step after obtaining the history is determining the blood glucose concentration with a reagent strip. Hypoglycemia is common and can be severe; values of 8 to 10 mg/dl (0.44 to 0.55 mmol/L) are not rare (normal: 80 to 110 mg/dl, 4.44 to 6.60 mmol/L). Blood glucose concentrations below 80 mg/dl (4.4 mmol/L) are abnormal; concentrations below 40 mg/dl (2.2 mmol/L) require immediate treatment. Although both hyperglycemia and a rebound hypoglycemia can occur following an intravenous bolus of 5 ml of 50% dextrose (Table 19–4) given over 30 to 60 seconds, this treatment will give enough time for a thorough physical examination and the careful aseptic placement of an indwelling intravenous catheter. Long-term control of hypoglycemia by maintaining blood glucose between 80 and 120 mg/dl (4.4–6.6 mmol/L) requires constant administration of a 5 to 10% dextrose solution intravenously. Noniatrogenic hyperglycemia is uncommon and is usually a spurious reagent strip finding, occurring in severe septicemia.

PHYSICAL EXAMINATION

Physical examination needs to be thorough to avoid focusing attention on an obvious problem such as convulsions and overlooking more subtle signs of septicemia such as hypopyon. Hypothermia (temperature ≤ 99° F, 37° C) is common. Often, severe infection occurs without fever, though if fever is present, it usually indicates infection.

Auscultation might reveal cardiac sounds suggesting or revealing a cardiac anomaly. Most likely, a holosystolic murmur in the first few days of life is due to a patent ductus arteriosus, a normal finding up to 4 days of age.

Lung sounds are more difficult to interpret because "normal" sounds can accompany severe pulmonary disorder. Because pulmonary disease is one of the major killers of foals and can be difficult to diagnose, frequent examination of a foal's lungs and repeated arterial blood gas analyses are essential in the management of very ill foals. Rapid breathing usually indicates either pulmonary disease (pneumonia, atelectasis) or acidosis. Slow breathing, especially if irregular, is often a sign of neurologic damage. Shallow breathing can be due to neurologic disease, acidosis, or pain from fractured ribs, particularly if the birth was assisted. A marked abdominal effort with each inspiration, especially if the chest collapses simultaneously, suggests pulmonary atelectasis and indicates an immediate need for ventilation. Arterial blood gas analysis, the most accurate and sensitive method of evaluating pulmonary function (Table 19–4), is feasible in the field if heparinized blood is not exposed to air and is kept on ice until analysis. Hypoxia and hypercarbia can be severe without external signs of pulmonary disease. Thoracic radiographs are also helpful in the diagnosis of pulmonary problems; good images can be obtained with a portable unit and rare-earth screens.

Pale or grayish mucous membranes, a weak pulse, or cold extremities indicate hypovolemia and a need for intravenous fluids. The foal can receive 1 to 2 L over 1 hour, and a lower maintenance rate can be used thereafter (3 to 4 ml/kg/hour). Red mucous membranes are a sign of shock and endotoxemia. Cyanotic mucous membranes are seen in both severe congenital cardiac disease and pulmonary disease; arterial blood gas analysis before and after oxygen administration might help differentiate between the two diseases. Oxygen can be given from a portable oxygen tank, and ventilation can be provided using a nasotracheal tube and Hope II pediatric resuscitator bag or similar device, although these are only short-term treatments. Long-term respiratory therapy care requires hospitalization. A brownish meconium staining around the eyes and ears noted in newborn foals is a sign of fetal distress at birth and a warning of possible meconium aspiration pneumonia.

Icterus is common and can be caused by neonatal isoerythrolysis, septicemia, or other processes affecting the liver. Transient icterus can also occur in otherwise normal newborn foals. Laboratory tests (packed-cell volume, serum bilirubin, hepatic enzymes) are needed to distinguish among potential causes of icterus.

The abdomen should be examined and auscultated. The passage of meconium should be ascertained. The inguinal region should be palpated, as inguinal hernias are common and occasionally can cause small-bowel obstruction. Gut sounds should be similar to those of the adult. The presence of gastric reflux should be assessed with a nasogastric tube. Ileus, bloat, and signs of pain such as lying on its back or grinding the teeth can be due to gastrointestinal ulcerations, meconium impaction, or peritonitis, or, more rarely, to gastrointestinal accidents (torsion, volvulus, intussusception) or congenital defects such as atresia ani. Premature and septicemic foals often tolerate oral feeding poorly and might require parenteral alimentation if ileus, bloat, and gastric reflux occur and persist. Diarrhea (except for foal heat diarrhea in the 1- to 2-week-old foal) is a cause for concern.

Abdominal radiographs are helpful in identifying gastrointestinal problems. High meconium impactions, peritonitis, necrotizing enterocolitis, and intussusceptions might be identified. Abdominocentesis, which might reveal peritonitis or compromised bowel, must be done carefully to avoid perforating bowel, which is more likely to occur in foals than in adults. Straining owing to constipation or meconium impaction should be distinguished from that accompanying dysuria. Foals squat to urinate but hunch their backs, often walking backward, if constipated. The presence of a ruptured bladder is possible whether or not the foal was seen to urinate.

ASSESSMENT OF ATTITUDE AND BEHAVIOR

The veterinarian should determine if the foal is alert and suckles and recognizes the mare. If the foal cannot stand, its strength and coordination should be assessed. Inability to stand might not be due to a neurologic problem; congenital defects such as ruptured extensor tendons, arthrogryposis, contracted flexor tendons, or bilaterally luxated patellas might make rising impossible. These conditions are easily detected by physical examination. In selenium-deficient areas, white muscle disease also can cause weakness and inability to suckle.

A quick neurologic examination will help detect central nervous system disease. Foals are generally "jerky" and hypersensitive compared to adults. A repeated lack of response to a test, rather than hyperreflexia, is probably more indicative of neurologic disease. The foal's general appearance and stance should be noted. A head tilt or circling can indicate unilateral damage to the vestibular system, perhaps owing to trauma or central nervous system bleeding. Some foals let the tongue loll but can retract it unless cranial nerves have been damaged.

Eyesight, although well developed in normal foals, is difficult to assess. Both pupils should constrict evenly in response to bright light, although an anxious foal's pupils might not constrict much. In response to a movement toward the head, a foal jerks its head away but will not usually blink until a few weeks old. Neurologic examination should reveal any ocular lesions such as entropion, corneal ulcers, hypopyon, or papillary edema. Entropion and corneal ulcers are common in dehydrated foals and should be treated rapidly to prevent permanent corneal scarring.

Foals will flinch away vigorously if a finger or pen is firmly stroked down either side of the back or tapped against the neck. The patellar and extensor carpi radialis tendon reflexes can be examined with the foal lying on its side, with the limb being tested uppermost and loosely supported. A crossed extensor reflex should be present up to about 3 weeks of age.

Although a thorough physical examination and some routine laboratory tests allow a clinician to arrive at an understanding of a foal's immediate problems, repeated examinations and laboratory tests are essential. Foals change rapidly, and a day or two of inattention can allow new problems to emerge.

PROBLEMS IN NEONATAL FOALS

WEAKNESS

Weakness, whether present since birth or starting some time thereafter, is often the first sign of a problem in a neonatal foal.

Weakness at birth often accompanies prematurity and dysmaturity. In full-term foals, causes of weakness include in utero infections (herpesvirus or bacterial), dystocia-induced neurologic disease, white muscle disease, and some congenital defects (such as severe cardiac anomalies). Foals in pain are reluctant to move and might appear weak. Foals weak at birth probably fail to drink colostrum and therefore often suffer the consequences of FPT, such as septicemia, pneumonia, or septic arthritis.

Foals that were strong at birth but deteriorate later might be suffering from a variety of problems including neonatal maladjustment, septicemia, metabolic disturbances such as dehydration, hypoglycemia, or uremia, or even simple starvation.

A thorough examination might reveal the cause of weakness, but usually hematology and serum biochemistry (muscle and liver enzymes, blood urea nitrogen, creatinine, electrolytes, and glucose) are needed to understand the problem. Serum IgG levels should be measured because of the increased chances of FPT. Although most neonatal illnesses are accompanied by some degree of weakness, three disease entities—white muscle disease, starvation, and septicemia—have few other symptoms, at least initially.

White Muscle Disease

White muscle disease occurs in selenium-deficient areas and can cause weakness and inability to suckle, with no other symptoms. Diagnosis is based on elevated serum aspartate aminotransferase and creatine kinase levels, low serum selenium concentrations, and necropsy findings (myopathy involving the heart, tongue, and most skeletal muscles). In selenium-deficient areas, the diet of pregnant mares should be supplemented, and an injectable preparation of vitamin E/selenium should be given at the recommended dosage to all newborn foals. This practice is preferable to waiting for laboratory results, and treatment can be repeated if necessary.

Starvation

Starvation is uncommon, but some mares provide little milk; their foals might suckle often but get thinner and weaker with few other signs. Such mares' udders are small and have little milk even if their foals have not suckled recently. Laboratory data are not helpful, and hypoglycemia is not a constant finding. The diagnosis can be made only by excluding other causes of weakness and hypoglycemia, and by the response to supplemental feeding starting with small amounts.

Septicemia

Septicemia causes weakness and depression, often with few other symptoms until the foal is dying. Most causative organisms are gram-negative (such as Escherichia coli, Klebsiella, and Enterobacter, although Streptococci and Actinobacillus are also found). The widespread infection, and sometimes endotoxemia, result in shock and simultaneous failure of multiple organs. In most cases the course of illness is short and the outcome fatal. In one study, despite appropriate treatment, only 25% of treated septicemic foals survived. Because of the high fatality rate, any foal with weakness, inability or failure to suckle, or other abnormal behavior should be considered septicemic until proven otherwise.

Symptoms of septicemia are vague and nonspecific. Abnormal behavior, sometimes progressing to convulsions or coma, is typical. Many septic foals have diarrhea. Other signs can include respiratory distress, bloat, colic, jaundice, swollen or painful joints, and uveitis. A patent urachus often accompanies bacterial infections. Laboratory tests are essential to arrive at a diagnosis. On the farm, reagent strips can be used to detect hypoglycemia, allowing for immediate treatment. Occasionally, a reagent strip will indicate marked hyperglycemia; this is nearly always a spurious finding, probably caused by bacterial metabolites in blood, and found just before death.

Blood should be drawn aseptically for blood cultures, whether or not the foal has received antibiotics previously. Only a positive blood culture is truly diagnostic for septicemia. Other useful tests include a complete blood count, a serum fibrinogen and biochemistry (urea, creatinine, electrolytes, aspartate aminotransferase, gamma glutamyltranspeptidase, sorbitol dehydrogenase, and glucose), as well as determination of serum IgG concentrations. FPT is nearly always present in septic foals. Blood gas analysis is useful because acidosis and pulmonary disease are often present. The white blood cell count can be low, normal, or high; neutrophil counts are low in about two thirds of the foals. A left shift and toxic granulation of neutrophils are found in about 90% of septic foals. Metabolic and occasionally respiratory acidosis are frequent. Other laboratory results vary with the degree of dehydration and the involvement of other organs.

Treatment of the septicemic foal is exhausting and time-consuming. Even well-equipped and well-staffed neonatal intensive care units find managing more than two or three seriously ill foals at one time difficult. Costs are high because of the continuous need for trained personnel and frequent sophisticated monitoring. Results of treatment vary, depending on early detection. Suspected or confirmed cases of sepsis in neonatal foals are usually best handled in a clinic with experience in such cases; farm treatment of most septicemic foals is often unsuccessful.

Treatment consists of rapid correction of FPT and aggressive antibiotic therapy (Table 19–5). Septicemic foals often need much larger amounts of plasma than other foals with FPT. Serum IgG concentrations should be raised above 800 mg/dl (8 g/L), although often this effort is hampered by an apparent rapid catabolism of antibodies. Colostrum might provide the gastrointestinal tract with some local immunity but cannot be expected to provide systemic protection for foals already ill. Serum IgG concentration should be determined 18 to 24 hours after treatment because often serum antibody levels do not rise as predicted.

Broad-spectrum and bactericidal antibiotics should be used (Table 19–5). Penicillin and an aminoglycoside are generally used simultaneously, because of the many possible causative organisms. Intravenous administration is preferable to obtain initial high serum concentrations. Therapy is modified as culture results become available and the condition progresses.

TABLE 19–5. ANTIBIOTIC DOSAGES FOR TREATMENT OF SEPTICEMIA

Antibiotic*	Dosage	Comments
Penicillins		Gram-positive predominantly
K	20–40,000 IU/kg Q4 hour IV, IM	Avoid if serum (K) is high
Na	20–40,000 IU/kg Q4 hour IV, IM	
Procaine G	22–44,000 IU/kg Q12 hour IM	Large volume, irritating
Ampicillin (Na)	22 mg/kg Q4–6 hour IV, IM	Gram-positive predominantly
Amoxicillin	30 mg/kg Q4–6 hour PO	Gram-positive, some gram-negative, discontinue if diarrhea occurs
Oxacillin	25–50 mg/kg Q6–8 hour IV	Gram-positive, β-lactamase producing Staph (rare infections)
Ticarcillin	50 mg/kg Q6–8 hour IV, IM	Pseudomonas, some gram-negative; less effective than penicillin against gram-positive
Aminoglycosides		Gram-negative, may be nephrotoxic Synergistic with penicillins
Gentamicin	1.75–2.2 mg/kg Q8 hour IV, IM	
Kanamycin	5 mg/kg Q8 hour IM	Less effective than gentamicin
Amikacin	7 mg/kg Q8–12 hour IV, IM	More effective against some gram-negative than gentamicin
Chloramphenicol Succinate	25 mg/kg Q6–12 hour IV	Less frequent dosage for foals under 2 days of age; Q6 hour if over 5 days
Erythromycin	20 mg/kg Q8 hour IV	Very irritating IM; discontinue if diarrhea occurs
Erythromycin estolate	20 mg/kg Q8 hour PO	
Cephalosporins		Gram-negative predominantly
Cephalothin	18 mg/kg Q6 hour IM	May cause pain on injection
Cefazolin	11–16 mg/kg Q6 hour IV, IM	More effective than Cephalothin against Escherichia coli, Klebsiella; penetrates bone and joints well
Cefotaxime	20–40 mg/kg Q6–8 hour IV	Very effective against gram-negative, especially Klebsiella, Pseudomonas. Not good against gram-positive
Ceftizoxime	20 mg/kg Q6–8 hour IV	Same as for Cefotaxime
Oxytetracycline	5–6.5 mg/kg Q12 hour IV	Discontinue if diarrhea occurs
Trimethoprim-sulfas	5 mg/kg Trimethoprim fraction, Q8–12 hour IV, IM, PO	Discontinue if diarrhea occurs
Metronidazole	7.5 mg/kg Q6–8 hour PO	Anaerobes—discontinue if diarrhea occurs

* Broad-spectrum antibiotics or antibiotic combinations should be selected initially (a penicillin/aminoglycoside combination is usually used). Once microbial sensitivities have been determined, the most effective antibiotic should be used, keeping in mind its cost and ease of administration.

TABLE 19–6. DRUGS COMMONLY USED TO TREAT GASTROINTESTINAL PROBLEMS

Drug	Dosage	Comments
Cimetidine	200–600 mg/45 kg foal Q6 hour IV, PO	H_2 antagonist (antiulcer)
Ranitidine	150 mg/45 kg foal Q12 hour PO	H_2 antagonist (antiulcer)
Sucralfate	2–4 g/45 kg foal Q6 hour PO	Gastric protectant (antiulcer) Administer on empty stomach, at least 1 hour apart from H_2 antagonist and other antacids
Antacids (such as aluminum hydroxide)	Adult human dose/45 kg foal Q6 hour	Administer at least 1 hour apart from other oral drugs
Activated charcoal	3–4 oz/45 kg foal Q8 hour	Suspend in warm water and administer via stomach tube; treatment of acute diarrhea

Supportive therapy is a time-consuming but essential part of treatment; without it, most septic foals die. Close monitoring and frequent re-evaluation are necessary because complications are frequent and serious. Serious complications include pneumonia, gastrointestinal ulcerations, peritonitis, septic meningitis, septic arthritis, osteomyelitis, renal failure, corneal ulcerations, and hypopyon. Because gastrointestinal and ophthalmic complications are the rule rather than the exception, preventive measures are routine in most clinics. Ophthalmic care includes correction of entropion, a common finding in dehydrated or ill foals, and treatment of any corneal ulceration. Medications to control gastrointestinal ulceration are usually administered throughout treatment, including H_2 antagonists (ranitidine, cimetidine), mucosal protectants (sucralfate), and antacids (Table 19–6).

Other common gastrointestinal complications in septicemic foals include ileus and gastric reflux, bloat, colic, and diarrhea. These are best treated conservatively by limiting oral feeding, relieving gastric reflux, maintaining hydration with intravenous fluids, and administering small doses of analgesics if needed.

Because septic foals are poor surgical candidates, surgical correction of a perforated ulcer remains a final effort, with a very poor chance of survival. Parenteral nutrition should be started in 24 to 48 hours if a foal is unable to tolerate oral feeding at all. Intravenous feeding is still poorly understood; it can be lifesaving but is expensive and difficult to implement.

Pulmonary function is best monitored by blood gas analysis, as well as auscultation and radiography (see Respiratory Problems). Fluid therapy, elimination of nephrotoxic drugs from the therapeutic regimen, and careful monitoring of intake and output of fluids constitute the usual treatment of renal dysfunction. Some premature foals with oliguria benefit from intravenous dopamine or dobutamine (Table 19–7) to improve renal perfusion. Any sign of lameness or joint swelling is cause for alarm in a septic foal (see Lameness). Hypopyon and uveitis are common. Therapy consists of systemic antibiotics and mydriatics to prevent formation of synechiae.

Urachal patency is a common but generally harmless complication of septicemia. The urachus usually closes with repeated silver nitrate cauterization and

TABLE 19–7. MISCELLANEOUS COMMONLY USED DRUGS

Drug	Dosage	Comments
Flunixin meglumine	0.25–1.1 mg/kg Q8–24 hour IV, IM, PO	Analgesic, antiinflammatory. Use lowest effective dose; may cause ulcers and renal damage
Phenylbutazone	2.2–4.4 mg/kg Q12–24 hour IV, PO	Same as for flunixin
Xylazine	0.5–1.1 mg/kg IV, IM	Sedative, analgesic; use lower dosage IV; severely hypotensive; use lowest effective dose, particularly combined with other sedatives
Butorphanol	0.02–0.1 mg/kg as needed IV	Used in combination with xylazine for sedation/analgesia
Acepromazine/ xylazine	0.01–0.02 mg/kg (acepromazine) + 0.3–0.6 mg/kg (xylazine) as needed IV	Good sedative combination for intra-articular drainage
Dobutamine	2–10 μg/kg/hour constant IV infusion	Treatment of hypotension; of oliguria in premature foals; correct fluid deficits simultaneously
Dopamine	2–5 mg/kg/hour constant IV infusion	Same as for dobutamine
Epinephrine	0.01 mg/kg as needed IV, or subcutaneously	Anaphylactic reactions; dilute to 1:10,000; administer slowly IV
Prednisolone Na succinate	0.25–2 mg/kg as needed IV	Anaphylactic reactions

improvement in the foal's condition. A persistently patent urachus might require surgical excision and closure.

ABNORMAL BEHAVIOR

Abnormal behavior includes depression, loss of the suckling reflex, failure to recognize the mare, aimless wandering, abnormal positions, "barking," convulsions, and coma. Many foals with these signs have neurologic disease, but other possible causes include metabolic disturbances (hypoglycemia, hepatoencephalopathy, uremia, and electrolyte abnormalities) and abdominal pain.

The examination of the foal with abnormal behavior should include a neuro-logic examination and routine laboratory tests such as a hematology and serum biochemistry. Many clinicians routinely do aerobic and anaerobic blood cultures.

Neurologic Abnormalities

Septic Meningoencephalitis. Severe neurologic signs (convulsions, coma) and symptoms or laboratory data suggestive of septicemia can suggest the presence of septic meningoencephalitis. Diagnosis is made by obtaining cerebrospinal fluid (CSF) (Table 19–8) from the altanto-occipital or lumbar sites. Elevated white cell counts, elevated protein, and decreased glucose concentrations in the CSF suggest the presence of infection

TABLE 19–8. CEREBROSPINAL FLUID
OF NORMAL FOALS

Color	Clear to pale yellow
TP (mg/dl)	90–200
WBC (/μl)	<20–25, predominantly monocytes and lymphocytes
RBC	Variable
Urinalysis reagent strip findings:	Protein < + + Glucose trace to + +

TP = total protein; WBC = white blood cell; RBC = red blood cell.

even if bacteria are not seen. Treatment is as for septicemia and prognosis is poor.

Neonatal Maladjustment. A common cause of abnormal behavior is neonatal maladjustment, a vague term encompassing most noninfectious neurologic diseases. Affected foals can be abnormal at birth, or can become confused and unable to suckle 1 or more days after an apparently normal start in life. Signs can progress to barking, convulsions, and coma. Suggested causes for the syndrome include hypoxia in utero or during birth and cerebrovascular hemorrhages. Cerebrovascular hemorrhages can be found in normal full-term foals but are more common in premature foals. Neurologic examination usually reveals a general symmetric loss of reflexes and perception. These foals often have abrasions, especially around the eyes, and entropion is common. Papilledema, a sign of cerebral edema, might be noted. Laboratory data are unremarkable in simple cases. CSF fluid analysis might show some increases in numbers of red blood cells or protein, but this increase might be found in normal foals as well. Many foals with neonatal maladjustment suffer from dehydration and FPT with its many consequences, as reflected in hematology and serum biochemistry.

Treatment is primarily supportive, and good nursing care is vital. Foals that are recumbent or thrashing benefit from head padding; particular attention should be paid to their eyes, and corneal ulcers should be treated aggressively. Dimethylsulfoxide (DMSO) has been used to decrease the cerebral inflammation and edema thought to be one of the causes of neonatal maladjustment. Its use is safe (Table 19–9). Mannitol is costly and might be contraindicated because of common cerebral or spinal bleeding. Corticosteroids should be avoided because of their potent immunosuppressive effect.

Diazepam can be administered to control seizures. Frequent convulsions might favor use of barbiturates, which last longer and are less expensive (Table 19–9). Treated foals do not usually have seizures for more than 1 or 2 days. Recovery is generally rapid and complete. Foals that continue to deteriorate or that remain comatose for 3 or more days have a very poor prognosis. A few foals take up to 1 month to relearn to drink. Some might have to be destroyed later because of recurring seizures or other behavioral abnormalities.

Postpartum Trauma. A less common cause of seizures or coma is postpartum trauma. Skull or vertebral fractures can result from kicks, falls, or collisions. Trauma should be suspected if bleeding from the nostrils or ears is observed or if neurologic signs are localized or asymmetric. Ataxia, paraplegia, or tetraplegia also can follow trauma or congenital lesions such as cerebellar abiotrophy and occipitoatlantoaxial malformations (both occur in Arabians). A neurologic examination facilitates diagnosis in most cases. Radiographs are particularly helpful if the lesion involves the cervical spine, and myelography can be rewarding. Laboratory data are usually unremarkable, although CSF analysis might be helpful. Although surgical repair might be at-

TABLE 19–9. DRUGS COMMONLY USED TO TREAT NEUROLOGIC PROBLEMS

Drug*	Dosage	Comments
Diazepam	0.05–0.4 mg/kg as needed IV, IM	Drug of choice for rapid control of seizures. Inject *slowly* IV
Pentobarbital	2–4 mg/kg, or to effect, IV	Respiratory depressant at higher doses
Phenobarbital	20 mg/kg initially, then 9 mg/kg Q8 hour or as needed IV	Lower doses may also be effective; dilute in sterile saline and inject over 30 minutes
Phenytoin	5–10 mg/kg initially IV, PO, then 1–5 mg/kg Q2–4 hour PO for first 12 hours; Q6–12 hour PO thereafter	Respiratory depressant at higher doses
Dimethylsulfoxide (DMSO)	0.5–1 g/kg Q12–24 hour IV	Administer diluted to 10–20% in isotonic saline or dextrose; may be used for up to 3 days

* The following drugs are not recommended for controlling seizures:
  Xylazine (severely hypotensive)
  Phenothiazines (potentiate seizure activity)
  Corticosteroids (immunosuppressive and ineffective)

tempted in exceptional cases, treatment of traumatic lesions is usually conservative, consisting of anti-inflammatory and analgesic drugs (DMSO, flunixin meglumine), rest, and nursing care. Prognosis varies. Foals with congenital lesions are usually euthanized.

Infectious Diseases. Infectious diseases can cause neurologic signs. Tetanus has been reported in foals as young as 7 days. Symptoms and treatment of tetanus are similar in foals and adults, although the prognosis is slightly better in foals because of their smaller size. Clostridium botulinum type B toxin is the cause of the shaker foal syndrome, affecting slightly older foals (2 weeks to 8 months). It occurs primarily in Kentucky. Affected foals are robust and grow well but develop weakness and shaking that can progress to paralysis. Treatment consists of administration of antitoxin and intravenous penicillin as well as nursing care. Mares can be vaccinated as a preventive measure.

Metabolic Abnormalities

Abnormal behavior such as depression, failure to suckle, convulsions, and coma

can also be caused by metabolic disturbances such as hypoglycemia, uremia, acidosis, hepatoencephalopathy, and electrolyte disturbances. Few of these conditions can be diagnosed without laboratory tests.

Hypoglycemia is common and can be life-threatening. Blood glucose concentrations should be determined with a reagent strip, and hypoglycemia corrected immediately. The most common causes of hypoglycemia are septicemia, starvation, and hepatic disease.

Hepatic disease can cause weakness, disorientation, convulsions, and coma owing to its resultant hypoglycemia and production of false neurotransmitters. Icterus is often present. In neonatal foals, hepatic disease is most commonly due to Bacillus piliformis (Tyzzer's disease) or in utero infection with equine herpesvirus type 1. Other organisms such as Actinobacillus and Salmonella can cause liver disease in septic foals. Toxins such as ferrous fumarate and bile duct obstruction after gastrointestinal ulceration are less common causes of hepatitic failure.

Diagnosis is based on laboratory data showing elevated liver enzymes, aspartate aminotransferase, gamma glutamyl-transpeptidase, and sorbitol dehydrogenase often accompanied by hypoglycemia and hyperbilirubinemia. Some clotting abnormalities can occur, and blood cultures can indicate septicemia.

Treatment is directed at eliminating the initial cause of the problem and supporting the foal until the liver heals. Broad-spectrum antibiotics (Table 19–5) are administered if the cause is infectious. A 5 to 10% intravenous glucose solution should be administered continuously to maintain blood glucose concentrations between 80 and 120 mg/dl (4.44–6.66 mmol/L) if the foal is hypoglycemic. Fresh plasma can be given if clotting abnormalities are suspected. Drugs metabolized by the liver (such as barbiturates) should be discontinued or used cautiously if they cannot be avoided. The prognosis depends on the cause of the problem. Tyzzer's disease is fulminating; foals are usually found dead and the diagnosis made at necropsy. Herpesvirus type 1 infections are also usually fatal, but other infections may be treatable.

Uremia also can be caused by decreased renal perfusion, as seen in severe dehydration or some very premature foals. Nephrotoxins such as nonsteroidal anti-inflammatory drugs (NSAIDs) (phenylbutazone, flunixin meglumine) or certain antibiotics (aminoglycosides) also can cause renal damage. Weakness and depression are the major neurologic signs of renal disease. Treatment consists of correcting the initial cause, eliminating or decreasing the dosage of nephrotoxic drugs, and restoring normovolemia with intravenous or oral fluids. Dopamine or dobutamine infusions can increase renal perfusion in oliguric premature foals (Table 19–7).

Bladder and Abdominal Abnormalities

If the foal appeared normal at birth and becomes progressively more depressed, weaker, and somewhat bloated by 2 to 4 days of age, it may have a ruptured bladder.

Foals of both sexes are affected equally. Signs appear later if only a small tear is present. Straining to urinate might or might not be present, and some foals appear to urinate normally. If the bladder is ruptured, amniocentesis will reveal abundant abdominal fluid that smells of urea if heated. The diagnosis is confirmed with laboratory tests. These foals have an elevated serum urea and creatinine concentrations, acidosis, and electrolyte abnormalities (hyponatremia, hypochloremia, and hyperkalemia). Abdominal fluid has a much higher creatinine concentration than serum has. The neurologic signs are most likely due to acidosis and electrolyte imbalances. If the diagnosis is in doubt, methylene blue can be instilled aseptically into the bladder and abdominocentesis used to detect its presence in the abdomen. The use of more sophisticated techniques such as radiography with contrast media is usually not necessary. The condition is treated surgically. Drainage of excess abdominal fluid and restoration of normal electrolyte balance by administering normotonic saline is essential before repair is attempted, as cardiac arrhythmias can occur under anesthesia. Prognosis is generally good. Uroperitoneum also can develop following urachal infections in which necrosis of the urachus develops followed by urine leakage. Signs and laboratory data are similar to those in foals with bladder rupture, although the hemogram suggests infection.

Finally, abnormal postures, depression, and anorexia can be signs of abdominal pain. Foals with meconium impaction might strain or walk backward. Most colicky foals throw themselves down and lie on their backs. Abnormal abdominal sounds, bloat or grinding of the teeth focus attention on the gastrointestinal system.

RESPIRATORY PROBLEMS

Respiratory disease is the major cause of death in newborn foals. Flared nostrils, tachypnea, dyspnea, exaggerated movement of the rib cage during breathing, and abnormal lung sounds are present in most cases, although some foals with extensive lung disease appear to be breathing well and even have normal lung sounds. Most foals with life-threatening hypoxia, and hypercarbia, unless moribund, have pink mucous membranes. Coughing and nasal discharge are common only in the resolving stages of the problem, or in foals with cleft palates. Congenital upper-airway problems (choanal atresia, tracheal collapse) can cause severe dyspnea but are uncommon.

Most respiratory diseases of newborn foals involve the lower airways. Foals stressed during birth can defecate in utero and inhale meconium, resulting in aspiration pneumonia. Premature foals are prone to pulmonary atelectasis and can lack adequate lung surfactant (the deficiency has been documented in premature neonates of other species). Surfactant reduces surface tension, preventing alveolar collapse during expiration. Pulmonary atelectasis creates a right-to-left vascular shunt, resulting in hypoxia, hypercarbia, and respiratory distress. Weak or premature foals are also likely to suffer from FPT, predisposing them to overwhelming pulmonary infections and respiratory distress.

Both viral (influenza, herpesvirus, adenovirus) and bacterial agents can cause pneumonia in foals. Common bacterial isolates include both gram-negative (Escherichia coli, Klebsiella) and gram-positive (Streptococci, Actinobacillus, Rhodococcus equi) organisms. Because of the often fatal outcome of untreated pulmonary disease, a particular effort should be made to detect it. Arterial blood gas analysis (Table 19–4) is invaluable because auscultation and physical examination fail to detect all cases. If blood pressure is very low and an arterial sample unobtainable, a venous sample can be useful.

Hypoxia (Pa_{O_2} <60 mm Hg, 8 kPa) can indicate vascular shunting or mis-matched ventilation and perfusion of the lung, as seen in pneumonia and atelectasis, or poor ventilation (in which case hypercapnia is also present). If severe, hypoxia is corrected by oxygen administration. Nasal insufflation of humidified oxygen (3 to 10 L/minute) can be done with minimal equipment. A soft plastic or rubber tube (a stallion urinary catheter works well) is placed in one nostril with the tip a few inches rostral to the pharynx. The tube is taped to the foal's muzzle, then connected to an oxygen tank by a longer plastic tube. Oxygen should be humidified before it reaches the foal to prevent drying of the respiratory mucosa. Foals tolerate nasal insufflation well and continue to suckle. A nasal discharge and some mucosal erosions are common but inconsequential sequels of therapy. Blood gases should be monitored regularly and oxygen flow adjusted to maintain the foal's Pa_{O_2} above 60 mm Hg (8 kPa) (preferably between 80 and 90 mm Hg, 10.6–12 kPa). Once stable, the foal should gradually be weaned off oxygen. Although ideally Pa_{O_2} should be above 90 mm Hg (12 kPa), as long as it is above 55 mm Hg (7.3 kPa) most foals with pulmonary disease do well.

Hypercarbia can result from severe pneumonia with right-to-left vascular shunts, and if mild, does not require specific treatment. Marked hypercarbia (Pa_{CO_2} above 60 mm Hg, 8 kPa) is a sign of hypoventilation, due either to neurologic disease or to exhaustion in the terminal stages of extensive, severe pulmonary disease. Respiratory stimulants such as doxapram are not helpful because they increase metabolic demands for oxygen without increasing ventilation. Such foals can be helped temporarily by placement of a nasotracheal tube (Fig. 19–1) connected to a Hope II pediatric resuscitator bag, which is compressed manually to inflate the foal's lungs. Oxygen can be leaked into the bag if needed. A nasogastric tube must be placed simultaneously to prevent bloat and to allow feeding. Frequent monitoring of blood gases is essential to ensure success. The goal is to maintain Pa_{CO_2} below 60 mm Hg (8 kPa) and Pa_{O_2} above 50 mm Hg (6.7 kPa). Long-term ventilatory support using a mechanical respirator is labor-intensive and expensive and requires sophisticated equipment; such cases are best handled in a large clinic.

White muscle disease (selenium deficiency) affects the muscles involved in respiration, as well as the heart, and should be considered in selenium-deficient areas.

Thoracic radiographs are useful to differentiate among pulmonary atelectasis, interstitial pneumonia, pulmonary abscessation, and aspiration pneumonia. If bacterial pneumonia is thought to be the cause of respiratory disease, transtracheal aspiration might identify the organism involved. Peripheral white blood cell counts can be elevated or low, neutrophils can appear toxic, and fibrinogen can be elevated if an infectious process is present. Further laboratory tests are not usually essential for diagnosis of a respiratory problem but will help detect any other concurrent disease. The foal should be re-evaluated frequently because its condition can change dramatically in a day or two.

Broad-spectrum antibiotics (Table 19–5) are used to treat bacterial pneumonia and are changed as dictated by culture results and progression of the case. FPT must be corrected if present. Bronchodilators (Table 19–10) might be useful. Aminophylline or theophylline, in addition to being effective bronchodilators, improve diaphragmatic contractility in other species, and thus might be useful in the treatment of weak neonates.

Nursing care for foals with pulmonary disease is vital. Foals benefit from being helped to stand or to lie sternally, because hypoxia and hypoventilation are much worse in lateral recumbency.

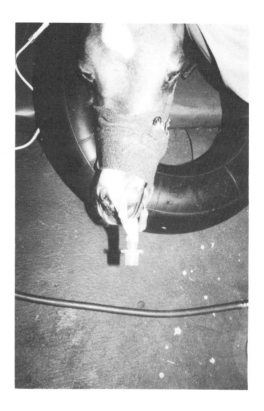

Fig. 19–1. Premature foal with a nasotracheal tube. The tube is well tolerated and can be used for ventilatory support.

Coupage (clapping cupped hands over the thorax) when a foal is standing or lying sternally helps clear secretions from the bronchi and trachea and should be done six to eight times daily.

Many foals with lung disease do not require respiratory therapy and can be successfully treated on the farm. Many of those that require oxygen need it only for a few hours to a few days and can be treated effectively in a small clinic if help is available constantly. Severely ill foals or those needing ventilation are best referred to a center experienced in the management of such problems. Prognosis, which varies with the extent of the lesion, is fair as long as the foal does not require ventilation. Foals that recover appear to develop into normal adults.

TABLE 19–10. DRUGS COMMONLY USED TO TREAT RESPIRATORY PROBLEMS

Drug	Dosage	Comments
Oxygen	3–10 L/min, *humidified,* by nasal insufflation	Adjust flow to maintain PaO_2 between 60–100 mm Hg (8–13.3 kPa)
Terbutaline	0.02 mg/kg Q4–6 hour IV (slowly), 0.2–0.3 mg/kg Q4–12 hour PO	Bronchodilator; up to 48 hours might be needed to see effect if given PO
Aminophylline	2 mg/kg loading dose IV, 1 mg/kg IV or 2 mg/kg PO Q12 hour maintenance	Bronchodilator; blood levels may increase if cimetidine is administered concurrently; decrease dosage or monitor blood concentrations to maintain 5–10 μg/dl
Theophylline	Dosage for neonates not established; adults 6 mg/kg Q6 hour IV?	Toxic side effects as for aminophylline: fever, gastritis, diuresis, and CNS depression or excitation

ICTERUS

Most ill newborn foals, as well as a few normal ones, are mildly icteric. Marked icterus, however, is usually a sign of severe liver disease (Chapter 14) or neonatal isoerythrolysis.

Neonatal isoerythrolysis is an acute hemolytic anemia caused by the foal's absorbing from colostrum maternal antibodies against the foal's red blood cells. It occurs when the foal has a different blood type than the dam (most often A or Q); the dam was sensitized to this blood type, generally during a previous pregnancy; and the foal had adequate transfer of maternal antibodies from colostrum.

Foals with neonatal isoerythrolysis are strong at birth and have suckled well. Usually they are not the dam's first-born. Depression and weakness, followed by jaundice, appear 12 hours to 5 days after birth. Prostration, tachypnea, and convulsions occur in severe cases, and some foals die before developing icterus. Urine can be brown or reddish. The speed with which signs appear and progress matches the severity of the disease.

Diagnosis is not usually difficult, as these foals are anemic, in severe cases markedly so, with a packed-cell volume of 6 to 10% (0.6–0.1 L/L). Plasma or serum is often yellow or reddish. Laboratory confirmation of neonatal isoerythrolysis requires demonstration of alloantibodies on the foal's red blood cells. Many false-negatives occur unless the presence of hemolysins is tested. Simple tests such as mixing the foal's blood with the mare's colostrum or serum are inaccurate.

Treatment depends on the severity of the disease and, more importantly, on the rate at which anemia and weakness develop. The packed-cell volume should be monitored at least twice daily. If the packed-cell volume is 12% (0.12 L/L) or less or is dropping rapidly toward that level, blood transfusions should be given to temporarily raise the foal's packed-cell volume levels, allowing for adequate tissue oxygenation (above 15%, 0.15 L/L). Unfortunately, blood transfusion is difficult. To avoid rapid destruction by alloantibodies still present in the foal's circulation, transfused red blood cells should be compatible with the mare's. The best red blood cells would be the mare's own, but because they must be washed free of serum before administration, a difficult procedure, a practical solution is to administer 1 to 2 L of whole blood from a universal donor, previously determined to lack Aa-or Qa-type red blood cells and alloantibodies. If such a horse is not available, a male pony is usually a safe donor because it is less likely to have the offending red blood cell type. Failing that, any male, except the foal's sire, can be used. Blood should be administered very slowly for the first 5 to 10 minutes and the foal watched carefully for signs of a transfusion reaction (elevated pulse and respiratory rates, abnormal color of mucous membranes). If none occurs, 1 to 2 L of whole blood can safely be given over 1 hour. If a reaction does occur, administration of blood should be stopped. Corticosteroid (Table 19–8) or antihistamine administration might allow the transfusion to continue at a slower rate, but sometimes administering blood to some foals is impossible. The foal's packed-cell volume should be monitored regularly; another transfusion might be necessary within a few days because the lifetime of transfused equine red blood cells is short (2 to 5 days). With careful nursing and supportive therapy, it is possible to save foals unable to tolerate blood transfusion.

All foals with neonatal isoerythrolysis should be kept well hydrated, despite the hemodilution thus produced, to prevent renal damage. Stress and excessive handling must be avoided. FPT is not a problem in these foals, although some authors consider these foals to be particularly vulnerable to infections and recommend prophylactic antibiotics.

A dam's future foals can be protected from neonatal isoerythrolysis by muzzling them at birth and feeding them colostrum (1 to 2 L) from a mare with no history of neonatal isoerythrolysis in her foals. The dam should be kept with her foal during this period and milked out often (every 2 hours or so). After 24 hours, the foal is allowed to suckle from its dam because any remaining alloantibodies can no longer be absorbed by the foal.

DIARRHEA

Most foals develop diarrhea sometime in the first few weeks of life. Although many cases of diarrhea are transient and resolve without treatment, its occurrence should be regarded with suspicion. Even mild depression, decreased appetite, or dehydration signal that further investigation and treatment of the problem are warranted. Foals can quickly become severely dehydrated, with sunken eyes, tenting skin, cold limbs, and muddy mucous membranes. Potential causes of diarrhea in foals are numerous, and determining which is implicated in a particular case can be difficult.

The most benign and common syndrome is foal heat diarrhea, occurring at 6 to 14 days of age and lasting 3 to 4 days. Affected foals are essentially healthy and alert, and they continue to drink and maintain hydration. Foal heat diarrhea occurs even in orphan foals or those maintained in sterile conditions. At present, the exact cause of foal heat diarrhea is undetermined, but an increase in small-bowel secretions, which the immature colon is incapable of reabsorbing, appears to be responsible. As long as a foal seems fine otherwise, further diagnostic workup or treatment is not warranted.

Occasionally a mare produces too much milk and the foal has soft feces owing to overeating. This problem is rarely serious and is usually self-correcting, because the dam's production will decrease on its own. Most mares that drip milk do so because the foal is not drinking normally, not because of overproduction of milk, and overeating should be diagnosed only after other possibilities have been eliminated. Bottle- or bucket-fed foals might also overeat and develop diarrhea.

Rotaviruses cause diarrhea that is most severe in the young foals; foals over 2 months of age are rarely ill. Rotaviral diarrhea is contagious and often endemic on large farms. Affected foals are at first depressed and drink poorly. A watery diarrhea develops 12 to 24 hours after the onset of depression and can last up to 3 weeks. Most foals start drinking again after 2 to 3 days, if they are not too severely affected. Fluid loss can be extensive; acidosis, electrolyte imbalances, and uremia deepen the depression, and renal failure and death can result. Recovering foals fail to gain weight for varying periods of time owing to malabsorption, but ultimately they recover completely. The few cases of persistent lactose intolerance reported in foals are thought to be secondary to rotaviral infections. Other viruses (adenovirus, coronavirus, parvovirus) have been found in the feces of foals with diarrhea, but their significance is unknown.

Bacterial enteritis is common and can be associated with systemic infections. Salmonella and Escherichia coli are the usual causative agents. Depression, poor appetite, purplish mucous membranes, mild colic, and occasionally fever usually precede diarrhea. Fulminating infections can be fatal. Feces vary from semiformed to fluid and foul-smelling, and dehydration and shock can be profound. Septic arthritis, osteomyelitis, or pneumonia are frequent complications, especially with Salmonellae. The role of Campylobacter and Bacteroides fragilis in foal diarrhea remains to be elucidated.

Clostridia can cause a severe necrotizing enteritis in 1- to 2-day-old foals. Affected foals are severely depressed and shocky. Those that do not die rapidly can pass bloody feces.

Parasitic diarrhea is not common in neonates, and Stronglyloides westerii is no longer thought to be a major cause of foal diarrhea.

Finally, foals are inquisitive and will often eat indigestible material; enteritis can follow excessive ingestion of sand, dirt, or other materials.

Although diagnosing diarrhea is not a challenge, identifying its cause can be. Patient history is useful; changes in diet or separation of dam and foal can cause transient nutritional diarrheas. An outbreak in many foals suggests rotaviral infection. A 6- to 14-day-old foal, perfectly healthy other than having soft to fluid feces, probably has foal heat diarrhea.

Fecal examination is important. A sample should be submitted for bacterial culture; typing of Escherichia coli is not useful because equine enteropathogenic strains have not been identified. Accurate and fast detection of rotavirus antigens in feces is easily accomplished with an ELISA developed for diagnosis of calf rotaviral diarrhea. A small number of parasite eggs in the feces of a neonatal foal indicate coprophagy and not a patent infection; if they are numerous, however, a prepatent infestation might be the cause of diarrhea. On the farm, occult blood in the feces can be detected with the use of a reagent strip, and the presence of sand or dirt can be detected by suspending feces in water.

Because septicemia is commonly associated with diarrhea, blood cultures should be taken from foals with signs of depression or systemic illness. Serum biochemistry and blood gas analysis (if available) are useful. Acidosis and electrolyte imbalances are common and sometimes severe. Hypoglycemia is not rare. A complete blood count can suggest septicemia. All ill foals should be tested for FPT.

Treatment is primarily supportive. Rehydration is important. Oral fluids containing sodium, chloride, potassium, and a source of bicarbonate can suffice for foals less severely affected or during the recovery period; solutions containing glucose might or might not be accepted by the foal. Most preparations sold for calves are adequate.

Intravenous fluids are needed by obviously dehydrated foals. An indwelling intravenous catheter should be placed aseptically, and rehydration started as soon as possible. Usually, lactated Ringer's solution or an isotonic multiple electrolyte solution are used; glucose can be added if needed. The first liter or two can be administered over 0.5 to 1 hour, and the rate then slowed to about 3 to 4 ml/kg/hour. Once laboratory results are available, specific deficiencies can be corrected as needed. Potassium chloride can be added at a rate of 20 mEq/L (mmol/L). Calcium should be added cautiously. Sodium and chloride deficiencies usually correct themselves gradually with the administration of isotonic fluids and rehydration. The base deficit can be roughly calculated by the formula

$$\text{deficit (mEq/L)} \times 0.4 \times \text{body weight (Kg)} = \text{total deficit.}$$

Only half of the calculated deficit should be administered over several hours because some correction occurs with rehydration, and overtreatment can be harmful. Plasma is given if FPT or hypoproteinemia owing to gastrointestinal loss are present.

Systemic antibiotics are useful only if septicemia or bacterial infection is suspected. Broad-spectrum antibiotics should be used initially and changed if necessary as culture and sensitivity results become available. Orally administered antibiotics are contraindicated as they eliminate the normal gut flora without affecting the causative bacterial agents, which are distributed systemically. Viral diarrhea and other diarrhea resulting from nonbacterial causes are not improved by antibiotics.

Other treatments of diarrhea are more controversial. Ivermectin or thiabendazole might eliminate prepatent parasitic infections. Many antidiarrheal drugs decrease gut motility but thus prevent the elimination of toxins and infectious agents. Bismuth subsalicylate, activated charcoal, or pectin (Table 19–6) are used by many clinicians. These drugs generally do no harm and can be useful in some cases. Flunixin meglumine decreases the signs of endotoxemia seen with Salmonella or Escherichia coli septicemia and diarrhea but must be used with extreme caution in neonates. NSAIDs can cause gut ulceration and renal tubular damage, particularly in dehydrated or hypovolemic foals.

Although malabsorption can be a problem with rotaviral diarrhea, most foals do best if fed as usual. If milk is thought to contribute to the problem, it can be diluted with electrolyte solutions; eliminating it from the diet could starve the foal. Foals unable to tolerate milk at all might benefit from supplementation with lactase (added to the milk 12 to 24 hours before feeding). Parenteral nutrition is necessary in some cases.

Most treated foals recover if complications do not arise, although diarrhea can persist for months. Secondary complications such as renal failure, septic arthritis, pneumonia, or meningitis indicate a much poorer prognosis.

COLIC

Colicky foals do not always behave like colicky adults. Mildly colicky foals are usually depressed and anorexic, often lying on their backs, propped against a wall. Foals with a meconium impaction will hunch, strain, and might back into walls. Some foals with abdominal pain grind their teeth. More violent signs such as rolling and kicking at the belly are usually seen when a displacement or torsion is the cause of pain. Premature or septicemic foals are often bloated but too depressed to show other signs of pain.

As with adults, the patient history and physical examination are the keys to correct diagnosis. If the foal is less than 3 days old and has not been seen to pass meconium, meconium impaction is likely. White foals born to Overo parents are likely to have lethal white syndrome, characterized by agenesis of parts of the gastrointestinal nervous system and subsequent hypoplasia of segments of the gut. Stressed or ill foals are prone to gastrointestinal ulceration, with or without perforation, especially if they have received NSAIDs.

Physical examination includes careful auscultation of the abdomen and localization of any gas caps, passage of a nasogastric tube to detect and remove excessive gastric contents, and palpation of the scrotum and inguinal canal in colt foals. Rectal examination with a lubricated finger allows detection of low meconium impactions or the rare imperforate anus. Abdominal radiographs are feasible with most small-animal equipment and can be extremely helpful. High meconium impactions (in the proximal rectum or in the colon), intussusceptions, peritonitis, and various displacements or torsions can sometimes be diagnosed radiographically.

Abdominocentesis (Table 19–11) is somewhat more difficult to perform in foals than in adults, as foals have a thin abdominal wall, and the bowel is easily punctured, particularly if the foal is bloated. Furthermore, most foals are recumbent when examined, which might make obtaining abdominal fluid difficult. Strict attention to aseptic technique is essential considering the neonate's reduced resistance to infection. A short intravenous catheter might be preferable to a bare needle for abdominocentesis, because the soft catheter can be safely advanced into the abdomen after the attached needle has punctured the abdominal wall. A sterile teat cannula can be used instead but tends to leave a large hole in the abdominal wall. Obtaining a sample might be impossible. Following abdominocentesis, the foal should have broad-spectrum antibiotic therapy for a few days. Other useful laboratory tests include a test for FPT and a complete blood count and serum biochemistry if anything other than a simple meconium impaction is suspected.

Meconium impactions are the most common cause of mild colic in neonates. Nearly all foals strain, hunch their backs, or back into walls or their dams before passing meconium. Several such short bouts of colic can occur, and foals usually nurse well between bouts. If signs persist beyond a few hours and no meconium is produced, treatment is warranted. Most cases respond well to enemas, especially if meconium can be felt on rectal examination. Phosphate-based commercial preparations or warm water work equally well. Any instrument inserted in the rectum must be well lubricated and used very gently. Warm water enemas, to which glycerine or mineral oil can be added, are given by gravity flow and repeated as necessary. Soapy water enemas can be irritating and are not recommended.

Foals that do not respond to treatment with repeated enemas and foals with a high meconium impaction often benefit from oral fluids (water or electrolyte solutions) given by stomach tube, in addition to regular feeding. If necessary, pain can be controlled by flunixin meglumine or a small amount of xylazine (Table 19–7), although frequent use or overdosage might produce gut ulceration or hypotension. The few foals that do not respond to conservative treatment in 24 to 48 hours might need surgery.

TABLE 19–11. NORMAL ABDOMINAL FLUID

Color	Pale yellow
Clarity	Clear
TP (g/dl)	<1.5
Specific gravity	<1.015
WBC (/μl)	<5000
Neutrophils	25–65%
Monocytes and macrocytes	20–50%
Lymphocytes	5–35%
Eosinophils	<3%

TP = total protein; WBC = white blood cell.

Newborn colts, especially Standardbreds, often have inguinal or even scrotal hernias. Most such hernias are painless and easily reducible with gentle manipulation and will correct themselves in time. Firm, cool, or painful hernias indicate that entrapment or strangulation of bowel has occurred. Immediate surgery is necessary, from which many foals recover uneventfully.

Any of the intestinal accidents, such as displacements and torsions, that occur in adults can occur in foals. Pain is often severe and the foal violent. The diagnostic workup and treatment of severe colic is discussed in Chapter 4. Survival rates appear to be similar to those of adults.

For unknown reasons, gastrointestinal ulcerations are common in foals and can result in perforation, peritonitis and death. Stress, NSAIDs, changes in diet, hypovolemia, sepsis, and shock can contribute to the formation of ulcers, but some cases occur without any obvious predisposing cause. In septicemic foals, peritonitis can occur in the absence of a specific gastrointestinal lesion, and in some cases aggressive antibiotic therapy is successful in resolving both septicemia and peritonitis. However, the prognosis in most cases is poor.

Signs of gastrointestinal ulceration include depression and anorexia, and some foals are mildly colicky or grind their teeth. Foals with severe ulceration can salivate profusely. Very ill foals such as septicemic or premature foals might show no signs at all. Gastric reflux is common in foals with strictures subsequent to ulceration. Gastrointestinal ulcers can be difficult to diagnose on the farm, and detection of occult blood in gastric reflux or fecal material is inconsistent. Abdominal radiography is useful, demonstrating a gas- or fluid-filled, distended stomach. Some ulcers or strictures are diagnosed with a barium contrast study. Free gas and large amounts of fluid are seen in the abdomen if an ulcer has perforated the gut. Abdominal fluid can be normal if ulcers have not perforated the gut or if a small perforation is sealed off by omentum; otherwise it can contain bacteria, food material, and numerous white blood cells.

Endoscopic examination allows for an immediate diagnosis of gastrointestinal ulceration but requires a long and narrow endoscope, prior fasting of the foal, removal of any gastric contents, and sedation or general anesthesia. The additional stress of endoscopy might not be justified. Most laboratory tests are not helpful, although in foals older than 2 weeks of age, ulceration should be suspected if serum pepsinogen concentrations are higher than 240 mg/ml.

Many clinicians simply assume that any stressed, ill or premature foal is likely to have or develop ulceration. Thus, most foals are treated empirically, and further diagnostic workup is done if pain persists or signs of shock develop. Perforation of a gastrointestinal ulcer is usually accompanied by signs of profound shock, depression, and death in a few hours. Surgical correction of a perforated gastric ulcer is sometimes possible, but chances of survival are poor.

Routine medical treatment consists of reducing unnecessary stress, discontinuing any ulcer-producing medications, and starting antiulcer medication—oral antacids, mucosal protectors, and H_2 antagonists (Table 19–6). A popular combination is sucralfate and one of the H_2 antagonists. The prognosis is good for foals that do not develop strictures or perforated ulcers.

Formation of duodenal strictures is signaled by frequent colicky episodes after feeding and accumulation of large amounts of gastric fluids. Contrast radiography and endoscopy (if available) are used to diagnose the condition; surgical correction is difficult but essential for successful treatment.

LAMENESS

Any sign of lameness in a neonatal foal is reason for concern; septic arthritis (joint ill) is the most common cause of lameness in foals, often causing permanent crippling and requiring euthanasia.

The lame foal should be examined carefully to detect any swelling, heat, or pain over joints or at the epiphyseal plates. All four limbs, not just the obviously painful one, should be inspected. A complete physical examination is essential because other concurrent problems are common. Fever might or might not be present. Many limb deformities such as abnormal angulation, flexor tendon contracture or laxity, and ruptured extensor tendons are not painful in themselves, but can prevent rising or walking. Thus, affected foals often suffer from FPT and are predisposed to bacterial infections. Lame foals tend to lie down a great deal. They might or might not be depressed and anorexic, and they soon develop decubitus ulcers.

The onset of lameness is often abrupt, and most owners are convinced that the foal has been stepped on or kicked by the mare, or suffered some accident. Unless obvious signs of trauma such as open wounds or fractures are present, it is best to assume that septic arthritis is the cause of pain, and to treat it quickly, because this infection progresses rapidly. Septic arthritis often develops in foals treated briefly for previous infections such as pneumonia or septicemia.

TABLE 19–12. SYNOVIAL FLUID ANALYSIS

	Normal	**Septic**
Color	Yellow to amber	Amber to bloody
Clarity	Clear	Turbid or flocculent
Viscosity	High	Low
RBC (/μl)	Rare	Few to many
WBC (/μl)	±800	>10000
Neutrophils	~8%	Predominant
Monocytes	~92%	Variable
Bacteria	None	Variable*

RBC = red blood cell; WBC = white blood cell.
* Bacteria often not detected despite sepsis; synovial fluid may be normal despite active bone infection.

Blood should be obtained to determine the foal's serum IgG concentrations. A complete blood count might be useful; white blood cells are usually normal but if abnormal indicate that infection is not localized solely to one or more joints. Blood cultures can be rewarding, especially if signs of sepsis are present. Synovial fluid from swollen, hot, or painful joints should be submitted for cytology and culture, although culture is frequently negative despite active infection (Table 19–12). Samples should be obtained aseptically with the foal well restrained and sedated (Table 19–8). Radiographs are extremely useful if a fracture is suspected or if lameness has been present for more than 1 or 2 days. The contralateral limb should be radiographed for comparison.

Septic Arthritis. Septic arthritis is due to bacterial colonization of areas in the growth plate and synovial membrane, where blood flow is sluggish. Commonly involved bacteria include Streptococci, Salmonella, and Escherichia coli; other aerobic and anaerobic organisms also can be responsible. Infection of the joint or periarticular structures results in accumulation of bacterial or cellular debris in the joint and poor drainage of the resulting exudate. Proteolytic enzymes released from white blood cells erode and destroy joint cartilage. Osteomyelitis of the growth plate often precedes joint involvement.

Treatment must be prompt and aggressive; delay can lead to irreversible cartilaginous destruction and permanent lameness. Broad-spectrum systemic antibiotics (Table 19–5) and joint lavage are the mainstays of therapy. A penicillin/aminoglycoside combination is used most frequently if bacterial cultures are negative. In some cases, if lameness and swelling are slight, systemic therapy alone can produce a good response, but most foals benefit from joint lavage.

By flushing out debris and proteolytic enzymes from the joint cavity, joint lavage helps restrict cartilage destruction. Joint lavage is best done after synovial fluid aspiration, while the foal is heavily sedated and well restrained. It can be performed aseptically on the farm if clean, dust-free surroundings and assistance are available. Two sterile needles or catheters are placed in the joint, and 1 or 2 L of sterile lactated Ringer's solution or any other isotonic sterile solution with a neutral pH are run in through one needle. The joint is repeatedly distended with the fluids and then allowed to drain by blocking the outflow needle as needed. The use of intra-articular antibiotics is controversial; many are irritating and must be buffered before use. Bandaging after drainage is optional. Foals with acute septic arthritis might need only one joint lavage if they are treated promptly and kept on broad-spectrum antibiotic therapy for an appropriate length of time. Foals that do not respond within 48 hours to one or two lavages in conjunction with systemic antibiotics, or foals first seen after a lameness lasting several days, might need surgical debridement of the affected joint because of extensive lesions. As the duration of the problem increases, the prognosis for future soundness worsens.

In addition to antibiotics and joint lavage, analgesics are sometimes necessary to allow the foal to get up and suckle. Phenylbutazone or flunixin meglumine (Table 19–7) are effective analgesics but like all NSAIDs can cause gastrointestinal ulceration. If analgesics must be used, the lowest effective dose is preferable. Antiulcer medication is often given whether or not foals receive NSAIDs, because gastrointestinal ulceration is commonly associated with septic arthritis. Foals should be stall rested for 2 to 4 weeks after successful treatment to optimize healing of joint cartilage.

Osteomyelitis. Osteomyelitis is treated in much the same way as septic arthritis. Large lesions might need surgical debridement and can result in abnormal angulation of the limb if they affect the growth plate. Foals must be examined frequently during treatment, because infection can flare up in previously uninvolved limbs and joints.

Trauma and Congenital Anomalies. Other causes of lameness in neonatal foals include trauma, which in turn can give rise to septic arthritis or osteomyelitis, and congenital anomalies. Diagnosis usually requires physical examination and radiography. Care should be exercised not to mistake some normal variations (e.g., two centers of ossification in the proximal sesamoids or the navicular bone) for fractures. Wounds and fractures are treated as they are in adult horses. Some longbone fractures that would require euthanasia in adults can be successfully treated in neonates.

Congenital anomalies can cause varying degrees of lameness. Soft-tissue abnormalities such as ruptured or lax extensor tendons and contracted flexor tendons often respond well to bandaging or splinting. Angular deformities that have not corrected by themselves in the first weeks of life might require surgery. Unlike agenesis of the third phalanx or of the navicular bone, these abnormalities rarely cause lameness in the foal. The latter conditions are rare and crippling; treatment is not warranted.

NURSING CARE

Often the quality of nursing care, rather than the sophistication of medical treatment, determines whether an ill neonate will live or die. Care of such foals is labor intensive but can be rewarding.

Foals that can suckle on their own, only needing help getting up every hour or so, can be managed on the farm or in a small clinic. The critically ill foal, which

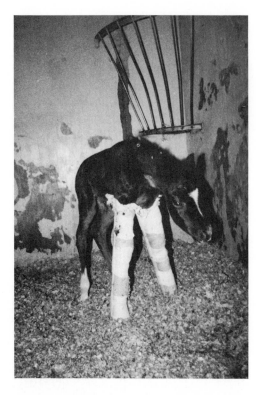

Fig. 19–2. Neonatal foal with bilateral forelimb splints. The shavings allow the foal to move more easily than straw bedding would.

might need close monitoring, respiratory therapy, parenteral fluids or nutrition, and numerous medications, is best managed in a hospital setting with constant help; these foals usually need an attendant at all times. Understandably such care is expensive, but most foals need intensive care only for a few days, and survival rates are steadily improving. Presently, about two thirds of all foals admitted to an intensive care unit survive, and most become normal adults.

HEATING AND BEDDING

Premature, weak, or ill foals thermoregulate poorly and need to be kept in a warm, sheltered place to prevent hypothermia and allow for easy monitoring and treatment. Unless a nurse-mare is readily available, the dam should be kept with the foal if possible. Barriers are needed to confine the foal to a small area, preventing indwelling intravenous catheters from being pulled out and the mare from stepping on the foal. Bedding should be dry and deep; straw is generally adequate, although shavings or sawdust are easier for foals with hyperextended or splinted limbs to move in (Fig. 19–2). Recumbent foals need the additional protection of a foam mat, air mattress, or water bed because they rapidly develop decubitus ulcers. Recumbent foals also get bedding in their eyes, causing corneal ulcers, and they swallow straw or shavings, which can contribute to gastrointestinal ulceration. Bedding should be covered by a blanket or sheet. Bedding gets wet very fast and must be changed often.

The foal's body temperature should be monitored frequently, and if it is below 100° F (37.8° C) or if shivering is noted, additional heat should be provided. Blankets, down vests, heat lamps, and water-heated pads are all useful; the latter can cause severe burns if not used carefully. Electric blankets are not safe. All electrical wires must be taped or tied out of reach of the mare and foal. Heating should be stopped as the foal's temperature rises above 102° F (38.3° C), unless continued shivering indicates that fever rather than overheating is the cause of the high body temperature.

FEEDING

Most mares produce enough milk to feed their foals. Weak foals should be assisted to rise and encouraged to nurse hourly. Often the first signs that a foal is not nursing well are drips of milk down its face and the fullness of the dam's udder. If the foal cannot suckle its dam, the mare can be milked by hand or with a breast pump. The udder should be washed, patted dry, and milked out every 2 to 6 hours, depending on the mare's output. Even with frequent milking, most mares will dry up quickly, and an alternative source of milk is usually needed. Nurse-mares are available in some areas but are usually expensive. Despite the marked differences between mare and goat milk, goat's milk is an excellent substitute. Alternatively, one author recommends 2% lowfat cow's milk to which 20 g/L of dextrose is added. Milk substitutes can also be used; excellent results have been obtained using goat's milk replacer, although most milk replacers intended for calves are of poor quality and are not tolerated by foals. Unfortunately, this unsuitability is also true of some of the mare's milk replacers on the market.

Newborn foals obtain their required 120 to 150 kcal/kg body weight daily by ingesting between 20 and 28% of their body weight daily. They gain 1 to 1.5 kg/day if well fed. Foals drink often and little at a time. When artificially feeding a foal, it is best to start with small amounts (50 to 100 ml) of milk every 30 minutes and to increase the amount gradually until the estimated hourly demand is met. Initially, hand-fed foals should be fed hourly because longer intervals between feedings can cause bloat and colic or a decreased intake and dehydration. Premature or septicemic foals are particularly prone to ileus, bloat, and colic, and intravenous fluids usually must be given simultaneously with oral feeding to maintain hydration. In some cases, premature or septicemic foals will not tolerate oral feeding and must be fed parenterally. Parenteral alimentation is expensive and practical only in a large clinic.

Milk should be heated to body temperature before feeding. Foals with good suckling reflexes can be bottle-fed (nipples for lambs work best); the bottle should be held low to prevent aspiration of milk. Weak foals with poor suckling reflexes or those with indwelling nasotracheal tubes should be fed only through a nasogastric tube (a stallion urinary catheter works well). One end of the nasogastric tube can be left in the esophagus near the cardia of the stomach or placed in the stomach. The other end of the tube should be sutured or taped securely to the muzzle (Fig. 19–3). The absence of gastric reflux and the tube's presence in the stomach should be ascertained before each feeding. If no gastric reflux is obtained, milk is given by gravity flow while the foal is propped up on its chest, to prevent aspiration. The nasogastric tube should be replaced daily, and correct placement verified often. Whatever method of feeding is used, the amount ingested should be recorded, as decreased intake, which can quickly lead to dehydration, constipation, or colic, is easily overlooked.

POSITIONING AND EXERCISE

Recumbent foals should be encouraged to remain in the sternal position with the help of pillows and blankets to facilitate pulmonary ventilation. They should be rolled from one side to the other every 1 to 2 hours to prevent pulmonary conges-

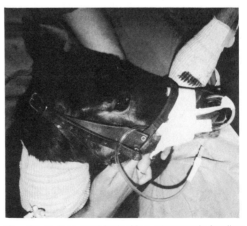

Fig. 19–3. Neonatal foal with a nasogastric feeding tube secured in place. The tapes do not obstruct the nostrils or the mouth.

tion. Foals should be helped to stand and suckle if they can. Limbs can be passively flexed, extended, and massaged in recumbent foals.

CLEANLINESS

Because foals urinate a great deal, they rapidly become soaked with urine and should be towel-dried frequently to prevent hypothermia or scalding. Long-term urinary catheterization is not recommended because of the high risk of infection. Foals with diarrhea often develop extensive scalds. Frequent cleaning and coating of the skin with petroleum jelly helps control the problem.

EYE CARE

Recumbent foals or those with neurologic problems tend to damage their eyes and face. Entropion and corneal ulceration are common and often prolong the period of veterinary care. Instilling ophthalmic petroleum jelly into each eye every 4 to 6 hours might help prevent corneal drying in premature or neurologically impaired foals and reduce the chances of corneal ulceration. Eyes

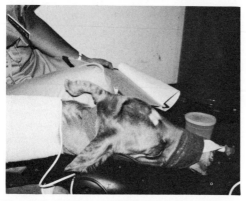

Fig. 19–4. The halter on the premature neonatal foal has been replaced by tape to reduce the risk of trauma. The ears are soft and the coat silky.

should be examined daily and stained with fluorescein to detect and promptly treat any developing ulcers. Padding the head, leaving holes for the eyes, ears, and muzzle, is helpful. Halters with buckles or snaps should be removed and replaced with tape (Fig. 19–4).

PARENTERAL MEDICATION

Because of the reduced immune defenses of neonates, more precautions are necessary than with adults. Indwelling intravenous catheters must be placed aseptically and kept clean and dry. Some authors recommend changing the catheter and culturing its tip every 3 days. The type of catheter used depends on personal preference; I prefer a short catheter in the cephalic vein or a long catheter (≤ 12 inches) in the jugular vein. The cephalic catheter is particularly easy to keep in place in a thrashing foal. Intramuscular injections are best given in the semitendinosus and semimembranosus muscles, after careful cleaning of the injection site. The neck should not be injected, because a stiff neck can prevent rising and suckling. Because foals have little muscle mass, medication should be given through indwelling intravenous catheters if possible. The injection cap must be cleaned before each use and the line flushed with heparinized physiologic saline afterward. Because estimating a foal's weight correctly is difficult, each foal should be weighed at the onset of treatment and every few days thereafter. Drug dosages and feeding amounts can be adjusted as needed, and hydration and weight-gain evaluated more accurately.

PREMATURITY AND DYSMATURITY

Foals born at 320 days of gestation or less are premature and have decreased chances of survival; those born before

300 days of gestation almost inevitably die. Premature foals are generally small and have short, silky coats, soft ears that do not feel cartilaginous, and bright red tongues (Fig. 19–3). Limbs are hyperextended if the foal stands, with a very low pastern angle; joints feel lax and can be flexed to a greater extent than in normal full-term foals. All reflexes such as righting, standing, searching for the mare's udder, and suckling are slow and weak if present at all. These foals might be unresponsive to stimuli.

Premature foals are generally acidotic and hypoglycemic and worsen with time. The packed-cell volume is usually elevated and the white blood cell count depressed. Pulmonary, urinary, and gastrointestinal systems also can be immature; respiratory distress, oliguria, and gastric ulceration and ileus are common. To survive, these foals require intensive nursing care as well as correction of FPT and treatment of ongoing diseases.

A few full-term foals are born with some of the characteristics of prematurity such as joint laxity. These "dysmature" foals might need the same nursing care as premature foals but appear to have better chances of survival.

MONITORING

Routine monitoring of recumbent foals includes determination of pulse and respiration rates, temperature, and blood glucose every 4 to 6 hours.

SUPPLEMENTAL READING

Baker, S.M., Drummond, W.H., Lane, T.J., and Koterba, A.M.: Follow-up evaluation of horses after neonatal intensive care. J. Am. Vet. Med. Assoc., 189:1454, 1986.

Bauer, J.E., et al.: Clinical chemistry reference values of foals during the first year of life. Equine Vet. J., 16:361, 1984.

Beech, J. (ed.): Symposium on Neonatal Equine Disease. Vet. Clin. North Am. Philadelphia, W.B. Saunders Co., 1987.

Harvey, J.W., et al.: Haematology of foals up to one year old. Equine Vet. J., 16:347, 1984.

Kosch, P.C., and Koterba, A.M.: Respiratory support for the newborn foal. In Current Therapy in Equine Medicine. 2nd Ed. Edited by N.E. Robinson. Philadelphia, W.B. Saunders Co., 1987.

Koterba, A.M.: Identification, diagnosis and treatment of the high-risk newborn foal. In Current Therapy in Equine Medicine. 2nd Ed. Edited by N.E. Robinson. Philadelphia, W.B. Saunders Co., 1987.

Koterba, A.M., et al.: Manual of Equine Neonatal Care. In press. Philadelphia, Lea & Febiger, 1989.

Madigan, J.E. (ed.): Manual of Equine Neonatal Medicine. Woodland, Live Oak Publishing, 1987.

Rossdale, P.D., Ousey, J.C., Silver, M., and Fowden, A.: Studies on equine prematurity 6: Guidelines for assessment of foal maturity. Equine Vet. J., 16:300, 1984.

Rumbaugh, G.E., and Adamson, P.J.W.: Automated serum chemical analysis in the foal. J. Am. Vet. Med. Assoc., 183:769, 1983.

INDEX

Page numbers in italics indicate figures; those followed by *t* indicate tables.